THE INDIAN WAR OF 1864

THE INDIAN WAR OF 1864

BEING A FRAGMENT
OF THE

EARLY HISTORY OF KANSAS, NEBRASKA,

COLORADO, AND WYOMING. .

BY

EUGENE F. WARE

Formerly Captain of Co. " F."
SEVENTH IOWA CAVALRY,
Who took part in the Indian Troubles of that time.

CRANE & COMPANY,
TOPEKA, KAN.
1911.

Title Page from the Original Edition

ILLUSTRATED WITH PLANS AND MAPS

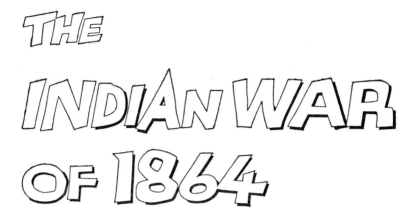

THE INDIAN WAR OF 1864

By CAPTAIN EUGENE F. WARE

WITH AN INTRODUCTION AND NOTES
By CLYDE C. WALTON
ILLINOIS STATE HISTORIAN

ST. MARTIN'S PRESS · NEW YORK

TABLE OF CONTENTS

INTRODUCTION

THE 7th Iowa Cavalry was unlike most other Civil War cavalry regiments. It was on active and arduous duty for more than three years in the service of the United States government, but its hard campaigns had absolutely no effect on the outcome of the Civil War. The regiment was recruited in Iowa in 1863, many of the first companies coming from the eastern part of the state. Companies A and B were mustered in April 27, 1863; C and D, April 28; E and F, June 3; G, June 16; and H on July 13. The remaining companies, however, joined the regiment by transfer on May 14, and it is these last four companies that helped to give the regiment its peculiar flavor. The Sioux City Cavalry, an independent organization already on duty in Dakota Territory, was designated Company I. Companies K, L, and M had originally been enrolled as Companies A, B, and C of the 14th Iowa Infantry but were transferred to the 41st Iowa Infantry and sent to Dakota Territory, and then finally transferred to the 7th Iowa Cavalry.

When the regimental organization was completed July 25, with the mustering in of its commanding officer, Colonel Samuel W. Summers, four companies were already on active duty on the frontier. And this was to be the fate of the regiment—no dashing regimental charges, with bugles blowing and sabers drawn; no fast-moving, brilliantly executed raids behind the Rebel lines; no bitterly contested advances upon Confederate earthworks; no regimental flag planted in a surrendered Southern fort.

Instead, the 7th Iowa Cavalry never served together as a unit and never fought a single engagement in Alabama or Georgia or Tennessee, or, for that matter, fired a shot at a Rebel soldier. Fragmented into company units (infrequently combined to battalion size), the 7th Iowa Cavalry fought its own war against the Sioux and Cheyennes in the Dakotas, Colorado, Wyoming, Kansas, and Nebraska. Its battles were White Stone Hill, Julesburg, and Mud Springs. General Sherman's great army split the Confederacy on its march to the sea; Colonel Summers' 7th Iowa patrolled and fought to keep the overland trail open from Fort Kearney, Nebraska, to Fort Laramie, Wyoming—and beyond.

Never serving together as a regiment seems to have given the soldiers of the 7th Iowa an intense and partisan loyalty to their individual companies. *The Indian War of 1864* is a reflection of the devotion of its author to his own company, "F." It is extremely unlikely that the men in this company even knew those in Companies K, L, and M, who were based on Fort Randall, Dakota Territory, beginning in December, 1861, and who marched and fought far to the north of the action covered by this book. Ware's account is not in any sense a history of the 7th Iowa Cavalry—no adequate, regimental history of the 7th exists—but it is a fascinating and detailed story of what happened to one officer of Company F, Eugene Fitch Ware.

At one time or another Eugene F. Ware was a soldier, farmer, statesman, poet, lawyer, and businessman. A man of unusual character, of appealing eccentricity and considerable ability, he deserves to be better known.

He was born in Hartford, Connecticut, May 29, 1841; his parents were Hiram B. and Amanda M. Ware; the father was descended from Robert Ware, one of the earliest settlers in Massachusetts. Young Eugene attended public school in Hartford, but while still a schoolboy he moved with his family to the energetic, growing Mississippi River town of Burlington, Iowa. There his education was continued, although the Ware family suffered severely from one of those little-understood economic phenomena, the nation-wide depression of panic.

Battered Fort Sumter had scarcely surrendered when the intensely patriotic young man determined to abandon his books and enlist in the army. He wanted to join Company E, 1st Iowa Infantry, but to his chagrin the company (formerly a local Zouave unit with which Ware had been drilling) already had more men than the army would accept.

> One night young Ware went in search of the captain to plead his cause. The captain was in a saloon. Ware went in to find him, and while searching he ran across a Kentucky man who was loudly proclaiming that the Yankees could not fight and that one southern man could whip five northern men. Ware took issue with this talk, and a fight followed in which Ware put the Kentuckian to sleep in two or three rounds. The captain of the company appeared in time to see the fight, and rewarded Ware by including him in the company.

He served until mustered out August 2 of that same year. This brief excursion into military life did not satisfy his desire to serve the Union, and on October 21, 1861, in Burlington, Iowa, he enlisted again, this time in a command known as "Pleyel's Lancers." This organization was being raised by Captain William Edward Harris of New York City and William Wells Woods of Burlington to become a company of the 1st U.S. Lancers. But the regiment was disbanded before "Pleyel's Lancers" could join it, and most of the men decided to join the 4th Iowa Cavalry, then being organized at Mount Pleasant, Iowa. They went as a group to that town, arriving November 19, were accepted as Company L, and were mustered into the service November 23, 1861. The regiment served in Missouri (Ware wrote about it in his book *The Lyon Campaign*), but Ware's career was routine until he was promoted 2nd Battalion quartermaster sergeant, January 15, 1862, and transferred to the regimental staff. When the internal organization of cavalry regiments was changed by General Order 126 of the Adjutant General's Office, his job was abolished, and he was mustered out October 25, 1862, at Helena, Arkansas.

But Ware still had not had enough. Once again he enlisted, joining Company A, 7th Iowa Cavalry, February 14, 1863. He was promoted sergeant major and transferred to the regimental noncommissioned staff July 27; on September 4 he was promoted second lieutenant of Company F. Three years later Lieutenant Ware was serving as aide-de-camp to General Grenville M. Dodge when he was promoted captain of Company F on May 11, 1866. He hardly had time to enjoy the privilege of commanding the company, however, because he was mustered out of service at Fort Leavenworth, Kansas, only six days later. One of his biographers suggests that Captain Ware left the army after Mrs. Washington L. Elliot told him to quit if he intended to marry; that the life of an army officer's wife was miserable; no home or family life could be established; the petty jealousies and bickerings of the officers' wives could not be endured. She painted a picture so dismal that although Ware then had no one in mind as his future wife, he decided to resign.

The young man did not stay in Iowa after leaving the army—but let him speak for himself:

> I used to be a newspaper man. I was on the Burlington *Hawkeye* away back in '66–'67. That was my first job after leaving

the army. I enlisted the day we got news of Fort Sumter, in the First Iowa regiment. I was just nineteen then. I belonged to a zouave drill company that was famous throughout the West for fancy drilling—all boys. Minute war broke out, nothing would do us but we must go. And such pulling and using of influence! Every one was afraid he'd be left out on that first roll and that the war'd be over in sixty days and he wouldn't get to go. I was delighted when I was taken. Well, I served out that stretch, and then I did three years in the Fourth Iowa cavalry. And still the war wasn't over. I went out again as a volunteer cavalry officer, and after peace was declared with the South we were sent north to fight Sioux Indians. Then we were mustered out and I went back to Burlington—twenty-four years old and looking for a job.

I contributed an editorial or so to the *Hawkeye,* which then was edited by a Mr. Beardsley. After him came Frank Hatton, and then Bob Burdette, you know. But they were after my time. Mr. Beardsley liked my stuff and offered me $75 a month to go on the paper regularly, and after consideration I took him up. I liked the work too. Pretty soon I evolved an idea. Mr. Beardsley liked to make running comments on the telegrams we got; for instance, "How does this strike you?" New York, such a date, and then the story. I was given charge of the telegraphic news and wrote my other stuff beside. I used to show up at one p.m. and work till four a.m. After about seven or eight months I began to feel sick. I didn't know what I had. I went to Dr. Nassau—he'd been surgeon of the Ninth Iowa—and told him I wanted access to his medical library. Then I began to read up. I found I had a fearful complication—heart trouble, consumption, liver complaint, sciatica, diabetes and incipient paraplegia. I was alarmed. I went to the doctor and asked advice. He took note of my symtoms [*sic*] and told me I was simply over-worked. He said all there was about it—I must leave the paper or collapse. He said, 'get in the open air.' I came to Kansas. Been here ever since, lawing. But that's how I started in the newspaper business.

It was to Fort Scott, Kansas, that Ware went in the spring of 1867. There he homesteaded a section of land and began to study law. He read the Kansas *Statutes, Walker's American Law,* and *Kent's Commentaries* and in 1871 was admitted to the bar, eventually practicing (as Ware and Ware) with his brother Charles. As a lawyer, one of his close friends said, Ware was unconventional, versatile, and ingenious:

Mr. Ware's war experience greatly intensified his natural ingenuity. The soldier learns to make short cuts, to jump the fences, to blaze new trails, to resort to wholly unprecedented means to accomplish an end. This was Ware's characteristic as a lawyer. He was a fine lawyer, a wonderful lawyer, but a wholly unconventional lawyer. His methods in any given case were more apt to be unprecedented than otherwise. Lawyers prefer beaten tracks. The train of precedent is very alluring—particularly to judges. Ware was very likely in any case to think out a new way. There was danger in this, because courts do not take kindly to novelty of theory and argument. Sometimes Ware's new ways would not work, but they were never without striking features which demanded the most respectful consideration.

In the early 1870's Ware was also working on the *Fort Scott Monitor*, and he was beginning to write poetry, using the pseudonym "Ironquill." Perhaps his first public recognition as a poet came about this time, after the publication of his poem "Neutralia." Best known of all his poetical work is undoubtedly "Washerwoman's Song," and this verse is a fair sample of his style:

> Human hopes and human creeds
> Have their roots in human needs:
> And I should not wish to strip
> From that washerwoman's lip
> Any song that she can sing,
> Any hope that songs can bring;
> For the woman has a friend
> Who will keep her to the end.

He always had a keen sense of the ludicrous, and his humor best expressed itself in a verse about Admiral Dewey, written soon after the Battle of Manila Bay:

> O Dewey was the morning
> Upon the first of May,
> And Dewey was the Admiral
> Down in Manila bay;
> And Dewey were the Regent's eyes,
> "Them" orbs of royal blue.
> And Dewey feel discouraged?
> I Dew not think we Dew.

In October, 1874, Ware married Miss Nettie P. Huntington in Rochester, New York; their union was blessed with four children, three girls and a boy. Mrs. Ware was described by a contemporary as a "woman of culture, of charming personality. . . . [She was] prominent in women's club work, high in the circles of the Daughters of the American Revolution, and identified with many of the good movements inaugurated for the benefit of society."

Ware took a keen interest in politics; an ardent Republican, he served in the Kansas State Senate for the sessions of 1879, 1881, and 1883. He was a delegate to two national conventions and was the choice for presidential elector-at-large in 1888. In 1902 he was appointed Commissioner of Pensions and moved to Washington for a few years, resigning, however, to return to his beloved Kansas.

He had moved to Topeka in 1893 and was for many years active in the affairs of the Kansas State Historical Society, serving as a member of the board of directors, as vice-president in 1898, and as president in 1899.

Aside from *The Indian War of 1864,* Ware published individual poems as well as a book of verse titled *The Rhymes of Ironquill,* a paper, "The Neutral Lands of Kansas," and another historical work about the Civil War, *The Lyon Campaign.* But his interests were varied, and he also devised his own "international language," an outgrowth of his unending efforts to know more about language.

All in all, Ware put his life to good use, for he was creative, active, and basically devoted to the advancement of human society. Still a celebrated figure in Kansas, he was known during his lifetime far beyond the borders of his adopted state. A close friend observed:

> Mr. Ware was popular and he was not. Few men in the state were better known. Few were better liked. Few were more heartily disliked. The men who disliked Ware were those who felt the sting of his criticism directed either at them personally, or, as was usually the case, at some favorite idea or hobby or institution. No man who thinks with absolute independence and expresses his convictions with soldierly emphasis can be popular with everybody. Ware had bitter enemies, some of whom, most of whom, were greatly to his credit. But enemies with him were taken as of course and did not seriously arrest his attention. He laughed about them and at them and forgot them.

A vigorous and energetic man, a creative and sometimes eccentric man, a man of independent thought with a fine sense of the historic, Eugene Fitch Ware made a considerable impact upon postwar Kansas. When he died in Cascade, Colorado, July 1, 1911, his passing was mourned in Kansas and noted in the newspapers all over the Middle West.

Although *The Indian War of 1864* was written long after the events it portrays, Ware says: "I kept a daily journal, and while in the service I frequently wrote to my mother long letters. Upon her death many years afterwards I found that she had saved them. So, the journal and letters and the company field-desk still in my possession enable me to write more fully and accurately than I otherwise might about the happenings of the year and a half hereinafter described."

Apparently Ware's letters and the journal are no longer in existence. Internal evidence indicates that Ware had to have them to be able to set down so much accurate detail about the overland trail, the army, and the Indians in 1863–1865. But the book is, after all, his recollection of those years, and should be read as a memoir.

In its own way, *The Indian War of 1864* is a classic bit of picturesque Americana. Nowhere else is there such a vivid description of the frontier during the Civil War and of the hard, dangerous, monotonous role played by the Civil War soldier who was sent west rather than south. Nothing escapes Ware—the scenery and landmarks, the weather, food, wild life, his fellow officers, Hostetter's celebrated Stomach Bitters, Spotted Tail weapons; he comments about everything.

But he was a man of severe prejudices. He bitterly hated Major Herman H. Heath; he thought the Indians deserved extermination—the typical attitude of the frontier; and he believed the Indians were hostile because agents of the Confederacy were inciting them to attack. While both the Confederacy and the Union did have agents among the five civilized tribes, the situation was not at all simple. Both sides also recruited from these civilized Indians—the Cherokees, Chickasaws, Choctaws, Creeks, and Seminoles—in what is now Oklahoma (then Indian Territory). The small engagements and shifting loyalties that resulted were complex and involved. But by no means did all the tribes in Indian Territory secede, as Ware says. The attempts by both North and South to win Indian support ended in devastating civil war in Indian Territory. The Indians were the principal losers, not only because the heavy hand of war was laid on their land but also because of the punitive treaties forced upon them by the North after the war had ended.

With the so-called "wild tribes" the North would have been satisfied merely to keep peace; but the South wanted their allegiance as well. The "Great Uprising" in Minnesota in 1862 was not, however, as Ware says, the work of Confederate agents but was brought about, rather, by a series of unfortunate (and preventable) events, including the late arrival of cash annuities due the Sioux. Although the government drove the Sioux out of Minnesota, news of the uprising proved to be exciting and unsettling —a heady wine—to the Plains tribes.

Even though many of the prewar Indian agents had been Southerners, they had little or no success in getting the less settled (and more dangerous) wild Indians—particularly the Navahos, Apaches, Comanches, Cheyennes, and Sioux—to join the Southern cause. The Navahos were placed on the reservation for good as a result of a vigorous campaign conducted by Colonel Christopher (Kit) Carson in 1863; both the North and South fought to subdue the Apaches, but this was a task that would occupy the army for another twenty years. The Comanches, Sioux, and Cheyennes, like the Apaches, were not concerned with the civil war to the east, and efforts to conquer them were not successful.

Despite Ware's lack of information on Indian affairs, he is generally accurate, particularly when he is reporting something he witnessed in person. Only when he describes events that he did not experience personally is he likely to be a little shaky. George E. Hyde in *Red Cloud's Folk* (Norman: University of Oklahoma Press, 1937) and George B. Grinnell in *The Fighting Cheyennes* (Norman: University of Oklahoma Press, 1956) are the best authorities on the Indians in 1864. They both point out what they consider to be errors made by Ware, but they, too, have their prejudices—they are wholeheartedly in sympathy with the Sioux and Cheyennes. And even though they occasionally disagree with Ware, they also disagree with each other; but they do not let their concern over minor points prevent them from using Ware as a source upon other points.

Now, from the vantage point of almost ninety years, it is easy to be sympathetic with the Indians and angry with white arrogance and stupidity. It is also easy, in sentimental reflection, to make the Indian something he never was. In 1864 the white man did not know how to deal with or understand the Indian; but neither did the Indian know how to deal with or understand the white man. To imply otherwise today is to be false to the indisputable facts of history.

The Indians—pushed here and there by the advancing frontier, suffering constant territorial loss, seeing the buffalo slaughtered (although too much has been made of this; the Indians slaughtered the buffalo too), and watching white soldiers spoiling for a fight and marching through their lands—were understandably nervous and apprehensive. The Sand Creek Massacre, November 19, 1864, was the culmination of a series of incidents which preceded the great raids of the year. At Sand Creek, Colorado, a force of Colorado volunteers led by Colonel John M. Chivington attacked a camp of Cheyenne and Arapaho Indians, killing and wounding hundreds, including women and children. This action—controversial then and still the subject of much emotional argument today—seems to have been an unprovoked surprise attack upon a friendly village. At any rate, from then on the die was cast, and savage war along the Platte followed.

Ware's descriptions of these days of confusion and terror are excellent, and although he missed the only real fight Company F ever had (the Indian attack at Julesburg, January 7, 1865), he knew what was going on. His is certainly the best record of what it was like to soldier in those extremely difficult times. Through his eyes we see a little of a phase of Civil War history which has always been somewhat obscure.

The Indian War of 1864 is, then, the personal record of a volunteer cavalry officer, a man with a vivid imagination and a gifted pen, who is, at the same time, remarkably accurate. Further, because of Ware's penchant for picturesque detail, the book is a classic bit of Americana.

. . . . . .

I am indebted for assistance and advice to many people, among whom are Nyle H. Miller, Secretary of the Kansas State Historical Society, Topeka; T. R. Walker, Curator of the John M. Browning Memorial Museum, Rock Island Arsenal, Rock Island, Illinois; Mrs. Agnes Wright Spring, Colorado State Historian, Denver, Colorado; Senator Clinton P. Anderson, who owns Herman Heath's letter books; and above all to Mrs. Ellen Whitney of the Illinois State Historical Library, Springfield, Illinois; and the incomparable Earl Schenck Miers of Edison, New Jersey.

The notes to the text are grouped by chapters beginning on page 431.

CLYDE C. WALTON

THE INDIAN WAR OF 1864

THE INDIAN WAR OF 1864

CHAPTER I

*The Summer of 1863 · Gettysburg and Vicks-
burg · Pea Ridge · Indian Prisoners · March to
Rolla · The Seventh Iowa Cavalry · September
19, 1863 · Omaha · The Camp · Sole in Command · Drilling by Bugle · The Loyal League
General H. H. Heath*

It was the summer of 1863. The battle of Gettysburg had
been fought, and the Confederates had retreated to the
south side of the Potomac. Pemberton had surrendered
Vicksburg with 27,000 prisoners, and the Mississippi River
had been opened to navigation for the people of the United
States. The Confederacy having thus been cut in two, its
government should have then seen that it was impossible to
succeed, and should have surrendered, thereby saving the
vast destruction of property and life which was ultimately
to ensue from the overrunning of its territory by the United
States forces.

All Europe deemed the Confederacy as no longer possible
of success. Its recognition by European powers was now out
of the question, and the United States was enabled to turn
its attention to matters of detail. And among these matters
was the question of the Indian nations then on the northwest,
west, and southwest.

In the last days of the Buchanan administration, while
preparations were being made for secession and war, the
South had arranged to carry with it the support of the Indian
tribes. The Indian tribes were governed by agents appointed
by a dishonest Secretary of the Interior, and the spirit of
rebellion was fomented among them as an incident to the

coming war. After the Southern Confederacy had been ushered in, and an army put into the field, in 1861, the Confederate Government immediately turned its attention to the utilization of the Indian. The tribes in the Indian Territory, then powerful and warlike, having long been treated as separate nations, exercised rights of sovereignty, and, under the influence of Confederate legations, gathered together in conventions, and formally seceded from the Union. This idea of secession, although ridiculous, because independent powers do not secede from one another, was nevertheless a strong factor in favor of the Confederacy, and a matter of great danger to the southwestern States of Kansas and Missouri and the weak frontiers thereof. But not only the tribes of the Indian Territory seceded, and put themselves in the scale of antagonism to the United States of America, but through their efforts the whole Indian population of the West was precipitated against the border States as far north as Minnesota, where barbarous massacres took place. When it was reported that the Indians of the Indian Territory were to be turned upon the Union forces, an intense feeling prevailed in the North against these Indians, and it recalled to mind the historical fact, known to every American, how the British did the same thing during our wars for independence, and even tried to turn those tribes against us in the Northwest in the War of 1812, and partially succeeded.

After the battle of Wilson Creek, which took place in southwestern Missouri, August 10, 1861, General MacIntosh, the senior Confederate in command, retired with his army to Arkansas, leaving General Price to look after the Missouri troops, and the Missouri field. While recruiting was going on for the Confederate service in Arkansas, and while fearing the result of Frémont's appointment to the command at St. Louis—a fear which was groundless—the Confederates took into their service a number of Indians from the Indian Territory. This fact was rumored around, and finally got into the Northern newspapers. As the methods of Indian warfare were known, and no one expected any quarter from Indians, the sentiment prevailed that every Indian caught in hostility to the Government should be summarily killed, and no feelings of humanity or sentiment seemed to oppose it.

At the battle of Pea Ridge, which was fought on the 6th, 7th and 8th days of March, 1862, a large number of these Indians were found among the Rebel forces. This battle, fought with grim determination on both sides, ended in crushing defeat for the Confederate General, his death, and the retreat and scatterment of the Confederate army there engaged. It so happened that eleven Indians were captured upon that field by persons so mild-tempered that they spared the lives of the captives. All the other Indians were killed outright. When these eleven Indians were got together, it was determined to send them North, for the purpose of (to use an expression of the day) "firing the Northern heart." It was believed that if these Indians could be exhibited as being captured with arms in their hands there would be an immediate outpouring of sentiment which would bring to the aid of the army, money and volunteers in increased ratio; although even at that time, sentiment was strong, because McClellan had gathered together and organized a fine army on the Potomac, which he was shortly to move, as was believed, to quash the Confederacy at Richmond. A large number of those captured at the Pea Ridge battle, "poor white trash," that did not know what they were fighting for except that they thought they were fighting to prevent the negroes from marrying into white families,—these most ignorant people, as a general rule, when captured, had things explained to them, were given the oath of loyalty; and they agreed to go home, not fight any more, and attend to their own business. But among the captives were a great many intelligent persons, men who had held official positions, civil and military, and these it was thought best to send up North to the military prison at Chicago. The writer of this book was detailed to go with these persons, numbering slightly over four hundred, including these eleven Indians, to the city of Rolla, which was the end of the railroad then projected from St. Louis to Springfield, Missouri. Rolla was one hundred and thirty miles from Springfield, and seventy miles from St. Louis.

The Pea Ridge battle-field was 80 miles southwest of Springfield. For the purpose of conveying these prisoners, together with wagons to haul back supplies, there was detailed a motley sort of guard. They were composed of convalescents who at Springfield had got out of the hospital, and who were believed equal to the light duty of convoying these prisoners, rather than the severe duty of campaigning down through Arkansas. In addition to these there were a few furlough men, who, after the battle of Pea Ridge, and the dissolution of the Confederate army, were permitted to go home for thirty days. There were also a few whose term of service had expired; there were a few Missouri Home Guards; there were a few cavalrymen detailed as wagonguards; there were some who were wounded so slightly that they could still do effective guard duty. The whole escort could, perhaps, be classed as a hundred cavalrymen, and fifty infantrymen. From Pea Ridge as far as Springfield, Missouri, the prisoners were escorted by several companies of cavalry who came along to take back from Springfield a lot of army supplies.

The route from Pea Ridge to Springfield was the most dangerous part of the route. From Springfield to Rolla the writer was not the commander of this expedition, but was a subordinate. Nominally, the officer in command was an Iowa Cavalry Lieutenant, named Patterson, who had been a very brave man, but had become ill through the exposure of the winter. The doctor believed that the Lieutenant had acquired the rudiments of consumption, and had suggested that the Lieutenant be given a furlough of ninety days to go home, and receive treatment. This officer was feeble, and as a fact, he never returned to the service, but died shortly afterwards; so that the responsibility of this trip was largely upon the writer of this. The orders were to keep the strictest guard upon these Indians, and not let any of them escape. It was desired that all should be taken safely and surely to the North, so that they might be exhibited as a show in the Northern cities, in a group. The indignation of the soldiers of our command towards the Indians was very great.

The line of march from Springfield to Rolla lay through a timber country all of the distance. The prisoners were marched compactly in the road. In the front was a slight cavalry advance guard; along each side marched some of the infantry and some of the cavalry. The cavalry rode one behind the other, with their revolvers in their hands. In front of the prisoners was a little squad of infantry, to keep the prisoners from running forward, and back of the prisoners another squad of infantry, to make them keep up. Behind came the wagons. When we camped at night these prisoners were herded together and compelled to build a stake-and-rider fence around themselves every night. They all knew how to build such fences, and they were hurried up in doing it. It was not possible, as the march was arranged, for any one to attempt to escape without being shot. The Indians somehow began to feel that they had no sympathy, not even from their co-prisoners, and seemed determined to take every opportunity to escape. In marching on the line, they would always manage to occupy the positions in the line from which escape was easiest and least hazardous. One after another of these Indians made efforts to escape, but the eyes of the guards and of the whole escort were upon the Indians, and every time that one of them made an attempt he lost his life. The result was that when we got to Waynesville, Missouri, which was about 28 miles from Rolla, there was only one Indian left, and during that night one of the guards killed him. The fact of the death of all these Indians was of course known to the Confederate prisoners, and word of it got back, soon, through them, to the South. The death of these Indians was proclaimed and really appeared in the light of a massacre or assassination. The result seems to have been that many more Indians immediately joined the Southern Confederacy, and formed regiments, and great hostility spread through the entire Indian country as far north as the Canada line; all of which was fomented by the Confederacy.

The Indians in 1863, outside of the Indian Territory, were numerous and powerful, and there were many forts guarding the frontiers and the lines of Western travel; but nevertheless, vast areas were not only unguarded, but even unexplored at that time. It was for the purpose of protecting the frontier that on September 19, 1863, eight companies of the Seventh Iowa Cavalry found themselves in Omaha, destined for the Indian country. The other four, of the twelve companies composing the regiment, had been in advance sent up and camped at Sioux City, Iowa, which was then called the "jumping-off place."

The companies which arrived on the date stated, in Omaha, were A, B, C, D, E, F, G, and H. The regiment was well mounted and had been provided with new uniforms, but was poorly armed. Each cavalryman had a Gallager carbine, an exceedingly inefficient weapon; a Colt's .44 calibre revolver, which loaded at the muzzle with a paper cartridge; a heavy dragoon sabre, which was becoming obsolete, and which, subsequently, before the regiment's term of service expired, was boxed up and stored.

The city of Omaha at that time was a straggling town scattered all over the second bottom of the river, the mud in places very deep, and adhesive, and the streets filled with wagon trains coming in from the west or going out. The transportation of that day was mainly by ox teams. The wagons were large and heavy and with boxes about four feet high, with bows and cotton-duck covers. They had a way of coupling one wagon to another, and of putting in front of the double freight, a dozen yoke of oxen, more or less, according to the load. There were a few mule teams, but not many, and much fewer horse teams. The transportation of the plains was effected mainly with oxen, which could be grazed upon the valley grass as they went. The city of Omaha did not seem to have much local business, but did seem to have a very great "freighting" business. The wind constantly blew at the rate of about fifteen to thirty miles an hour. While we were there upon a street I noticed a large roll or pile of damaged tin roofing, and upon asking a bystander what it meant, he said they had a building upon the hill which they had used for a Territorial capitol building, but the wind had blown the roof off. The saloons were many in number, and miserable in quality. It is probable no town ever sold, per capita, more mean and destructive whisky. Fights were constantly in progress, and somebody was being killed every day. There were a large number of persons wearing some portion of a Confederate uniform, but they all disclaimed having been in the Confederate army, and either said they had bought the piece of uniform or captured it. As a matter of fact, the city was full of deserters from the Confederate army. We were camped out on the western edge of town; our tents were in rows double-guyed to resist the wind, and with holes dug in the ground in which to cook, so that the wind would not blow the fire out over the tents. We got our camp made about sundown of September 19, 1863, and in a short time a large number of our men were in various stages of intoxication, and telling how they were going to punish "Mr. Lo," as they called the Indian, as soon as they could get out where he was. Alas! some of these very men were buried out in the Indian country with their boots on. The first night in camp in Omaha was a very convivial occasion.

There was then one large hotel in Omaha, called the Herndon House. It had been built as a sort of boom hotel. It was named after a Lieutenant Herndon, of the United States service, who, by his then recent exploration of the Amazon River, had made quite a reputation. General McKean was commanding the *District* of Nebraska, or "Nebraska and the Plains," as it was officially called. He had his headquarters in this Herndon building, with a large staff, mostly young men, who were a very jolly set of officers. Besides these there were galloping around over the streets frequently, groups of officers who had come down from the plains, or down the river from above, or were connected with the supply department. On the edge of town were many freighters' camps. I remember the first night that we were there a woolen-shirted, sombrero-hatted teamster came into our camp with a guitar, and sang all the army songs of the period. He also sang "Joe Bowers," and also "Betsey from Pike." I had heard "Joe Bowers" often sung before in the army, but had never heard "Betsey from Pike." The song represented a woman going overland with her husband to the mines, and the trials, troubles and tribulations of the road. I remember only two verses, which were as follows:

"The wagon broke down with the tear of bull-crash,
And out of the end-gate rolled all kinds of trash;
A small volume of infantry clothes done up with care
Looked remarkably suspicious, though all on the square.

Says a miner to Betts, 'Won't you dance along with me?'
'Oh, I will that, old hoss, if you don't make too free;
But don't dance me hard, for I'll tell you the reason why,
Dog-gon you, I'm chuck-full of alca-ho-li.'"

We drilled during the second afternoon of our stay in Omaha. It was entirely by the bugle. Indian-fighters must be drilled by the bugle, and the men must be taught the bugle-calls, and constantly exercised lest they forget.

That night there was some kind of a show in Omaha, theatrical or otherwise—I do not remember. It just happened, as the regiment was then organized, and at that particular time situated, that I, being a Second Lieutenant, was the youngest officer in rank immediately with the regiment. So the Colonel after supper turned over the command of the regiment to the Major, who was next; and the Major turned it over to the Senior Captain, and the Senior Captain turned it over to some one else, and all started for town on horseback. Finally it got down to the Lieutenants, and by eight o'clock my immediate superior had turned the regiment over to me. There was no commissioned officer to whom I could turn; they all outranked me, and I had to stay up, and take care of the regiment while all of my seniors went into the city. By nine o'clock the regiment was boisterous. Reveille was sounded, then tattoo, and afterwards "taps." By the time taps were sounded, I found a large part of the regiment drunk, and once in a while some soldier in a shriek of ecstasy would fire his revolver at the moon. Then I would take the Corporal and guard, and put the man under arrest. In a little while I had the guard tent full, and still things were as lively as ever. I finally got a crowd of about twenty-five sober men, and went around and gathered up the noisiest and set a sergeant drilling them. But they soon ran, helter-skelter, and the camp guards could not stop them. My escort and I smashed up all the whisky we could find, and finally got to tying the loudest ones up to the wagons with lariats, and by about eleven o'clock there was some semblance of order. Finally the officers began to string in, but I had a bad three hours. This all sounds worse than it really was; the men were going out on the plains, and intended to have a celebration before they went. They carried it further than they should. I was glad when all was over that no one was killed.

At the wharf were a lot of steamboats unloading supplies. They were light-draft Missouri boats. Omaha was a great steamboat town. Everything had to be brought there by steamboat. The boats were stern-wheelers. There was yet no railroad to Omaha. Vast quantities of supplies were being piled up, on the wharf, and it was said that we were waiting in Omaha so as to escort a train, and so as to take out a large amount of supplies for ourselves. The only way we kept the men from carousing was by drilling. And while they were well drilled to the word of command, they were not thoroughly up on the bugle-calls. They were drilled constantly; in the morning on foot, obeying in a modified way the bugle-calls, and drilling on horseback in the afternoon, and then we had classes in the evening, and sounded the bugle-calls, and had the pupils give the equivalent military command.

Shortly before our arrival in Omaha I had met and been introduced to a man who was a national organizer of the Union League. It was called the "National Loyal Union League." Only such officers were let into it as were of known loyalty. The army was so honeycombed with disloyal men and Rebel sympathizers that it was difficult to know always whom to trust. These were to be weeded out, and the obligation of the Loyal League was administered only to those of whom the organization was dead sure. It was a strange thing to me to be approached by one whom I did not know, and be talked to upon the subject. He said there were persons in my regiment who were Rebels, and who were disloyal; that he was authorized to give me admission to the order. This was before we reached Omaha. He said it cost nothing, but it must be kept profoundly a secret. He said that it had a civil branch, and a military branch; that the obligations were different, and the object different; but that any officer or soldier who belonged to the military order could make himself known, and could be admitted, and visit a lodge of civilians. I expressed a thorough appreciation of the plan, and he took an hour, and put me through a verbal drill, and gave me some signs, and passwords. The day before marching into Omaha, while riding on the road with my company, a farmer with a load of hay alongside of the road gave the hailing-sign. I stopped, and talked with him a few moments, and he told me that near where we were stopping that night was a large Union League organization that had arrested and put in jail a gang of Confederate deserters, and that they would be glad to see me present. When our command went into camp, I rode that night into the village, and I had gone but a short distance before I got the "hailing-sign," in both instances given in the same way. I found out where there was to be a meeting of the lodge that night, and I went up, and attended it. The hailing-sign was a remarkable invention. It was "two and two." In any way that two and two could be designated, the hailing-sign was made. For instance, if the hand should be held up and the four fingers divided in the middle, two on each side. With a bugle it was two short notes, then an interval, and two short notes. It could be made almost any way; two fingers to the chin. The persons who hailed me, as stated, put two of their fingers in their vest pockets, leaving their other two fingers out. Nobody in the regiment that I know of, was initiated when I was, and I was told where to make reports in case I had something to communicate. I did not know whether there were any persons in the regiment, when I got to Omaha, who belonged to the Loyal League. But the third day while I was there, I was lying down in the tent, late in the afternoon, with my feet near the mess-chest. My Captain came in, and as he was a warm-hearted, true-blue Union officer of great gallantry, and great courage, it occurred to me that he might belong to the Loyal League, so with my foot I tapped on the mess-chest two couplets of raps. Captain O'Brien looked up at me and said, "What sort of a sign is that?" and I said, "How do you know it is a sign?" And he said, "When did you join?" And I said, "What do you mean? Join what?" Then he put out his hand and gave me the grip, to which I responded. The grip was a two-and-two grip. I had been recently promoted into the company. Thereupon he told me who belonged to the Union League in our regiment, and told me who was suspected. Among others was our senior Major, who was believed to be thoroughly "secesh," although professing quite the contrary. His name was H. H. Heath, and afterwards, in 1866, one of his letters was found in the Rebel archives, and read upon the floor of Congress. He had arrived in 1865 to the rank of Brigadier-General, but had offered his services to the Confederates for a remuneration of magnitude during the dark days. Once at roll-call shortly afterwards, in the presence of my men, while the first sergeant was calling the roll, I gave the sign, and some half-dozen of them responded. How or where they got into the order I never knew, but I tied up to them afterwards.

We had a number of accidents in Omaha. Several of our men were sick and our company became reduced to about 80 effective men.

I kept a daily journal, and while in the service I frequently wrote to my mother long letters. Upon her death many years afterwards I found that she had saved them. So, the journal and letters and the company field-desk still in my possession enable me to write more fully and accurately than I otherwise might about the happenings of the year and a half hereinafter described.

CHAPTER II

ON SEPTEMBER 26, 1863, our company started on the march
west. We went over the high tableland, rough and rolling,
and after twenty-three miles came to the Elkhorn River.
Upon this day's march I remember the first appearance
of a very strange character, to whom I shall hereafter
refer. It occurred this way: Shortly before we started to
march, a grown, mature man, who gave his age as thirty-
six, came and wanted to enlist. He said he had been on the
frontier, and had served in the regular army. As we were
going out there again, he wished to go; he declared his in-
tentions to be loyal to the Union, and that he would enlist
in some command for three years or during the war. His
name was James Cannon. About one-third of the boys when
we started in the morning were more or less intoxicated.
Cannon was talkatively full. He wanted to ride at the head
of the column and talk with me, the most of the trip. Finally
I reached out and took his canteen, which I found half-full
of whisky, and poured it out on the ground, and told him
if he did not sober up and quit drinking I would not send
in his enlistment papers, and would let him go without
either muster-in or discharge, and he promised he would
never drink any more.

The condition of the country between Omaha and the
Elkhorn River was that of a wild Western country. The road
was a well-beaten track, four or five hundred feet wide, on

which an enormous traffic for years had been operating. The country was rough, and timberless; there were no settlements of any note, except, there might be seen, here and there, far off down some long swale, a haystack, or a shack of some kind, or herd of cattle handled by one or two men, but far off from the road. The wind had blown almost all the time since we had been in Omaha, and as we went over this upland the road was hard and smooth as a floor, for the dust and sand and gravel had been blown off from it by the violence of the wind.

The companies of our regiment while in Omaha were formed into two battalions of four companies each; companies A, B, C, and D forming the first battalion, and E, F, G, and H, the second. The companies had been sent out of Omaha one at a time, so that they might scatter along the road in their progress west, and have better grass and forage than if they all went together. Those companies went out first which were ready, and provided for, first; several companies went ahead of our company, and several companies came behind us. In going over to the Elkhorn River we met long trains of wagons coming in. Almost all of them were ox trains, and their wagons were mostly empty. It was no uncommon sight to see three yokes of oxen pulling three or four wagons coupled together in a sort of train. The Elkhorn River did not have much timber on it, but in its valley new farms were being opened.

Upon September 27th we marched through Fremont, and camped on the Platte valley two and one-half miles west of town. At this point the country was level, and somewhat settled. That evening a soldier who had served in the war, and been discharged, came into camp, and when he found that we were an Iowa company, he told of a couple of Iowa soldiers who were living about a mile from camp. When he gave their names, I thought I remembered them; so I went out to see them. They were two brothers, unmarried, keeping "bach" in a little cabin made of the trunks of cottonwood trees, daubed up with mud ready for the winter. They had each taken a quarter-section, and settled

upon it as a homestead. One had been discharged from the
hospital, his health having been impaired down near Vicksburg. The other was severely wounded at the battle of
Shiloh, and was discharged on account of wounds received.
Neither one was drawing a pension. They spoke at considerable length of the difficulties which they encountered
with their neighbors, saying that several of their neighbors
were old Confederate soldiers who had deserted and left
the Confederate service, but who were still strongly against
the "Abolition war." Each one of these boys had two revolvers, and a rifle. They said that there had been a Union
League formed at the village of Fremont.

On September 28, 1863, we started early in the morning, and camped on Shell Creek. It was quite a long, deep-
cut stream, but apparently not flowing much water. We
camped on the stream a half-mile above where the road
crossed it. Captain O'Brien and I went out hunting for
ducks, the Captain having bought a double-barrel shotgun
and ammunition at Fremont. The Major commanding our
battalion, with an escort, joined us in the afternoon, shortly
before we went into camp. He was one of the old pioneers of
the West, Major John S. Wood, of Ottumwa, Iowa. He had
been to California with the forty-niners, and in camp that
night he told us of a battle which he and his wagon train,
over fourteen years before, had with Indians on the bank of
Shell Creek. The Major was not a man who praised himself
very much, and when he told the story of the Shell Creek
fight it was very interesting to us. In the morning he took
us out to where he said he had dropped an Indian with his
rifle.

The country along the route of the day's travel was considerably settled. I would say that one-fourth of the quarter-
sections had occupants—that is, down in the valley; the
upper lands seemed to be entirely uninhabited. We passed
a large number of trains during the day coming in, and some
few going out. Those that were going out seemed to be
loaded only for Fort Kearney, or else were the wagons of
private ranchers along the line to about a point of two

hundred and fifty miles west of the river. It was a sort of custom of the place to talk to everybody and ask everybody where he came from, and we, being on horseback, had time to ride back a few yards with the boss of a train to talk with him further regarding the grass and water, and where the best camping-places were. We passed during this day several little bands of Indians, generally not more than four together. They were mostly in pairs, bucks and squaws; hardly any children. They seemed to be sort of migratory; to be in camp a great deal, and to make but little progress in their wandering. The settlers said the Indians were apparently friendly, and nobody showed any fear of them. They seemed to be wanting the protection of the whites. One woman at a ranch near the road where we stopped to water, said that they kept walking around the house, and looking in the windows, and at first scared her considerably, but finally she got so she would go and order them off without any fear. But there were vivid rumors of the warlike conditions of the Western tribes, and of murders, burnings and difficulties a few hundred miles west.

Upon September 29, 1863, we marched to Loup Fork, and camped a half-mile from Columbus. Captain O'Brien was dissatisfied with the shotgun he had bought at Fremont. In fact, it was a weak gun, and at Columbus he looked around until he found a man who had a large, powerful duck gun, and the Captain traded off his old gun for almost nothing, and bought the new one. As the game would be consumed by our mess, we agreed that the cost of all of the ammunition should be charged up to our officers' mess. It was a gun of the old type, with a wooden ramrod, but it shot well. The Captain was a couple of years older than I, and we together had to manage the company. It was a tough company to manage. The Captain had been in the service for a long while, and had been down South, was in the battle of Perryville, and was a brave and reliable officer. I was on the rolls as a "veteran volunteer," which under the law gave me a sort of preference. We had formed a fast and enduring friendship, and pulled together always in all emergencies. Our

First Lieutenant was a white-haired, gray-whiskered, incapable man, of good family and good birth, but without the slightest military ability in the world, and had got his First Lieutenancy on account of political influence. The men had no respect for him, and didn't mind him, or care for what he said.

Our company was composed of fellows who had a natural longing for a fight, and the Captain and I each of us had more than once a personal conflict with some of our men; but the men had got into the habit of minding us when we gave orders. The First Lieutenant was being utilized as a sort of commissary and quartermaster, and was not with us at this particular time. At Columbus there were but few houses; it was entirely a frontier village, and had some wild and frontier characters in it. Among them was a man named North, who was a great Indian fighter, and a great authority on Indians. He was highly esteemed by the Pawnees on account of various acts of bravery. This man North, many years after, went in with "Buffalo Bill" and organized the "Wild West Show," which made fortunes for many. It happened that Captain O'Brien and I ran onto North immediately after our entrance into the village, and formed an acquaintance which lasted forever afterwards. In this narrative of mine, North will be hereafter referred to.

In the little village of Columbus was a long, low one-story building which had painted on it in large letters nearly four feet high, "W. W. W." I inquired what it was, and was told that the letters stood for "White Wheat Whisky," and that there was a German there distilling whisky. I went over to take a look, and see what sort of place it was, and sure enough, I found some of my men in there loading up their canteens. I had to make them unload, and compelled the distiller to pay back their money which he had received. This was a disagreeable matter, for the boys were about half full, and the man himself was a good deal of a bully. They had paid him for all they had consumed. I thought it best to keep whisky out of the camp; in fact, such were the orders; from our superior officers.

The Loup Fork at the time was not a very large river; its name was the French word for "wolf." This was on account of the Pawnee Indians, who had settled at some distance up the stream; "Pawnee," in the Indian language, meaning "wolf." The Pawnees gave the name "Wolf" to the river, which the French, who were the first traders and scouts into the country, translated into "Loup," which has ever since remained.

The night at Columbus was a very eventful night. One of our companies that had preceded us had marched up the Loup River to protect the Pawnees, it being understood that the Sioux were determined to raid them, and the Sioux at that time were an extremely powerful tribe. That night Lieutenant Norris, of the company spoken of, came down to Columbus with some of his men, and having been there in that neighborhood long enough to find out where everything was that was bad, the whole posse got drunk, and the camp was a considerable of a pandemonium. We, however, got the men herded into their tents, and the sober ones guarded the others. Nothing in particular took place except the men shouted, played poker, and shot holes through the top of the tent until after midnight. We were joined by a young man from Ottumwa, Iowa, long since dead, who claimed to have received permission to trade among the friendly Indians along the frontier. He was a very nice young man, who got delightfully and amiably intoxicated on all occasions, was more congenial when drunk than sober, and who played poker with the men for postage stamps, and made himself a general good fellow.

In the morning there came along a paymaster of the United States, with orders from the District headquarters to take escorts wherever he wanted them, and could find them. He presented his credentials to us, and requested that we go with him to the headquarters of the Pawnee tribe up Loup Fork. At that time the Northwestern country was made into a department with headquarters at Fort

Leavenworth. This department was divided into districts, and the district which we were in was the District of "Nebraska and the Plains"; it went west into what was then Colorado, and "Idaho Territory" north of it. This district was divided into sub-districts, and the "Eastern sub-district of the District of Nebraska" had headquarters at Fort Kearney, which was then a large live fort with a wide reservation. This paymaster of the army desired us to go with him because he had to pay off the Pawnee Indians, and the employés of the United States at the Pawnee agency, and go from there to Fort Kearney.

On September 30, 1863, we took up our march with the paymaster and went up Loup Fork to the Pawnee agency, which was said to be twenty miles from where we camped. As near as I can now tell the Pawnee agency was near the mouth of Beaver Creek, on the north side of the Loup Fork, in the eastern part of what is now Nance County. It rained very hard during the night before we started, but in the morning the porous sandy soil had soaked the water up, and we got to the agency about noon. There was a Government agent in charge of the Pawnee Indians at that place, and he came to meet us. His name was Lushbaugh. He had brilliant red, fluffy, bunched side-whiskers under his ears, a variety of whiskers that was not entirely uncommon in those days. They differed from the "burnsides" in that they disconnected from the moustache in front. The Burnsides were a very common method of wearing whiskers in those days. They were so called from the manner in which General Burnside of the regular army trimmed his beard. The name was finally transformed into "sideburns." The variety that Lushbaugh wore had several names, but our boys began adopting them after that, and called them "Lushbaughs," and for several years after that in various places in the West I heard that form called "Lushbaugh." This agent, Mr. Lushbaugh, was very fond of ardent spirits, and the moment we got into the agency he proceeded to tank up. He showed us everything—the Council Chamber, and the little blacksmith shop, and a few things that indicated a fair degree of civilization. A large number of the Indians were out after buffalo, so that there were not very many of the Pawnees in. But the little Indians were around in squads with bows and arrows shooting at marks, and it seemed to be their principal variety of amusement. Mr. Lushbaugh said at that time there were 1,400 good capable warriors in the Pawnee tribe. The squaws had raised some corn, potatoes, and a large quantity of pumpkins that summer. The corn was the nubbin-eared corn of the Pawnees.

The Pawnees were an agricultural tribe to the extent that they had time out of mind raised corn and pumpkins. We went over the village, looked into the tents, and with an interpreter did some talking with the people. There were a few old men and crones smoking and enjoying the sun. We went down towards the river to see where the crossing was, as we expected to move soon, and we noticed the women in great numbers along the river. They were strong, masculine, animated and chatty, and were giggling all the time. We passed a number of squads where these women were cutting up pumpkins into ringlets, and hanging them up in the trees to dry. We went up and down the river for nearly a mile to select the best crossing, and the trees were all hung full of drying pumpkin-rings. No women in Europe or America of any race ever seemed more light-hearted and happy and talkative than these Pawnee squaws, and they shouted words at us which we, of course, did not understand the meaning of. I had been of the opinion that all Indians were taciturn until this, my first large experience with them. The squaws seemed stout and muscular, and to be superior to their husbands. Those male Indians whom we saw around the village seemed to be inferior in strength, good-nature and appearance to their spouses. And every once in a while we saw an Indian who was considerable of a dandy, and had himself decked out in very artistic Indian costume made of fine tanned deer-skin, elaborately embroidered with beads, and porcupine quills. I don't see where all the porcupines came from for this lavish decoration, and am of the opinion that other quills were worked in to meet requirements.

While we were there in the Council Chamber one Indian after another came, and stood at the window looking in, and to my remark that they ought to be taught better manners, Mr. Lushbaugh said that the Indian thought by such attention to us he was doing us great honor, and that we ought to consider that we were being complimented. In a little while the paymaster was ready to go, and we concluded to cross the Loup Fork with him and camp on the other side, so as to get a good early start in the morning. The paymaster's wagon with its big heavy iron safe drove into the stream with several of the mounted soldiers ahead, and several behind. The wagon did not follow the track exactly, and the first thing we knew the mules were floundering, and the wagon was sinking. We rallied around the wagon, unhooked the mules, and then finally used our lariat-ropes, and all pulling together we managed to extricate the light wagon, and the safe, but the safe was down under two feet of water when we got it out. We snaked it to shore, and put it on its side, and let the water out. The paymaster got the combination, and found a large amount of his United States paper money all soaked up with water, saturated as wet as could be; so we had to go back to the Pawnee village. We got the safe into the Council room, opened it, and got the money out. The bills were spread around on the floor to dry, and on tables and chairs and everything. He had quite a large sum, more than we thought he had; no specie—specie had become obsolete. The paymaster stayed on the inside with the door locked. I detailed four men to march a square beat on the outside of the building, one to each side, and I got a chair and mounted guard, and the balance of the boys went into camp on the bank of the river. Mr. Lushbaugh stayed up with us till about 12 o'clock, telling of the various times when he had drunk a great amount of whisky and laid somebody out; and every once in a while he took a drink himself by way of illustration.

Owing to Sioux rumors other troops were sent of our

regiment, following us, up to the Pawnee agency. There were two companies, but I do not remember their letters. They camped below the agency, and several of the officers came up, and came to the Council house to look through the window about sundown and see the money scattered around. These officers had evidently provided themselves with "W. W. W." before leaving Columbus, because they were quite talkative, and wanted to bet on something, and bragged on their horses. About dark two of the officers got to betting as to the relative speed of their horses, and bantered each other for a race. Finally it was agreed that they were to run down with their horses to Columbus, and back, forty miles, and the one that came out ahead was to have $100. So in the gloaming of the twilight, near the Council house, the word "Go" was given, amid a lot of Indians, squaws and pappooses standing around, and most of the soldiers of the different companies. When the word was given both of them started off like the wind, and they were soon lost to view. Each one of them had a canteen swinging over his shoulder. It is my impression that they did not go over two miles, because about midnight they both came back slowly, riding together in a hilarious condition, pretending that they had gone to Columbus, and had just got back, and that it was an even race, and nobody won anything. They soon had everybody in the camp around them, and Captain O'Brien, who was the senior officer, ordered them both under arrest back to their quarters, to which they proceeded to go. One of them, however, objected considerably, and said that he had been a staff officer of General Quimby's and didn't like to be treated that way. General Quimby was one of the noted Brigadier-Generals of the war at that time. Both of these officers turned out to be of no account, and the Quimby young man succeeded afterwards in getting himself dismissed from the service. I was guarding the Council house and had considerable responsibility. It would have taken no flight of imagination if half a dozen of the soldiers, with good horses, had broken into the Council room, driven off the guards, and carried away the money. There were two or three in my company I felt would do it if they had an opportunity; they were toughs, and afterwards deserted. So I stood on post until towards morning, when, the money having got dry, the paymaster got it back into the safe. At a late hour in the morning with a guide we crossed the Loup Fork, and started south to hit the road along the Platte. A prairie-fire, a few days before we came there, had swept the country between Prairie Creek and Loup Fork, and for many miles we marched over a black, barren and desolate country. On the night of October 1st we camped at Warm Slough. I cannot tell from any map that I can now find, where Warm Slough was, but it was not far from the river, and I would say in the eastern part of what is now Merrick County.

CHAPTER III

ON THE evening of October 1, 1863, as stated, we went into camp early at Warm Slough, and there were a good number of travelers on the road. We passed train after train going west, and several trains passed going east. While we were in camp I took Captain O'Brien's shotgun, and went out to get some prairie-chickens. It was a good deal of a feat to shoot prairie-chickens on the wing from horseback, but both the Captain and I became quite expert owing to the intelligence of our horses, who, the moment a bird flew up or we made a demonstration, stood stock-still. As I was coming in at twilight by myself, Captain O'Brien, who had remained in camp, came up to me, and told me to go and put on my saber, and both revolvers loaded, right quick, and join him. He said the whole camp was drunk; that they had got some whisky from a passing train, and were raising Cain. I was soon equipped, and went with him. The Captain pulled out his saber, and went among the men, and began to take them by the neck and shake them up, and order them to be still, and I followed at his side. The Captain went at it rather violently, but succeeded in getting the men hushed up. Order was restored, and we returned to our tent, which was pitched about three hundred feet from the men. In a little while yelling and shooting broke out, and the Captain jumped up and put on his saber and revolvers, and bade me do the same. We went over to the tents, and the Captain began to punch some of the men around, and compel them to be still. There were several of the men and some of the

23

non-commissioned officers who were sober. Some of the men were ugly, and the Captain immediately detailed five sober men with picket-ropes, of which each man carried one (which was a thirty-foot rope with an iron pin for picketing horses), and he took one man after another, who was ugly drunk, to the wagon, and compelled the sober men to tie them to the wagon-wheels. This was an exceedingly dangerous performance, but the Captain had all kinds of nerve and never feared to do his duty, and never feared his men. I accompanied him on the round backwards and forwards to the wagons, until some of the men gathered around the wagons with their guns and threatened to loosen the men who were tied up. So the Captain stationed me to guard the men while he brought others up and tied them. I walked up and down with a revolver, and had the men stand back. He tied up sixteen of them to the wagon-wheels of six loaded wagons which we had at that time. There was an appearance of a mutiny, so the Captain went in and out of the tents giving the men considerable harsh talk, and saying that he would shoot the first man that did anything that looked like a mutiny; that he proposed to handle the company as it ought to be handled, and didn't intend that drunkenness should impair its discipline. In a little while several shots were fired inside of a tent up through the canvas. Then the Captain gave a great "bluff," and went up and down through the camp ordering silence. He and I together kept things going, guarding the prisoners alternately and walking around among the tents, until finally the whisky died out, and the men became more sober, but not less ugly. We released the men who were tied up after about all of them had fallen asleep from drunkenness. Things quieted down about midnight, and finally the men were all released, and the next day matters went along as if nothing had happened; but it was a very trying situation. We put our soberest man on guard that night at the picket-rope where the horses were tied, so that none of the men could go and saddle a horse and desert. The Captain's prompt and decided vigor had a good effect upon the company. And although we had many troubles after that, we never had at any time a difficulty which seemed so likely to break up the company. The Captain expressed gratitude for the assistance I gave him, and the men made up their minds as to who was in command of the company. A considerable while after that I had occasion at midnight to go in front and stop a large detachment of my men bent upon a vicious purpose which I will hereafter describe, but the incident at Warm Slough enabled us afterwards to command the attention of the men, and to keep them fully in line of duty. A company of volunteer soldiers will grow clannish and inclined to hang together for good or evil, and to see how far they can disobey the military law, and how far they can scare or baffle their officers; and when they are all out by themselves with no other corps or regiment or strange troops to bring them into line, and when they are by numbers the masters of the situation, they are liable to play havoc with all military principles, and to run over an officer, if they possibly can. When on detached service, such as we were on, it is sometimes about all an officer's life is worth to maintain his own standing, and the discipline of his company.

Ought I to tell these things in writing of my illustrious company? Well, it is history, and future times will want to know what manner of men wrought out the surprising details of that age.

Captain O'Brien was exceedingly rough, but his conduct was exactly the right thing. There was no better man in the company, physically, than the Captain, and next to the Captain in that respect I thought I was a very close second. The troubles we had with the men came largely from whisky. As to the doing of any dangerous duty the men had no lack of courage, nor of will to go into any fight, or into any dangerous place, or to do any valiant military act. They were all right as fighters, and as soldiers, with the exception that being volunteers and being taken out of the great body of people along with their officers, they felt that they were about as good as their officers were, and that they had a right to a will of their own. They thought that if they wanted to drink and raise Cain it was all right, providing they were ready to fight when the emergencies of the service demanded it. The volunteer soldier of that day was a very strongheaded, willful, obstinate fighter. He had been brought up from his boyhood to fight. The men fought around among themselves, pounding each other up, and exercising the same sort of a feeling of emulation that a lot of roosters would in a barnyard. When they wanted to stand off in a ring, and fight each other according to what were then considered "prize ring rules," we as officers never interfered. They had to fight somebody at some time, and little private fisticuffs were only an outlet for the energy and vigor of the men individually. In fact, one night without our knowledge, one of our sergeants got into a fist fight with one of the men, and they went at it, when a ring was formed, "hammer and tongs." I never knew anything of it until the next morning at roll-call, when I noticed the sergeant's face all black-and-blue. I asked what was the matter; he said he had been hurt. I guessed immediately how he had been hurt, and pursued the inquiry no further. It was, of course, against good order and military discipline that a private soldier should pound up a non-commissioned officer, but I did not deem it wise to take notice of such things if the non-commissioned officer did not care to say anything upon the subject. We took occasion some time afterwards to reduce this sergeant to the ranks, on the ground that when he made out his reports he did not write plainly enough. Our non-commissioned officers were sturdy young fellows, and kept pretty good order, and assisted us very greatly to keep and establish discipline.

Every man in the company could sign his name, and the large majority of them could write well. Although the company was a sort of fiery and untamed company, still the Captain and I could not help having a good deal of affection for the men, because there was one thing they wouldn't do —they wouldn't get scared. And they wouldn't dodge any hardship or danger, and would march all night and all day, and all night again, with perfect composure, and the more difficult and dangerous the work and necessities of the occasion, the more good-natured they seemed to be. But whisky changed it all when they got too much of it.

In the morning of October 2, 1863, the Captain desired me to go on ahead to Fort Kearney, and arrange for quarters at that place, or pick out a camping-ground, and see about rations. I moved along with the command until we got to a place called the O. K. Store, which I think was the beginning of what is now the city of Grand Island. I remember hearing Grand Island spoken of, and remember of one of our Corporals going down to what he called the "North Channel," at which place he killed somebody's hog, skinned it and brought it into camp with all appendages cut off, and called it "antelope." Captain O'Brien and I had some of it for our supper, and having served in the army down South, we distinctly identified the flavor, and knew that it was pig. We sent for the Corporal and asked him about it, and he said that it was wholly wild, and nowhere near any habitation, and he thought it was too good a thing to let go by. Upon which we told him that if anybody made complaint we would pay for the hog and see that it came out of his pay-roll, to which he with apparent readiness consented.

At the O. K. store there was a telegraph station of the Overland Telegraph, and the Captain desired me not to wait, but to take that night's stage and go through to Fort Kearney. In order to do that I had to telegraph on down to Fremont or Columbus to know what the condition of things was, and whether there were any vacant seats in the coaches. I was up that night trying to get this information until two o'clock in the morning, at which time a stage came, loaded down to the guards with passengers. Every available person that could get on the stage was there. On the inside they were sitting by turns on each other's laps. The settlement around the store seemed to be German. The person in charge of the store was a German, and they had a very large stock of goods. There was another stage coming along, shortly after the two o'clock stage, as was believed, but I could not reach it by wire, and finally, having sat up all night, I went around to the company and took breakfast.

On October 3rd we marched along the road and camped on Wood River at a place which was then called "Center." On Wood River, near where we camped, Major Wood, who had rejoined us, took us out and showed an old crossing of the river where his train had a fight with the Indians over fourteen years before. These Indians he thought were the Pawnees. Upon the trip this day we passed a camp with several tents of Indians. The Indians which we had seen farther down called themselves Omahas. These Indians called themselves Ponkas, and we were told that they were a part of the same family as the Omahas. These Ponkas seemed to be a kindly, lazy, inefficient set of Indians, but the women had the same industrious appearance as other squaws. The men had a sort of effeminate look. They seemed to have small feet and to be more feminine than the women. They were strutty, with a sort of Indian pride. The women did all the work, and appeared to think that it was the proper thing for them to show off their husbands all fixed up; they thought that they would not be considered good housekeepers if they could not show a well-dressed, idle husband. The squaws all appeared to be of such fiber that they could trounce their husbands easily, and throw them out of the tent when they wanted to. In fact, it seemed to me that the women were about fifty-five per cent masculine, and the men about fifty-five per cent feminine. I think that some of the contempt which the early settlers had for the Indian was due to his effeminate actions and appearance. In addition to this, the Indian grew no whiskers, and had a general inefficient manner, and was not in stature and build the equal of the white boys that were in our company.

The travel on the road continued incessant. The greater part of the travel, however, was towards Omaha. I was told that the heaviest trains and the greatest travel westward started with the grass in the spring. It now appeared as if the main travel was back towards Omaha, it being autumn, and that the trains had herded and left the greater part of their oxen somewhere west and with ox teams reduced in number were hauling back the empty wagons coupled together. With them were a great many returning travelers riding on horseback with their trunks in the wagons. These travelers were engaged in having a good time on their return and in hunting game along the route. There were a good many greyhounds with the trains. Jack-rabbits had become very plentiful after reaching Wood River, and antelopes were seen from time to time in great numbers towards the hills. These travelers and riders wore no coat or vest. They wore heavy woolen shirts with silk handkerchiefs around their necks, and one or two revolvers buckled on. I always stopped and talked to the wagon-masters of the trains, and it was the custom of the plains to give each other all the information possible in regard to the routes. As these people were all very observant, we could always tell pretty nearly what there was ahead of us. The Indians had entirely disappeared from the route. We were told that there were buffalo over in the hills both north and south of the river, but they seemed to stay away from the valley, being frightened by the hunters. Many of the wagons began to have large pieces of buffalo-meat hung up on the bows which supported the wagon-covers. At one point about noon of this day (October 3rd), I saw in the very great distance the black specks indicating buffalo, but they were too far off for us to bother with them.

A little while before we went into camp at Center we made a halt to let the horses graze upon the luxurious grass down in the valley. The wagons were parked and the horses unsaddled and picketed. The Captain and I went out into the road to await the coming of a train which was ahead of us. Suddenly we heard a lot of shooting, and the Captain and I immediately with great anxiety directed our steps in that direction. It seems that a buffalo had been discovered down near the river-bank, and, endeavoring to escape, had plunged into the water and quicksands, and the boys had rallied around it and killed it. It was pulled out onto the bank and skinned and put into our wagon, and that night we camped at the place called Center, where there were a couple of houses, and the whole company sat up until late at night frying and eating buffalo-meat. We divided some of the meat with a party of "pilgrims" as they were called, who overtook us going west. Everybody traveling west in those days was called a "pilgrim." The next day, October 4th, we marched, crossed the river to the south side, and went into Fort Kearney, where we arrived shortly after noontime.

CHAPTER IV

FORT KEARNEY at that time was an old frontier post. It was said to have been established in 1848. It was situated south of the river, and somewhat east from the crossing of the Platte, so that the trains going west, and crossing the river, would not come past the post, but would cross above and west of it. There was a tough collection of frontier habitations just on the west edge of the reservation; this place, called Dobytown, was two miles west of the Fort. All of the buildings, so far, west of Columbus, had been covered with clay roofs. We first noticed them at Columbus. The roofs were made of poles, in the interstices of which willow brush had been placed, over these swale-grass from the bed of the river, and on top of it all from six to ten inches of hard clay dug out from the lower portion of some of the gullies. This clay had been tamped and pounded down, forming a complete shelter from rain and cold. It was almost like cement. In fact, there was nothing in the country to make any other kind of a roof out of. There were no shingle machines, or wood from which shingles could be made. Dobytown was a collection of adobe buildings of Mexican style, containing the toughest inhabitants of the country, male and female.

Fort Kearney was at the junction of the two regular roads, one coming west from Omaha, and the other up to the Platte from Fort Leavenworth, the trail being augmented by roads from Weston and St. Jo. These all united at Dobytown and went together in one track west. The volume of travel was much the larger on the southern prong, and these two great currents of overland commerce meeting at Dobytown fixed the spot there where the toughs of the country met and had their frolics. Large quantities of the meanest whisky on earth were consumed here, but, strange as it may appear, there were also quantities of champagne sold and drank here. Persons suddenly enriched, coming from the west and the mines, met here with old chums and cronies and with them drank champagne; or met old enemies, and with them fought a duel to the death. The cemetery was larger than the town. Three of the men of my company disappeared immediately upon our arrival, and it was suggested that I would find them in Dobytown. The next morning a man who lived in Dobytown being down at the Fort, offered to go up with me and go around, as he was acquainted with the places, and help me find the men. There was a row of telegraph poles between the Fort and Doby-town, and after we had started, this new acquaintance of mine, who had on two Colt's pistols, told me he could ride the line as fast as his horse would run, and put six bullets out of each revolver into successive telegraph poles; that is to say, he could hit a telegraph pole with every shot. Being somewhat experienced myself from a couple of years' service in the cavalry, I did not think he could do it, but I rode along with him, and he did it with the missing of only one tele-graph pole in twelve shots. The road along was about eighteen feet from the poles. He afterwards told me he had practiced on it hundreds of times. I often practiced on it myself after that, but never could quite attain so good an average. His name was Talbot.

There was at Fort Kearney a vast warehouse in which supplies for the west were stored in great quantities. In this big warehouse were rations enough for an army. And this at that time was needed, because under the law as it then stood, the commissary had the right to sell provisions to indigent and hungry persons who made a requisition ap-proved by the Post Commander, and these sales were made at the Government cost price. There were a great many people who through accidents and improvidence ran out of provisions in the wild barren country, and there was a constant sale by the post commissary. Post commanders were very particular in these matters, and quite frugal in their way of giving orders, yet nevertheless in the aggregate the sales were large, and it was necessary that large storehouses of provisions should be kept, so that Fort Kearney and other frontier posts west of it could be supplied in cases of emergency. In addition to that, a post commander always had the right to gratuitously feed the Indians, and the Indians were very prone to come in and see, in their way of expressing it, "What the white brother would do for them." These stores were all rated at cost according to a schedule prepared by the assistant quarter-master-general at Leavenworth. When we went there this great warehouse was almost full. And in the warehouse there was a large room almost as big as a small house, which was built up with heavy planks. The commissary unlocked it one day to show me, and there he had racks in which barrel upon barrel of liquor was stored. He said that there had been liquor piled in there since 1849, and that owing to the difficulties and troubles which ensued from its sale and use, it was carefully handled and only used for issue to fatigue parties. He then said, "The report is that you are going west to build a fort, and if so I will let you have a barrel, at cost price." He then kicked the head of a barrel in one of the lower racks, and said: "There is a barrel that has been here since 1849, as you see by that mark. That is rye whisky, invoiced at twenty-six cents a gallon." It was fully fifteen years old. He said, "There must have been considerable evaporated out of it, so you will have to buy it at what its marked capacity is." Thereupon I told him to save it for me in case the time came. There was also a large quartermaster depot for everything in the shape of necessary tools, and frontier utensils. There were axes, whip-saws, anvils, blacksmith and carpenter tools, shovels, spades, plows, and almost everything that would be needed at a frontier post.

The post itself was a little old rusty frontier cantonment. The buildings were principally made out of native lumber, hauled in from the East. The post had run down in style and appearance since the regulars left it. The fuel was cottonwood cordwood, cut down on the island of the Platte. The parade-ground was not very large, and had around it a few straggling trees that had evidently been set out in large numbers when the post had been made; a few had survived, and they showed the effect of the barrenness and aridity of the climate. They looked tough. On the south side of the square was the largest building, and on the second floor of it was a large room which seemed as if it had at one time been used as a sort of officers' club. There was a large brick fireplace, and above it the masonry of the chimney had been plastered with a hard, smooth finish. Upon this white surface on the breast of the chimney were written a large number of names. It looked as if it had been a sort of register of all the officers who from first to last had ever visited the post. Each one had taken a little space and written his name. And it was one of the most interesting experiences of my stay there that I put in the afternoon reading the names of Captain So-and-so, Lieutenant So-and-so, and Major So-and-so, who since that time had become well-known celebrities in the military service, North or South, in the civil war then pending. It seems as if about all the officers then being distinguished in the war from the regular army, had at one time registered their names upon that chimney-front. Among them was Lieut. R. E. Lee. I will speak more particularly of Fort Kearney further on.

There was no cultivation whatever in and around Kearney. It was too desolate and arid. A little garden was in use, down a distance from the post, surrounded with some barriers made of post and brush. The refuse of the stable had been spaded under, a shallow well dug, and soldiers from time to time on fatigue duty had been put to work in those gardens. But the result was very feeble, and outside of that nothing was raised. I remember during the few days that we were at Fort Kearney there came up a violent wind-storm which carried the sand and gravel freely, and the next morning I was up at Dobytown, and saw them shoveling away from the doors the accumulated drifts. In some places the sand and gravel had piled up against the doors fully a foot high. Out on the tableland the sand was on the surface, except that in the swales there was grass. I was told that Fort Kearney marked the western line of the rights of the Pawnee Indians; that they were forbidden by either military order or treaty from going any farther west than the line of Fort Kearney. There was also said to be a buffer territory, and that the western Indians were not allowed to come east within forty miles of Fort Kearney; so that there ran a strip north and south of forty miles wide upon which no Indians by right could go. But it was only a talking point. As a matter of fact, the Indians went where they pleased. The travel from the west at this time was very great, and the trains were full of armed men, and they all reported that rumors of Indian trouble were prevailing all through the west towards Denver.

Around Fort Kearney at that time was a large number of splendid greyhounds. Major Wood, of our regiment, to whom I have heretofore referred, was directed to take command of Fort Kearney. He did so, and acted as post commander until further orders. The greyhounds around the post seemed to be sort of common property, and Major Wood gave Captain O'Brien one, and me one— two of the most beautiful animals of the kind I ever saw, and to which the Captain and I became very much attached. The origin of these greyhounds was as follows, which I give as it was told to me: Sometime back in the '50s an English nobleman by the name of Lord George Gore came to this country for the purpose of hunting big game. As one person described it to me, Lord George Gore came with forty horses, forty servants, forty guns, forty dogs and forty of everything else. He stopped at Fort Kearney and hunted, and several litters of those greyhounds, and some of the original bunch, were left at the post, and became sort of public property, subject to the direction of the post commander.

The moment of our arrival at the post we had all our horses re-shod, and were told we would be sent to build a fort at Cottonwood Canyon, one hundred miles farther west. We drew from the post quartermaster axes, saws, augers, chisels, bar iron for horseshoes, anvils and bellows, and all the necessary paraphernalia to start housekeeping out in the wild country. And I had the commissary take the barrel of whisky which he had promised, fill it from another barrel, and box it up as hardware. It was loaded in the wagon with our other stuff, so that when we moved we started with eight large Government wagons piled high with rations, supplies, corn, ammunition, and tools for the creation of a frontier post.

On October 7th Major Wood, the post commander, desired to bid us adieu by having a buffalo-hunt. Large quantities of buffaloes were over in the hills south of the post. So, at noon, Captain O'Brien and I and the Major, with a scout, went out to look for the buffalo, but were charged to be careful, because Indians from the west might be following the buffalo, and they might take advantage of the situation and get us before we got back. But we never saw any Indians. We went out with nothing but Colt's revolvers, calibre .44, and we had a very exciting afternoon. The buffalo had a strange way of moving across the country. The bulls would be together in large flocks off on one of the wings of the moving herd. They were the most exciting game. They were savage, and often put up a good fight. Our horses were much scared, and it was with great difficulty we could get anywhere near the buffalo. During the afternoon, while we killed several buffaloes, it is a fact that the buffaloes chased us as much as we did them. Captain O'Brien had a very ornamental "McClellan cap," as it was called, an officer's cap embroidered with a gold corps badge, and cross-sabers, and on the inside of it in the top was a piece of red patent leather. The Captain picked out the biggest buffalo of the bull herd as they were going, and managed to get near enough to hit the buffalo, and slightly wound it, not seriously. The buffalo started after the Captain, and his horse became frantic. In the jolting that ensued the Captain's cap fell off, and the red top showing up attracted the eye of the buffalo. He got down on his front elbows and bored his horn right through the top of that cap and pranced off with it on his left horn. The Captain was unable with his revolver to bring him down. We cut out the tongues of the buffaloes we killed, and brought them back after sunset. Swarms of wolves were seen in every direction, hanging on the flanks of the buffalo herd.

All arrangements having been made to start west, we bade adieu to the officers of the various companies after supper, and went to our tents, which were pitched near the Fort, ready to start early in the morning. In a little while an officer came out to us, and told us they wanted to have some ceremonies before we started, as we would not meet again soon, and we went with him to the quartermaster's office and a jollification began. Among those present was an officer of a Missouri regiment. I do not now remember his regiment, but he was a First Lieutenant. He had been sent with dispatches through to Colorado, and was on his way back. This officer along during the evening suggested a game of poker; to use his language, "ten cents ante and one dollar limit"; and he said, "I'll be banker." Soon a party of six were engaged with this Missouri officer, who acted as banker; he issued the grains of coffee which were used upon the occasion. About one o'clock the party broke up, and lo and behold! the banker had had bad luck, and was unable to redeem the chips. He had gone broke, and more too,—he owed every one around the board. Being unable to pay out, he was asked why he had suggested a game like this when he had no money to go into it, and he said that he was going back to St. Louis and he thought he could make enough to pay his expenses. Thereupon Captain O'Brien took out his pocket-knife and cut one of the buttons off of the officer's coat. "I will take this in full of what you owe me."

The buttons on the officer's coat, although he was in the United States service, were not United States buttons, but were gilt buttons of the State of Missouri. The arms of the State were on them; they were such as had been used by the officers of the National Guard of the State. But State pride of this officer had caused him to use these buttons on his United States uniform. In about two minutes the officer had very few buttons on his uniform. Each one of us took a large one from the front row, and gave a verbal receipt in full. We never heard of him afterwards. I sent the button home by mail for preservation, and owing to its ridiculous history have preserved it ever since and still have it.

The next morning, October 8th, we left Fort Kearney, and went west to a fortified ranch called Gardner's Ranch, which was kept by a Mr. James Heemstreet.

CHAPTER V

OUR course was now west along the south bank of the river. From time to time we passed pools that had sticks driven near them, upon which some person had written "Alkali," meaning that the water was so impregnated with alkali that it might be harmful. The wind seemed to blow constantly from the time that we left Fort Kearney. The road was a broad, smooth, beaten track, fully three hundred feet wide, swept clean by the wind, and along the sides for some distance the grass was pretty well eaten out. We fed our horses morning, noon and night, each time a quart of shelled corn. We had a wagon-load or more of it in sacks; each sack held sixty-four quarts, and was said to weigh one hundred and twelve pounds, net. In the evening of the second day, October 9, 1863, we camped near a new cedar ranch, with sod inclosure for stock, built by a man named French. There was some very good grass down near the river. Mr. French had been keeping everybody off from grazing on it, and endeavored to keep us off, but it was Government land, and we were in the service of the Government, and we did not recognize his sovereignty over the broad country. Mr. French became very boisterous, and we had some words with him. Afterwards we were told that he was a Confederate deserter from a Southern regiment, and was not very fond of blue uniforms, and felt inclined to be as disagreeable as possible.

That evening we were overtaken by a stage going through under an escort, and out of the stage jumped a Mr. William Redfield, who notified us that he was one of the Vote Commissioners of Iowa. While the soldiers were away from home the Legislature had given the soldiers the right to vote, so that they could keep down the Copperhead element, which was strong in some portions of the State of Iowa, as also elsewhere. These Vote Commissioners mustered the troops, examined their muster-rolls, and found out who were voters. And having fixed the voting strength of the various companies and regiments, checked up the voting returns afterwards, and delivered them in Iowa. French's ranch was said to be fifty miles west of Kearney.

Buffalo were visible with a field-glass on both sides of the river, but in small numbers, and much scattered. They were not in herds. With a field-glass the antelope could be seen on the north of the river in myriads, and in great numbers towards the hills south and in front of us. In the road I captured a prairie-dog. He was large and fat, and was going from one mound to another. I headed him off, and finally caught him on foot. Our two dogs, "Kearney," owned by Captain O'Brien, and "Lady," owned by me, given to us, as stated, at Fort Kearney, were great companions. They were constantly coursing out and around, and stirring up game; wolves and jack-rabbits were frequent. The dogs gave some beautiful runs after antelope, but the antelope, having much the start, was able to outrun the dogs. Here we found out for the first time that the "jack-rabbit" was swifter than the antelope. A pilgrim on the road who watched our dogs run, told us that if we wanted to have good fun we must get a stag-hound to go with the greyhounds, because, he said, the greyhound courses by sight, and often misses the game, but the stag-hound by scent will keep the track, and recover the pursuit. So, thereupon, we kept our eyes open, and bought a stag-hound of a passing train, and named him, from his loud, sonorous voice, "Bugler," and with the three afterwards we often caught antelope and jack-rabbits.

From Fort Kearney, for many miles up, there was no water in the river. The water seemed to be in "the underflow." We not infrequently rode down to the river, and with shovels dug watering-places in the sand of the bed. We always found permanent water within eighteen inches of the top, no matter how dry the sand on top appeared to be. We were told that 75 miles of the river were then dry, and that generally about 125 miles of it were dry in the dryest season. At French's ranch the water began to appear on the surface in the shape of damp places and little pools.

The next morning, being the morning of October 10th, another stage with escort passed us, and we were joined by the assistant surgeon of our regiment, who had been ordered to overtake us, and act as our medical attendant at the post which we were about to establish. We started bright and early in the morning, and having made about fifteen miles, halted to rest the horses. Buffalo were noticed over in the hills south of us, and many antelope. The hills were constantly rising higher, and canyons were running into them south from the river. Leaving the company to proceed to a certain designated place seventy-five miles west of Kearney, called Smith's ranch, Captain O'Brien and I and the Doctor and the Vote Commissioner, Mr. Redfield, went out into the hills. Our horses were fresh, and we saw the buffalo scattered seemingly at great distances, as far as the eye could reach, all apparently driving to the south. We had now got into the country where Indians were making occasional raids, stealing horses, and killing heedless travelers. We did not care to pursue the buffalo nor kill them unnecessarily, but we desired to watch their movements, and to view the country. We found a tableland as level as a floor as far as the eye could reach, with buffalo scattered over it, that was ever and anon disappearing. The reason of it was that the canyons were cut down straight from the level of the plain, and showed no signs of existence; nor could the depressions be noticed until arriving almost at their brinks. Then beautiful valleys were seen, narrow and deep, full of enormous cedar trees, box elders, hackberry, plum trees, and shrubbery. There were always places that we could find to descend into the canyons, and come out on the other side. We rode along this plain, over these beautiful valleys, for fully ten miles. Down in the valleys the buffalo were plenty, and there were very many deer; wolves in droves were observed sneaking along the sides. Our two dogs were constantly hunting and developing game. There had never been an ax put into these canyons, except a little at their openings near the river. The cedar trees were as straight as arrows, very numerous, and all sizes up to two feet in diameter. They grew mostly from the bottom of the canyon, yet no tree-tops were seen rising above the level of the plain.

Having killed what buffalo we wanted, and taken the tongues and humps, we turned obliquely towards the river to resume our place with the command. At a point on the corner of a canyon as it opened out into the broad plain of the Platte River we came across a new Indian grave. It was on a scaffold made of four poles. These poles had evidently been lodge-poles, and were set into the ground. About ten feet from the ground, thongs had been stretched across from pole to pole, and a scaffold made; the Indian, wrapped up in a fresh buffalo-hide and bound up with a horsehair lariat, had been left to dry. Some portion of a horse had been tied to each lodge-pole; perhaps the horse had been quartered, and the legs tied up; at any rate, there were the bones off which the wolves had eaten, but they had not been able to get up to disturb the Indian, who had probably been killed soon before in a raid down the road. The Captain and I rode northwest, while the Doctor and Vote Commissioner, separating from us, went north towards the river. We could from our high elevation see our company of cavalry in the rear, miles away, coming slowly and silently up the plain, with a cloud of dust drifting to the north.

The wind had very much freshened, and as we got down into the valley, which was here two or three miles wide on each side of the stream, Captain O'Brien started to light a cigar. This was a great feat for any one to do, in such a wind, on horseback. But the Captain from his former service in the army claimed that he could light a cigar in a tornado. The Captain did light a cigar and threw the match away, which he thought had gone out. In a flash a blaze started up in a northerly course towards the river. The grass was fine and silky; the "prairie-grass" had not got in that country at that time, and there was only short, matted buffalo-grass. The flame went with the speed of a railroad train, enlarging as it went. Towards the river the blaze widened and the fire went with a hoarse rumble. In the track ahead of this fire were some cattle grazing. They immediately took flight, and fled towards the river in front of the fire. The fire soon reached the river in a path about one-half mile wide, and became soon extinguished. Several of the cattle were injured jumping down the river-bank, and a man rode out to us and demanded pay. The Captain told the man that the circumstances were entirely an accident, and sympathized with the man, and drawing up his canteen, which was nearly full of whisky (which the Captain partook very little of), he handed it to the man, who pulled away at it as if he had met an old friend that he had not seen for years. The result was that he rode down with us to the river, and when they saw the cattle there, our teams soon came up, and we got the few injured cattle out, killed and skinned them, hung them up to dry over-night, and Captain O'Brien gave a voucher to the man for so many pounds of beef, averaging five hundred pounds to the animal, at six cents a pound. It turned out all right. They were nice fat cattle, and we needed the meat, and the man got his pay through the department quartermaster.

We camped for the night between seventy-five and eighty miles west of Fort Kearney. At the place where we camped the water was visible in the river, but there was no distinct current. The nights were becoming chilly, the elevation higher, and the wind more constant. About every ten miles from French's ranch west there was a store-building with a high, thick, sodded inclosure used as a corral.

These places were also stage stations, and some had sod structures like bastions, built out on the corners, so as to make places of defense. And with each of these places there was generally a herd of cattle, a bunch of Indian ponies, some herders, and a lot of Indian-trading goods; for during the previous summer the Indians had come in to trade all along the line of the Platte valley from French's ranch west. They brought in lots of well-tanned buffalo-robes, quantities of antelope-skins, tanned and untanned, great quantities of buckskin, and many other articles of peltry. But trading with the Indians had stopped, for there was a growing feeling of hostility, although there were still some white men living with the Indians, who had joined them years before, learned the languages and married into the tribes. But unless the white man could speak the language and had lived among them for several years, and had married into the tribe, he was not liked, and his life was in danger. These white men had all come in, and were to be found idling away their time at the various ranches which we passed; some were acting as herders. There were also white hunters and trappers who picked up a great deal of fun, and much money, along the Platte, because at certain places there were beaver and other fur-bearing animals.

We started early on October 11th, and passed Gilmans' ranch, which was built of cedar, and, going fifteen miles farther, camped at a spring called Cottonwood Springs. A man by the name of Charles MacDonald had built a cedar ranch at the mouth of Cottonwood Canyon, which canyon came down to the river near Cottonwood Springs. Cottonwood Springs was merely a seep in a gully which had been an old bed of the river, and which had curved up towards Cottonwood Canyon. The water-bed of the river being largely composed of gravel, the water came down in the underflow, and seeped out at a place down in the bank where there had grown a large cottonwood tree. This spring had been dug out, and was the only spring as far as then known along the Platte for two hundred miles. It was at the mouth of Cottonwood Canyon that we were to build our military post. The place was a great crossing for the Indians going north and south. The valley here was several miles wide. There was a large island in the river of several thousand acres, upon which grew the finest grass to be found in the country, and there were some scrubby willows and cottonwoods; so that the Indians coming from the north found it a good stopping-place to feed their ponies either in summer or winter, because in the winter the ponies could eat the cottonwood brush. In addition to this, Cottonwood Canyon gave a fine passage to the south. A road went up on the floor of the canyon, between the trees, until it rose onto the tableland twenty miles south. The canyon furnished fuel and protection. It was for the purpose of breaking up this Indian run-way that we were ordered to build a post at the mouth of the canyon. We arrived there at eleven o'clock in the morning of October 11, 1863.

CHAPTER VI

COTTONWOOD SPRINGS, when we arrived there, was one of the important points on the road. MacDonald had a year or so before our arrival, built, as stated, a cedar-log store-building. The main building was about twenty feet front and forty feet deep, and was two stories high. A wing 50 feet extended to the west. The latter was, at the eaves, about eight feet high and fifteen feet deep in the clear. Around it in the rear was a large and defensible corral, which extended to the arroyo coming out of the canyon. It had been a good trading-point with the Indians, and there was a stage station there, and a blacksmith shop kept by a man named Hindman. In the stage station was a telegraph office. There was also on the other side of the road a place where canned goods and liquors were sold, kept by a man named Boyer, who had lost a leg, and whom the Indians called "Hook-sah," which meant "cut leg." MacDonald had dug, in front of his store, and cribbed up, an inexhaustible well, which was said to be forty-six feet deep; it was rigged with pulley, chain, and heavy oaken buckets. MacDonald and those at the place had formerly had a good trade with the Indians, but now it was all ended, and they were in danger.

We immediately pitched our tents, and marked out the quadrangle for company quarters, officers' quarters, and guard-house. The next day was spent in unloading our supplies, putting them under shelter, and organizing the squads for going up into the canyon for cedar logs. We had only about seventy-five men that were really effective for hard work, but many of them were very skillful in the use of the ax, and many knew how to handle tools. The end room of the wing of MacDonald's cedar structure was used as "pilgrim quarters." It had a heavy clay roof, and a large simple cast-iron cook stove, with sheet-iron stovepipe running up through the roof. Our "Post Headquarters" used that room for office and mess, but we slept in our tents. On October 13th we started up the canyon; six of our men had worked in the pineries, and were expert axmen. They went to work as three couples to fell the trees. Their axes were sharp, the weather stimulating, and they tumbled the trees rapidly. Other squads trimmed the branches; others with a cross-cut saw worked in constant reliefs, cutting the logs the right length. Our quarters had been planned to be built of twenty-foot logs. These logs were about a foot in diameter. We had our pick. After getting down a lot of the logs, we organized squads with our team mules to snake them out of the canyon. The men made rapid work, and every night every man who had worked in the canyon got a good snifter from my barrel of 1849 whisky. We were racing against the weather, and I never saw men work with more activity. The main barracks for the men were designed as six square rooms, which made a long building one hundred twenty feet long by twenty feet wide on the outside. Among our number were those who had built log cabins, and knew how to "carry up a corner," as the expression was. So the logs were snaked down, and with assistance the men at the corners notched them up, and it was but a few days before the cabins seven feet high in the clear were ready for the roof. The best logs were kept out to build Company Headquarters with. In a little while we had the pole roof on, with the interstices filled with cedar boughs, and about ten inches of good hard clay tamped down; but we were still without doors and windows, although we had places for them sawed out in the log walls. The large logs, of which there were many over twelve inches in diameter, were reserved for lumber. We dug out a place on the bank of the arroyo as a saw-pit, and having two whip-saws, the men were started sawing out lumber one inch in thickness. The men took turns at the top, and the bottom, with the saw, sawing the length of a log. Then they were relieved by two others, so that the whip-saws were kept running all the time, but no one had more than one round a day at that particular work. With smaller cedar poles cut, and used as joists, we soon had bunks made in each of the rooms of our company's quarters. We had drawn "hay bags" from the quarter-master at Fort Kearney. These we used as straw-ticks, and filled with whatever the soldiers wanted to put in. The boys chose partners, and began to occupy the bunks. We had drawn a lot of sheet-iron for the purpose of making stoves, and stovepipes. Our blacksmith rapidly fixed the company up with sorts of funnel-shape sheet-iron stoves, in which the cedar chips burned like tinder. These company quarters were rather close, there being no communication between the different rooms. Sixteen men occupied a room, and between the bunks was a space where they had their mess-cooking, and their mess-eating. With the whip-saw, lumber enough was got out for a door in front of each room, and a window shutter in the rear.

One or more non-commissioned officers were established in each room, and the north end room was a non-commissioned officers' mess. In our kits were two broadaxes, and there were men who knew how to use them, so the Company Headquarters building was made of logs that had been "scored and hewed." The scoring was a simple process. The man stood on the top of the log, and chopped into a line through the whole length of the log, and then the man with the broadax hewed in and straightened it. By working in reliefs, in a few days the Company Headquarters building, eight feet high and twenty feet square, with a puncheon floor and cedar door, and with an oil-paper window, was ready. Then we put up a house in which to store supplies. This was forty by twenty. Then across the road—for we had built alongside of the road and quite near to Mac-Donald's ranch—across the road we put up a hospital building of twenty-foot square-hewed logs, with a sort of porch. These buildings were all "chinked and daubed." That is, blocks and chips were driven in between the logs, and clay was mixed into mortar by the wagon-load down near the springs, and hauled up, and the walls plastered up inside and out so that they were air-tight. Afterwards, the roof having become settled, the clay was dampened and plastered with a trowel. Then we built a guard-house twenty feet square, divided across the middle so that the back half of it was as dark as a dungeon, with a big heavy plank door with hinges extending across, which our blacksmith had made. Then it became necessary to look after our horses, and to build a stable to protect them. These were built upon the palisade principle. We made the outline of our stable just about two hundred feet long, although it bent with an angle so that we could fill in the other angles, and have a square with an open interior. We dug a trench three feet deep. We cut the posts only twelve feet long, and putting them on end in the trench, we filled the trench, leaving the posts standing side and side. When the walls were up, which did not require very long time, the tops of the posts were sawed off level, and a plate-rail spiked on top of them, with spikes made by the blacksmith, one to a log. Upon this we placed a roof, and then fitted up the interior with poles, and got our horses under cover. Between these upright palisades we drove blocks, put in filling, and on the west and north plastered them up. It was very interesting to watch work go forward in such a case as this. There were men in the company who collectively knew how to do everything, and do it well. Everyone was desirous of getting fixed before the cold weather, and there was no laziness or shirking.

Upon Tuesday, November 3, 1863, the election came off. A strong Copperhead and "peace-at-any-price" party had grown up in Iowa, and the election was centered upon the governorship. The National Democratic party had Mc-Clellan for a nominal head; it was trying to bring the war to a close, and was propounding all kinds of arbitrations and compromises. The only position for the soldiers to take was that of fighting the thing right straight through to the bitter end, and making the United States, in the language of Lincoln, "All slave or all free." Such was the grim determination of the men in the field, and in the ranks; such was the sentiment of most of the officers. There were several in the company of whom I had begun to have suspicions, but I think by desertion afterward they mostly eliminated themselves, and their influence, from the company. Capt. O'Brien got the company together at noon on election day, and made them a speech. So did I. It wasn't very much of a speech, only I told them we couldn't afford to let Iowa get into the hands of the Copperheads, because then they would stop recruiting, and try to bring the war to a close. We made the speeches a little bit bitter, and got the men worked up pretty thoroughly. I was the election officer who was to receive and count and forward the ballots. The Captain was as ardent as I was, and a better talker. I was pleasantly surprised that the men stayed with us; only eight voted the opposite ticket. Capt. O'Brien was much delighted. I made every effort to find out from among the boys who it was that voted those eight votes. It was, of course, somewhat difficult to find out, but I think five of the eight became deserters, and of the other three one was killed by whisky, and two had poor military records. Assisted by the soldier vote, the State of Iowa was saved, and retained in the ranks of loyal States. On looking back it seems to me strange how hard we had to fight, and yet how much exertion we had to put forth to control those in the rear so that we could be permitted to put down the Rebellion. As I look back on it I don't see how it was that the Union was saved; and I cannot comprehend, although I was in the middle of it, how it was that we managed to keep things going until the end came, in a satisfactory manner.

At a ranch below us, where there was a good valley in

the Platte, a man had brought out a mowing-machine, and had put up for the use of the overland travelers about two hundred tons of hay. After we arrived, he came to see us, and told us that although grass was dead, and dry, that he could still cut considerable more of it, and that horses could live upon it. We made arrangements with him for some of this poor hay, and also enough of the other to carry us through. In addition to this, squads of horses tied together by the halter, two and two, were sent out under charge of a soldier to allow them to graze and frolic day by day; and our horses, having nothing else to do at the time, improved and kept in excellent condition.

On November 28th we were all under cover, and although there was still much to do, we determined to celebrate Thanksgiving, supposing that to be the day. Down at Gilmans' Ranch, fifteen miles east of the post, they wanted to furnish us some fat cattle, and some additional hay. Captain O'Brien and I rode down there, and found the "Gilman Brothers." There were two of them. They had been engaged in the Indian trade. They told us that the Indians were liable at any time to make a lot of trouble, and they told us much about Indian character, disposition, and methods. The elder of the two had a strange history. He had joined the Walker filibustering expedition which went to Cuba years before, in which so many were garroted. He said that he was a young man, and was from Portsmouth, New Hampshire, and understood the sea and understood the Cubans. And instead of going ashore in Cuba, he got onto a piece of wood or wreckage and stayed out in the Gulf Stream until he was picked up by a freight vessel. He said that if he had gone ashore the Spanish officers would have executed him. After that he started for California with his brother. Their team got wrecked, and they stopped, got to trading with the Indians, and finally built their ranch. They now had a very fine built and defensible ranch. They told us how they made their money. They said that the train oxen not being generally shod, their feet on the overland travel finally became sore, and the oxen became unable to pull, and that the ranchmen traded one well animal for two footsore animals,—even trade, two for one. Then they kept the footsore animals for a time until their hoofs grew out, and traded again. By keeping a supply of well-broken oxen which could be put right under the yoke, they had managed to build up a large business, and occasionally to sell yokes of oxen at large prices for cash, and they had made considerable money. They had a large stock of goods.

There was an Indian sitting down in front of this ranch when we went there, but the Gilmans said that the Indian was a poor, worthless and harmless fellow, who would do nobody any injury. The Indian name of the elder brother, J. K. Gilman, was We-chox'-cha, and of the younger, Jud Gilman, the Indian name was Po-te'-sha-sha. I was told that the first name meant "the old man with a pump," and the other, "red whiskers." There was an iron pump out in front of the house, and the younger had red whiskers. The Indians gave every white man a name. They could not understand why a white man should have a name that did not mean anything. We made arrangements with the Gilmans for beef for the post, subject to the approval of the district quartermaster. And also arranged that they should not sell all of their hay, so that in case we needed some in the spring we could have it. The Gilmans told us that the Indians would not begin their depredations until the grass was high enough for their ponies. That we might expect trouble about the first of June next. All the prophecies J. K. Gilman made came true, and the information which he gave proved to be sound and sensible. He was a very capable, intelligent man, as was also his brother, although the older was better informed. They were men who would make good citizens anywhere, and how they should be out there in that lone ranch trading with Indians and pilgrims, was a great deal of a mystery, unless it could be explained by the profits of their business. The elder Gilman told me that their stuff there around them was worth more than $50,000, and that they had large quantities of supplies in back rooms for the purpose of handling the trade. They also said that they had gotten acquainted with all the chiefs of the Sioux and Cheyennes, and had induced men as agents to go out and live with them, and sort of take orders; that is, to influence trade to come to them, the Gilmans, on a percentage.

Gold was discovered in Colorado May 7, 1859, at Idaho Springs, by a man, it was claimed, named George Washington Jackson. Soon afterwards a heavy emigration from the States to there set in.

Shortly after Thanksgiving, about the first of December, a large train came down from the west. There must have been fully two hundred persons in it, and about the same time some travelers came up from the east, so that one evening MacDonald, the owner of the ranch, announced that they were going to have Masonic services in the second story of his ranch building. I was not a member of that organization, but I saw a number going there, and it was a surprise to me how all of the persons of that congregation could get into that one upper room. I afterwards spoke of it to MacDonald, and he went and got out his Masonic apron and a lot of paraphernalia, and said that he had been at the head of a lodge in the East, and was going to establish one as soon as enough people in the country could come to it.

One thing that was remarkable was the number of skunks in the Platte valley. They were playing hide-and-seek all over Fort Kearney while we were there, and ranchmen said that they were plentiful, and a great nuisance. We had hardly got established before they were in and out the floors and the stables, and other places where they could hide, and they appeared to be as tame and playful as kittens. It was not long before in our new post they became an insufferable pest.

We still kept on at work improving our quarters. We dug and curbed up a well. We made a flag-pole out of cedar trees trimmed down, and joined up by the blacksmith. It was a great occasion. It was a beautiful tall and slender pole, and we set it deeply in the ground. We needed some more supplies; and were told that we could have two twelve-pound mountain howitzers from Fort Kearney. So we sent down our teams with an escort of a sergeant and ten men that brought us back the two howitzers, a lot of artillery ammunition, new tools, rations, and supplies. These two howitzers we mounted on the parade-ground. Captain O'Brien had belonged to the artillery early in the war, and thoroughly understood the handling of these light guns. Squads were put to work drilling on these howitzers, so that in course of time every man in the company could fill any place on a gun squad. About the fifteenth of December, while drilling the squad, some Indians were seen over on the island of the Platte north of the post. It was thought best to give them a scare; so the two pieces were run to a good place north of the post, near the river, and fired at the Indians. Our shells fell short, but the Indians scampered to the north bank, and were soon out of sight. In a day or two afterwards there suddenly appeared in the post an old Indian, together with a young buck of about twenty. He came up to me, saying, "How-cola, How-cola," the word "Cola," in the Sioux language, meaning "friend." He made a sign that he wanted something to eat, so I took them both to the storehouse, and told the commissary sergeant to draw out a quart of molasses into a mess-pan, and give it to the Indians with a box of hard-tack, and let them eat what they wanted. The amount which they consumed was enormous. I went out to inquire how these Indians got in, and where they were from. Some civilian whom I didn't know, talked with the Indians, and they said they were with their tribe a long distance south, but had come north to see their white brother, and see what their white brother would do for them. They were probably spies. Several of the boys stood around in wonderment, watching these Indians eat. Each one of them ate as much as five men ought to be able to hold. The weather was cold, and they were not very warmly clad, but each one had a fine tanned buffalo-robe as soft and flexible as velvet. I wanted to find out something from them, but while I was hunting for the man that knew, these Indians started on a trot, and went up the canyon one behind the other, and were seen no more. We ought to have put them in the guard-house and held them.

Ever since I came to the post I had made it a custom to give the Loyal League hailing-sign to the men who were passing in the trains, but I rarely got a response. Not one man in five hundred knew what it meant. Not one in five hundred seemed to care whether the Government won or lost in the Civil War. They were either deserters from the army, North or South, or were out for cash only.

CHAPTER VII

GOING back in a retrospective way over our proceedings at Cottonwood Springs (concerning matters which I did not wish to break the thread of my relation to give), I will recur to a wind-storm that came on October 17th. The air was dry and arid, and a sudden wind came up in the forenoon from the north, unaccompanied by dampness or snow. The wind just blew, and kept increasing in force and momentum. All of our tents were blown down during the afternoon, and during the gale it was impossible to raise them. Our stuff was blown off from the flat ground and rolled and tumbled over until it struck the depression of the arroyo of Cottonwood Canyon. It was a straight, even wind. We soon found out what it was necessary for us to build in order to resist the climate. The pilgrim quarters at MacDonald's ranch was soon stored with what we were obliged to save. Incredible as it may seem, the wind blew down the stove-pipe into the stove, so that it turned one of the covers over to get exit. This heavy iron cover was about seven inches in diameter. When we put it back the stove rattled until again the cover turned over. Jimmy O'Brien said it was an "Irish tornado,"—that the wind blew "straight up and down." Along in the afternoon, our horses that were tied up with picket-rope became frantic, and began breaking away. A two-inch rope was torn from its moorings and the horses started up Cottonwood Canyon. There were less than half a dozen horses that were left securely tied. These were immediately saddled, and soldiers detailed to corral the stampeded horses, and to keep them together in the canyon. By using iron picket-pins and lariat-ropes some few of the tents were got up again, toward night, and held in place. The wind blew a gale all night, and got somewhat chilly. Boxes of clothing and hard-bread were rolling over the prairie, bound for the arroyo. We all of us slept where we best could, but most upon the lee bank of the canyon-bed. The wind immediately subsided as the sun rose in the morning, and we had no more trouble with it except to gather up the things. The difficulty with the wind was that it carried the sand and gravel in the air, and made it painful and almost dangerous at times to be where the full effect of the current came, which was mixed with the sand and gravel. The latter seemed to come in streaks. A herder of the ranch told a funny story about a window which was exposed to one of these sand-and-gravel storms, and he said that it had been changed into the appearance of ground glass, and had been rendered almost opaque. But he made light of the storm, saying that he had seen much worse ones. Afterwards we did experience one equally as bad, if not worse, while going from Lodgepole northwest to Court House Rock. Sand and gravel banked up against the pilgrim quarters in places about two feet high above the level, as the consequence of this storm. We kept the horses herded up in the canyon until the storm was over, and did not lose any.

About two weeks after that we were told that some prowling Indians had been seen in south of Gilmans' ranch, headed towards our place, and Captain O'Brien thought I had better reconnoiter a little up the canyon, so as to forestall any surprise. Instead of taking a party of men with me, I thought I would prefer to go alone, as I had a most excellent horse, which I will hereinafter describe. I rode up on the east rim of the canyon, and looked over the country with my field-glass pretty fully. By keeping up on the rim, I could see the canyon inside and out. I went around about ten miles, and saw a lot of fresh pony-tracks. I also saw a large lone buffalo down in the canyon. I rode past it to see whether or not there was any Indian looking for him, and making up my mind there was not, I went down into the canyon to get the buffalo. I only had two Colt's calibre .44 revolvers in my holster. I carried neither saber nor carbine. The time that I had with that buffalo in the canyon I shall not soon forget. He chased me a great deal more than I chased him. The matted hair upon his forehead was filled with mud, and he faced me at all times. My revolver bullets glanced off from his forehead apparently as if it were a piece of granite, and they only seemed to irritate him. It was fully two hours before I laid him out, and I had fired thirty-one shots.

About a week after that, Captain O'Brien desired to make a further reconnoissance, in view of reports which came in. I got well acquainted with the ins and outs on the east side, and the shortest and best routes from one crossing to another, which were deeply worn by buffalo trails. And here I got my first idea of the extent to which game and wild animals make the shortest and best roads through a country, and the most accessible roads, which in after time are followed by the white man, and become the highways from place to place. On this occasion I carried my target rifle (a Smith & Wesson, calibre .44) and a field-glass. When about eight miles from the camp, I saw in the distance a bareheaded Indian going over a ridge on foot with great speed. I hastened to catch up with him, but when I got to the ridge where he disappeared I considered that it would be safer for me to be careful lest I should fall into some kind of ambuscade. So I rode around on the high ground, and examined the gullies for about a mile, but the Indian had successfully eluded me, and I was in no condition to go down and hunt through the canyon. He was probably some lone Indian who was acting as a spy, or reconnoitering. An Indian on a pony could be easily tracked, but an Indian on foot could slip around and secrete himself, and be quite safe. There were always down in the valley along the road some half-breed Indian traders who also acted as spies, and would communicate all necessary information to the Indians and sell them what was called "Pilgrim whisky"; hence the Indians, as we were informed, reconnoitered on foot, and it was one of these I had probably seen.

The pilgrim whisky of that day was a bad compound. Owing to the distance which it had to be carried, alcohol was substituted for whisky, and when a person out in that country got a barrel of alcohol, he would take a quart of it and mix it with a quart of water, and stir in molasses and a touch of red pepper, and it made a compound that would bring out all the bad qualities of the consumer. This was the kind of whisky that the Indians would get from traders. They dealt surreptitiously, because it was a penitentiary offense to sell whisky to the Indians. The ranchmen fought the contraband fiercely, and there were stories of herders and ranchmen taking some half-breed and lynching him when they had found that he had sold that kind of stuff to the Indians.

By the first of December we had got pretty well acquainted with our surroundings. Captain O'Brien with four men went out to reconnoiter the canyon fully, and he took the west bank. He went nearly to the end of the canyon, and explored it fully, and then going west came down back through another large cedar-filled canyon. I afterwards, in about a week, also made the reconnoissance of the canyon from the west bank about ten miles of distance, and at a certain place where there was a wall of indurated clay I carved name, date, Company, and Regiment. It was necessary for us as officers of the company to know the country, and to familiarize ourselves with Indian matters. Ten miles west of our post was Jack Morrow's ranch, of which I will speak hereafter. Between it and our post there were several ranches that had been deserted, on account of the Indian scare, but which were reoccupied after our arrival. In fact, as soon as we camped at Cottonwood Springs, the safety of the place being assured, many people seemed inclined to take up land, or to accept employment in the neighborhood. On the first of December, on the suggestion of Captain

O'Brien, I tabulated all the civilians fit for military duty within twenty-five miles between Gilmans' ranch and Jack Morrow's, and found that there were nearly one hundred and fifty men. They were frontiersmen as a rule, all well armed, and more or less engaged in the "pilgrim trade," some in cattle, and some in hunting and trapping. The largest number was probably at Gilmans' ranch. The Gilmans had two hundred cows, but never milked one. The ranch had a number of herders. There were herds along the river at various other ranches, attached to which were herders of various kinds; some full-blood French of the Canadian variety, and some adventurous spirits from the East who, in addition to their work at the ranches, made considerable by hunting and trapping. All of the ranches sold steel traps of various sizes, from muskrat up to bear. The population had increased principally during our occupation. There were down at Gilmans' ranch, besides the Gilmans themselves, several who were very wise in Indian lore, and with whom we often desired to talk. From time to time we felt obliged to know things, and to go to Gilmans' ranch for the purpose of having consultation. The fifteen miles down to the ranch was over a country as level as a floor, beaten down hard and swept by the wind. It took an hour and a half to go there; so we could leave at two o'clock and get back at seven, and have two hours' consultation. From them we obtained information, and drew rough maps and diagrams of the country both north and south. They told us where the bunches of timber were, both north and south, and where the water was among the valleys in the hills, and the routes which the Indians used.

All of this time, however, the work at the post was going on rapidly, either the Captain or myself acting as boss. Our first Lieutenant looked more particularly after the supplies. I had two horses, one a good, average cavalry horse, but I managed to become the owner of a large, raw-boned iron-gray horse, of which I will speak more hereafter. I got him before coming to Nebraska, and paid $135 for him. The horse formerly belonged to Colonel Baker, of the Second Iowa Infantry, who was killed in the battle of Pittsburg Landing. The horse was not afraid of firearms nor musketry. He had a mouth that was as tough as the forks of a cottonwood log, and I had to use a large curb bit on him with an iron bar under the jaw, made by our company blacksmith. Without this terrible curb, I could do nothing with him. He was afraid of nothing but a buffalo, and as a wild buffalo is more dangerous than a bear, I was always afraid that sometime he would act bad and get me hurt. He was also very much frightened at even the smell of a buffalo-robe. This large iron-gray horse would start out on a dead run for Gilmans' ranch, and keep it up for fifteen miles without halting. I never saw a horse with more endurance, or more of a desire to go, and he kept himself lean by his efforts and energy. I knew that when I was on his back no Indian pony nor band of Indians could overtake me, and hence I scouted the country without apprehension. The buffalo which I killed as last alluded to, was the last buffalo we saw around Cottonwood Canyon. Our fort was called "Cantonment McKean," but the War Department afterwards named it "Fort McPherson," after General McPherson, who was killed while with Sherman near Atlanta, Georgia; but the fort was popularly known as "Fort Cottonwood." Among our men was a fine carpenter who had worked at cabinetmaking, and from the boards which we whip-sawed out, he made lots of chairs, a company desk, tables and furniture as needed. It is strange how simply furniture can be made, and yet equal to the best in comfort and convenience. Our furniture was all made out of beautiful red cedar.

Along on the side of the hill west of our post, and about five hundred yards from it, we put up a palisade of logs sunk in the ground, and forming an eight-foot square target. I practiced with our howitzers upon this target until I got the exact range and capacity of the two guns. They varied but little; we had to know how far the guns would shoot, and the number of seconds on which to cut our shell fuses. We had a large number of shrapnel shell fitted with Bohrman fuses. Our powder was separate, in red flannel bag cartridges, so made as to fit the rear chamber of the gun, which was smaller than the calibre. Attached to the shrapnel shell was a wooden block made accurately to fit the bore of the piece. The powder was first rammed down, and then the shell rammed down on the wooden block, which was called a "sabot." The "sabot" was merely a wad. The fuse of the shell was towards the muzzle of the gun. The explosion of the powder went around the shell, and ignited the fuse in front of it. The gun was fired with what were called "friction primers," which, being inserted in the touchhole and connected with the lanyard, were pulled off, and threw the fire down into the cartridge. But, before the friction primer was put in, a "priming-wire" was thrust down to punch a hole through the flannel bag of the cartridge. The process of loading was somewhat complicated for so simple a gun. One man brought the powder cartridge and inserted it, and it was rammed home by another man with a wooden rammer. Then another brought the shell with sabot attachment, and that was immediately rammed down, sabot first. Another man used the priming-wire, and inserted the friction primer. The chief of the piece then sighted the gun, and gave the signal to the man who held the lanyard. The shrapnel was made as an iron shell about five-eighths of an inch thick, with an orifice of about an inch and a half, on which the thread of a screw was cut. Then the shell was filled with round leaden balls, and in the interstices melted sulphur was poured. Then a hole was bored down an inch and a half in diameter through the bullets behind the open part, and this was filled with powder, leaving the sulphur and lead arranged around the powder; then the fuse was screwed in. The utmost angle of safety in firing the howitzer was fifteen degrees. Anything more than that was liable to spring or break the axle on the recoil. At an angle of fifteen degrees, unless the trail was fixed properly, the piece was liable to turn a summerset. After a great deal of experiment of the two pieces I prepared a little schedule of distances and seconds, which I furnished to my sergeants. All of the sergeants were instructed in sighting the piece and in cutting the fuse. The fuse was a tin disc, and was cut with a three-cornered little hand-chisel. My experiments differed somewhat in result from the artillery manual, but was accurate in regard to the two particular pieces, and was as follows:

Yards of Range	Elevation	Fuse
450	2½°	2″
500	3°	2¼″
700	4°	2¾″
800	4½°	3″

Upon a smooth floor of the valley we could shoot one of these shrapnels, and after the first graze at fifteen degrees, the ball would go bouncing along for quite a distance. And by cutting the fuse at about the end we could get the utmost range out of the piece. An elevation of 8 degrees was considered safe, but more than that was liable to strain the piece, because the charge was so heavy and the gun so light.

After we had got well established in our quarters a new company was sent to our post to assist us, there having arisen rumors that we might be attacked. Company "G" of our regiment arrived, and immediately proceeded to do as we did in the building of company quarters, and with them came Ben Gallagher as Post Sutler. He hired men to build him a sutler-house, and he also hired some men to get out some cedar telegraph poles to repair the telegraph lines. Company "G" worked rapidly, and we sheltered them and their horses during the worst days, and they had a comparatively easy time of it. They soon got into good quarters, and in good condition.

During the time, an empty train coming down from Denver by order of the quartermaster's department brought us ten thousand pounds of pine lumber. This was hauled at the rate of one dollar per hundred pounds per hundred miles, and the amount in feet of the pine lumber was *four thousand*. It cost the Government to haul down this four thousand feet of lumber, $282.96. That is, over $70 per thousand.

The arrival of Company "G" made our place a two-company post, and George M. O'Brien, Major of the regi-

ment, was appointed Post Commander. I was made Post
Adjutant, and we built a post headquarters. Preliminarily
we were obliged to take all of the wing of the MacDonald
ranch, and one half-room in the building of "Hook-sah,"
whose real name was Isador P. Boyer. In order to hurry up
the work for post headquarters, Washington Hinman, William A. Anderson and John W. Lewis were employed as professional carpenters. We also had to have a corral for beef
cattle, and this we constructed.

Ranchmen on the line of the road who had at certain
grassy spots along the river cut considerable hay, offered
us this coarse hay, cut while it was green, for $15 a ton, and
a lot of it which was cut dry and withered, after we came,
they offered for $10 a ton. For a short while, during the illness of our First Lieutenant, I was made Post Quartermaster
and Commissary, and I found that we had at that time seven
army wagons complete, with six mules each. That we had on
hand unused 413 hewed cedar logs, 347 round logs, and 322
large cedar poles, piled up awaiting further construction of
buildings. Our veterinary department had been reinforced
by a lot of horse medicine, tar oil, spirits of niter, etc. We
had anvils, vises, sledges, rasps, monkey wrenches, a portable forge, 10 augers, 21 chisels, 10 planes, 6 broadaxes, together with a line of blacksmith tools and carpenter tools, 56
felling axes, 18 shovels, scales and weights, complete grindstone, 500 pounds of nails, 100 pounds of horseshoe nails,
500 pounds of horseshoes, 130 pounds of rope, 20 sides of
leather, 80 ax-handles, parts of wagons to make repairs, several hundred pounds of various kinds of iron for making
horseshoes and for making spikes and nails, a lot of charcoal,
a large number of trace-chains, a dozen tarpaulins, and
shortly after that we received a consignment of white lead,
linseed oil, and putty. The current prices at the ranches during the winter of sales to the pilgrims as they went by for
horse feed was two and one-half cents a pound for hay, and
four cents a pound for shelled corn. From time to time we
sent trains down to Fort Kearney, and on their return they
bought feed, and vouchers were given. Of the ranchmen

along the line whose places we usually stopped at, the following is a complete list: Thomas French, Thomas Mullally, Daniel Freeman, B. S. Blondeau, Daniel L. Smith, Peniston and Miller, J. K. Gilman & Co. (Jud Gilman). The prices of articles of clothing furnished to soldiers as sold by the quartermaster for cash, to the officers, were as follows: Coat, $7.00; cavalry trousers, $3.55; flannel drawers, $0.90; peg boots, $2.92; blankets, $3.25. The blankets were shoddy blankets, and the boots were very rough and coarse. One day two citizens came in and wanted to buy some of the empty corn-sacks, and the post commander ordered the sale. They were bought by S. F. Burtch and I. C. Beatty, who paid the price of twenty cents apiece for them, $57. This money was then, by order of the post commander, expended for shelled corn from a passing train at the rate of $2.07½ a bushel. On the first of January, 1864, we had on hand at the Post Commissary about twenty thousand pounds of flour, five thousand pounds of bacon, ten beef cattle, twenty-seven hundred pounds of beans, sixteen hundred pounds of coffee, four thousand pounds of sugar, together with a good supply of the other articles belonging to the Government ration. The sales to officers permitted by the regulation prices fixed by the Government were as follows: Ham in barrels, nine and one-half cents a pound; hard-bread, four cents; white sugar, sixteen and one-half cents per pound; sperm candles, thirty-seven and one-half cents; molasses, sixty-one cents per gallon; dried apples, eight cents a pound; hominy and grits, two and one-half cents a pound; soap, seven cents. Other stuff could be bought from other sources cheaper than the Government price. The regular Government ration of that period was as follows:

12 oz. pork or bacon, or in lieu thereof 20 oz. fresh or salt beef.
22 oz. soft bread or flour, or 20 oz. corn-meal, or 16 oz. "hard-tack."
15 lbs. beans or peas (dried) . . . . to 100 rations.
10 lbs. rice or hominy . . . . " " "
10 lbs. green or 8 lbs. roasted coffee . . . . " " "
In lieu of coffee, 24 oz. of tea . . . . " " "
15 lbs. of sugar . . . . " " "
1 gallon of vinegar . . . . " " "
20 oz. star candles . . . . " " "

4 lbs. soap .... " " "
60 oz. of salt .... " " "
4 oz. pepper .... " " "
1 quart of molasses .... " " "
30 pounds of potatoes (when practicable) .... " " "

I wish to state here, as this is a retrospective chapter, that our work at Cottonwood Springs was fully appreciated by our superiors. That is about all the glory that a person gets out of the subordinate phases of military life. We were inspected on November 11th, 1863, by an officer sent out especially to see what we were doing. He reported as follows:

"Nov. 11, 1863. Inspected Cos. 'F' and 'G,' Seventh Iowa Cavalry, at Cottonwood Springs; Major O'Brien Commanding.

"Military bearing and appearance soldierly. Discipline and system of military instruction good. Officers efficient and well instructed. Orders duly received and promptly published and enforced. Police of quarters and camp good."

Thereupon the Commanding General of the Department sent the report to the General Commanding our district at Omaha as follows:

"HEADQUARTERS, DEPARTMENT OF THE MISSOURI. ST. LOUIS, MO., *December 1, 1863.*

"Respectfully referred to Brig.-General Thomas McKean, Commanding the District of Nebraska, for his information.

"The Major-General Commanding the Department of Missouri is highly pleased at the assurances contained in the report relative to the efficiency of Major O'Brien's command at Cottonwood Springs, as shown by the care taken of the command, the soldierly bearing and appearance of the officers and men, their discipline and instruction, for all of which the Major-General Commanding highly commends and sincerely thanks every officer and soldier of the command.

By order of
JOHN M. SCHOFIELD,
Major-General Commanding
I. H. MELCHER, Lt. Col., *Insptr. Genl.*"

The originals are among the private papers of the estate of Major (afterwards Brigadier-General) George M. O'Brien.

The General Schofield was afterwards Lieutenant-General and at the head of the armies of the United States.

Company "F" had some wild-western defects, but for the purpose for which they were organized and brought together they had no superiors. Before we get through we will say the same of the First Nebraska Veteran Volunteer Cavalry, with whom we were afterwards associated.

CHAPTER VIII

DURING all this time the stage service was kept up. The stages did not seem to have any regular service, except this, that as fast as they got a coach-load they went through. People in the coaches were all armed. Sometimes two or three coaches went through at a time. The service was not irregular as being neglected, but was irregular because it was overcrowded, and the condition of the country unsafe. The dangerous part of the line was considered at that time to be between Fort Kearney and our fort, "Fort Cottonwood," as it was generally called. The stage stations were about ten miles apart, sometimes a little more and sometimes a little less, according to the location of the ranches. Stores of shelled corn, for the use of the stage horses, were kept at principal stations along the line of the route. Intermediate stations between these principal stations were called "swing stations," where the horses were changed. For instance, the horses of a stage going up were taken off at a swing station, and fed; they might be there an hour or six hours; they might be put upon another stage in the same direction, or upon a stage returning. It was the policy of the stage company to make the business as profitable as possible, so it did not run its coaches until each coach had a good load, and they were most generally crowded with persons both on the inside and on top. Sometimes a stage would be almost loaded with women. From time to time stage company wagons went by loaded with shelled corn for distribution as needed at the swing stations. All of the coaches carried Government mail in greater or less quantities. Occasionally when the mail accumulated a covered wagon loaded with mail went along with the coaches. These coaches were billed to go a hundred miles a day going west; sometimes they went faster. Coming east the down-grade of a few feet per mile enabled them to make better time. They went night and day, and a jollier lot of people could scarcely be found anywhere than the parties in these coaches.

The coaches were all built alike, upon a standard pattern called the "Concord Coach," with heavy leather springs, and they drove from four to six horses according to their load. The drivers sat up in the box, proud as brigadier-generals, and they were as tough, hardy and brave a lot of people as could be found anywhere. As a rule they were courteous to the passengers, and careful of their horses. They made runs of about a hundred miles and back. I got acquainted with many of them, and a more fearless and companionable lot of men I never met. There seemed to be an idea among them that while on the box they should not drink liquor, but when they got off they had stories to tell, and generally indulged freely. They gathered up mail from the ranches, and trains, and travelers along the road, and saw that it reached its destination. They had but very few perquisites, but among others was the getting furs, principally beaver-skins, and selling them to passengers. Most of them had beaver-skin overcoats with large turned-up collars. We soon understood the benefits of these collars, and the officers of our post put large beaver collars on their overcoats, and the men of the company fitted themselves out with tanned wolfskin collars, which were equally as good. Wolves were so numerous that there was quite an industry in shooting or poisoning them, and tanning their skins for the pilgrim trade.

The commanding officer of our post was, as stated, Major George M. O'Brien, of the Seventh Iowa Cavalry. For a while I acted as Adjutant, Quartermaster, Commissary, and Ordnance officer combined. Major O'Brien was a fine-looking, highstrung Irishman, educated in the University of Dublin. He was the oldest brother of Captain O'Brien of my company. Major O'Brien took an active interest in the establishment of the post, and getting it ready for the outbreak which was to come in the summer. A squad from one or the other of our companies was sent down with teams nearly every week to Fort Kearney for supplies. The teams would go down one week, and come back the next. The distance was called one hundred miles.

On December 23rd the officers of our posts were invited up to Jack Morrow's ranch to dinner. Myself and Captain O'Brien went up, leaving the company in charge of our First Lieutenant. A couple of the officers of the other company, the First Sergeant and the Post Sutler (Ben Gallagher), were in the party. Jack Morrow's ranch was out on the prairie, nearly south of the junction of the two Platte rivers. North Platte had much more water in it than the South Platte. Between our post and Jack Morrow's the high hills of the table-land ran far north in a bold promontory, broken at the point into a sort of peak, which could be seen a long distance both up and down the river, towards which it projected. We had to go past this to get to Morrow's ranch. This point was called the "Sioux Lookout." Going up, we detected with a field-glass an Indian's head peering over the top of the ridge at us, but he afterwards scudded away and disappeared. We were told at Morrow's that the Indians were keeping constant lookout from that point, although the weather was exceedingly cold. There was a canyon came in near there called "Moran Canyon," also filled with large cedars. Jack Morrow was said to have cut out five thousand cedar logs from the canyon for his own use, and for sale to other persons; and to have got out two thousand fine cedar telegraph poles. It was also said that he would not allow anybody else to cut any timber in that canyon. Morrow had as large an outfit, nearly, as the Gilmans. He claimed to have cattle and goods and improvements worth $100,000, but he overstated it. He was a tall, raw-boned, dangerous-looking man, wearing a mustache, and a goatee on his under lip. He was said to be a killer, to have shot a man or two, and to have passed his life on the plains. He was said to have daily altercations with pilgrims, and to have gone on drunks that were so stupendous in their waste of money and strange eccentricities that he was known from Denver to Fort Kearney and very largely in Omaha. He was said to have had an Indian wife, although I never knew whether that was true or not. He had a very large stock of goods, and a row of "pilgrim quarters." His ranch-house was built of cedar logs, and was two and a half stories high and sixty feet long. The third story was divided into rooms, and the cross-logs were not sawed out to admit doors, so that in going from one room to another it was necessary to crawl over six feet of cedar-log wall to get into these rooms. Yet he had people sleeping in those rooms a great deal of the time. He stored away great quantities of furs, robes, dried buffalo-meat and beef, and other stuffs, for shipment, in a sort of annual caravan, which he made down to Omaha. He had a very capable and accomplished First Lieutenant who acted as foreman, salesman, and cashier. His name was Hewey Morgan. When Morrow went on a spree Hewey Morgan's authority began, and he must have exercised it very capably, because Morrow trusted him implicitly.

About five o'clock in the afternoon—it was after sundown, when we arrived there—Morrow was either two-thirds full or pretended to be. My opinion of it was that it was merely pretense. In a little while he brought out a basket of champagne, and after we had paid our attention to it our dinner began. It was broiled antelope heart, baked buffalo hump, fried beaver tails; a regular pioneer banquet, and Hewey Morgan poured out the champagne in tin cups all around. There were two or three residents at the table, neighboring ranchmen from down near the post. Among others a young man named Sam Fitchie, who could recite poetry, and was a regular declaimer, and impersonator, and withal a fine-looking and well-educated young gentleman. He was out there trying to work into the stock business, and had not been there very long. Many years afterwards I met him as a prominent minister in Ohio. His Indian name was Wa-pah-see-cha (bad matches).

When the banquet was over, Morrow got out his paraphernalia, and offered to deal faro bank. We agreed to battle away at his bank for thirty minutes while the horses were being saddled and brought around, which we did without any material loss to anybody. Captain O'Brien whispered to me that he thought the whole business looked as if Jack Morrow was after a Government contract with our post. I sort of received the same impression. Just before the leave-taking began, Hewey Morgan wanted to ask me a question privately, and I went out with him. And the question was, whether he couldn't get a contract to furnish the Government with one hundred thousand pounds of shelled corn at five cents a pound, and if I would not use my efforts with the post commander. I told him that I certainly would not; that the corn could be put down much cheaper than that, and that I couldn't recommend it. He took it good-naturedly, and on the way back to the post, when we got to comparing notes on the point, Hewey Morgan or Jack Morrow had each spoken to every member of the party. This whole proceeding was so raw that none of us ever made any visit again to Jack Morrow. Captain O'Brien was an honest man, and was very indignant.

A few days after that a little short, stubby Irishman named Burke came into camp, and said that he and the people with him wanted a job of work. I sent him to the post commander, Major O'Brien, and Major O'Brien sent for me. This man Burke had left Denver with some empty wagons, and had agreed to haul about fifty men through to Omaha at a rapidity not less than twenty-five miles a day, and was to furnish transportation for men, trunks and baggage, and feed them en route; he made a through rate. It was a train pulled by horses and mules. He said that he had to halt his train; that his animals needed shoeing; that their feet were badly worn; and while he was there he wanted to get something for the men to do. Major O'Brien suggested that he put in a bid for cedar cordwood; that he should go up in the canyon, take the tops, limbs and refuse of our cutting, make it up, and cord and stack it near the post. He went up, and came back and said he would do it for $4 a cord. Major O'Brien sent for me, and asked me what I thought about it; we concluded to offer a voucher for $3 a cord piled up near the barracks, at a point which I should designate. Burke and his men debated the thing the whole day, and finally came back, took the contract and piled up the four hundred cords of wood. Burke said afterwards that there was about $20 profit in the contract; that he "would liked to have made ten cents a cord on it," but hadn't done it—had made only five.

During the months of January and February at least twenty coaches of Mormon officers and missionaries went past our post, going and coming. They traveled all by themselves; asked no protection nor odds of anybody. They always said that they did not fear the Indians, and that the Indians never harmed a Mormon. So, they passed by us, went up the North Platte and through the South Pass without an escort of any kind. Along in January a large mule train came up, loaded with shell corn and flour from Denver. As they neared our post a most terrific blizzard set in. It was, indeed, a fearful one. It caught this train three or four miles east of our post, down by the river. The train parted, its wagons got scattered, some of its horses and mules were literally blown away. They got started before the wind, and they could not be overtaken nor caught. The result was that the train was wrecked. They came to the post and asked us to take their corn and flour. Having no authority to buy, I told them that I would take it, receipt for it, and store it, and that they could return to the river, and if I received word from the Quartermaster-General there, I would take the stuff up on my accounts. This was satisfactory. The train immediately fastened the empty wagons together with what animals they saved and had recaptured, and pulled back to Leavenworth, from which place I got an order to take the property up on my returns, it having been bought by the Government.

Along about the latter part of February the weather became very severe. Storms came down from the northwest, one chasing after the other in close succession, that kept us very closely hived up in the barracks. Considerable snow fell upon the level ground, which blew over into the canyon, and in places there it was quite deep, so that our cordwood was a very great benefit to us. We took the horses out whenever we could, and rode them around and exercised them, but they were getting soft and unfitted for hard campaigning. We had always taken good care of our horses; in fact, when we left Omaha we adopted a frontier custom of placing a gunny-sack under the horse-blanket. I never saw that practiced anywhere else, except on the plains: Every soldier smoothed out a gunny-sack when he saddled his horse; it prevented the woolen horse-blanket from scalding the horse's back. The wind and alkali and sand had made it necessary to take care of the backs of our horses, and we arrived at Cottonwood Springs with our horses in good condition, but the keeping of them penned up was reducing their effective capacity very much. We did not dare to turn them out loose, to play, for fear some unexpected Indian might turn up and stampede them.

When the bad weather set in, it was our principal duty and object to keep our horses up, and we rode them around as best we could, occasionally trying to go through the forms of a drill. Owing to the fact that we were among the Indians, we adopted the bugle-drill almost entirely, and all movements were executed not by word of mouth, but from the note of the bugle. And in order to keep the men and subordinate officers efficient in that, we practiced considerably at nights in the barracks, to keep the men's ears alert to distinguish the calls. Most of the men were inclined to forget.

While this rough and inclement weather was in progress a man named Gardner came to our post, and went to headquarters. He represented that he was the Government agent among the Cheyennes, at a considerable distance southwest of us. Gilman had said that there were twenty thousand Indian warriors within three days' ride (one hundred fifty miles) north of us, and an equal number south of us, but nobody knew exactly where they were. This man Gardner was not particularly specific, nor do I remember where he said the headquarters of the tribe were which he represented. The first thing that I heard of the matter was the end of a heated conversation with Major O'Brien, in which he demanded of Major O'Brien that the Major send out a company of cavalry with a brass howitzer, and arrest the head chief of the Cheyenne band; this the Major refused to do, but said he would consider. Gardner went out in a very lofty way, went across to Mr. Boyer's, where liquor was to be had, and I didn't see him until the next day. Major O'Brien said that this man Gardner had reported that he had been to the tribe to see about certain annuities and the carrying out of certain treaty obligations, and that the head chief had insulted him and slapped his face and told him that he was a coward and that the Government of the United States couldn't do anything with the Cheyenne tribes, and that they didn't care whether there was peace or war, and so on, and so on. The Major was of the opinion that as Gardner was a Government officer and had a right to call upon troops, something ought to be done, because, if the matter were left to go, there was no telling where the end might be in our dealings with those Indians. And he told me to think it over, and get ready and plan what I would do, because if that trouble arose he would want to send me out on the expedition. As I came out of headquarters to go and tell Captain O'Brien about it, I met J. K. Gilman near our company line, who was going to make a call upon Captain O'Brien, and I asked him to come in so that we could talk it over. Gilman's idea came quickly to the front. He said: "That man Gardner is a worthless, drunken fellow, who has been put in through political influence, and don't know how to handle himself, the Cheyennes, or anybody else. If you go out and demand the surrender of the chief or any of the head-men they will refuse to do it, and all you will have to do is turn around and come back. If you go to showing fight your posse will last about thirty minutes." He said: "My advice for you is to go out there and take this man Gardner with you, and a good interpreter, and not to go nearer than five miles of their village. Send in for a delegation of their head-men and have a little preliminary council, and listen to the complaint those Indians have got to make, and then come back." The next day at the post Gardner was rip-roariously drunk, and not much business was done. In two or three days, however, he had got Major O'Brien up to the idea of sending me out, and Major O'Brien told me to get ready and start within seven days. Thereupon I outlined the policy which Mr. Gilman had suggested, and Major O'Brien considered it wise, and sensible; so he sent for Gardner and outlined it. Gardner refused to go with me; said that it wasn't his business; that it was his business to call for Government troops to do what he ordered them to do, and he accused Major O'Brien of trying to shirk his responsibility. This made the Major very indignant, and he rose up in his wrath, and being a great big, strong man himself, he ordered Gardner out of headquarters, and told him not to come back until he was sober. Gardner went out, got onto a stage and went down to Fort Kearney. In a little while instructions both by wire and letter came, saying under no circumstances to send out a force against the Cheyennes; that the General commanding the District had the matter under consideration, and would give the necessary order when the time arrived, and for the post commander to take no orders from any civilian whom-soever. The rumor of our sending out a hundred men to the Cheyenne village with a brass howitzer went around with great rapidity, and it was not long before different ranchmen came in and said that it would simply precipitate the Chey-enne war, which would come anyhow as soon as the Indian ponies could live on the grass; that it was folly to send less than one thousand armed men, and that no cavalry company could get within ten miles of the Indian village before it would be annihilated; that it would bring a raid on the Platte valley, for which nobody was quite ready. Major O'Brien took the consensus of opinion and forwarded it with his own recommendations down to headquarters, and I felt somewhat relieved when I knew definitely that I was not to go out on such a forlorn expedition.

Turning from the subject of Indians to another far more interesting, I will relate an occurrence that happened early in March; but I must go back into the past. I had been with the first army of General Curtis that marched down through Arkansas from Pea Ridge to Helena in 1862. We arrived at Helena, on the Mississippi River, shortly after the river was opened up by the gunboats at Memphis, the bombardment of which we heard over in Arkansas. As the Rebel gunboats were chased down the river the transports came from the North, and, as we were quite ragged, clothing was issued to us, and I drew a Government blouse. In the pocket of this blouse, August, 1862, at Helena, Arkansas, I found a letter substantially in these words: "I would like to know where this blouse is going to. If the brave soldier who gets it will let me know I will be very much obliged to him." It was signed Louisa J. B———. The letter was from a town that was one of the suburbs of New York City, in New Jersey. I immediately answered it, although the blouse had been some time coming, and a correspondence grew up which had run considerably more than a year. The correspondence consisted of my detailing matters concerning the campaigns that I was in, and the military duties which I was performing. The answers from New Jersey consisted in telling briefly what the newspapers said about the progress of the war, and the actions of the President. About the first of March, 1864, I received a very nice letter, in which the writer said that she was the mother of the young lady who had written me. The letter was a very fine and delicately written letter, so sensible that it was impressive. She said:

"I think you may be able to comprehend how devoted an interest a mother must take in her daughter's welfare, and her correspondence. My husband had large contracts for the army, and while my daughter was home from school visiting her father, who was making a large shipment of clothing, she wrote the note that you found in the blouse. It was the romantic idea of a school-girl. Your letters have been so interesting that it is not unreasonable for you to imagine that she has become interested in receiving them. The correspondence has gone on for some time. She has read me your letters, and they have been in every respect interesting and proper; but I fear that this matter may go too far. I wish, if you will permit the request, that you write no more to her, at least for the present. If at some future time you should be able to satisfactorily establish your character and standing, and shall visit the East, we shall be pleased to receive you. But you must know that her parents feel considerable interest in the matter, as you are such a total stranger, and we have no knowledge of your family or your social standing."

It was one of the nicest letters ever written; it produced a very great impression on me. I had a sister of my own whom I thought a great deal of, and I couldn't help thinking that I would feel the same way if she were writing to some one under the same circumstances. After cogitating over the letter I returned it to her, telling her that all correspondence so far had been destroyed, which was the fact; that I had only the last letter, which I returned herewith; that I appreciated her feelings exactly, because I had relatives of my own; and that I would assure her that the correspondence was ended. About a month or more after that I received all my letters back from the young lady, and they were fragrant with roses, and had pencil-marks, underscored sentences, and query-marks on the edges, and all that sort of thing. After reading them consecutively through from one end to the other, I placed them gently upon the cedar coals while the aroma floated out upon the thirsty air. And that was the last of the episode, for I have never heard of any of the persons since; and as nearly fifty years have now elapsed I probably never will. I never interested myself further in the matter. There was another girl.

I tell this story to illustrate what happened constantly in the army. There were probably in my own company forty cases of correspondence not much unlike the one which I have depicted. Of course I supposed I was writing to the girl who *made the blouse,* for the girls who made the blouses and coats and clothing put such notes in, so that there was hardly any soldier who did not draw some kind of address like this during the Civil War, and many of them got more than one. In fact, it was not unusual, when there appeared in the newspapers notice of some movement of troops, naming some certain officer, that he would get half a dozen letters from persons he never heard of before, and perhaps never heard of again. And this was not wholly on our side. We had often captured the mail of Confederate regiments, and there was hardly any soldier in our army who did not carry around at some time some letter which some Southern girl had written to some Southern soldier. We had thousands of them, and I suppose the Confederates had similar experience.

The girls both North and South kept the soldiers feeling that their services were appreciated, and the boys in the ranks were bound that the girls should not be disappointed; and so, the war was long and severe. And the girls helped fight it. And neither side wanted to give up.

CHAPTER IX

TWICE before March 1, 1864, I went to Fort Kearney on business connected with the supply of the post, and made quick trips; always rode fifty miles a day on these trips, and took two days going, and two days coming. Generally stopped at the ranch of Thomas Mullally, who was not quite half way. One of the celebrities along the line of the road was a telegrapher who was called Sloat. He was known to everybody, and went up and down the road looking after the telegraph line, which had not been long in operation. As the telegraph line was of immense importance, it was looked after most diligently. This man Sloat told many marvelous anecdotes connected with his adventures; I traveled with him more than once, and was much interested in his stories and exploits. There was afterwards another telegraph operator whom I may refer to, whose name was Holcomb, and both of them were men who were exceedingly expert, considering the then condition of the art. It may be thought strange that the Indians did not secretly destroy the telegraph line. There were a number of strange stories connected with it, and with Indian experience. In order to give the Indians a profound respect for the wire, chiefs had formerly been called in and had been told to make up a story and then separate. When afterwards the story was told to one operator where one chief was present, it was told at another station to the other chief in such a way as to produce the most stupendous dread. No effort was made to explain it to the Indians upon any scientific principle, but it was given the appearance of a black and diabolical art. The Indians were given some electric shocks; and every conceivable plan, to make them afraid of the wire, was indulged in by the officers and employés of the company, it being much to their financial advantage to make the Indian dread the wire.

About a year before we were there, a party of Indian braves crossed the line up by O'Fallon's Bluffs, and one Indian who had been down in "The States," as it was called, and thought he understood it, volunteered to show his gang that they must not be afraid of it, and that it was a good thing to have the wire up in their village to lariat ponies to. So he chopped down a pole, severed the wire and began ripping it off from the poles. They concluded to take north with them, up to their village on the Blue Water River, about as much as they could easily drag. It was during the hot summer weather. They cut off nearly a half-mile of wire, and all of the Indians in single file on horseback catching hold of the wire, proceeded to ride and pull the wire across the prairie towards their village. After they had gone several miles and were going over the ridge, they were overtaken by an electric storm, and as they were rapidly traveling, dragging the wire, by some means or other a bolt of lightning, so the story goes, knocked almost all of them off their horses and hurt some of them considerably. Thereupon they dropped the wire, and coming to the conclusion that it was punishment for their acts and that it was "bad medicine," they afterwards let it alone. The story of it, being quite wonderful, circulated with great rapidity among the Indians, and none of them could ever afterwards be found who would tamper with the wire. They would cut down a pole and use the wood for cooking, but they stayed clear of the wire, and the operation of the telegraph was thus very rarely obstructed.

Shortly after the first day of March, 1864, Major O'Brien, our Post Commander, was ordered down to Fort Kearney on some command, and my Captain O'Brien was made Post Commander. Our First Lieutenant and our Company Sergeant were both sent for, to come to Fort Kearney, and that left me in command of the company, and I was relieved from all duties of Quartermaster, Commissary and Ordnance Officer. My duties had been exceedingly onerous because there was so much company duty to do in addition to the general duties referred to, and I got but little time for leisure, although the scouting of the country around south of our post was indulged in upon all opportunities. Captain O'Brien took turns with me in that, and he generally went alone, as I did myself. We became thoroughly acquainted with every feature of the ground within fifteen miles of the post, south of the river, and we knew whereabouts Indians might hide, or might be found, should they want to come near us from the south.

When I went into command of the company, Captain O'Brien suggested that it was about time for earnest drilling of the company to begin, although we were constantly engaged in finishing and improving our post. I started in by his order to drill twenty-five different men every day with the bugle skirmish drill, and to have the company adopt it for Indian warfare. We had heard a great deal about the Indian manner of fighting and the various engagements which the regular army had had with them for ten and fifteen years back, and what was necessary to be done to successfully meet the manner of fighting which the Indians adopted. We drilled entirely by skirmish drill. We deployed at from twenty to fifty yards intervals. We raced over the prairie, wheeling, deploying and rallying on the right, left and center, all by the bugle. We also adopted a drill on foot, in which the ranks would count off one, two, three, and four. The number "four" would hold horses, and numbers one, two and three would deploy to the front as skirmishers, in which case the command was, "At ten paces take interval —march." Then we would drill in firing and loading on the ground. Then, on a bugle-call, each number "one" would rise and rush forward twenty to fifty paces according to order, and lie down. Then number "two" would rise and make a dash, and pass number "one" fifty paces, and lie down, firing and loading. And then number "three" would go forward to the front in the same manner, everything being done on the double-quick, the men going to earth on the call of the bugle, while the number fours would follow from behind at considerable distance with the horses. We practiced this drilling day after day, generally with twenty-four men and a sergeant. And the men ran for miles all over the Platte valley in every direction, practicing their skirmish drill by the bugle. They got so that they rather liked it, and it was good exercise. The horses got used to the firing, for we expended much ammunition; and they got hardened up for a campaign.

One day Mr. Gilman and a nice-looking stranger came out and rode around with me on the drill. Our bugle-calls were from the army regulations, and had probably been handed down from Revolutionary days. The bugler, mistaking one of my orders, gave the wrong call, and this stranger spoke up and called my attention to it. This very much surprised me, and I said to him, "How do you know?" And he said, "Well, I have a good ear for music." Afterwards Mr. Gilman told me that the man stated, after we had separated, that for some time he had been in the Confederate cavalry and was familiar with the calls. As he was a fine-looking man and was going west, I always imagined he was a refugee from the Confederate army; the war was then going on. Most probably he was a Confederate officer, who had some sense and was willing to quit.

It is of some interest to know how we managed to keep from being lonesome. As a matter of fact, the men all seemed to be very proud of the new nice cedar encampment they had built, and proud of the condition of the company. We got lots of newspapers. In fact, every stage that went by threw us a bundle of newspapers, and in the barracks after supper, men were reading the war news aloud, and we kept up with the movements, battles and skirmishes of the war. But of all amusements in the company, the greatest amusement was the man Cannon, of whom I have spoken heretofore. It turned out that Cannon had been in the regular army for a number of years before the war, and had been all over the great Southwest, from the Indian Territory and Texas clear through to the Pacific Coast. He was, perhaps, the most talented and monumental liar that had ever been in the Government service. His stories were inexhaustible. He put in all of his time when at work or drill, thinking up something that he would give the boys when it came night. Night after night and month after month he was telling stories of wonderful adventures. Once in a while he came around to headquarters and started in at night to practice on the Captain and me. For a patient, interesting, and versatile prevaricator I had never seen his equal. According to his story he had been confidentially detailed by every officer in the regular army whose name had appeared so far during the war. He knew the secrets, the history, the private life and the capabilities of everybody that had ever graduated from West Point. He was not of very great benefit to the company as a soldier. He was inclined to shirk his duty, and once in a while liquor would get away with him, and he would have to be put in the guard-house. But when he went into the guard-house he always had the guard, and the corporal of the guard, hanging with breathless interest on his stories of flood and field, of Indian warfare, and of adventures with wild beasts, wild birds, Mexico, and everything else. He finally went by the name of "Jimmie," and he is one of the last ones that the company would ever forget. He was not fit for promotion of any kind. He was good-natured, but in all respects he was absolutely unreliable. But next to the newspapers which came to the camp, he was the chief means of relieving the men from a feeling of lonesomeness or discontent. His stories were ninety-nine per cent pure fiction, at least, and sometimes about one hundred and ten.

There is in all military bodies a feeling of homesickness, much more aggravated in some than in others, but which once in a while breaks out, and becomes contagious. We had several spells in our company in which the men became homesick. In fact, almost as soon as we reached Cottonwood Springs, in October, 1863, and camped upon the bleak and desolate land, some of the boys nearly broke down. One of them I remember particularly, and I felt very sorry for him. He was a German named Hakel, over twenty-one years of age. He had a sweetheart in Dubuque, Iowa. Something must have gone wrong, because he got a case called in military medicine "nostalgia," and he drooped around and seemed to take no interest in much of anything. He wouldn't even interest himself in the taste of the fine old whisky which I got from Fort Kearney. One day he said that he believed he would go down to the bank of the river and clean his revolver. There was no need of his going to that place, but he did go to the place, and shortly after we heard the sound of a firing, and on investigation he had killed himself. It was impossible to tell whether he had done it accidentally or not. But I made up my mind that the proper thing to do was to give him the benefit of the doubt, and it being my duty to report the fact to headquarters, I did so, and the way I reported it was quite brief. I gave his name and full description, and I stated the cause of death to be "accidental suicide." I thought the term "accidental suicide" was about as brief as I could make it. The Colonel of our regiment was an aged lawyer from an Iowa village. He immediately directed the regimental Adjutant to return the report to me for correction, saying there was no such thing as "accidental suicide." This illustrates the littleness of so many officers. The great affairs of the regiment, their supplies, drill and efficiency were taken little or no notice of. Except for the meddling at long intervals, we hardly knew we had a colonel. In this case this was the first time I had heard from the Colonel for a long while. But he claimed to be a lawyer, and he claimed that there was no such thing as "accidental suicide." So in my second report I described the death with a circumlocution that I think must have give him a pain. I described the death in about the words of a legal indictment, and stated that Hakel had come to his death from the impact of a leaden bullet, calibre .44, propelled by a charge of powder contained in the chamber of a Colt's revolver, calibre .44, number 602,890, which pistol was held, at 3:45 P. M. of said day, in the right hand of the said Hakel. I also set forth that the discharge of the said revolver was not intentional, but was an involuntary action on the part of the said Hakel, etc., etc. I managed to describe accurately and with considerable minuteness the portions of his shape through which the bullet went, and the result. The Colonel down at Fort Kearney, where he was then located, had made considerable fun of my statement of "accidental suicide," and I had received privately some letters containing his wise and oracular disquisitions upon the English language. So, when I afterwards sent a copy of my second report to some of the officers, it tickled them very much, but it produced a bad feeling between the Colonel and me; I had more friends in the regiment than he had. Some time afterwards, the strength of the regiment having been reduced by casualties to a number slightly below the minimum, concerning which no notice would have been taken except for the general opinion in which the Colonel was held, he was ordered to be mustered out. We shed no tears. He afterwards went back to Iowa, and was killed in a runaway while he was out driving a buggy. This death of Hakel took place on October 14, 1863. Four of our men had already died of disease, but they were men whom we had left behind us, and four others had deserted before we had reached Omaha. During the entire history of the company we had nine desertions, and here I wish to speak of two men particularly.

We had a man in our company by the name of John Ryan. He was a young Irishman from Dubuque. He was not inclined to get drunk, although he drank somewhat, but he was seized with the most intractable spells as to his disposition. He had wanted as a young man to be a prizefighter, and had taken lessons in pugilism. He would get along all right for two or three weeks, and then he would sort of get on the war-path, and he wanted to fight. Before he got through he had a dozen of them, and although he may have knocked over and whipped ten out of the dozen, he generally wound up by somebody pounding him up good and hard. I determined to see if I couldn't bring about a change, and I had a talk with him. The difficulty about it was that he was about as old as I was, and seemed to think that he understood, as well as I did, what ought to be done. I finally had a personal collision with him, and put him in the guard-house. Then he talked out openly that he proposed to shoot me before my term of service was over. I sent for him, and told him that he had committed a crime, and that I could have him court-martialed, and sent to the penitentiary; but, if I should have him court-martialed for threats, he might vainly form an opinion that I was afraid of him, and wanted to get away from him; that I did not propose to humor him by anything that would give him the opinion that I wanted to separate from him. I told him that it cost the United States a thousand dollars to get a soldier drilled up to efficiency, and it was my duty to see that he performed the work that the Government had paid him for; and that whenever he wanted to try determinations with me we would take a couple of revolvers and go up the canyon. He made no reply, and the interview ended. Ryan kept a-going from bad to worse. He seemed to have got an idea that he wanted to whip every soldier in the company. He wanted to have it understood that he was the best man in the company; once in a while, there being a good many men in the company of fine capability, some good man in the company who would get a cross word from Ryan would make a pretext of jumping onto Ryan, and, getting in the first blow, beat him up. I will have occasion to refer to Ryan further on, and the circumstances under which he finally deserted.

This brings me to the description of a man who came into our company after we had been at Cottonwood Springs for a couple of months, and desired to enlist. His name was Robert McFarland. He came to me and told me that he wanted to enlist, and said that he was a Scotchman, and that he concluded that he would like to learn to be a soldier. I didn't like his looks very well, and referred him to Captain O'Brien. Captain O'Brien had him sign up enlistment papers, and swore him in, and he was assigned to one of the barracks in the company. He appeared to be a very dumb, ignorant sort of fellow for a while, say for three or four weeks. He claimed to be a farmer boy, although his record showed him to be twenty-five years of age. My opinion is that he was, in fact, about twenty-eight at that time. He was always writing lots of letters. One day the Orderly Sergeant came to me and said that there must be something wrong about McFarland, because he was writing so many letters. I told the Corporal of his squad to keep an eye on him, and see what he could make out of his actions. McFarland was a man who was inclined to shirk his duties, but he seemed to learn soldiering with wonderful speed, for after he had drilled a couple of days he seemed to drill as well as anybody. One day he was sent on a detail to go down to Fort Kearney and back. And while he was down at Fort Kearney McFarland fortunately got drunk, and he confided to one of his new friends in the company that he, McFarland, was an Irishman, and that he lived in New Orleans, and that he belonged to a military company there before the war. And when the war broke out he joined the Louisiana Tigers, and that he had been sent up to Virginia and was with Stonewall Jackson and in the battles of the army of the North Virginia until after Gettysburg, and until after Lee had returned to Virginia. And that he, McFarland, had made up his mind that the Confederacy was whipped, and that there was no use in fighting any more, and that he and several others had deserted with the intention of going out to the mountains and entering the gold-fields. He said that when he was coming along and saw a company of soldiers, he sort of made up his mind that he wanted to be a soldier again. As he was not fighting against his brothers in the South, he thought it wouldn't make any difference; that he wouldn't be captured by the Southern Confederacy and punished for deserting. And he also said that his name was not Robert McFarland, and that he had assumed that name for the purpose of enlistment. This was the brief of a long drunken story that lasted about all night, and was told to and listened to with great interest by one of our Iowa farm boys, who immediately came to me and gave it to me in detail; and I recognized the fact that the story was so coherent that it was without doubt true. So, one day while I was in command of the company, I sent for him and had a talk with him, and he with great reluctance admitted the facts. I told him then that he must brace up and be a better soldier, and do more work; that he was shirking a great deal; that the boys would notice it, and as he had been in the Confederate army they wouldn't like it. I had some writing which I wanted to do in some of the reports and returns, and I asked him how well he could write, and found out he was a most excellent penman, and I put him to work on writing. But he was a man who had a bad face, a bad disposition, and made a bad impression. He was not only a deserter, but he was evidently a great deal of a rogue. I will speak of him again further on.

Along the latter part of January, 1864, two men who were driving on a train passed the Fort; came in and said that they had had a row with the wagon-master and wanted to enlist. One of them was named Joseph Cooper and the other John Jackson. Jackson was about thirty, and Cooper was somewhere between forty-five and fifty, but gave his age forty-five, because that was the age limit. We were about to reject Cooper, but he said that he was a practical veterinary surgeon, so we took them both into the company. As they were both absolutely worthless and had probably been thrashed out of their train by the wagon-master because they were worthless, the boys soon got down on them, caught them in little, petty thievery, and we dumped them both into the guard-house and kept them in there off and on for quite a while, making them work under the supervision of a corporal when they were out. We found them stealing rations and selling rations from their comrades to the pilgrims. And upon the suggestion of the Captain I made life such a burden for them that, having given them an opportunity to desert, they embraced the opportunity and we heard of them no more.

We also lost two men by the fact that one of them was a minor and his mother took him out of the service with a writ of habeas corpus. This was before we got to Omaha. Another was a deserter from the Eleventh Iowa Infantry, then in the field; having been detected, he was placed under guard and sent to his regiment to be court-martialed.

In March, 1864, we received a consignment of twelve recruits, which brought our company up again to a good standing. These men were Iowa farm boys, and twelve as good men as could be found in the army. Three of them had already been in the service, been honestly discharged from wounds received, recovered fully, and reënlisted. Four of them were discharged as sergeants and corporals when our company was mustered out in 1866, one being Milo Lacey as First Sergeant.

The way that recruits came to a company during the Civil War was something like this: The boys at home were growing up, and wanted to get into the service, or for some reason obstacles to their enlistment had vanished, and when they got ready to enlist it became a question with them where they wanted to go. Each of them had several boy acquaintances or relatives who were already in existing regiments. Each one may have had two or three chums in some certain regiment, so when he made up his mind to enlist, he would enlist in a regiment in which he had friends or relatives. As the newspapers were full of the exploits of the regiments at the front, it often happened that some exploit would determine the recruit to go to that regiment if he had a friend or relative in it, in preference to some other regiment where he had a friend or relative. It so happened that the boys of our regiment had a great many friends and relatives in eastern Iowa, and these recruits would be brought together at some point and drilled preliminarily, and taught soldiering say for two or three or four months, and then they would be forwarded in squads to the regiment. If a regiment

was not receiving the recruits that it wanted or thought it
ought to have, it was common for the Colonel to pick out
some good recruiting lieutenant and get him a recruiting
furlough and then send him back where the bulk of the regiment had been recruited, and let him go to work. Many regiments were kept up to the maximum in that manner. Our
company received subsequent batches of recruits, of which
I will speak hereafter. Our company had first and last one
hundred and fifty-one members. The casualties of the service
were always heavy. For instance, we lost by death twenty-
seven men, by desertion nine, and by transfer to other regiments and by other causes, nine. Then again while the
majority of the company had enlisted for three years or
during the war, there were a few who had enlisted for only
one year. Nevertheless, many of these stayed in, and were
either killed in battle or died of disease.

CHAPTER X

I HAVE referred to the store which Boyer kept where
liquors were sold. We managed to get pretty good police
regulations in our company in regard to liquors. My barrel
of 1849 whisky didn't last very long, so that soon afterwards
on one of my trips to Fort Kearney I went to the post commander and told him what my men were doing, and that
they must have a ration of whisky if they did this hard
pioneer work, that is, if they wanted the ration. I sat down
with him and computed what it would take to build the fort
for *two companies* and to make the work speed along
rapidly. And I pointed out to him that it was the cheapest
thing for the Government to give that inducement. After a
considerable consultation he agreed with me that I might
take out a supply that would last until the completion of
the post, as they had much on hand and there did not seem
to be a great demand. In short, I drew seven more barrels
of good corn whisky as rations. And the arrangement which
we made, and which was satisfactory to the men, and which
worked exceedingly well, was this: Every man who worked
as an axman or builder, or in other words did hard work
that was strictly outside of military service, got a drink in
the morning if he wanted it, and one in the evening if he
wanted it, when he was through with his work. And if he
shirked during the day, he did not get his evening drink.
The men all seemed to be inspired, and they all wanted to

work, and those who did work, as a rule, did well. The number of shirkers was not many. In order that there should be no intemperance in the morning, when the time for a jigger had arrived there was poured out in a tin cup a gill, and he drank it right there. The captain didn't allow him to carry it off. Our great big Corporal Forbush, who was the Hercules of the company, and who had passed a great deal of his life swinging an ax in the Northern pineries, was the man who gave the boys their drinks. He was liable to drink a little too much himself, but he was a good disciplinarian, and the boys could not get any whisky and carry it off. They drank it on the spot, and in his presence, morning and night. A gill is a pretty good-sized drink, and was all a man should have at one time. The seven barrels would not have lasted long if it had not been economically administered, and only to those who did the hard work. There was very little constitutional intemperance in our company. It was sporadic. None of the ranchmen would sell liquor to our men, nor would the sutler. And if a man was caught with liquor he was put at work on fatigue duty without liquor, so that we had but very little trouble during the winter.

That good old ancient time was an era of drinking. There was no such thing known then in the West as "prohibition," and nearly everybody drank a little. It was also the age of bitters. Sometime back in the early '50s the manufacture of artificial bitters had been introduced. Before that time an old invention called "Stoughton" had been for a long while in vogue. In every saloon was a bottle of "Stoughton bitters," and if anybody wanted any bitters he called for some Stoughton and put it in. It was only occasionally the Stoughton was used, but the Stoughton bottle was always at the bar, and the synonym for an idle fellow, always in evidence and doing nothing, was to call him a "Stoughton bottle." And frequently men were spoken of in politics or religion or in a story as a mere "Stoughton bottle." That is, they were in evidence, but nobody paid much attention to them. The simile survived for a lifetime after the Stoughton bottle had gone. But someone afterwards invented "bitters" as a beverage; three celebrated kinds were thrown onto the market, and made great fortunes for their inventors, as they were early occupants of the field. The first in order was "Plantation Bitters"; next, "Hostetter's Bitters"; third, "Log Cabin Bitters." By the time the war broke out these bitters had been advertised with an expenditure of money which at that time was thought remarkable. Plantation Bitters appeared in 1860, and every wall and fence and vacant place in the United States was placarded with the legend, "S. T. 1860 X." For several months everybody was guessing what the sign meant. It was in the newspapers. It was distributed in handbills on the street. It was seen at every turn, "S. T. 1860 X." After the world had long grown tired of guessing, there appeared the complete legend, "Plantation Bitters, S. T. 1860 X." Plantation Bitters became the bottled liquor of the age. It was made out of alcohol, water and flavoring, and was really very attractive as to taste and results. The Hostetter and the Log Cabin followed closely behind in popularity. The Log Cabin got into sutler tents all over the district which the army occupied. Its principal advertisement was the strange glass bottle made in the shape of a log cabin. At about the time I speak of all three of these liquors were on sale at Boyer's. The legend of the Plantation Bitters was that it meant "Sure thing in ten years from 1860." That is, when the inventor had made the decoction, and submitted it to a friend as an invention and marketable article, the friend, so the story goes, told him that it was a sure thing for a fortune in ten years. So, acting on this thought, he had billed the United States, "S. T. 1860 X.," and spent half a million advertising "S. T. 1860 X.," before anybody knew what it was all about.

In March, 1864, while we were at the post, Artemus Ward, the great humorist, came through on a coach; and hearing that he was coming, Captain O'Brien and I went to the coach to greet him. It was late in the afternoon. The first thing he did was to ask us to go and take a drink with him, and Boyer's was the saloon. Artemus Ward went in, with us following him, and said, "What have you got to drink here?" Boyer said, "Nothing but bitters." Ward said, "What kind of bitters?" Boyer said, "I have got nothing but Hostetter; some trains went by here and they cleaned me out of everything but Hostetter." So Ward said, "Give us some Hostetter," and the bottle was shoved out on the cedar counter. We took a drink with Ward, who told us about some Salt Lake experience he had recently had. In a little while the driver shouted for him to get aboard. Ward turned to Boyer, and he says, "How much Hostetter have you got?" Boyer looked under his counter and said, "I had a case of two dozen bottles which I opened this afternoon and that is all I have got, and I have used up five of them." Said Artemus Ward, "I have got to have eighteen of those bottles." Boyer said, "That only leaves me one bottle." Ward said, "It don't make any difference; your mathematics are all right, but I want eighteen of those bottles." The bottles sold for $1.50. Ward said, "I will give you $2 a bottle." In a short time the money had been paid. Ward went to the coach with the box of eighteen bottles under his arm, and we bade him an affectionate adieu. The crowded coach greeted him with cheers, and I have no doubt that they finished the whole business before morning, on the coach.

Our company kept constantly improving. Captain O'Brien had been a sergeant in the Fifth Wisconsin Battery, and I had been a sergeant in the Fourth Iowa Cavalry, and we had both served from the beginning of the war. Our First Lieutenant, of whom I have spoken, was a gray-haired and gray-whiskered man, who said he was only forty-five. He was a very gentlemanly, placid old man, without the slightest particle of military instinct or habit. The other company at our post was officered by three as inefficient men as could be found in the regiment. They were of no account whatever. The Captain and First Lieutenant were well along in years, and had got their places because they had been the relatives of somebody, and had managed to get the appointment. The Second Lieutenant was the son of the senior Major of our regiment, Major H. H. Heath.

This man Heath had served in the First Iowa Cavalry, and had been made a Major of our regiment through the influence of a very giddy wife, who was the daughter of a Syracuse barber in New York. Major Heath himself was a fine-looking, dressy, showy fellow, but a great scoundrel. Through the influence which his wife had with Senator Lane of Kansas, Heath became finally brevetted as a Brigadier-General. Heath was a self-important, dictatorial wind-bag, and he succeeded in getting his worthless, drunken son as Second Lieutenant in the Company. The elder Heath coquetted with Jeff Davis to get a Brigadier-Generalship in the Confederate army. He was willing to be a traitor to his country or do anything else. He was absolutely without principal. I have referred to him once before, but will repeat. When the Rebel archives were captured at Richmond, Heath's letter was found among the many other similar documents, and when Heath under President Andrew Johnson wanted an appointment, Major-General G. M. Dodge, who was one of Sherman's corps commanders and happened to be a member of Congress at that time from Iowa, got hold of the Heath letter, and read it on the floor of Congress, and Heath became a refugee, fled to Peru, and died a pauper and a tramp. Heath, on account of his rascality, at the close of the war was recommended to be cashiered, but his wife, in a beautiful blue moire antique dress, went on to Washington, saw President Johnson, saved him, and had his dismissal remitted to a discharge from the service. I am anticipating history somewhat in giving the pedigree of Second Lieutenant Heath. I had so much trouble with him in the barracks that I had made up my mind that I would have him court-martialed and disposed of, because he would fill himself with whisky and become offensive and insulting. He would go down among his private soldiers in the barracks and play poker with them and win their money, and he would cheat at cards, and if a soldier playing with him, protested, he would send him to the guard-house. On the afternoon of March 21, 1864, Heath was sent out with a squad of men to scout along the south side of the river to see if there

were any Indians or tracks to be seen. He got in just about
sundown, and as he was going by his own barracks close to a
door, a gun went off in the hands of one of the soldiers, and
the bullet went a dead shot through his head and killed him.
It was believed that one of the men had taken advantage of
the situation to arrange the accident. I was directed by the
Post Commander (Captain O'Brien) to inquire into the
cause of the death, and make report. The soldier said that
it was an entire accident. Everybody seemed to be pleased
with the circumstance; nobody seemed to find any fault
with it, and there being no evidence to the contrary, and
it being entirely to the benefit of the United States service,
I reported the testimony, and nothing was done except to
bury the Lieutenant. Major Heath showed no particular
interest in the death of his only son. He was a son by a
former wife, and was the only child he ever had. He did not
attend the funeral, nor were any arrangements made except
to put the Lieutenant under the ground. Then the Captain
of the company summoned all the power he had to get his
own worthless brother-in-law in as Second Lieutenant; but
the other officers of the post objected, and succeeded in beat-
ing him before the Governor and Adjutant-General of Iowa,
who made the appointments.

For twenty-five miles along the line, including Jack Morrow's ranch, and Gilmans', there were ten ranches, and
farm-houses. Wives and relatives of these settlers seeing
the post well established, came out on stages from the East
and joined their husbands and relations. Along about the
first of April MacDonald said he was going to take the stuff
out of his store-building as much as he could, and get up a
dance on the first favorable opportunity. This plan was
carried out, and women were there from the whole twenty-
five miles. There were about twenty of them. Fiddlers were
easily obtained, and the dance lasted until breakfast-time.
I did not get much of an opportunity to be present except
occasionally, up to twelve o'clock, after which I went on
duty as officer of the guard. But it was a regular frontier
dance. I have put down in my memorandum only two of the

tunes that were played, and I give the names that the fiddler gave me. One of them was "Soapsuds over the Fence," and the other "Turkey in the Straw." All the men in the country were there except the soldiers, and a great deal of liquor was consumed, and several rough-and-tumble fist fights were had out of doors on the flat; but I arrested nobody, and let them all have just as good a time as they wanted to. Captain O'Brien was the mogul of the evening.

Matters upon the road began to get very busy about the first of April. The grass was not up so that the ox teams could travel, but the early pilgrims with smart mule teams began to go through in large numbers. The weather was very stormy and unpleasant in the latter part of March, and considerable snow fell, which the wind would sweep off into the gullies, and fill up almost level, although they might be ten or twenty feet deep. The sand, gravel and snow would be swept off by the wind from the road, and the river-bottom, leaving the roads entirely passable.

Word came from Fort Kearney that an effort would be made to have a big Indian council about the middle of April, and that word had been sent to all of the Sioux, both north and south. The Cheyennes and Arapahoes had not been invited, because it was believed if the Sioux could be influenced the others would remain neutral. So we planned for a reception that would strike terror into the red man when he came in to see us. The hospital which we had built was practically unused. The boys did not like to go to the hospital, and remained in their bunks until they recovered or got in pretty bad condition. And when they got in bad condition, if they could go we sent them down to Fort Kearney, where they could get good care.

One day early in April, 1864, John Dillon, the actor, was passing through on a stage. He was coming from the west. Some telegraph operator notified the operator at our post. Captain O'Brien knew John Dillon personally, and as they were fellow-Irishmen, it was but natural that the Captain should warmly greet him, and I went along. The result was that we got Dillon to stop over. We had built an addition to the hospital so as to make it twenty by forty. We got everybody out of the hospital, hung up some blankets at the end, and we had as good an entertainment from John Dillon as we had ever listened to anywhere. Dillon had been playing in Denver, and was on the way to the States, and we organized him a house, fifty cents admission. We had no chairs nor anything to sit on, so the front row sat down on the floor, and formed a semi-circle about five feet from Dillon, all around in front of him. Then the next row sat on cracker-boxes, flat side down, and the next row sat on cracker-boxes on edge, and the balance stood up. The entrance was through a window. Dillon was about two-thirds "full," and had a little monologue play to start on, in which he had some real drinking out of a real Hostetter bottle, and he kept the thing up for about three hours, to the amusement and delight of us all. We were packed like herrings in a box, and if John Dillon hadn't been one of the greatest comedians in the United States we could not have been kept there under those circumstances. When the show was over he came over to our quarters, and we all played poker until breakfast.

During April a vacancy as Second Lieutenant took place at Fort Kearney, in Company A. The First Sergeant, Tom Potter, and I had been friends, and I had been working to help him get into the vacancy, and during April I was very much grieved to hear that he had failed in being commissioned. This Tom Potter finally became an officer of the company. Our relations were exceedingly friendly, but at this time he had no money, few friends, and no relatives. There was nobody to help him. He was alone in the world, and promotions did not always go upon their merits. Our friendship lasted for many years, until his death. He afterwards became president of the Union Pacific Railroad at Fifty Thousand Dollars a year, and worked himself to death. But in the very height of his powers in the army, he was unable to become Second Lieutenant, owing to the petty little rivalries and dishonest instincts of his superiors, until long afterwards.

On April 9th we were visited by Captain Logan of the First Colorado Cavalry. Captain Logan was making the tour down the Platte from Denver to ascertain the condition of things, and the probabilities of an Indian war. He stayed with us a couple of days. He had talked with the ranchmen and settlers along the line. He told us that unless we could win the Sioux over at the approaching convention, we would have all kinds of Indian trouble. He said that he had been detailed to send out half-breed Indians as runners, and to assist in making complete the convention which was to meet at our post the middle of the month. We afterwards met most of the First Colorado Cavalry. They were a good regiment, and had saved New Mexico from going into the Confederacy. There is no more interesting regimental history than that which a young man named Hollister, who belonged to the regiment, has written of it. The regiment was a regiment of pioneers who were inured to the open air, and life on horseback; and as for being fighters, there were none superior, and we Iowa boys always liked them. Before we went out onto the plains, there had been part of the Eleventh Ohio Cavalry regiment sent to Fort Laramie, which was about two hundred and seventy-five miles northwest of us, on the Salt Lake trail. Once in a while we saw one of the officers or men of that regiment going down to Fort Kearney to get supplies.

On April 13, 1864, Harry Dall reached our post, and, being tired of staging, thought he would stay over a day and rest. I ran across him shortly after he got out of the stage, and he told me his story. Secretary Seward had sent him from Washington to go to Alaska, and he was going to go and report upon the botany, biology and climate of Alaska. I never saw him before or since. He was one of the most companionable men I ever met. We went out with our greyhounds, and caught an antelope and gave Dall a good time. It is impossible for me to say what he afterwards did, except that he made a long and interesting report upon Alaska, which was widely published; and he was about the first of the Americans who knew anything of the land which Secretary Seward purchased from Russia. Those who in those days opposed the purchase, called it "our national ice-house." He was with us at the same time that a Mr. S. F. Burtch, of Omaha, was with us. Burtch was one of those breezy young men of the Western country, who had business all over it, got acquainted with everybody, and liked everybody and everybody liked him. Burtch and Dall came together accidentally at our place; they made a great team.

One day a discussion grew up as to the amount of travel on the plains. Those who had lived on the plains for some time said that the travel from January 1st to April 1st, 1864, had been the heaviest ever on the plains, for that season of the year; and that the probability was that the year of 1864 would show more travel by far than ever before. Various persons began to tell about the trains which they had seen. Many persons told of trains that were from ten to fifteen miles long, being aggregations of several independent trains. They told of eight hundred ox teams passing their ranches in a single day. Mrs. Mac-Donald, the wife of the ranchman at our post, said she had many times kept account of the number of wagons which went by, and that one day they went up to nine hundred, counting those going both ways. That may sound like a very large story, and it is a large one, but is entirely credible. These ox teams would pass a store in their slow gait about one in a minute and a half or two minutes, after they had begun to start by. But that would only make from three to four hundred in ten hours; but when trains were going both ways as they were, it is not incredible by any means that nine hundred wagons passed a ranch in one day. I have stood on the "Sioux Lookout" with my field-glass, and have seen a train as long as I could definitely distinguish it with my glass, and it would stretch out until it would become so fine that it was impossible to fairly scan it. As the wind was generally blowing either from the north or the south, the teams had a vast prism of dust rising either to the north or south, and the dust would be in the air mile after mile until the dust and teams both reached the vanishing-point on the horizon. Fully three-fourths of this traffic was with oxen. The wagons were large, cumbersome wagons which I have heretofore described. And in addition to the description I will say that they had wooden axles, and were of what they called the thimble-skein variety. On the end of the heavy wooden axle was the iron thimble which revolved in another iron thimble in the hub, which was called the skein; the axle was held on by a linch-pin made by a blacksmith. The thimble-skein was lubricated with tar, and the tar-bucket hung on the rear axle. At every ranch were lift-jacks, so that these wheels could be raised, taken off, and the axles lubricated. The wind and the whirling sand and dust made it necessary for this to be frequently done.

The drivers were called "bull-whackers," which was abbreviated down to "Whackers." They had long gads, and a long lash with whang-leather tip; this they could make pop like a rifle. And they could hit a steer on any part, with the whang tip as it cracked, and it could nip the hide out just like a knife. They generally drove walking along the left side of the team, but when the dust was heavy they walked on the clear side, whether right or left. The wagon-master was boss, he was king, and generally the most dangerous man in the lot. He carried a revolver or two, and his altercations with the whackers were very frequent. The wagons were piled full and the curtains drawn, so that it was not very easy to steal anything. One time Jack Morrow was at the post and was inebriated as usual, and he confided to me how he got his start. He said: "I came from Missouri, and got to whacking bulls across the plains; after a while I got onto a Government train loaded with ammunition. I unscrewed the boxes, took out the ammunition and sold it to the ranchmen, filled the boxes with sand, and screwed them down. Then before we got to Laramie I had a rumpus with the wagon-master and he pulled a pistol and I skinned out for somewhere else and nobody got onto it." He said, "I never heard a word from it ever afterwards, but I sold a big lot of ammunition." This statement might have been true, or not, but it was nevertheless the fact that in the commerce of the prairie, a great difficulty lay in guarding against theft in transit, and this was one of the main duties of the wagon-master in conducting his train.

It is perfectly safe to say that for several months during the summer there poured into Denver no less than a thousand tons of merchandise a day, and this seems almost incredible when we consider the hardship and privations which made it possible. But there was a class of people in the West, Missouri and Iowa, that liked fun, enjoyed freedom, despised luxury, and took no note of danger or privation; and they were not of the dumb and stupid class of society. Many were educated, some of them were gifted. They were full of fun, wanted to see the world, and tried to shoot each other up whenever they came in angry contact. I remember one of them standing up and reciting for ten minutes from memory one of the bucolics of Virgil. He had it in the original from end to end, and said he came from St. Genevieve, Missouri. As I now look back, the prominent, noticeable, rollicking dare-devils seemed to come principally from Missouri.

CHAPTER XI

UPON April 16th an old Indian came in, and hunted me up, and with him was a man who could talk Indian. This old Indian was the vanguard coming up to the council. When I saw him I recognized him as the one who had appeared in camp some time before, and to whom I fed the molasses and crackers. He came up and was very profuse with me in his hearty handshake and "How-cola?" (Cola means friend.) I was very much surprised. The interpreter told me that the Indian's name was O-way-see'-cha, accent on the third syllable. This word means in the Sioux dialect "bad wound," "see-cha" meaning bad. The Sioux, like the French, put their adjectives after the noun. Wah-see-cha means "medicine bad," *i. e.,* white-man. I was told that he acquired his name from a fight with the Pawnee Indians down north of Fort Kearney several years before; that he was so badly wounded that they carried him off on an Indian litter between two ponies; and he finally recovered to be as well as ever; and then, Indian fashion he took a new name. He greeted me with an expression which the interpreter said meant that I was "his long-knife son." I asked him if he was hungry, and he said "No." Then I went to Ben Gallagher's sutler store with him and bought him a plug of chewing tobacco, which in the manner of that time, and the trade, was a foot long, three inches wide, and an inch thick, and for which I paid a dollar. This I gave to O-way-see'-cha and he patted me on the back, and bade me an affectionate good-by. He was camped upon the Platte valley two or three miles above the post. Nobody saw him come there, and it was supposed that he came down there stealthily, got himself all fixed at night, and made his appearance at the post the next morning. During the day we heard that Sioux Indians were coming in from every side; we had an inspection of arms, and put ourselves in such condition that we could fall in, and begin business at a moment's notice. The men were ordered to stay around the barracks, to wear their revolvers, sleep in their uniforms, and be ready, because we did not know what tricks might be played upon us. We also had the cannon loaded with shrapnel cut one second, set a post guard, and put pickets all around a half-mile from the post.

On April 16, 1864, General Mitchell and Lieutenant Williams, coming from Fort Kearney, arrived at the post. This was Brigadier-General Robert B. Mitchell. He was born in Ohio; came to Kansas as a pro-slavery Democrat. The conduct of the Missourians, and the early Kansas troubles, made him an anti-slavery Democrat. When the war broke out he was for fighting, and became immediately the Colonel of the Second Kansas. He was in the Lyon campaign in Missouri, and was badly shot up at the battle of Wilson's Creek. I was in that campaign as a soldier in the First Iowa Infantry, and our regiment was brigaded with the Second Kansas for a while, and I remembered Colonel Mitchell very well, and when he was said to have been shot, and taken from the field. After he recovered he was made a Brigadier-General, and sent with the army to Kentucky, and was in command of a brigade of cavalry. He was in the battle of Perryville, where he said he lost seven hundred men in seven minutes. He was in a very great number of fights and skirmishes, and used to say that up to date, he was in two more battles in number than any Brigadier in the service. His two biggest battles were Wilson Creek and Perryville, and it so happened that I was in the Wilson

Creek battle and Captain O'Brien was in the Perryville battle. So, when he arrived at our post, we introduced ourselves to him and he took a great fancy to our company, and nearly ignored the other officers of the post. Lieutenant Williams, who was with him as A. D. C., was a little Kentucky cavalry First Lieutenant who had distinguished himself at Perryville by charging and cutting through a regiment of Confederate infantry, and then forming in the rear and cutting back through a battery of artillery. On the evening of the 16th Captain O'Brien and I had a fine visit with the General.

In the meantime the Indians were coming in, and camping together near the river outside of the two miles limit. We had all of our men fully armed, and everything ready to prevent a surprise of our post. The Indians were ordered not come within two miles of the post, except that they might send a delegation in of one hundred, to accompany their speakers to the place of rendezvous. Our sutler, Ben Gallagher, had started in to build a large sutler store, twenty-five feet square. Holes for the doors and windows had been sawed from the logs, and most of the roof was on. But it had no floor nor any furnishing. It had a large doorhole in the north and one in the south; the opening on the south side faced our camp. With great pomp the Indians to the number of about one hundred, all fully armed and finely mounted, came down towards our camp about nine o'clock. Then seventeen chiefs threw off their weapons, leaving them behind with their escort, and came forward to the new sutler-house with great pomp and ceremony. Then all of the officers of the post, coming up to within about fifty feet of the building, took off their sabres and revolvers and left them in a pile with a guard. We had three interpreters, the principal one of whom was named Watts. He had been with the Indians and traded with them for many years. His usual name was "Snell," which was an abbreviation of his Indian name, which was Wah-see-cha-es-snel-la (The "lonesome white man"). There were two other interpreters besides Watts. Among the Indians there was an Indian who, it was said, readily understood English.

The Indians formed a semicircle, in the building, sitting down on the ground, and we formed one, sitting on cracker-boxes opposite them, except that General Mitchell sat in a large camp-chair. He looked like a king. He was an exceedingly handsome man, with a full, dark-brown curly beard and mustache. Major George M. O'Brien sat on his right, also a fine-looking man, standing six feet one inch. He afterwards practiced law in Omaha, and on his death was buried there.

On the left of the General sat Captain O'Brien, six feet high. I was six feet, and we tapered off at both sides, making a pretty good showing, in full uniforms, with our red silk sashes on, which hadn't seen the light for several months. Back of the General was a man whom the General had brought along with him, and from whom he appeared to take advice as to preliminaries and procedure. I didn't find who he was. To the left front of the General, and immediately in front of Captain O'Brien, on a cracker-box, sat the interpreter, Watts. The Indians all through this matter seemed to be unusually important, and punctilious. They all had their blankets on, and although they had ostensibly left their arms behind, every one had probably a sharp butcher-knife in the folds of his blanket. At least, Watts said so. As a sort of stand-off, we, who had left our arms behind us, each had a pistol in his hip pocket so as not to be taken unawares. Nothing was said for several minutes, and we all sat in silence. Every once in a while an Indian made a sort of sign or signal, and it would go around like penitents crossing. It was some kind of a slight significant sign made instantly and simply, which would be taken up and gone through with as if it were a signal of some kind, or an invocation of some kind. Directly opposite General Mitchell was Shan-tag-a-lisk, which is translated as "Spotted Tail." He was the greatest warrior in the Sioux nation, said to be the greatest either past or present. He was said to be able to count twenty-six "cooz." He belonged to the Brulé Sioux. On his right was my friend, "Bad Wound." On the left were "Two

Strike," and "Two Crows," and the "Big Mandan." On the opposite side were "Prickly Pear" and "Eagle Twice." These are all the names I have preserved. "Two Strike" was said to have killed two Pawnees with one bullet. These Indians represented the four tribes of the Sioux that were nearest to us. Those south of the river were the "Ogallallah," of whom "Bad Wound" was chief. Northwest were the "Brulés," of whom "Shan-tag-a-lisk" was chief. North of us and east of the Brulés were what were called the "Minne-kaw'-zhouz." The latter word signified shallow water. The "shallow water" Sioux lived upon the streams which through a great scope of country were all shallow. "Two Strike" was said to be their chief. East of them on the Missouri river were a lot of Indians represented by the Big Mandan. The word Brulé, which is a French word, means "sun-burnt"; it was derived from the Indian name which in the Indian tongue meant "burnt-thighs." Their thighs exposed to the sun were sunburned in their constant riding on horseback. The words meant more than at first appeared; for, Indians who walked on the ground did not get their thighs burned more than other parts, especially as the Indians went practically naked when the sun was hot. Hence the words "burnt-thighs" meant that the Brulé Indians were riders; that they belonged to the cavalry, that is, the Chivalry; in other words, they were of the equestrian class. The words constituted a boast that they were better than others and were the Rough-Riders of the plains. Such was the tradition of the name. Peace or war upon the plains, as to us, depended largely upon our satisfying all these Indians.

Strange as it may appear, all of the Indians had extremely feminine faces, except the Big Mandan. Spotted Tail looked exactly like a woman; and in short, as I had already observed, and often afterwards observed, the Indian men seemed to have a feminine look and the women to have a rather masculine look, which increased as they grew older. An old Indian woman had a much more dangerous-looking face than an old Indian man. So much has been written about the noble looks and appearance of the red man, and his fine physique, and all that kind of stuff, that it seems strange to contradict it; but, as a matter of fact, the Indian warriors as a whole looked more like women than like men, and their extermination, I believe, is due to the fact that they did not have the surviving power nor the sufficient fibre. In addition to this, these Indians had revolting and beastly habits and vices, just as bad as could be, and their names, many of them, were such that no interpretation in the English would be printable.

The word "Ogallallah" meant "the split-off band," because in former years the band had split off from the main Sioux tribe, and gone down into what was said to have been Pawnee territory. But concerning those facts I could never get anything but contradictory stories. The "split-off" must have been a long while before. They called themselves Lah-ko-tahs. The interpreter told me that the separation had been so long, and so distant, that one part of the Sioux tribe had lost the consonant "d" and the other the use of the consonant "l," and one called themselves "Lah-ko-tahs," and the other "Dah-ko-tahs." Once I talked with two Irish travelers in regard to the Indians. One of them asked me what the word "Ogallallah" meant, and I told him that it meant "the split-off band," and he spoke up and said, "That is a pure Irish word, and in the old Irish language means, 'secessionist.'" I may say here that it was not unusual for persons in referring to the language of the northern Sioux to say that there were words in use among them that were distinctly Irish and Welsh. I took no note of them at the time, considering them to be merely accidental coincidences, and now I remember only the word "Ogallallah."

It was very interesting, the silent way in which we sat on both sides and gazed at each other. When it came to muscle and physique, our men, man for man, could have thrown them all outdoors and walked on them, except perhaps as to the "Big Mandan." We were all larger than the Indians except him, and he was about six feet four, and about a yard across, about forty years of age, and very light-colored for an Indian. It would have been a close tussle between him and Major O'Brien. Finally, one Indian got out a pipe from under his blanket. It had a stem about two and a half feet long. It was made of red pipestone, and had a good-sized bowl, but the orifice was scant for the tobacco. It was filled with great pomp and solemnity by the man who took it, and he did it little by little, as if it was a great function. He felt the weight and importance of the ceremony. Then he passed the pipe down to the end of the line, and there an Indian with a flint-and-steel and a piece of punk started the pipe. Then it went from mouth to mouth, the parties each taking three whiffs. When it had gone along the entire Indian line, it struck the end of our line. We were all trying to look solemn. The Indians were dreadfully solemn. They acted as if they thought they were doing the greatest deed in their lives; we did not wish to hurt their feelings by impairing the solemnity of the occasion, so we just looked as wise as we could. But when the pipe struck the end of our line, where Lieutenant Williams was, before he put the pipe into his mouth he drew it under his sleeve, saying as he did so, "I don't believe I want to swap saliva with that crowd." This being said in a ponderous and thoughtful way, perhaps impressed the crowd on the other side as being a mental benediction on receiving the utensil. We all kept looking solemn, however, although it was hard work. When the pipe got to the General he pulled out his silk handkerchief and polished off the mouthpiece, took three profound whiffs, and passed it on. After it had gone through with our line it went across to where it had started from.

Finally Spotted Tail said something which, being interpreted, was: "The white brother has sent for us. What does the white brother want?" Then General Mitchell, with much assumed and natural dignity, combined, began to tell the Indians how the whites and Indians had lived side by side in peace for so many years, and how the Indians were prosperous through contact with the whites, and were getting guns, and killing game more easily, and having a better time of it generally; and how persons had conspired to bring about a want of amity and friendship; and how it was his desire to meet the red brother, and tell him what the Great Father in Washington wanted. It was a long preamble which General Mitchell had evidently conned over in his mind, because he wound up with a statement that the white man wanted peace, *and wanted the Sioux to keep out of the Platte Valley.*

Thereupon the Big Mandan rose up, throwing off his blanket, and standing out with nothing on but breech-clout and moccasins. He commenced a speech which started out slow and low, beginning to rise in volume and increase in rapidity, until he was spouting away like a man running for office before a county convention. No report that I know of was ever made of what took place at this powwow, and my notes concerning it are meager. But the "Big Mandan" told about how in former days they had fought the Chippewas clear up to the Lakes in the east, and now they were being crowded away from the Missouri River; that they owned the land, and they owned the buffalo, and the antelope, and the deer, and the wild ducks, and the geese; and how the white man was pushing them all the time, and killing their cattle, and their birds, and catching their fish, and making it harder all the time for them to get a living. It was the old, old story. During his speech the Indians all sat and looked mutely at the ground. All at once at a passage of the speech they brightened up, and grunted an applause. I said to the interpreter, "What is that sentence?" He said, "The Indian coined a new word." It appears that it is one of the characteristics of the Indian language to run words together; to take a vowel from one and a consonant from another, forming a combination of thought, and boiling it down into a word. And it was the part of an orator to make new words which his hearers could immediately comprehend the meaning of, and it was on this occasion that the Big Mandan had met the dramatic situation by the coining of a new word for the Sioux vocabulary.

General Mitchell made a speech, a brief reply, sitting in his chair, intending to assuage the sentiment that the Big Mandan had raised. Major O'Brien wanted to make a talk, but General Mitchell would not allow anybody to talk but himself, fearing the matter might break up into something which would resemble a town row. Then another of the Indians got up and went over the story again; how they were a hungry people; how the white brother had everything, and they had nothing; how the white brother had flour and bacon and sugar and everything else in vast quantities more than they wanted, while the Indian had a continual struggle with poverty, and had nothing to eat but dried pumpkin, and buffalo-berries, and jerked meat. General Mitchell replied to this speech by saying that the Government gave them blankets enough and clothing enough, to clothe them for all seasons of the year; that the Government gave them flour, bacon and supplies, which if prudently used would always enable them to have plenty to eat; that the Government desired them to live in houses, and had offered them carpenters and blacksmiths, and to teach them how to build houses; and how to become civilized and live like the whites, but they would not do it, and that their troubles arose from their perversity and want of thought.

Then another of the Indian orators got up, and began to talk about the white people sending whisky into their villages, and cheating them out of their beaver-skins, and the mink and otter and muskrats, and buffalo-robes, and how the Indians were getting fewer and poorer all the time from the "drunk-water" which the white man sent out. To this General Mitchell replied that there were bad white men as well as bad Indians; that the white man put chains on those who sold whisky to Indians, and kept them in confinement, when they could be caught; that such white men were bad white men; that the Indians ought to kill them on sight when they brought whisky into their village; that the difficulty with the Indians was they wanted the white man to bring the whisky in, and would not punish him; that they wanted the whisky, and therefore they were complaining of themselves, and not of the white men.

And so it went, speech after speech, General Mitchell always replying to every speech. He had thought it all up, and I must say he beat the Indians in their controversy. He told the Indians that they had no right to claim all of the land. He told them that the good Manitou, who put us all on earth, intended that each one should have his share of the earth, and the Indians had no right to take ten times as much land per head as they allowed the white people. And he pointed out that the white people had to live all penned up and in discomfort, so that the Indian could have ten times the amount of land that he ought to have, and kill the buffalo which belonged to everybody on the earth alike, but which the Indians claimed the entire ownership of. And that the Indian had kept the white man back, and the latter was so crowded that if the lands which the white man had were divided, each white man would have only a small piece, so small that an Indian could shoot an arrow across it, while the Indian had land he could not see over.

The manner of discussion was that the Indian would speak a sentence, and then the interpreter would interpret it. Then the Indian would speak another sentence, and that would be interpreted. When the General spoke, his speech was put into the Sioux language, and the man behind the General was there as overseer to see that "Snell" translated it correctly, and several times the overseer interfered to have the translation explained, the great object being to have the true idea which each one brought forth, presented to the other. The debate ran on, and the pipe was relit and passed around several times during the silences which ensued. Silences of five to ten minutes ensued after each of General Mitchell's speeches. Then the pipe would go around with the same formality. Spotted Tail, sitting quietly, said: "Why are we here? Why has the white brother asked us to come?" Then General Mitchell said: "The object of this meeting is to have an understanding, and make a treaty, so each will know what he ought to do. We want you Sioux to stay off from the Platte Valley. You can come down to the hills on the edge of the valley while you are hunting, but you must not come down into the valley, for it scares our women and children traveling, going up and down, and it scares the women and children that are living in the houses in the valley. If you wish to cross the road, and go north or south of the river, you must send in word during the daytime to one of the posts, and then you will be escorted across the valley from the hills on one side to the hills on the other, and then you can go where you will. But you mustn't come down in the valley or allow spies, beggars, or bad Indians to come down into the valley. You must restrain your bad men; we will hold you responsible; this is an ultimatum. This we insist upon your doing. If it takes more to feed you, if it takes more bacon or blankets and corn, we will give you more, but you must stay out of the Platte Valley."

This speech of General Mitchell's seemed to nettle them all. Shan-tag-a-lisk was their greatest warrior, but he was not much of a talker. Their principal orator was the Big Mandan, but Shan-tag-a-lisk got up with his blanket on, and his arms folded across his breast, and began talking in a low, hesitating tone. He said: "The Sioux nation is a great people, and we do not wish to be dictated to by the whites or anybody else. We do not care particularly about the Platte valley, because there is no game in it. Your young men and your freighters have driven all the game out, or killed it, so we find nothing in the Platte valley. But we want to come and trade in the Platte valley wherever we please. We want places where we can sell our beaver-skins and our buffalo-robes. The Platte valley is ours, and we do not intend to give it away. We have let the white man have it so that he could pass, but he has gone over it so often now that he claims it and thinks he owns it. But it is still ours, and always has been ours. It belonged to our forefathers, and their graves are along the hills overlooking the valley from the Missouri river to the mountains, and we do not expect to give it up. We are not afraid of the white man, nor are we afraid to fight him. We have not had in late years any very serious difficulties with the white men. Trouble has been brought about by 'drunk-water.' Bad whites have given it to bad Indians, and they have got both of us into trouble. The donations which the white men have been giving us are not sufficient; they are not adequate for the concessions which we have made. The goods that were brought us at Woc-co-pom'-any agency were neither as good as had been promised us, nor were they in amount as had been promised us. The Great Father through his army officers makes us great promises, but the agents, who are not army officers, cheat us, and do not carry out the treaty obligations. Last fall at the Woc-co-pom'-any agency, when the agent asked us to sign for our goods, we would not sign, because they were not what they should be in value or amount, and one of the army officers who was there told us not to sign, and he swore at the agent, and told him he was a thief, and was cheating us. The army officers treat us well enough, but those who are not officers cheat us when they can, and we do not want to deal with any but the army officers. Besides this, we will not give up the Platte valley to you until we have a regular treaty, and until we have all agreed to it, and have been paid for it. It will soon be that you will want other roads to the west. If we give you this you will want another, and if we give you that you will want a third. Before we will agree to anything you must stop the surveyors that are going west at this very time on the river Niobrara. All of these things must be considered before we will make a treaty."

Then General Mitchell asked if anyone present knew about the Niobrara, and some one of the party spoke and said that a surveying party was going west up the Niobrara with an escort. The Niobrara river was a river running west from the Missouri river parallel with the Platte, and about a hundred miles north of where we then were. Spotted Tail said that the Niobrara river went through their good country, and that they would resist the white man putting a road through, and that unless the work was stopped they were going to drive off or kill the expedition. And he also said that he wanted the road out on the Smoky Hill closed up, because it went through their best buffalo country. And he further said that they would not for the present carry out the wishes of General Mitchell until their demands were agreed to. The speech of Shan-tag-a-lisk wound up with a regular bluff, and it made General Mitchell a little angry; he got up, and told the Indians that he was not there to coax them, but was there to tell them what to do. That he would stop the survey up on the Niobrara river until there was another conference; that the Smoky Hill route was a route much used, and was necessary for the white man, and it would not be closed. And he wound up by saying that if the Sioux did not keep away from the Platte river he would station a soldier to every blade of grass from the Missouri River to the Rocky Mountains. This counter "bluff" on the part of General Mitchell brought Spotted Tail immediately to his feet. He got up and said that the Sioux nation was not afraid of the white people; that there were more Sioux Indians than there were white people; that the Sioux nation had twenty-six thousand Ar-ke'-che-tas (organized warriors), and could put more soldiers into the Platte valley than the white people could; that they knew all about the white people, and the white people were not smart enough to fool them; that the white people were all the while trying to fool the Indians and deceive them as to numbers so as to scare them. That the whites were parading before the Indians all the time so as to show off their numbers; that the same people that came up the Platte valley went back by the way of Smoky Hill. "We have seen them, and recognize them time and again. Some of them come back by way of Platte river, but that is only to fool us. The white men are marching around in a ring so that we may see them and be led to believe that there is a great number of them. They cannot fool us. We recognize the same people, and they are too few; we are not afraid of them—we outnumber them."

It had got well along into the afternoon; no headway had been made, but General Mitchell seemed to think that the ground had been broken for a future conference. It was finally decided that the conference should adjourn, and meet again at the same place in fifty days. Nothing whatever had been gained. Both parties had been bluffing, and neither side was afraid of the other. But General Mitchell promised to stop the Niobrara expedition, and to get permission from the Great Father at Washington to make a new treaty, that would cede the Platte valley; that every one present should think the matter over; and come back in fifty days; and that the Indians should bring other chiefs with them if they wished. Then General Mitchell with great formality took Spotted Tail by the hand and said, "How cola?" and had the interpreter tell him that they would all be fed before they left the post. Thereupon the Indians were all taken to the cookhouse, where everything had been kept in readiness, and they were given all they could eat, which was an enormous amount. The boiled beef and coffee and hard-bread (which the boys called "Lincoln shingles") were spread out with panfuls of molasses, and things went along all right. A lot of supplies had been sent to the Indian camps during the day. The Indians invited our officers to go over to their camp and have a dog feast. It was not considered advisable for more than three to go, together with some civilians who were there. Captain O'Brien was one of the officers, and he requested me to be on guard until he came back, and have the horses all saddled and the men ready to mount on a moment's notice. He wanted to go to the Indian camp, and did not know what might happen, but he never seemed to fear any danger. One of the Indians asked the visitors to bring some coffee; so one of them, on his horse, took a little bag of roasted coffee, perhaps ten pounds. Captain O'Brien's story is that they were entertained by the principal chiefs; that they had dog to eat, and that the dog wasn't so bad after all. That the Indians put coffee into a big camp-kettle, and commenced boiling and kept filling the camp-kettle and boiling coffee until he came away about ten o'clock at night. He said the Indians drank coffee hot by the gallon, and didn't seem to be able to get enough of it. He said they appeared to be all right, and friendly; he didn't believe there would be any Indian trouble.

The next morning there was not an Indian in sight, and current matters at our post went along in the same usual way. General Mitchell left as soon as the Indians did. I will speak more of him further on, but will say here that his honored grave may be seen on one of the sunlit slopes of the Arlington National Cemetery near Washington.

Shan-tag-a-lisk was over forty years old, but claimed to be about thirty. Pioneers said the Indians would not tell the truth about their ages, because they thought it might give the white men some occult advantage over them.

CHAPTER XII

DURING April, several detachments of the Eleventh Ohio
Cavalry passed us going northwest to Fort Laramie, and we
got acquainted with them. On the 19th of April we had quite
a number of visitors. John K. Wright, a Lieutenant of the
Sixteenth Kansas Cavalry, with a detachment was going to
Denver. Wright was afterwards State Senator in Kansas,
and a very prominent citizen. With him was R. B. Hitz, a
surgeon of the United States Army, who afterwards arose to
distinction. He was going to Laramie. There was also Lieut.
Jenkins of the Second Colorado Cavalry and Lieut. Rockwell
of the First Colorado. The latter officers were going west,
and the party had two hundred and forty unassigned recruits. With them was a strange character, Captain Alfred
de Watteville. He was a Captain of "guides" in Geneva,
Switzerland. He was in the Swiss army. He pronounced the
word "guides," gwiids. He had his servant, and special team.
He called himself Baron. He was a large, fine-looking, gentlemanly fellow, and spoke English well enough to make himself understood. We took him out antelope-hunting, both
the Captain and I. While he was there, five days, we caught
two antelopes after a chase from eight to twelve miles each.
He was very much delighted with his entertainment; told
about the European service; had visited our armies in the

field; and was on a general tour of education. We took a fancy to him, and parted from him with great regret. De Watteville, Wright and Hitz departed together, going towards Denver, which was then merely a frontier town.

On the 24th of April, 1864, a large detachment of the Eleventh Ohio Cavalry went by, going west; we went down and took supper with the officers. The commanding officer of the regiment was Lieut.-Col. Collins. He was a very fine old gentleman, rather old for military service, but finely preserved, energetic and soldierly. He had a son as a Lieutenant whose name was Casper. Casper was a wild, heedless young man, and was afterwards killed by the Indians. Fort Collins, in Colorado, was named after the Colonel, and the town of Casper, in Wyoming, was named after the son.

While all of these officers I have spoken of were at our post, Ranchman MacDonald had another dance. And some of the passengers in the stages, including several women, stopped to attend it. There had in the meantime several new girls come into the neighborhood, and the dance was quite well attended. One of the young ladies from Cincinnati, quite interested in the dance, confided to me privately that she liked to attend dances, and dance with the officers of the army. One of the fiddlers upon that occasion was the First Lieutenant of Company G, of our regiment, who was at the post. He was a strange man to be made an army officer. He was a red-headed, fiddling farmer. He afterwards got himself dismissed from the service. He got his place because he had done good recruiting through the farms of his vicinity, and got enough of the boys in to give him a First Lieutenancy. That was the kind of stuff our armies were officered with at first, and it must ever be so in the volunteer service, at the outstart. In the first place we must have recruits, and the fellow who gets up the recruits must be paid for it by making him an officer. The man who is the best recruiter is the worst officer. Then it takes the attrition of six months or a year, or perhaps more, to get this stamp of fellows out, and get in those who have some military inspiration. It was the same both in the North and in the South during the Civil War. Both armies had to weed out worthless officers, and get the right men into command, before discipline and efficiency became potent. The South started out better equipped than the North in the Civil War, but in the course of time the North caught up. To illustrate: The Third Louisiana had its first battle at Wilson Creek; its Colonel and Captains had served in the regular army in some capacity. The First Iowa Infantry, who held their ground against them, had only three officers who had ever been in the service.

Along in the latter part of April, one of our men claimed that he was ill, and went to the post surgeon, Dr. LaForce. The Doctor said he thought it was a case of smallpox. Upon consultation the following plan was suggested: That a tent be put up on the island nearest the post, and the man be taken there, and some soldier be detailed to take care of him who had had the smallpox. This duty fell upon a brave, nervy little Irishman by the name of Jimmie O'Brien, whom I will speak of again hereinafter. One glance at Jimmie told that he had had a very severe case of smallpox, for his whole face was pitted up so that it looked as rough as a rasp. Jimmie accepted the detail with genuine Irish good-nature, and, taking a supply of firearms and ammunition, went over onto the island and set up a tent, and took care of this comrade. Cooked rations were served by leaving them on the banks of the river, and Jimmie waded across and got them and took care of his comrade until he was finally well. Then we took Jimmie some matches and a lot of hay, and left some new clothes for both on the banks of the river. Jimmie burned up the tent and the old clothes and everything. Both parties took a good wash in the river, came out and dressed themselves in their new clothes, and the contagion never spread, nor did we ever have another case of it.

While stationed at Cottonwood Springs, the post commander had some assumed political duties, and among others he had to act as Justice of the Peace. I was post adjutant all the time, and these matters were very largely submitted to me. I prepared the cases, obtained the facts, and brought the parties before the post commander, who would hear my statement, listen to anything that either side wished to submit, and then render judgment. These matters consisted of complaints by "whackers" against the wagon-bosses, assaults, thefts, borrowed-money matters, and a great variety of other trivial things. The post commander did not only decide the cases, but he carried his decisions into effect. For instance, if a wagon-master wrongfully quarreled with a whacker in such a way as to justify the latter in leaving, and then refused to pay him, the post commander ordered the payment to be made in his presence, and if there was any hesitation or demurrer to it, the defendant was immediately stuck into the guard-house. We had such a summary way of enforcing justice that there was no appeal, and what was decided went as accepted, and that was the end of it. If some man unjustly quarreled with the wagon-boss we put the man into the guard-house until the train had got ten days on its journey, and then let him go to take care of himself. If a man with a team committed an assault, and was unable to pay, we just took enough of his stuff to pay the plaintiff. It might be a sack of corn, or a saddle, or something. Everybody was made to behave; and, it being well understood that we were there for that purpose, it served as a useful check upon the lawlessness of the plains.

Major O'Brien, the post commander, was a good lawyer, and had practiced law, and he knew how to get at things quickly, and knew how far he ought to go. The decisions of Major O'Brien were sought by the people up and down the road for a hundred miles, and he was not a bit backward in assuming jurisdiction in any kind of a case, and carrying his decrees into force. Several men who were charged with having committed crimes were put under ball and chain and delivered down at Fort Kearney, which had become the headquarters of our district. The commanding General of our military district, Gen. R. B. Mitchell, of whom I have spoken, was a good lawyer himself, and his adjutant was John Pratt, of Boston, a most accomplished gentleman, also a lawyer. The General made headquarters at Fort Kearney instead of Omaha (as his predecessor had done), and he was very anxious that justice should be dispensed through his district, and that civilized methods should prevail. Although there were no civil officers, General Mitchell worked out the whole scheme through military instrumentalities in very good shape. From time to time he instructed his subordinate post commanders how to carry on their civil functions, and protect life and property. He was a great stickler for protecting property, and if some pilgrim stole a saddle or a lariat, it was his theory that the man should be arrested, and punished, even if a soldier had to chase the man for two weeks and it cost the Government $1,000. Hence it was, that our duties were civil as well as military, and we were obliged to briefly report all civil infractions, decisions and punishment. Once or twice we put people into the guard-house and they appealed to the General; he sent for them to be forwarded under escort with the next train to Fort Kearney, where he re-heard the case. One of the peculiarities of the civil jurisdiction was that people applied to the post to enforce the payment of bets which they had made. Parties would make bets, and then when they lost, sometimes would not pay. It was a betting age, and a betting country. We did not go according to the statute law in this matter. We recognized that the payment of bets was an obligation which persons should honor; that betting was recognized by the community as legitimate, and the non-payment of bets tended to disturb social conditions and make enemies, and bring about aggressions. But the debt must either be proven in writing or admitted by the defendant. We enforced gambling debts when reduced to writing and signed. More than once men had the alternative given them of paying a gambling debt or a bet fairly proven, or else of going to the guard-house. If they didn't have the money, they went to the guard-house anyway. There had to be some punishment.

Along early in April one of our best men, having been recently appointed sergeant, played a very nice scheme upon our post. He said that our post needed a laundry; that we ought to have a building in which the soldiers could do their washing, with a well and appurtenances; and that we ought to make some nice tight, cedar boxes for washtubs, etc., etc. This struck us as a good thing, so we went to work and built a laundry building twenty feet square, but without a well, because it was not far from the stockade where our horses were, and where there was a good well. Now it happened that sometime in February a woman left a train that was going west, came to MacDonald's ranch and asked if they wanted to employ a cook, or woman to assist in the work of the house. It was exactly what MacDonald wanted; his wife had been trying to get somebody for quite a while. The applicant was a woman, tall, slim, razor-faced, about six feet three inches high, and she looked like a human being that wasn't afraid of wild man or wild beast. She started in with MacDonald and did a power of work—washing, cleaning up the store, and everything else; she was a perfect giantess to work. She said that she was raised on a farm in Missouri, was unmarried, and was thinking of going through to Denver where some relatives were, but had concluded she had gone about as far west as she wanted to go. MacDonald was very much pleased with her work and services. As Captain O'Brien used to say, "She was as ugly as a mud fence." She obtained the nickname of "Lengthy." After a couple of months this nickname was reduced to "Linty." One day this Sergeant of whom I spoke above, came to us and suggested that we employ "Linty" as a laundress and give her the laundry-house, and arrange it so that whenever she did any washing for the soldiers it should be reported and taken from the soldier's pay at the pay-table. That was in accordance with the army regulations, providing the company should approve of it. We called up the company and stated the proposition. The Sergeant in the mean time worked the company all right, and the company without objection all agreed that their washing might be taken out of their pay if done by "Linty," but that they had the right to do their own washing nevertheless, if they wanted to. MacDonald objected a great deal towards letting the woman go, but she went, and took up quarters in the new laundry, and curtained off a part of it where she kept her trunk and bedstead. She went to work washing for the boys. She understood it well. She was very strong and industrious, and was doing very nicely, when one day, on May 6, 1864, this Sergeant and "Linty" appeared before the post commander and demanded to be united in marriage. The Captain had never married anybody before, but he had the right as post commander to perform the rite. So the Captain sent for me as the company commander to be present. The Captain fixed up a good deal of ceremony and it was pretty near a mock marriage, except that it was strictly legal. The Captain asked, "Who giveth this woman away?" and I said, "I do," and we went through the ceremony in great shape. Thereupon, arm-in-arm the Sergeant walked down with his bride to the new laundry-house, and started to take up his abode there. Some of the boys, finding it out, determined to have some fun. Late in the evening they got mess-pans and about a hundred of them surrounded the laundry and commenced giving an old-fashioned "shiviree." They ought all to have been arrested, because it was about nine o'clock at night, but the Captain and I concluded we would let the boys have some fun. All at once the noise stopped, and the next morning I heard that the Sergeant had gone to his wife's dress, got her pocket-book, took all the money she had, $5, gone out in stocking-feet and had given the money to the boys and told them to go off and get drunk, and leave them, as, he said, that was all they both had. Thereupon the Sergeant took up his headquarters at the laundry and stayed there. Under the army regulations he drew rations for himself and his wife separately, and we saw that from first to last the Sergeant together with the woman had studied up the whole plan. *They had worked us.* We held this against the Sergeant until things had calmed down, and then we reduced him to the ranks; afterwards, having been a blacksmith, we put him over with Woodruff, the other blacksmith, shoeing horses and repairing wagons. They were not discharged from the service until they were mustered out, in May, 1866, and the couple stayed together as well as any married couple I ever saw, for in all future marches and expeditions of the company this woman went along, and followed the troubles and dared the dangers of the service, so that we finally got to thinking more of "Linty" than we did of her husband.

Owing to troubles reported from the south, Company "G," which was at our post, started May 2nd for Fort Kearney, from which post they went directly to Fort Riley, Kansas. Fort Riley was at the junction of the Republican river, upon which the Indians were very numerous, and, owing to emissaries from the Southern Confederacy, that country was becoming very dangerous ground. From time to time we heard that emissaries from the Confederacy were making inflammatory speeches, and doing their best to alienate the southern Cheyennes, and the Ogallallah Sioux. But this influence did not extend strongly across the Platte to the northern Sioux or Cheyennes, because such emissaries would be shot if they fell into our hands. Nevertheless, there were rumors that efforts were being made in the Indian villages north and northwest of us. From a Sergeant, Ellsworth, who afterwards was an officer in Company "G," the fort and town of "Ellsworth," in Kansas, was named. Shortly after the departure of Company "G" from our post, Company "C," Seventh Iowa Cavalry, arrived and occupied their barracks. Schenck, who was First Lieutenant of the company, had been detailed at Fort Kearney. The company was poorly officered and the captain was shortly afterwards court-martialed.

On May 7th a Mr. Trivit, of Denver, entered complaint against Ingram & Christie, who had a train passing our post. Trivit alleged fraud of considerable amount. Captain O'Brien, the commander of the post, was down at Gilmans' ranch trying to make some arrangements for the cutting of a lot of hay during the summer. I swore Trivit to the truth of his statement, which I had my First Sergeant reduce to writing. Thereupon I arrested the other two persons, but sent them under arrest with their train to be halted down at Gilmans' for trial by Captain O'Brien. He tried the matter out, made his finding, and it was complied with, and the matter ended.

During May two professional gamblers, one from Ottumwa and one from Denver, confederated together, got into our quarters, and got into games of poker with our men. They were quite liberal in buying sutler's stuff, and distributing it among the men in the quarters, but they were also very cunning in regard to it. They slept around wherever they could find a place and played poker whenever they could find a victim. Finally I heard of it, got them into my quarters, had a squad of soldiers come and peel off their clothes. They each had several decks of marked cards, and a lot of money. This I took from them, and then put them both into the guard-house until I could ascertain how much they had won from the men. After arriving at what I thought was a fair conclusion, I gave the balance back, although it was a good deal more than I thought they ought to have, and I started them out of camp in opposite directions, two miles each way. I never saw or heard of them again. After they had gone several of the boys put in application to have their money refunded to them. To those applying, I returned no money at the time, but gave them first a few days each of extra work around the stables. Afterwards the money was returned to the losers; some of the boys had wives and families at home, who would be very much benefitted by it.

We had received requests from headquarters to prepare maps of the country as far as we knew. So we got up maps of the country, making them accurate as far as we were acquainted with the lay of the land, by observation or by advice of pioneers and others, as best we could. Along where we were, from Gilmans' to Jack Morrow's there were five cedar canyons, and we had explored them all pretty well, and we could make our maps so as to comprise a radius of twenty miles south of the river. I afterwards saw where, in the Chief Engineer's office at Leavenworth, our maps had been worked into a large Nebraska map, of which a copy had been forwarded to the War Department. It is from such sources as this that maps of a country are first made.

Some person going East from Denver had stopped at our post, which had been put up hastily, and which occupied a place that seven months before had been vacant. This person going East had published in an Eastern magazine a full account of the rapidity with which the work had been done, the value of the post, and its fine situation; in the article appeared my name among others. In one batch of mail I received letters from five different girls who wrote saying they had seen the article, and suggesting correspondence. One was from Monroe, Wisconsin, one was from McGregor, Iowa, one from Ottumwa, Iowa, one from Broadhead, Wisconsin, and another from Waterford, Pennsylvania. Captain O'Brien got a number, but we answered none of them.

On the 15th of May there came into camp a tough-looking woman who said that she had been assaulted by eighteen Cheyennes. She said that on the road east of Morrow's ranch, "Eighteen Cheyenne chieftains ravished my person." The woman was about forty years of age, and a very bad-looking character; but fearing that she might be telling the truth, and as she was talking about it to everybody that would listen to her, Captain O'Brien ordered me to take ten men, and immediately proceed to the place, and try to ascertain what were the facts. Going up to Jack Morrow's, I passed several persons who had been on the road and had seen nothing, and heard nothing. When I got up to Morrow's ranch and related the story the woman told, and asked them if they had seen any Cheyennes they all broke out into immoderate laughter, and one of them said: "You better go back to the post; that woman is 'Salt Lake Kate.' She is the toughest female on the road. Better have her leave the post; send her East as soon as possible." Afterwards one of the party said there had been some Indians seen out on the bluffs that day; that they did not seem to be stealing cattle, but to be very shy and acting as spies. I turned back, and while on march to our post, with my field-glass I kept my eye upon the Sioux Lookout, hoping if by chance I might see by accurate and intense observation whether some Indian would put his head up far enough for me to see him. After a little while I beheld a little piece of an Indian's head spying over the ridge. My first impulse was to try to capture him, but as he had a mile or so the advantage of me, and could divine my movement in a minute, I did not attempt it. On my return we started "Salt Lake Kate" down the road with a passing train, and never saw or heard of her afterwards. But events followed rapidly which made us suspicious that she had really been telling the truth, because on the next day or the day after, John Gilman came up to the post, and said that he had seen twenty Cheyennes over on the bluff near them, and that he demanded protection from the United States, and would hold the United States responsible if he lost anything through want of protection, and he served this notice upon us in writing. We didn't like this movement on the part of Gilman, and gave him some harsh language, and told him that if he wanted to be protected to come on up to the post. However, he went back, and put his ranch into a fortified condition so as to stand a siege.

At Gilmans' there was staying a peculiar man who came up with them, and stopped at our post. He was a wandering tailor. He had a wagon with cloth and buttons and stuff in it, and went up and down the road making good clothes for people who wanted them. As there were no tailors in the country, and as there were large numbers of people who had worn tailor-made clothes, he seemed to have done a pretty good business. He couldn't always give the people the kind of goods they wanted, but he could really make a nice tailor-made suit, and he was really a professional tailor. The ranchmen of the best order provided themselves with stuff to be made up, and this man Farley, who was a jolly fellow, and a rapid workman, had quite a patronage. He happened to have some blue cloth suitable for uniforms, and he made me one of the best suits I ever had. It cost me about three prices, but it would be difficult to have excelled it in fit, and workmanship, and I was always glad to remember the man, and afterwards to recommend his work farther up the road.

CHAPTER XIII

ON MAY 17, 1864, traveling with an escort, there came to our
Post the Chief Inspector of the Department, to give us and
the Post an inspection, from which we afterwards heard as
follows from the Chief of Cavalry, from whose report I make
the following quotation:

"HEADQUARTERS DEPARTMENT OF KANSAS.
OFFICE CHIEF OF CAVALRY,
FORT LEAVENWORTH, *July 7, 1864.*

Captain N. J. O'Brien,
Co. 'F,' Seventh Iowa Cavalry,
Fort Cottonwood, Nebr. Ter.

"CAPTAIN: The cavalry inspection report of Chief of Cavalry,
District of Nebraska, shows . . . your company is reported as
having no ammunition on hand, and this is the second month that
it is so reported. *In all other respects the report is perfect,* and
the District Chief of Cavalry in his remarks adds:

'COTTONWOOD SPRINGS, *May 19, 1864.*

'Inspected Companies G and F, 7th Iowa Cavalry, this day.
COMPANY F, before reported, is in good condition, well drilled,
and well disciplined, horses in good order; twelve men are reported sick; some of them are confined to quarters by reason of
very sore eyes. I report the companies without ammunition because the Post Commander takes charge of the ammunition, and
only issues to the companies as needed for immediate use.'

"Respectfully forwarded through headquarters, District of
Nebraska.

Very respectfully,
B. S. HENNING, Major,
Chief of Cavalry."

This report of the eyes is a fact of which I have spoken before. The incessant wind which blew upon the plains, and kept the sand and alkali in circulation, affected the eyes of the men, and there were constantly some of the men who were unable to do much until their eyes were well; and this was so general a matter that all of the ranches kept large spectacles or goggles to sell to the "pilgrims," and we had a lot in our company to be used by the men when they felt that they were beginning to suffer.

I have spoken briefly of the arrival of Company C, May 19, 1864, which came to take the place of Company G. A circumstance happened on the arrival of Company C which it always made me sorry to recollect, and it was in this wise: My big iron-gray horse didn't get exercise enough, and was always hungering and thirsting for a run. We knew of the coming of Company C, and I saw them when they got within two miles of the Post. For my horse I had had the blacksmith make an iron band as a curb to go under his jaw. I imagined I could stop him any time with such a curb bit, or else break his jaw. I whistled up the two dogs, Fannie and Kearney, and started down to meet Company C. After I had got about a half-mile below the Post, a jack-rabbit jumped up, and the two dogs started yelping after it towards the bluffs. In my effort to turn the horse away from the dogs and rabbit, and get him towards the company, I pulled heavily upon the reins, so much so that the curb broke, and it left me with nothing but a straight pull on the bridle-bit. The horse, full of vim and vigor, kept on after the dogs. While chasing one rabbit, another would jump up in front of him, and the dogs would go off after the second rabbit. In about ten minutes I had passed Company C, and was going down the valley, my horse following the dogs as if he were a greyhound himself, and enjoying the sport as much as they. I endeavored to turn him around, back onto the road. He kept going like the wind, and I pulled and tugged on him until I was as weak as a kitten. I always thought I could ride a horse (having been in the cavalry service for over two years) wherever I wanted to go, but this horse and the dogs just seemed to play over the prairie and there was no stopping it. By throwing all my weight upon one side of the bridle, and pulling and sawing, I happened to get him turned a little, and away from the dogs. But soon they passed me on a fresh trail, and I found myself floundering among the banks of the river. The horse and dogs plunged and ran, and I stayed on the back of the horse, absolutely powerless to check him. The horse ran around with me as hard as he could go for nearly two hours, and when the rabbits got away the dogs would run alongside the horse, and jump and bark at his bridle-bit. Finally the horse and dogs got started back towards the Post, and I went with them. I was just riding, just staying on the back of the horse. I had pulled and pulled until I was so tired I couldn't pull a pound weight. I had a sort of gone feeling, was covered with perspiration, and had lost my hat. Company C had come to the Post and gone to their quarters, when finally the horse made up his mind to go to the Post, and with every effort which muscle and speed could show, the horse came up the road to the Post. Seeing that I must be in the presence of my soldiers, I made an effort and took hold of the reins and appeared to pull. Just as the horse was going through the parade-ground one of the soldiers ran and jumped in front of him. The horse stopped stiff-legged, and I went on over his head, over his ears, and onto the top of my head and back of my neck, and I just remember the appearance of the soldier and the beginning of my flight. Several hours after, I woke up in the hospital, and the doctor was rubbing me with alcohol and a soldier was letting well-water fall from a canteen held high above my head, and dropping upon my forehead. There were several hours of a thought vacuum in my memory. The doctor still kept at work after I came to, and a lot of the soldiers stood around to see whether I was going to make it or not, because the doctor could not tell the extent of my injuries. As a matter of fact, I was not injured much. I was just entirely used up, and I struck on my head just hard enough for it to thoroughly stun. I wanted to show that I was not injured, and the doctor said he couldn't find any fractures or apparent injury; so in the morning I got them to help me up and dress, and at roll-call, which we had at half-past five, I got out, with very great effort, and stood in front of the company, and attended the performances and disbanded the company, and sent them back to the barracks, and then went back to the hospital and collapsed for a couple of days. Then I got up, and was as well as ever.

The question then arose with me, what I should do with my iron-gray horse. If I had been in a fight with the Indians, I should have certainly lost my life. I had the blacksmith put in another bar on the bridle-bit, but I made up my mind that I would not keep the horse. An Iowa Colonel had been shot off from him at the celebrated battle of Pittsburg Landing, and I thought I would not take any chances. I will anticipate my story somewhat by saying that I put up a sign at Mac-Donald's ranch, reading "Horse for Sale." A little while after that I was up the river from the Post, drilling the company and riding this horse, when a wagon train went by. A man came up to me and asked me if I was the man who had the horse for sale. I told him "Yes," and that the price was $150. He felt the horse all over, looked in his mouth, held up his feet, and finally said, "I'll take him." He said, "I promised to get my wife a horse," and I said, "You don't want this horse. This is no horse for a woman to ride." In the mean time the woman had come up, and she said that she could ride as fast as any horse could run, and they thought I was trying to back out from the sale. Thereupon I had them wait until I finished my drilling, then I took my company back to the Post, and the man walked back, paid me the money, and took the horse. I told Sergeant Howe to go back with the man and see the woman and to tell her that the horse was very swift, might run away, and that she would have to be careful. Howe delivered the message, and the woman scoffed at it, and said that a horse couldn't run any too fast to suit her. She got on board of the horse and the train started on. Howe stated that in about five minutes the woman was scudding across the prairie and away from the road on the horse, lightning speed. He said he watched her until she went clear to the bluffs, and disappeared. Then he came down to the Post as fast as possible, and said that we might have to send somebody up there to help them. But to all that I was quite indifferent, and thought that I would not act until I was requested. I am glad to say that I never heard of the matter after. I was now left with only one horse.

According to army regulations, a cavalry officer should have two horses—one for himself, and one for his orderly; the army regulations allowed issue of rations both to the orderly and the two horses. I had one good horse, and although I had no particular use for another at that time, I immediately began looking around for one. I finally succeeded, as will hereinafterwards appear.

The inspection which we had got from Major Armstrong was a very full and thorough one. Our drill captured the Major entirely, and the condition of our horses pleased him very much; he told Captain O'Brien that our company was the best drilled and disciplined company along the Platte river or in the entire command. The Captain told the Major that he was very pleased to hear it, and for the Major to give me half of the credit for it, which was very courteous on the part of Captain O'Brien. The Captain was not only one of the best officers in the United States service, but he was very fair-minded, and didn't try to steal all the glory there was afloat. He never shirked any duty himself, and he never hesitated to give credit where credit was due to any of his subordinates. For that reason my recollection of my service with him remained most delightful; and was entirely different, I think, from that of any other junior officer in the regiment. There was no other company in which there was not bickering and quarreling and disputes between the officers. In fact, it is almost incredible that there were so many quarrels as there were, although I know from experience in my former regiments that the same conditions elsewhere prevailed. Superior officers were always trying to unhorse some subordinate, and get him out of the service so as to get some friend or relative in his place, and subordinates were keeping black marks upon their superiors so as to get them court-martialed and dismissed from the service. There was never any of that feeling in our company. The officers of our company all stood together, and the men appreciated it, and did their part towards making the company an exceptionally good one.

In our company was a little young Irishman by the name of Murphy. Murphy was ambitious, and talkative. He enlisted at the age of nineteen. He had a fine, rich brogue, and it was a pleasure to listen to him. He was fond of drink, and began to get bad after we got to Cottonwood Springs, but he still did a lot of work. He was very handy with the ax, and could do about two men's work in chopping. Murphy wanted to be promoted. He was anxious for distinction, and when he couldn't be corporal, he thought the next thing was to get drunk. He was a fascinating little fellow, and where he got his whisky was always a great puzzle to us. Finally we got to putting Murphy in the guard-house, and by the first of November, 1863, he had developed a great thirst for liquor. In addition to that, he was a great politician, and was always shouting for Gen. George B. McClellan, who he said was the greatest Irishman in America. A large portion of our soldiers didn't like McClellan, and he had long since been relieved from the command of the Army of the Potomac; had been relegated to the rear, and was being talked of by the Democratic party as President of the United States. Murphy was everlastingly shouting for McClellan, whether drunk or sober,—generally the former, in the guard-house. The result was that the guard-house was a sort of Democratic headquarters for Murphy and McClellan. Along in the latter part of May, 1864, Murphy had been much drunk and had made a lot of trouble. I determined to set out a row of trees, principally box-elders, around the parade-ground, and I took Murphy out of the guard-house, gave him a spade, and detailed a corporal to keep him going. I got a corporal that did not believe in political democracy, and he kept Murphy digging day after day in good shape. But in spite of everything we could do, although Murphy was taken back to the guardhouse, and was carefully watched, and kept digging day after day, he kept half drunk all of the time. How that man managed to get whisky was one of the greatest of puzzles. It seemed that he could absorb it from the air, or suck it up from the sandy and arid plain. Murphy, from being one of the most active and capable young men, became just the opposite. He went to pieces, and finally died in the hospital a total wreck, about eight months after the last date named.

And so it was in the army. The army was a most wonderful school. Many of the men improved from the moment they got into the company; they kept improving, educating one another, and building up right along in physique and in mind. Others who were good men seemed to go wrong, and from bad to worse, until they were of no account whatever. I never could understand it. The army is a great school and builds men up, and gives them benefits which they could nowhere else obtain; but to obtain these benefits they have to take unknown chances, and assume the risk of becoming utterly worthless.

About the middle of May, 1864, there came into our camp a strange person. I made no memorandum of it at the time. He was a fellow with hardly any clothes, and was sunburned, tanned, covered with mud and scratches, and made a bad appearance at the Post. Several soldiers gathered around him, and he said his name was John Smith. As everybody who was a fugitive from justice called himself "John Smith," we paid but little attention to him. He did not tell his story, but he looked like a man who had been a tramp, and had slept in all kinds of gutters, had been kicked around, and had just awakened from a prolonged spree. My suggestion to him was that he should get out of camp, and move on. He disappeared, but soon thereafter returned and cut much of a figure; further on he will be heard of.

There also came into camp a man who said his true name was Gray, and that he had made hunting an occupation; they called him "the hunter," which had been abbreviated finally to the name, "Hunter." In a short time he appeared in company with John Smith, who had got washed up, dressed up, and shaved; he was now quite a presentable-looking fellow. We told him and Hunter that if they would

bring in buffalo, deer-meat or wild turkeys, we would pay
for it by the pound, just the same as for beef. They went off
hunting, I don't know where, and came in with several
horseback-loads of meat, amounting to about $30.

About the time of the full moon in May, 1864, (20th,) it
was suggested that we ought to go over to the other side of
the island and find the best ford across the North arm of the
river. Sam Fitchie, one of the trappers around the Post, and
"Hunter" proffered to guide us, but thought we had better
not go until evening, because, as the trapper said, "We will
probably go up towards the head of the island, and there's a
lot of beaver and otter up there, and if you never saw them
playing it would be a sight which you would enjoy." We
started late in the afternoon, about sundown, and found the
river running pretty high. Going up towards the head of the
island, there was an old arm of the river which had been obstructed, and we found a great number of places where the
beaver had cut down cottonwood trees and made a marsh.

As the hour grew later and the moon was up brightly, the
guide took us into a clump of short cottonwoods and willow
brush, further up toward the head of the island, where a little
thread of the river was running rapidly between banks that
were about ten feet high. He cautioned us to be quiet and
to get off our horses, tie them, and walk a short distance
until we would come to where he said we would find the
wild animals playing; and sure enough, there they were. On
the bank, down into the river, had been cut sliding-places,
and the beaver and otter were crawling up out of the water
onto the bank in one place, and, all wet with the water, were
sliding down a gap in the bank in another place. The otter
were sort of snarling all the time, and the beaver were sput-
tering away at each other. There were three of the slides
running down to the water, and when these animals were
coming up out of the water and sliding down as fast as they
could make it, they were like a lot of little boys sliding down
a hill. They came up at one place through an accessible gap
in the bank, and then slid down through the other. The otter
would slide down and go under the water and not come up

again for twenty or fifty feet; then they would head again for the bank and take another slide. The beavers, as they slid down the bank, kept patting it with their broad, trowel-like tails and as they came down into the water they would sniff, but not go under. Other little animals were soon around, but they were not on the slide. The guide said that they were mink and muskrat. One time a little flock of them all went down in a company in the stream, sporting and playing about. It was a most interesting sight, and we watched it for an hour. We had no desire to interfere with their play, nor did we dare to fire a gun, not knowing but what Indians might be secreted in the neighborhood. The moon shone very brightly, and lit up the stream so that everything could be plainly seen. The sliding was all done on the north bank of the stream across from us. We kept back in the shade of the willow brush, and were not seen. However, all at once, through some cause or other, every animal quickly disappeared, and not a thing of life was visible, although we waited for nearly half an hour. They had evidently gotten acquainted with our presence and had communicated it to one another. "Hunter" declared that he could see the outline of a big bull elk in the willow brush across the stream opposite us, and tried to point it out to me, but I could not see it. "Hunter" had many of the Indian superstitions; among others was one that wild animals understood the language and signs of all of the other wild animals, and that if one wild animal or bird gave a note of fear, surprise or warning, all of the others understood it, took notice and acted upon it. "Hunter" said the bull elk gave us away; at any rate, every living thing suddenly disappeared.

The only result of our ride was that we found that just at that time the north bank of the river at that point was difficult to cross. It seemed that the coming warm spring had melted the snow on the mountains on the North Platte, and the river was running high and full and cold, on the north side of the island.

CHAPTER XIV

ON MAY 21st two old hunters and stage-drivers, one, a half-breed, called "Joe Jewett," and the other, "Sharp," came and told us that the combined Cheyennes and Brulés, down on Turkey Creek, about forty miles southwest of Fort Kearney and about seventy miles southeast of us, were having a fight; that they had surrounded a body of Colorado soldiers, and an Indian runner had said that ten of the soldiers had already been killed; that they were the soldiers who worked the artillery belonging to the detachment; that the artillery was consequently worthless, and that the Indians had surrounded the soldiers to prevent reinforcement, and were trying to starve them out. This information we forwarded to Fort Kearney by wire, but we never got any reply, nor received any orders in regard to our own action; it is probable that the rumor was an exaggerated one, although we prepared affidavits for Joe Jewett and Sharp to sign concerning the whole business, and they swore to the affidavits on information and belief, and we forwarded them. All of the women on the road were immediately sent down to Fort Kearney, which was a safe place, and perhaps none remained upon the road along its line from Kearney to near Denver except Mrs. MacDonald at our Post, and our laundress, "Linty," hereinbefore referred to.

The Indian runner was the Indian telegraph of that day. The Indian was given a message. He conned it over and learned it. He delivered it word for word; that was his business and his only aim. If he told a lie it was not his lie. It was the lie of the man who sent him. He remembered the message, word for word.

Our understanding was that the Cheyennes and Comanches had been thoroughly aroused by Confederate officers, and there were reports that some bands of Indians, not desiring to join the uprising, had killed some of the Confederate ambassadors. I afterwards remember seeing a report that the Osages had killed eight Confederate officers under like circumstances, in one bunch. At any rate, the Confederate officers had arrayed the Indians against us as far as Kansas and southern Nebraska were concerned, but the Brulés were principally north of the Platte River. It was about this time that through Mr. Gilman we were informed that an Indian runner had said a Cheyenne chief had been up through the bands of the Brulé Sioux north of the river, showing a sergeant's cavalry jacket, his watch and paraphernalia as trophies, and was instituting war dances. We were told that this would, of course, eventually precipitate the Brulé Sioux upon us. We kept careful guard around our Post, to prevent an ambush or surprise. We could be surprised only from one quarter, and that was towards the south. One man could keep view of the country east, west and north of us, but there was nothing to prevent the Indians from hiding in the ramifications of Cottonwood Canyon, and making a dash at the Post.

So we had Cottonwood Canyon and its prongs inspected every day, and at night after dark we ran a picket-post well up into the Canyon, and had the pickets signaled every thirty minutes. The way was this: After dark we went up quietly with a strong body, say twenty men, on foot, and nestled into some protected corner, and then put out pickets. We had no loud hailing or calling of pickets, but the one who visited the picket was to go stealthily or crawl on the ground. The hailing-sign was by raps with a pebble upon the saber scabbard. If he could not find the picket when he thought he had gone near enough, the inspector gave three raps, to which the picket should respond with two, then a reply of one, and counter reply of one.

I was out on one of these picket stations one night, along in the latter part of May, and the men were located at a certain washout. I settled myself about twenty yards farther up, in a little swale. Everything had been still for a while, but I had kept wide awake. Around upon one side of me I heard a stealthy noise as of some one crawling, and I made up my mind it was an Indian. I, with great caution and quiet, turned over and brought my revolver to bear upon the indistinct object. In a very short time John Ryan of my company, of whom I have spoken, rose upon his hands and feet and found me with a revolver presented at his face. He had threatened to kill me as before stated, and he was in all probability now bent upon that object. By having been awake, and anticipating danger, he found when he came up in the dark that I had the drop on him. He never raised his revolver, but remained motionless, knowing that his life was in my hands. I asked him what he was doing, and he said he was trying to find the picket-post. He had come out that night with the detail, and knew where it was; I pointed out the way to go, kept him covered with my revolver, and he went back. The next day I brought him up standing; told him that there was murder in him, and that I must see that he was properly taken care of. I took him, and put him in the guard-house myself, and preferred charges against him. The final outcome was that he and two of his pals, Jackson and McFarland, whom I had put in the guard-house for stealing coffee from the mess, managed to saw out, get horses and two revolvers each, escape, and all get away. They dashed straight down south into the Indian country, knowing that they could not travel the roads east or west. Whether they ever lived through it or not, I do not know. I have never heard of them since. They were three of about the worst men that I ever saw. Jackson and McFarland without doubt were deserters from the Confederate army. The three were incorrigible thieves, and suffered a good part from the treatment which they deserved and got. They were under guard and doing fatigue duty, and sleeping in the guard-house, a good deal of the time.

In order to carry out the sequence of individual narrative, I have gone ahead of my story. Coming back now to May 23rd: We noticed a wagon going up the river on the other side; who the people were we did not know, but the Indians made a dash upon them right opposite the Post in broad daylight, killed two men, set fire to the wagon, and ran off with the horses. We could not get to them. We went down, and crossed the south branch of the river, which was pretty high, and which was very dangerous, but having all succeeded in getting across and reaching the stream of the North Platte on the north side of the island, we found a torrent coming down from the melted snows, and a stream fully eight feet deep. It was impossible to cross it, and the Indians knew it, and they bade us defiance, and shook their fresh scalps at us. Indians were reported all along the line of the road; they were on the bluffs on our side, scrutinizing the road; at night we saw fire-arrows go up on both sides of us, and on the opposite sides of the river. During the day from time to time we saw the puff-signals of smoke. The Indians had an agreed set of signals which we did not understand, but which were plain to them, and by which they signalized everything of importance along the line. One was a smoke-puff, which was made by gathering a light pile of dead grass, not much of it, so that it would burn quickly, almost instantly. Sometimes they were made with gunpowder in the grass. The number and manner of these puffs conveyed the signal. The puff would seem to last only about four seconds. With my field-glass I could get up on the hill near the Post, and see smoke signals by day and fire-arrows by night from time to time, although there were but few on the south side, and these off at a distance.

On the 25th of May, 1864, Captain O'Brien went down

the road with twenty-five men to ascertain some facts and he came back with a great quantity of Indian rumors, which were current along the road. May 26th General Mitchell arrived, coming back with Captain O'Brien and a small escort, and with the General was one of his aides-de-camp, a Lieutenant Williams, of whom I have heretofore spoken as being a brave young officer from Kentucky. My former acquaintance with General Mitchell made his visit a very pleasant one to me. We furnished him an escort, and he went up the road some little distance, and came back, and started John Smith and "Hunter" on an Indian scout. Smith and "Hunter" claimed to have a hold upon the Cheyennes, and to be well acquainted in the villages, and said that they were not afraid to go down into the Cheyenne country and see what was going on. To anticipate my story, I may say that they were gone about a week, and came back, having been chased by the Cheyennes. They were unable to find out anything about matters, and all they could report was that the southern Cheyennes, that is, the Cheyennes south of the Platte river, extending down across Kansas, were all hostile, on the war-path, and knew no friends. Reports frequently came that they were ravaging the Kansas frontier, which was then in eastern Kansas; that they had sealed up the Smoky Hill road from central Kansas west to Denver; were fighting pilgrims along the Arkansas river, and were harassing the Colorado settlements east of Denver and Colorado City down on the Fountain river.

In the meantime a large number of Brulé Indians came in, all declaring their friendship; they camped down on the south side of the river, a couple of miles above our camp. There was a large band of them. They were principally Brulé Sioux, and were under the command of "Shan-tag-a-lisk," called by his translated name, "Spotted Tail." There was also the chief of the Ogallallah Sioux, who was one of the most peaceful of them all, "O-way-see'-cha," going by his translated name of "Bad Wound." There was a new one, representing some northern band, said to be the Minne-kaw'-zhouz. This chief was called Zheul-lee. He went by his translated name as "The Whistler." We had another Indian council, which was practically a duplicate of the one hereinbefore described. About the same persons were present, except the Big Mandan; he was reported to have gone up the Missouri river. In making further inquiry as to why the Big Mandan was ever in a Sioux council, the interpreter told me that the Big Mandan was probably a Mandan boy who had been captured, and raised by the Sioux; that as he grew to be a very large man, and an important man, and had no knowledge of the Mandan tribe, and was now in reality a Sioux, he had got as his adoption name the title of "The Big Mandan."

General Mitchell ordered the issuance of a lot of rations to these Indians, and fed them up, good and hearty; gave them lots of bacon, coffee, and hard-bread, also killed some beef, and let them have the head and all the entrails, and offal, which they seemed to prefer to the meat. At any rate, they ate up all the insides of the beeves which we killed. Captain O'Brien went up to see them upon some order, I don't know what, but the men in the Post were kept under arms all the time, although it was perhaps unnecessary, for the Sioux would not have made a dash when they had their women and children present, and there were in the camp a number of each. The Sioux seemed to have changed their ideas but little since the last council meeting. The surveyors had been called in from the Niobrara river, and that source of trouble was quieted. General Mitchell promised that their distribution of stuff at the Woc-co-pom'-any agency, upon the North Platte, should not be disturbed, or withheld, and that there should be added to it some provisions, bacon, molasses, and hard-bread, on condition of their not taking the war-path. The same kind of speeches was practically made as before; the Indian wanted to know what his white brother would do for him, and the white brother knew that it was cheaper to clothe and feed him than fight him. General Mitchell insisted, as he did before, that the earth belonged to the people on it per capita, and no Indian had any more right to increased acreage than the white brother had. And he also pointed out to Mr. Indian that here the Indian had no primary right to the soil, but that it belonged originally to those from whom the Sioux had taken it when the Chippewas, their ancient enemy, had driven them west. And that rights to land, if accumulated by conquest by the Indians, could be accumulated by the whites. Mitchell had his speech well in hand, as he had before, and he argued with the Indian at every point. The council was entirely uneventful. The pipe of peace was passed around, and we all smoked it with a stoic and reverential silence. The Indian being told that he had no right to the Platte valley unless he wanted to use or cultivate it, appeared to see the propriety of letting those have it who could use it. At any rate, he preferred molasses, hard-bread and bacon to the occupation of the river valley. He knew there was no game along the river-bed where the wagons were constantly going, and it was of no value to him whatever; therefore three-point Mackinaw blankets that were nice and red, appealed to him strongly. Shan-tag-a-lisk had a daughter who was very ambitious. General Harney in former days had given the mother an Episcopal prayer-book, and she carried it as a talisman of good luck all her life. The daughter had made up her mind to not marry anybody who was not a "Capitan," which was a Spanish name the Sioux used, and which comprised any officer from corporal up to general. Of this daughter I have written elsewhere, in a magazine; see supplement hereto.

But the Indians did not seem to be satisfied. They would not sign anything nor come to any definite conclusion. They still wanted the Smoky Hill route between Kansas and Denver closed. They seemed willing to permit travel west on the Arkansas and on the Platte, but all north of the Platte to the Upper Missouri and all south of the Platte to the Arkansas they wanted to be left alone. They also wanted to come and go across the Platte as they pleased. General Mitchell was inflexible; he demanded that they stay away from the Platte, and that they let the Smoky Hill route alone. And Mitchell told the chiefs plainly that they must control and restrain their young men or there would be war. In order to bring about a permanent understanding, Mitchell told the chiefs to talk with their people fully, and meet him again. So he made another postponement of fifty days, and told them to all be back and that he would come up and meet them. He also told them he was determined to stop them from warring with the Pawnees; that he wanted a treaty of peace between all of his Indians, and that at the next meeting it must be fixed up. Mitchell wore a full Brigadier's uniform with a yellow silk sash over his shoulder, and looked like a king. He was a good deal of a king, and he certainly talked like a king, and the Indians understood him. He tried to impress on them that if they were friends of his, the chiefs must restrain their young men. The party broke up with the understanding that they would meet at Cottonwood Springs in fifty days and come to a better understanding, and if possible a final understanding, upon the subjects involved. General Mitchell issued them some rations, and they promised to control their young men so that no overt acts would be committed during the coming interval. I do not want to get ahead of my story, but as a matter of fact, O-way-see'-cha afterwards went north across the Platte to get out of the way of the Cheyennes, and Spotted Tail went, and hid his band up in the Big Horn range. So that, so far as the Sioux were concerned, the fights with them, which took place soon after, were only fights with wild, erratic war parties of young men who could not be controlled. It was stated to me by a person who claimed to know, that after O-way-see'-cha got back from this council to his tribe south of the Platte, several young men, stated by one person to be eleven in number, and by another to be seventeen in number, started out to raid the Platte valley, and that they did so, and killed several, doing much damage, with a loss to themselves of a couple killed. And it was stated that O-way-see'-cha, the moment that he had heard that they had left his camp, got his head-men and warriors together, took the tents and property, all which they could find of these raiding young men, and burned it up, and killed all of their horses and dogs. This was said to have put an end to the Ogallallah branch of the Sioux trouble, but it was these war parties from the various Sioux bands that made trouble hereinafter related. The difficulty was that the chiefs could not control their people. The Indians were a wild, bloodthirsty set of barbarians, and one half, at least, of them deserved killing as much as the wolves which barked around their tepees.

The time of these conventions was generally set by a formula; the Indians could not go by the days of the month, so the date was fixed for a certain number of moons ahead, and the time set was "when the moon is straight up at sunset." When the moon was overhead at sunset it gave time for the pow-wow, and then the Indians had a full moon in which they could ride night and day going home.

CHAPTER XV

IN THE mean time the travel along the road had been very much interfered with; trains were consolidated, and sent through with military escorts. About half of our post was continually on the road, every day escorting stages and trains. The trains went in a consolidated manner with many armed men, and at night they were corralled and regular picket guards established. Indians were seen around at all times, but in small numbers, and nothing of particular event took place except theft and stampedes of loose stock. During June we were constantly on the go. Among one of the caravans that passed us was a Mormon train that must have been five or six miles long, twelve yoke of oxen to each wagon. It was a train the like of which passes belief, except to those who have seen one of them. Large bull-wagons, loaded to the top of the bows with merchandise of which no outsider knew anything, passed slowly up the river at about the rate of a mile an hour. They said the freight ran 7,000 pounds to the wagon. It was all day passing us, June 23rd.

The most ignorant of foreign immigrants composed the train. Among them was a large proportion of women—old, coarse-looking, cruel-looking, and ignorant, and with the features and appearance of being persons who had had an exceedingly hard lot in life. There were but few young women, and these were of an ignorant, coarse-looking class. The persons who were in control were smart, intelligent-looking people, who handled the others with apparent ease. Everybody was carrying something. Some had large and bulky loads. There were push-carts in the train, and wheeled light vehicles pulled by men and women. The oddity of the situation, the altitude, the exhilaration of the climate, seemed to have infected them all with good-nature, and a sort of coarse happiness. I went out and looked at the train, and marveled greatly that there should be a religion which could make absolute slaves out of people, and that the slavery would be such a change of conditions as could be enjoyable. It did really look like a big missionary scheme that had some sense and some reason to it. These Mormons paid no attention whatever to the Indians. They traveled along as if there were no such thing as Indians. They even seemed to be dissatisfied with being protected by us, but we rode with a squad in advance of them, and a little squad in the rear of them, which, together with a flank patrol, could rally on a bugle-call, if necessary; but to the Mormons there never seemed to be any such necessity. There was a sort of Masonic understanding of some kind between the Indians and the Mormons which we never understood, and which will be noticed by events further on.

On July 1st, while everything was excitement as regarded the Indian scare, I got word to go to Fort Kearney immediately as a member of a court-martial. General Mitchell was there, and some officers had been doing improper things, and there were several soldiers that needed trying for desertion, murder, and other offenses. So the General desired a court-martial to meet there, and quickly clear up the docket. The General was a man who was quite firm, and decided. It was told of him that during an engagement down in Kentucky he was not pleased with the way a Lieutenant acted, and as soon as the skirmish was over he called up the Lieutenant, and hailing an orderly sergeant who was passing by, made the orderly sergeant cut off the Lieutenant's shoulder-straps, escort him out to the edge of camp, and tell him to "git."

Knowing the Indian custom of not doing any fighting

at night, I started for Fort Kearney and rode down fifteen miles to Gilmans' ranch that night, with an escort of two men; the next day I rode fifty miles, and sent the escort back. The next day I got into Fort Kearney promptly, and very much to the satisfaction of General Mitchell. Coming down the Platte, the mosquitoes and buffalo-gnats were very annoying. They seemed to be suddenly rising from damp places along the river; but as the breeze was from the south we did not get the full force of the inconvenience. When there was a lull in the breeze we suffered considerably, and our horses much more. I got into Fort Kearney before noon, having made the hundred miles in about 42 hours. The road was on the south side of the river, at that time.

Immediately after dinner the court-martial convened. Lieutenant Schenck of Company "C" was Judge Advocate of the court. Captain O'Brien, my captain, was already at the post, having been summoned there for consultation before I came. The president of the court-martial was a Colonel from somewhere, and the number of the court was nine besides the Judge Advocate (Lieutenant Schenck), which made ten. The court-martial was not a particularly eventful one, and I would not undertake to describe the method of the proceedings if it were not for the change that has taken place in those matters since then. The court-martial as then held was held on the old-fashioned plan, and the proceedings were somewhat as follows:

The indictment against the officer was framed in the shape of "charges" and "specifications." For instance, charge first—"Conduct unbecoming an officer and a gentleman." Specification first—In this, that he did so-and-so. Specification second—In this, that he did something else; and so on and so forth. Then charge second—"Insubordination." Specification first—In this, that he spoke so-and-so to somebody. Specification second—In this, that he kicked somebody; and so forth and so forth.

It was the rule that the court-martial should have a majority of its members of a higher rank than the accused, and that they should sit around the table in the order of their rank on each side in full uniform. So in this case the Colonel sat at the head of the table, and the officers tapered down in rank right and left until at the end was the junior officer (myself), and the Judge Advocate opposite me. In those days there were no shorthand reporters nor typewriters, and all the evidence and proceedings had to be got up in long-hand, certified up to the commander, so that appeals and arguments might be made thereon. The accused was brought in, the charges and specifications read to him, and to each of the specifications he pleaded "Not guilty," and then to the charge as a whole, "Not guilty"; then to the next specifications and to the next charge. Then the accused was asked to become a witness, and to be sworn, but was told that he was under no obligation to give any evidence against himself if he did not want to, and he might refuse to be sworn, and might refuse to testify. In some instances the accused said he preferred to testify, and then he was examined like any other witness. The Judge Advocate was the prosecutor, and in the condition of the art as it then existed, he had a large tab of blank paper in front of him, and began writing down the questions. Every question must be written down, and then the answer must be written down. And around the table sat the court in full uniform, nothing being left off of official decorations. As to cavalry officers, they even had on their spurs and silk sashes.

If there was any officer who had neglected any portion of his official dress, the accused had the right to challenge him until he got himself properly clad. But he had no right to challenge any of the party otherwise except for cause, which very seldom happened. The slow progress of writing out questions and writing down the answers was most aggravating. Then the witness always took plenty of time to answer, and often flanked the question. Then the prosecutor would write out another question, and as fast as these questions and answers were made they were stuck together by paste into a long roll, to be transcribed.

Ever and anon some member of the court who thought he was gifted with superior intuition, would object to one of the questions put by the Judge Advocate, and the court would look around to see whether anybody seconded the objection. If nobody seconded it, the presiding officer would say, "Do you insist upon your objection?" and if the officer said, "Yes," then the court would order the accused to be taken out of the room by the man with a bayonet who had him in charge. Then the door would be closed and an executive session would begin. Then the officer would fully state his objection, and the objection would be voted upon, and the youngest in rank voted first. It just happened that I was the youngest in rank, most of them being Captains, and I generally had the first say, and I was always delighted when my view was concurred in. And if it was decided that the question should be put, the accused was brought back, and the question put, and with deliberation answered.

The result was that we made slow headway, but the method was in all respects observed. There is generally in every court-martial some simple, meager, vain fellow who wants to show off, and be conspicuous, and take a great deal of a part in the proceedings. He makes a court-martial as irritable and petulant a proceeding as can well be imagined. And for slowness there is nothing equal to it as carried out under the old régime. Every once in a while some member of the court would want to ask a question. So that a member of the court would write out a question, and hand it to the presiding officer. He would stop the proceedings so he could read the question, and if he did not want to have it put he would ask the member if he insisted. If the member said, "Yes," out went the accused, and the question was read and voted on by everybody present. At times every member of the court-martial would be writing questions, and they would be flooded onto the Judge Advocate. If the presiding officer thought a question all right, he would send it down to the Judge Advocate to be asked. Then somebody on the court would object, having the right to object, and then out would go the accused, under guard, and the matter would be discussed. Besides this, there was always somebody who wanted to make a show of philanthropy, and thought his principal duty was to be humane, and impede the prosecution. Then the Judge Advocate would lean to the other side, and ply questions with great speed and fertility. When the evidence was all in, it was a great pile of scrap-paper stuck together with paste. Then the court listened to anybody who wanted to address the court, only they were limited to time if it were thought best. Sometimes the Captain or some soldier who was being tried, would come in and make a talk on behalf of his man. Once in a while a lawyer was brought up, who acted pompous and pretended to know it all, and read authorities from law books that were not pertinent. Finally the court came to vote, and began at the bottom; the youngest in commission got up and verbally expressed his opinion first, then wrote it, and handed it to the presiding officer. If there was any difference to talk over and discuss, they did so, and generally arrived at some compromise verdict. After the verdict came the sentence; then all this quantity of literature that had been formed was copied off and sent to the commanding officer for his approval. This writing was done by hand, and if they wanted three copies, which was sometimes the case when an officer was tried and determined to appeal, one person read aloud the record, sentence by sentence, while three simultaneously copied it. A court-martial in July, in full uniform, all buttoned up to the chin, with a sash on, is very uninteresting and unpleasant work.

In order to make speed at this court-martial, we worked nights and Sundays, right along, and at the end of two weeks we had convicted and sentenced various soldiers for various crimes and misdemeanors, and had disposed of two officers,—one officer for general worthlessness, drunkenness, want of discipline, and the spending of and embezzlement of his company's fund; and another officer for a very strange and unofficer-like proceeding. He had come to Fort Kearney and was detailed there, and he sent for his wife and young son, a boy about ten or twelve years of age. The officer immediately began buying for family use from the commissary a great amount of flour, sugar, and dried apples. As he got these at what it cost the Government, it was about half-price as they sold outside of the post. He got several barrels of sugar, several large sacks of dried apples, and a great quantity of flour. It was finally discovered that in one of the neglected kitchens of the officers' quarters, the Captain's wife and boy were making apple pies and selling them for fifteen cents apiece. As the Government furnished the wood and sold supplies cheaply, the boy made a great quantity of money by selling these pies to the overland immigration, and to the soldiers, and persons around the post. As near as we could figure, they had made six or seven hundred dollars net on it, and the Captain had furthered the whole scheme. We considered it the limit, and let him out of the service, and put an end to that sort of business at the post.

All at once, while the court-martial was going off, news came of Indian depredations west of Fort Laramie, and I was relieved from services on the court-martial and was told to proceed as rapidly as possible to my post. General Mitchell told me in the morning to get ready to go with him on a little expedition which he contemplated, and to have thirty days' rations for my men and horses loaded and ready in two wagons. I left Fort Kearney after dinner, and rode that afternoon thirty-five miles up the river. There had been a rain. The breeze changed from the south to the north and the air was moist and hot. Anticipating the gnats and mosquitoes, I had got a small piece of mosquito netting at a store at Dobytown. I had not gone far upon the road when I ran into clouds of gnats. After a while my horse showed symptoms of great pain. The gnats were in dense quantities. I had the mosquito netting over my face. The horse was suffering very much both at his nose and eyes, and he was constantly shaking his head to keep them out of his ears. I took the mosquito netting off my own face, and put it over my horse's and tied my handkerchief over my face. The wind blowing over the river kept the road filled with swarms of mosquitoes and gnats. I finally got to a ranch, and wanted a larger handkerchief. The only handkerchief large enough was a yellow silk one costing $5. This I bought, and, cutting some willow boughs from a place on the edge of the river, I made two large whisk brooms, one for each hand, and dropping the reins on the saddle I rode the horse on the run, switching at every step either on the right or left of his head with these bush brooms which I had in my hand. Finally, towards the evening, I got past these clouds of mosquitoes and gnats, and felt greatly relieved. The mosquitoes and gnats would hover around one another in the air, and made heavy, cloud-like banks that you could see plainly long distances ahead, and feel plainly the resistance of when you rode into them. I made this trip alone, without any escort, but was in no particular danger, because I was frequently passing large trains not very far apart which had escorts. I was up bright and early on the 16th, and rode into the post, a distance of 65 miles that day, stopping at Gilmans' and getting a fresh horse after I had ridden my own horse fifty miles.

When I got into our post that night, I found a great number of campers and pilgrims at the post. They were afraid to go ahead, and there were nearly a thousand thus camped. And there was quite a number of women among them, and they were having a dance at MacDonald's store, and out on the hard flat ground in front of his store. There were several stages full of ladies going through as passengers on the coaches from the west, and some of them were really nice people. I had ridden only sixty-five miles that day, and didn't feel very tired, so I got into the dance, and we ran it until daylight. And as I had some experience in calling cotillion figures, I served about an hour after midnight as reinforcement in that particular. The people had to do something, and they might just as well have some fun as to sit around the camp-fire and look at the wind blow the ashes away.

The next day I got the company all out, inspected their arms, clothing, horses, equipment, and everything. I also packed up thirty days' supplies and got the wagons ready. This was done in the manner Captain O'Brien ordered, whom I had left at Fort Kearney, and who was coming up with General Mitchell. He told me to have the company look its best, and I told the boys to brush up their jackets, and get on some style. We put in the whole of July 18th in getting in shape to move, as the General had promised to come along, and be there on the morning of the 19th.

CHAPTER XVI

July 18, 1864 · Return from Fort Kearney · Indians at Cottonwood · Council Overdue · Preparation to March · General Mitchell Arrives · Pawnee Battalion · The Council Meadow, July 19, 1864 · The Council · The Flight of the Indians · The Return to Cottonwood · Start for Fort Laramie · Camp at Jack Morrow's · Ben Gallagher and John Smith · Line of March

WHEN I got back to the post, July 18, 1864, as stated in the former chapter, I found camped two miles up the river a large number of Sioux Indians of various bands, all avowedly friendly, with some few Cheyennes, so it was stated, among them. The Sioux had come to hold the third and final council, adjourned to fifty days from the second. The council was three or four days overdue, General Mitchell being absent, and the Indians had waited and been fed in the mean time. The presence of this large body of Indians near the post practically blockaded the road at this point, hence the number of travelers at the post, and hence the dance of which I spoke. The Indians appeared quiet, but rumor had it that there were more "buck" Indians there than usual, and but few squaws and no small children. Nobody felt quite safe, and the post was carefully guarded and picketed, and the pilgrims and the travelers were organized for complete defense. "Hunter" and John Smith had been up to the camp and seen the Indians and tried to talk with them, but found them to be unsociable and non-communicative, and reported their belief that the third council would be a failure. General Mitchell was reported as coming up the river with a battalion of Pawnee Indian scouts, said to be 200 in number, but in fact about 80. Trouble was feared, although we knew we could repulse any Indian attack.

General Mitchell arrived early in the forenoon of July 19, 1864, with Company "D" of our regiment, as an escort, and Lieutenant John K. Rankin, a very brave and capable cavalry officer from Kansas, who had served down South, and from the very beginning of the war. He now resides at Lawrence, Kansas. General Mitchell left the Pawnee scouts back about three miles in camp, but came in with his escort, Company "D," an ambulance and two horses, one extra each for himself and Lieutenant Rankin.

As both the Sioux and Cheyennes were now committing overt acts through the raiding parties of their young men, General Mitchell seemed to think that a council would be unproductive of results. Upon consultation he determined that he would not risk a failure, lest it might result in immediate trouble; but he thought that he would try his Pawnee Indian peace scheme and see how it would work. He had to try something, so that the Indians would not think they had come on a fool's errand. So he sent word to the Sioux to send their chiefs and head-men to an arroyo two miles east of the Post, and be there at two o'clock with the officer as a pilot and guard, who was sent with the message. This was Lieutenant Rankin, who had the interpreter "Snell" (Watts) with him. Then Mitchell caucussed with his officers and prepared his plans.

There was a very wide grassy meadow three miles east of our Post, and the arroyo was on the west side of it. The Sioux Indians began moving, and instead of a few going east to the place of rendezvous they all went, tepees, horses, dogs and all; and at two o'clock every Indian in the country round about, that we knew of, was there. They were all ready for traveling, and were racing their horses around and yelling, and evidently some of them had obtained some pilgrim whisky. A mile east of them was the "Pawnee Battalion," in a close group, with their horses all saddled and in hand. Between the two gangs of Indians was the escort of the General, already referred to, composed of Company "D"—65 men, of our regiment. The Pawnees and the Sioux had been engaged in exterminating each other for several years.

Finally the Sioux party crossed the Arroyo, came east a little, and spread out towards the river, with everything in seeming readiness for a hasty movement, and they began shouting at the Pawnees, and the Pawnees, feeling safe, began shouting back. Up at the Post all of the soldiers were out under arms, and mounted, with Major O'Brien in command. All of the pilgrim trains were corralled and the men prepared and ready for trouble. General Mitchell left the Post before two o'clock and went down to the rendezvous, the grassy meadow, taking with him one hundred men from the Post, of which fifty men were from our company, "F," and fifty from Company "C," the latter being under the command of its first sergeant. Captain O'Brien rode with General Mitchell and I took charge of the detail from our company, together with one of our brass howitzers. With General Mitchell rode all the interpreters he could get, about ten. General Mitchell was worried and angry.

Captain North, of Columbus, Nebraska, of whom I have already spoken, was in command of the Pawnee Battalion, and said he preferred war to peace with the Sioux. He understood and spoke the Pawnee language well, and had with him two other men who could do the same.

As General Mitchell came down with his troops and took a position on the side of the wagon-road, a little distance south of the meadow, the Indians on both sides seemed uneasy and began milling around on horseback and edging up nearer and nearer to one another, shouting and yelling at each other like a lot of demons.

The first thing that General Mitchell did was to run a long thin line of cavalry from Company "C" between the Indians clear down through to the river. They were set about fifty yards apart from each other and were faced alternately east and west, with drawn sabres that flashed in the sun. Then General Mitchell ordered the howitzer to be unlimbered and loaded with shrapnel, with fuse cut two seconds. He then through the interpreters ordered the Indians on both sides to get back. Then he ordered a soldier to go forward to the center, take his sabre and stab it in the ground and leave it there to mark a talking-place; this the soldier did by sticking it in a big ant-hill that happened to be at about the right place. This sabre standing there stuck into the ground marked the talking-place. Then through the interpreters the General ordered each side to send their speakers dismounted and unarmed, not exceeding ten in number, to places on each side about one hundred feet from the center. He told them also that he would make a speech, as directed by the Great Father at Washington, and then he wanted to hear from them alternately, beginning with the Sioux. The stations on each side of the center for the oratorical delegates were marked out, and the delegates from each side took their respective places, coming from their tribes on foot with a slow, pompous step. When they had taken their stations, General Mitchell, in full uniform, in an imposing way, on his magnificent mahogany-bay horse, rode out to the center, which was about one hundred yards north. Close behind him was Captain O'Brien, all togged out, finely mounted and looking like a duke. With him was our company bugler. Behind them rode two interpreters for the Sioux language and two for the Pawnee. The General on arriving at the center halted, turned and saluted the Sioux, then turned and saluted the Pawnees; then he gave a signal to the bugler; he came forward and gave some loud bugle-calls to the Pawnees, then turned and gave the same thing to the Sioux. Then by command of the General, after about two minutes of dignified silence had elapsed the bugler passed to the rear and sounded, "Forward," at which signal I moved up with my detail, as did also the howitzer and about a dozen citizens and the escort Company "D" and the balance of Company "C." Altogether there were about one hundred and ninety white men, eighty Pawnees, and about four hundred Sioux and their associates. The white command was drawn up to within about fifty feet of the General, and by his order the howitzer was put in position, pointing at the Sioux and masked in between an open-order arrangement of the cavalry.

The General had been advised to put as much pomp and ceremony into the proceedings as possible, and right well he did it. When all was arranged and in order, he directed the interpreters to come out in front of him, and then he, sitting on his horse, facing north, turning neither to the right nor left, nor towards the Indians, began his speech. He stopped at the end of each sentence, and the head interpreter shouted and translated the sentence to the Sioux. Then the other interpreter did the same thing, shouting the translation to the Pawnees. It was very deliberate, and plenty of time was given after each sentence for the Indians to get it straight among themselves. The general had told the interpreters what his speech was, and they had the translation all studied out. I was where I could hear it all, and it was easy for me to write it down, it went so slowly. His words were as follows:

"BROTHERS: The Great Father in Washington sends me here to tell you that it makes his heart ache to see his red children fighting with each other. [Pause.]

"He wants to see them all living in peace with each other, for they are all equally his children. [Pause.]

"There is land enough and water enough and game enough and grass enough for all. [Pause.]

"The Great Father wants his red children to live peaceably with his white children and with each other, because they are all brothers. [Pause.]

"As long as the red children war with each other they cannot make progress, nor have so much to eat, nor as many horses, nor as many children. [Pause.]

"The Great Father wants to see his red children become numerous, and have horses and cattle and children, and plenty to eat. [Pause.]

"He wants you to pledge yourselves on each side not to interfere with each other's hunting parties, and not to cross the neutral strip on the north side of the Platte. [Pause.]

"And he wants you both to promise not to steal each other's

horses, and not to kill each other, and not to prowl around each other's villages. [Pause.]

"Then, if you do this, the Great Father will be glad because you obey him, and he will help you, and if you suffer he will have rations issued to you so that you will not starve. [Pause.]

"Now, speak out your minds on this subject, and talk straight and say what you will do, so that I may tell the Great Father what you think, and how you feel and what you will do. [Pause.]

"If you do not agree, I will speak again."

Here the General stopped, but he never got a chance to carry out the threat of his last sentence. Having finished and the last word having been interpreted and delivered, the General gave a signal to the trumpeter, and he came forward as before and gave a blast to each side. Then a very awkward silence set in, and for ten minutes not an Indian stirred. There was a decorum and deliberation to the actions of the Indians that impressed us all that the General had undertaken an embarrassing and difficult job. The waiting became oppressive, and the Indians were grouped together in a compact and motionless mass on each side. After the General spoke, then one Indian from each speaking station went back to tell his people what the General had said, but the Indians kept silent after receiving the messages.

Finally, a Sioux dressed and decorated with eagle feathers and paint came forward to the center where the sabre was sticking in the ant-hill. He carried something that looked like a long buckskin bag with a cane in it. He began to talk slowly, and his words were first translated into English and then by another interpreter shouted to the Pawnees in their own language.

This first speaker opened out in a conciliatory way which promised well. He said that he wanted to please the Great Father and wanted to please General Mitchell. He did not think that the Pawnees amounted to much, and was willing to leave them alone. Then he went into a swaggering talk of how great a nation the Sioux were, and how brave they were. It looked as if he were talking one word at the

Pawnees and two at General Mitchell. The latter sat on his horse, looked disgusted and said nothing.

The Sioux speaker went back to his station, and after a long, deliberate wait, out came a Pawnee, bareheaded and with a pair of blue army trousers on. He proceeded to say that the Pawnees in olden times had owned all of the land south of the Platte, even the country they were then standing on, but that smallpox had scourged them and they were now settled on land which they liked, and which the white man conceded them, and that they preferred peace, and would be willing to live at peace with the Sioux and Cheyennes if the latter would be peaceful.

Then a Sioux came forward, after a prolonged silence, and made a dreary and unemotional speech, most of it a boast as to who his ancestors were and what they had done, but he was willing to let the Pawnees alone if the Great Father wanted it done.

Then a Pawnee replied in much the same strain, and to the effect that the Pawnees were not afraid of the Sioux, and never had been, but would live at peace with them or anybody else that the Great Father requested.

The first three or four speeches on each side looked as if they might get down to business and accomplish something at last, or agree to something. The speeches were not made by the warriors or leaders, but by the talkers. They were probably a cheap lot who represented the tribe only in a slight way and were put forward just to say nothing and commit their sides to nothing. The interpreters said that the speakers were a snide lot, and that the real fighters and leaders were not heard. The substance of the speeches was mostly brag, and under the circumstances seemed childish and inappropriate. The speakers did not seem to want to grasp the situation. Perhaps they did not dare to commit their sides to a policy for which they might be killed in a week. At any rate, the talking grew tiresome, and nothing to the point.

Then a Sioux speaker came in on turn after several had

spoken; he said that he did not see any particular reason for changing present conditions—that the Sioux nation was getting along all right. That if the Great Father could not stop his white children from fighting, how could he expect to stop the red. This was a palpable hit—a good one—the Civil War was then being strenuously fought every day. The General sat on his mahogany bay listening to every word, and now he smiled a faint and sickly smile.

The Pawnee speakers seemed to favor peace and raise no impediments to an agreement, but the Sioux began to grow worse and worse, until they began to abuse the Pawnees roundly. One after another spoke, and still the Pawnees held their temper, and when they spoke generally consented to a trial of peaceful relations.

About sundown a Pawnee speaker closed his speech by saying that the Pawnees were listening to the advice of their Government agents and the army officers whom the Great Father had sent among them, and had not done anything lately of which the Sioux could complain.

Just as the sun was setting the last Sioux speaker took the center and gave a violent harangue with much gesticulation, working in much of the sign language which the Pawnees could understand but we could not. "Liar, liar," said the Sioux orator as he thrust forward from his chin his right hand closed with the two front fingers spread and extended, signifying forked tongue,—"Liar; they all are forked tongues; while these few are up here talking peace to us the moccasin-tracks of their young men can be seen all around our villages, trying to steal our horses and scalp our children. Besides all this, what are they doing up here now, and whom are they going after to fight?"

The speaker spoke with such rapidity and vehemence that he soon outran the interpreters and they quit, but the Pawnees knew from the signs that were made what was being said, and they began to murmur and shout back. But the Sioux speaker was wound up and set going and he had to run on until he ran down. He was talking to himself and the universe, and did not heed and could not wait for an interpreter.

Finally General Mitchell rode up and called a halt; the bugler blew a call; the sun had set; the convention was a failure. He ordered the Pawnees back; he ordered me to deploy my men down the center. Then he ordered the Sioux to cross the river, go north, keep out of the Platte valley, and not stop for three days. The Sioux Indians began howling and shouting; in a body they plunged into the river and soon were across; but they kept on yelling as they went north, and we heard them for a couple of miles until their yells died out in the distance. We hurried back to the Post, followed by the Pawnees and Company "D."

We waited at the Post but a few minutes, and all started off on the march toward the west, except Company "C"; it remained back to guard the Post. We took our two pieces of artillery and our wagons. We were now headed for Fort Laramie, a distance of about three hundred miles. The Pawnee Indians were taken along.

Our line of march was as follows:

First, an advance guard of ten cavalrymen of my company, in my charge. *Next*, General Mitchell, Major Wood, Lieutenant Rankin, and John Smith, the guide, on horseback. *Next*, the General's ambulance, and the two horses of the General and Lieutenant Rankin. *Next*, came about a dozen civilians, guides and interpreters on horseback. *Next*, six wagons, each drawn by six mules, being one for headquarters and the civilians, two for each company, and one for the Pawnees. *Next*, our Company "F," in command of Captain O'Brien, seventy men. *Next*, Company "D," in command of Captain Fouts, with sixty-five men. *Next*, the Pawnees. Including drivers and all we numbered about 160 white men and eighty Indians. Major Woods was in charge of the escort, and no better man could have been found. Captain Fouts was an old man, brave but inefficient; he was shortly afterwards killed in battle with the Indians. We got into Jack Morrow's late, and found there about forty citizens, all under arms. We had two days' cooked rations with us, and when we got into camp we got some cedar wood from Morrow and cooked a little coffee. It was hot, and we posted our guards and pickets and lay down on the prairie, to sleep.

I had forgotten to say, that along with General Mitchell there had come up from Fort Kearney with him Major Armstrong, who was Chief of Cavalry and Inspector of the District. He was making a careful inspection of all the posts and troops in the command. He was very strict, and put in his time faithfully and very industriously. He examined our stables, barracks, horses, and supplies. He watched us march; he looked us over, and into everything. We never knew what conclusion he came to or what was the result of it all until when, nearly two months afterwards, the Captain got the following letter:

"HEADQUARTERS DEPARTMENT OF KANSAS,
OFFICE OF CHIEF OF CAVALRY,
FORT LEAVENWORTH, *August 1, 1864.*

"*Captain N. J. O'Brien,*
Commanding Co. 'F,' Seventh Iowa Cavalry,
Cottonwood Springs.

"CAPTAIN: The Cavalry Inspection report of Chief of Cavalry, District of Nebraska, shows eight enlisted men of your company as 'present sick,' and it is properly explained in remarks of Chief of Cavalry.

"On close examination I find that in every particular the report is very satisfactory, and shows a company that you should feel proud of, and which is an honor to the regiment of which you are a part. The District Chief of Cavalry in his remarks adds:

"'COTTONWOOD SPRINGS, July 19, 1864.—Company "F," Seventh Iowa Cavalry, inspected this day, and Company marched same day after inspection. Clothing, camp and garrison equipage in good order.'

"Respectfully forwarded through Hd. Irs. Dist. of Nebraska.
Very respectfully,
Your Obt. Servant,
B. S. HENNING,
Major and Chief of Cavalry,
Department of Kansas."

This letter when received, long afterwards, was read at the head of the company for at least a week at evening roll-call, after which the Captain gave it to me to preserve.

Headquarters, Department of Kansas,
Office Chief of Cavalry
Fort Leavenworth, *August 1st* 1864

Capt. A. J. O'Brien
Comdg Co "F" 7 Iowa Cav
Cottonwood Springs

Captain

The Cavalry Inspection Report of Chief of Cavalry, District of Nebraska, shows eight enlisted men of your Company as "Present Sick", and it is properly explained in remarks of Chief of Cavalry.

On close examination I find that in every particular the report is very satisfactory, and shows a Company that you should feel proud of and which is an honor to the Regiment of which you are apart. The District Chief of Cavalry in his remarks adds,

"Cotton Wood Springs July 19 1864 Co "F" 7 Iowa Cavalry Inspected this day, and Company marched the same day after Inspection. Clothing Camp and Garrison equipage in good order Respectfully forwarded through N° 2oo, Dist of Nebraska.

Very respectfully
Your Obt Servant
B. I. Henning
Maj & Chief of Cav, Dept of Kansas

THE CHIEF OF CAVALRY'S COMPLIMENTS TO CO. "F," 7TH IOWA CAVALRY.

It was so flattering that to preserve my reputation for truth and veracity I feel that I ought to append a photograph copy, which I do.

Returning now to our camp, at Jack Morrow's, that night, I will add that Ben Gallagher, our post sutler, together with "John Smith," the guide, came with us. That evening, when our horses had all been tied to the picket-rope between our two company wagons, we all lay down on the prairie with our heads in our saddles to go to sleep. General Mitchell was in his ambulance and the companies were off one side. What took place that night I will leave for another chapter. It was ten miles from Cottonwood Springs to Jack Morrow's ranch. We had had a busy day of it. It was a beautiful, bright moonlight night.

CHAPTER XVII

The Camp at Jack Morrow's · John Smith's Story ·
The Soldiers' Suggestion

I WAS lying on the prairie at midnight, all alone, with my head in the saddle, about midway between General Mitchell's ambulance and my company, each about fifty yards distant, thinking of the strange events of the day, and wondering what the Indians would do next. Captain O'Brien was about one hundred feet from me, going to sleep with Lieutenant Rankin. I had taken a final look at the bright, beautiful moon, and had about got into a doze when along came Ben Gallagher and "John Smith," leading their horses. Ben Gallagher went to his saddle-pockets and pulled out a yellow earthen bottle made in the form of a book, and labeled on the back "History of the War." It had an aperture and cork at the top, and held about a quart. He handed it to me; I examined it and read a page or two. John Smith said, "Let's camp with Lieutenant Ware." So they both took their saddles off, spread their blankets near me, took their horses to the picket-rope, tied them, and came back. Gallagher and Smith began alternately taking little chapters from the "History of the War," and finally they lay down on the ground near me, and we looked up at the moon and were about to go to sleep. The whisky had loosened up the tongue of "John Smith," and as we lay there on the wild flat prairie, out in that wild flat country, with our heads near together in our saddles, and while the wolves out in the hills were howling, Smith told the following story, of which I made full notes at the time, and which I can remember now as well as if it were told yesterday, so profound was the impression it made.

169

I will repeat practically what John Smith said, in his own talk, as I put it down afterwards:

"After I graduated at Yale College I thought that literature was what I wanted to follow, and I tried my hand on a newspaper in Iowa, but finally determined to go West, and as everybody was striking out for Pike's Peak—it was 'Pike's Peak or Bust'—I concluded to try Pike's Peak, and if I didn't like it I would go on through to California. I got to Omaha, and finally got in with a train; I had some horses, and I went along with the train, paying my bills for myself and my horses. I got right awful sick, and they thought I was going to die, I didn't know what I was about; thought so too; didn't much care what happened, and they left me at a ranch not far from Gilmans'. And I surprised them all by finally getting well, but I had been sick a long time, lost everything, and I didn't get well very fast. There were Indians around all the time. I heard them talk, and sort of picked up the language. I had studied Latin and Greek and French, and knew something of the other languages, and I found it wasn't difficult for me to pick up the Cheyenne language, and the Sioux. I finally got well so I could ride a horse, but I didn't have a cent left. Somebody got my horses, and I got cared for. Don't know exactly how it was arranged, but I was very much scared about myself. I didn't get my strength back very fast, and I was afraid to do anything much. I went up to Gilmans' one day, and Gilman asked me if I didn't want to go over on Red Willow Creek and trade with the Indians some for him. After negotiations, finding out that Gilman would furnish me a half-breed interpreter, and give me a good show on the profits, I went over there, and I picked up their language right off, both the verbal and the sign, and made myself agreeable to all the chiefs, and did pretty well. Gilman was pleased, and I kept going backwards and forwards, and I made Gilman a whole lot of money, and made something for myself. After I had been with the Indians for a while I got a big disgust on with civilized life, concluded there wasn't much to it, and that I would rather live like an Indian than a white man. I had a talk with Gilman, and Gilman was so satisfied with my work that he offered to back me right along as a sort of partner. Well, I got sort of stuck on Indian life, thought I would rather be an Indian, and I married the daughter of the chief in the band there on the Red Willow. He wasn't the head of the Cheyennes, but he was the head of that band. And I got a nice tepee (tent), and some horses and dogs and two children, one of them a boy and the oldest a girl, and I was considered one of the band. When there was anything to come up, they asked me what I thought about it, and I never tried to become chief, nor anything of that kind, and consequently I didn't have any trouble with any ambitious Indian; I was living there all right until they tried to get the Cheyennes into this war. I saw there was going to be a whole lot of trouble. Indians from the south came up there, and things got distracted. They called a large meeting down near the mouth of Red Willow where our camp then was, and there came in Cheyennes from down below. The meeting was a big meeting. We had a big bonfire, and the young bucks were all talking war, and I didn't know exactly what to do. My wife told me that there was going to be trouble, and that if I wasn't careful some of them would shoot me. One evening at a big camp-fire there was an Indian who said he was a Kioway. I don't know whether he was or not. He was an Indian that spoke a different dialect from any that I knew of, but he could talk Cheyenne as plain as anybody, and he talked long and loud. He had set up a post near the fire, like a fence-post, and he had put a soldier's hat on it, that had the brass cross-sabers and trimmings of a cavalry soldier's hat. He would talk and get excited, and with his tomahawk he would chop into this hat on the post. I tilted up the corner of the tent and listened to all of it, and my wife went out to listen better. I saw the uproar getting greater and greater, and some of the young bucks got excited, and went to shooting their guns into the air. My wife went and got a pony as if leading it out to grass, and took it outside of camp up in the brush, and put a saddle and bridle on it, and told me where to find it. Then she told me to slip out, and get on it and skip, while she went and sat down near the scene, and watched what was going on. I thought things might cool down, but the spasm grew worse, and they got to howling and yelling and singing war-songs, and everybody was around the camp-fire. I kissed my two children good-by, little half-breeds, but mighty pretty for Indians; I slid out, and got onto that horse and rode. I struck for Cotton-wood Canyon. It is a pretty long trip, but I rode pretty fast, and I got up to the head breaks about dawn, when right up out of the grass in front of me rose two Cheyenne Indians, both of them with bows and arrows, and I didn't have a gun. I was a refugee. I didn't dare have a gun. They took me prisoner; I said to myself, 'Now my time has come.' They asked me where I was going, and I told them that I was going down to Cottonwood Canyon to get some ammunition, supplies and whisky. My pony was plumb used up, and they made me get off, and one of them said, 'Come with us,' and I said, 'No,' I wanted to go down and get my stuff. Then the Cheyenne drew an arrow up to its head, and punched it up against me, and I, of course, knew if he let go of the bow-string the arrow would go right through me. I supposed they would take me down to the canyon, tie me up to a tree, build a fire around me, and have some fun. I had to go, but I kept thinking, and watching for something to do in the way of an escape, when all at once they stopped, and one of them went into some bushes and pulled out a little keg of In-dian whisky. Then I saw that they both had been drinking, and that their actions were due to drink. The whisky was awful stuff, made out of alcohol, water, red pepper and molasses, and these two Indians had got this keg hidden up in the breaks at the head of Cottonwood Canyon, and were having a great time. One of them had a big tin cup, and he filled it plum full, and handed it to me to drink. I said to him that it would kill me, that I couldn't drink it; and they told me that I must drink it, and I took a sip. Then they told me to go on drinking; then they would draw arrows each one up to its head, and with the bow thus drawn, punch me with the sharp point of the arrow. They would punch me in the ribs with it, they would punch me in the neck with it. I knew if they would relax just a little and the arrow was released I was a dead man. I said to myself, they're going to get me drunk and then roast me. I would take a sip and they would laugh in a diabolical manner, and draw the arrow up again to the full, and punch me with it, and say, 'Drink.' Well, I kept sipping, and expostulating, but it wouldn't do. I concluded I would rather be roasted drunk than sober. One of them would laugh and howl as he watched the other one punch me with drawn arrow, and they would take turns at this, and take turns at laughing. Well, I don't know, but I guess I drank it all up. I bade myself good-by, and farewell, and did it more than once. I know I kept sipping and they kept prodding me with drawn arrows. I remember falling to the ground, and trying to get up, and I remember those fellows dancing around, shouting and having fun, while I was thinking my end had come.

"Well, sir, I wasn't hurt. I woke up with hardly any clothes on. They took my moccasins and my coat, but when I woke up the sun was shining down on me, hot and blistering, and I didn't know where I was, and I didn't know whether I was dead or alive, and such a raging thirst and fever I never had. My head was bursting wide open, and my mouth all dry and crisp. My tongue was rough like shark-skin. I tried to get up, but fell over, and it sort of began to dawn on me that I was alive. There was nobody around, and I couldn't tell where I was, and I finally saw the depressions of the ground, and I made up my mind that I must find water. I went stumbling down the grade, and every once in a while I would fall over, and lie there, and after a while I would get up, and I thought I would choke to death, and never find any water. From time to time I went on down and would fall, and have a momentary lapse of memory, and finally I struck a little muddy pool, and I went into it, and drank and vomited, and drank and rolled over in the water and mud, and lay there. Then I got out, and went farther down, but I went mighty slow, and every once in a while I would strike another little pool full of alkali and trash, and I would go into it, and roll in the mud and rub my hair with the water and mud, trying to ease my headache, and finally I got down to where there was some water that was drinkable, and then I began to revive. Finally I struck a place where I just lay down in the water and went to sleep, and I kept waking up; and that's the way I went down to Cottonwood Canyon. I got up from one of those mud-holes where I had rolled and slept all night, and then went down to the camp where you first saw me, which accounts for the horrible appearance that I made. I had, I guess, drank a quart of that whisky; it was a wonder it did not kill me.[1]

"Now, in fact, I wasn't in the danger I thought I was in. These Cheyennes had been out on an expedition to get some whisky, and didn't know what was going on in the village. I thought they had been sent ahead to intercept me, but as a matter of fact they didn't know anything about what was going on. They were having some private fun with me. That was an Indian way of having some fun. But I never expected to get through without being tied up to a tree and burned. I have not been back, couldn't get back, but I would like to see those two children, and have no doubt that I will. My Indian wife is all right, first-class for an Indian, but I got about through with my wanting to live the life of an Indian."

The next day one of the men of my company, as I was riding alongside of him, said to me: "I believe I know that John Smith. I used to live in Ottumwa, Iowa, and there was a fellow came on there from Yale College, and cut a good deal of a swell, and edited a newspaper, and got in a woman scrape, and skipped the town. I have forgotten his name.

[1] NOTE.—"John Smith's" first appearance at our camp will be found in Chapter 13.

It was several years ago, but it wasn't John Smith, and I believe he is the same fellow." To this I made no reply, except to say: "You are so liable to be mistaken that you hadn't better say anything about it; you may have a controversy and this man will call you out, and you will have to shoot him or he will shoot you. I don't care about losing any of my men, and I guess you hadn't better say anything about it at the present." He did not know John Smith's story, as told to me in the moonlight. I never found out Smith's true name.

CHAPTER XVIII

THE NEXT DAY, JULY 20, 1864, Major Woods, of our regiment, in command, we marched west. The weather was
hot, and the wind from the south came over the baked plains
dry and lifeless. A cloud of dust floated to the north. The
trains, what few there were, were all corralled at stations,
waiting for escorts. They were waiting to fall in with any
escorted train going their way. General Mitchell was urging
his men forward, and we were going west at a pretty rapid
rate, so fast that no train could long keep in sight of us.
There were rumors of herders being killed, and of Indians
being in the hills along our route. Wherever we saw a train
corralled, the pilgrims had stories of seeing Indians in the
hills and of seeing Indians crossing the river stealthily. But
no Indians were yet visible to us. During the day Lieutenant Rankin came and rode with me, and we talked over
the Indian council. Rankin said the General was angry and
mortified over it; that if it had been successful it would have
been a great achievement and much to his reputation and
credit; that it was not Mitchell's idea, but that a lot of
preachers had got at President Lincoln and insisted that the
preachers should have the control of the Indian situation,
and that the various sects should divide the control among
themselves—that is to say, the Methodists should have so
much jurisdiction, the Catholics so much, the Baptists so

much, and so on, and that they were worrying Lincoln a
good deal, and that they wanted him to take immediate steps
to have an universal Indian peace between all the Indians.
Lincoln yielded to much of it and had sent for Mitchell and
told him to take up the matter and see what he could do.
Mitchell did his best, but failed, and was now studying up,
as he rode along, what his report and recommendations
should be. He was telling Rankin from time to time how to
prepare the report and what to put in it, and was adding here
and there an occasional malediction on the preachers.

On the evening of July 20, 1864, we reached O'Fallon's,
where there had been a ranch kept by Bob Williams.
O'Fallon's Bluffs was about 50 miles west of Cottonwood
Springs, and was another of the great crossing-places for
the Indians going north and south, and General Mitchell
afterwards ordered it to be fortified and guarded by a company of cavalry. At this point I made a discovery of a mistake, which I think I ought to record here. The evening
before I left Fort Kearney, a young man came to me and said
he wanted to have a little private talk. We went off to one
side, and he said he was in a train that was camped near
there that evening, and was going back to the States. He
said his father was a wealthy man, and had made him a
present on his birthday of a very fine gold watch which cost
$200; that as a pilgrim he had been out west, and had had
bad luck, and was now trying to get home. That he had run
out of money entirely, and had nothing left but his father's
present to get him back home to Indianapolis. He said he
hated to part with the watch very greatly; that it was en-
deared to him by many associations, but that he had to
have something to eat, and he had to get back home, and
that his health was not very good anyway, and he wanted
me to let him have money enough to get home, and I hold
the watch. I asked him how much he wanted, and he said
$50. He said that he had inquired about me, and found that
I was all right, and that he wanted the privilege of sending
me by express the money for the watch, and getting it back
again as soon as he could get home. That as I was in the army

he could always find me, while these other people were so light-footed that they were here today and somewhere else tomorrow. He told me that the watch was an elegant time-keeper, and he hoped that I would take good care of it until he sent for it. In the light of a solitary candle the watch was very beautiful and polished, and I handed the man $50, and he grasped my hand with emotion, and bade me an affectionate good-by. The latter part of the transaction was in the presence of two or three others, and while they did not know the facts, they knew that I had got the watch. I had not given the watch any examination until I got up the morning at Jack Morrow's, and it somehow or other had tarnished considerably since I got it, three or four days before, and I gave a good look at it, and saw that I had been fooled. I showed it to Lieutenant Rankin, and he said it was a "pinchbeck" watch. "Pinchbeck" was a compound mettle made to resemble gold, and in those days was the synonym for bogus gold. I saw in a moment that I had been badly fooled, and fearing that it might get out, and be a good joke on me, I called up the First Sergeant of my company and told him that I had had opportunity of buying a cheap watch for him which I desired to make him a present of, and I succeeded in escaping the ridicule which otherwise might have followed me for quite a while. I told nobody anything, but I afterwards heard of several similar circumstances. The watches were worth $48 a dozen, and this man or a body of men had scattered them along the road to ranches and pilgrims, from Denver to Omaha. It was in those days a new industry, and the right kind of man could make $1,000 a month at it in the Western country, until discovered.

On July 21, 1864, we went about twenty-five miles, and camped at an abandoned ranch which had belonged to a man named Jereux. Ben Gallagher remained at O'Fallon's Bluffs, but our scout "John Smith" went with us. On the march up the river we met several large caravans of wagons, all armed. None of them had less than one hundred armed men, together with a squad of cavalry and from three to half a dozen stages loaded with passengers.

All day long on both sides of the river we saw smoke signals. In the evening at Jereux ranch the wolves howled around us in great numbers. We generally got up early, went into camp early in the afternoon, and grazed our horses until sundown. The grazing of horses was very hazardous. We took our horses and hobbled them by the left fetlock with the halter-strap, tying their left hoof within eighteen inches of their heads, so that when the horse lifted up his head he pulled his foot up from the ground. They were hobbled in that manner successfully, and then the whole company was detailed out between them and the hills on foot, armed, remaining on guard until sundown, when the horses were brought in and tied half-and-half on each side of the picket-rope; then each of the horses was fed a quart of corn, and a guard was stationed out to prevent a run or a stampede.

During the howling of the wolves at night, every once in a while John Smith would say, "Do you hear that wolf?" pointing in a certain direction, and would say, "That isn't a wolf—that is a Cheyenne," and he told us that the Cheyennes by their wolf-calls had a method of signaling or communicating to those far back or in the distance, and communicating many things, such as the number of soldiers which they saw, and whether it was dangerous to attempt an attack or not, and so forth. He said he did not understand the signals, because they were agreed upon for the occasion only, and differed with the occasion.

We noticed while marching that the ground rose in sort of steps on the plateaus and that we were getting up to a higher altitude. These steps were many miles apart, and the surface was getting, if possible, more dry, arid and desolate than it had been.

The Salt Lake trail went by Fort Laramie. The old route crossed the South Platte a considerable distance east of Julesburg, and went over the dividing ridge to Ash Hollow, and down Ash Hollow to the North Platte. But the hills of Ash Hollow were very steep, and another road had been laid out.

On the south side of the South Platte, perhaps about

a mile east of the mouth of "Lodgepole Creek," a Frenchman by the name of Jules had started a trading-post. The place was a great Cheyenne crossing-ground going north and south, and a frequent place of Cheyenne rendezvous. It was also much used by the Sioux. The Cheyennes had a great liking for the country on the South Platte at the mouth of Lodgepole, and had had camps there for many years. Jules was said to be a half-breed French-and-Indian trader, and to have established this post for the purpose of trading with the Cheyenne Indians. It was said his name was Jules Beni, but everybody called him "Jules." He was a man of keen native shrewdness, an exceedingly dangerous man, with a peppery, fierce disposition. He had killed several persons, and had become a great deal of a character in the country. A man who had known him several years told me that Jules once killed two persons of local celebrity, cut off their ears, dried them, and carried these four ears in his pockets. That every once in a while he would take them out and show them to somebody. They were great trophies, as he thought. He kept supplies for the pilgrims, and at one time had a large stock. An old pioneer told me that one time Jules got half drunk, and brought out several sacks of flour which he was selling for a dollar a pound, made a mortar-bed out of it in front of his store, knocked in the head of a barrel of whisky which he was selling for $10 a quart, got a hoe, poured in the whisky, and got to making mortar in a manner as, he said, he had just seen a fellow doing down at Omaha, where he had been getting a stock of goods. This drunken freak represented the waste of several hundred dollars' worth of his stock. He got to be so bad and dangerous that Slade, the superintendent of the stage company, had to kill him.

At the time of which I write, nothing was left of the Jules ranch; it was gone, but the stage company had a large stable there, and a large boarding-house, a blacksmith shop, a telegraph station, a large sod corral, a wareroom built of cedar logs, and about eighty tons of shelled corn in sacks stored therein. There were quite a number of men there—blacksmiths, relays of telegraph operators, perhaps a dozen stage-drivers, and men who were taking care of horses. I would say there were fifty men there, all armed to the teeth, and with everything arranged so they could fight behind sod walls, and make a desperate resistance.

Ben Holladay claimed to be the owner and proprietor of all of this stage line and property, clear through to the Pacific Coast. He was a great celebrity. He was reputed to be very rich, and yet he had a reputation for great daring and a love for wild and dangerous life. His organization of this stage line across the continent in its then unsafe and lawless condition was a wonderful achievement. I saw him twice, passing on the road—once at Fort Kearney and once at Julesburg, and he impressed me as a man of restless and untiring vigor.

"Julesburg Station," as it was then called, was situated well down on the flats near where the course of the river then turned, and the main wagon-road ran alongside of the houses. There is a present town Julesburg, but it is on the other side of the river, and several miles farther down. The wood that was used was most of it cedar, hauled from Jack Morrow's canyon, and the balance of the building material was sod.

Near this place, which I will call Old Julesburg, the river-crossing started in a little east of the station, not very far down the river, and went around in a curve, coming out say a quarter or half a mile farther up the river. There was another crossing farther up the river, that crossed over west of the mouth of Lodgepole; the two trails went up Lodgepole Creek on opposite sides, until they joined several miles farther up. Those present at that time were in the habit of calling the lower one the "California crossing," and the west one the "Mormon crossing," because it appears that the Mormon trains crossed there and went quite a distance up the west side of Lodgepole.

The fact that General Mitchell was coming up the Platte to make an inspection, and organize military protection, and visit Fort Laramie, was noised around in advance, a great deal, and before we got to Julesburg wagons for the

Salt Lake route had congregated in great numbers at Jules-burg, and wanted to go up the road behind General Mitchell. As we approached near Julesburg, we came to a place where the river had at one time flowed close to the bank. There was a long stretch of dry sandy arroyo about eight feet below the sharp edge of the perpendicular bank. Along this bank ran the telegraph line.

Before we reached the place a heavy storm was lower-ing. The air swirled around, and a cool wave descended. All at once a terrific storm broke in upon us from the south-west. We could hear it coming with continual resounding peals of thunder. Crash was following crash so loud, heavily and quickly that, fearful the horses would become terri-fied and break away, General Mitchell ordered the horses all to be taken down on the sand under the bank. Finally the General's horse, and the mules from the ambulance, and all were taken down under the bank. The storm at first went over our heads without rain, and furnished us a grand electrical display. The noise finally ceased for a little while, and there came a calm, and the boys got up on the edge of the bank above the horses, sitting down and holding their horses below them in the arroyo by the bridle-rein. We all thought the matter was about over, and were congratulating ourselves that we had not been soaked with a rain. We watched the electric storm roll over on the North Platte hills, when all at once came a flash of lightning and shock of thunder that knocked almost the entire company over. Several were stunned, several fell over the bank, and the balance jumped down. The lightning had struck one of the telegraph poles not far from us, and splintered the poles or damaged them for a great distance on each side. It was such an astonishing peal that it was a little while before anybody spoke. As we saw the wire lying on the ground, and the neighboring poles shattered, General Mitchell ordered two of the soldiers to go each way, and see how many poles were affected by that blow of lightning. The men reported that, taking the poles that were shattered, or to some extent visibly damaged, there were thirty-three in number, which was nearly a half-mile on each side of us.

In a little while it began a drizzling rain, and after it had rained enough to wet us all through, we arrived, July 22, 1864, at Julesburg, and found nearly three miles of wagons there. They wanted to go through on the Salt Lake Trail. They were camped along the line of the river; the grass had been pretty well eaten out; everybody in the pilgrim trains was mad, and most of them quarreling. Having no organized head, they did not intend to go across the river until they knew that General Mitchell had crossed the river with his soldiers, and had started up. They wanted to feel safe. Major Woods of the Seventh Iowa Cavalry was with us; he was a most active, daring and capable man. I have spoken of him herein before.

The crossing of Platte River in those days with a train was a matter of very serious moment; but we had got used to the theory, and knew how to do it. It was to find a route that was the most firm, and then puddling it by marching one horse back of another until the quicksand became settled; then the road became firmer. The horses sometimes floundered greatly, but that served to settle the road. They were ridden across about ten feet apart.

So the first thing to be done on this occasion was to pick out a road for the crossing of the present train. The action of the water in the river was such that a good crossing to-day might be a poor one next week if untraveled, and so each crossing was a matter of its own. There was at this time plenty of water in the river at Julesburg.

On this occasion Major Woods started out with his horse to pick out a road across the river. He laid it out in a general way, so that he knew where he had been, and could see his own tracks. Then he came back, and the line of soldiers went over again right after him, and back, and made the road. In the mean time the wagons were ready, and the Major at the head of the wagon train, each wagon about one hundred feet behind the other, started across, with men of the train along the line standing in the water on both sides with whips to keep the horses stepping fast. If a horse should stop he would in course of time sink down in the quicksand, and the object was to have each wagon, one right behind the other, go as fast as the horses could pull it. The wagons started, and it was a roar of yelling from the time the first one went in, during all the afternoon, and well up into the night. The travelers had lanterns, and at night men with lanterns stood in the water on both sides of the track; and the Major kept bossing the job, hour after hour, riding backwards and forwards between the wagons, and once in a while changing his horse.

Along about midnight one of the mule teams got balky, and the mules turned out of the road, and in the effort to get them back the wagon was halted until the mules could be backed again into line, and the result was that the wagon began sinking. The mules were taken out, and succeeding wagons went around the wreck, which was soon down to the bed in the mud. There was no way to stop a wagon alongside of the wreck, and take off its cargo, and Major Woods with some assistance struggled in vain to keep the wagon from sinking faster on one side than the other. In the work, and heroic tugging, which Major Woods did, he strained himself so that he himself had to be taken out of the river and carried over to his tent. The wagon slowly sank until it disappeared from sight in the fathomless sand below. Some of the natives around managed to save and confiscate some few things of the load, such as the bows and cover, meat, the driver's bedding, etc., but the wagon and almost its entire cargo disappeared—went down where it was never recovered or could be found afterwards. In the morning the train was almost all across, with a reported loss of the wagon and two mules which were being led or driven, and which got where they could not be relieved, and sank out of sight. The lost wagon was reported to have been loaded with nails.

Major Woods was put into an ambulance, and I saw no more of him until after we got to Laramie some days afterwards.

When the train was all across, General Mitchell called

the drivers together, and the different separate wagon-bosses, and told them that they had got to keep together, stay together, help each other, and fight for each other; that otherwise they were liable to be disbanded, murdered and plundered. He picked out what he thought were the best three wagon-bosses in the lot, and told these people that they must select one of them to be the boss during the trip, and that he would see that the one selected did the right thing, and if not he would put him in the guard-house at Fort Laramie when they passed. This arrangement proved very satisfactory, as the train went on through, presumably in good order, for it never reported any trouble after that. At the mouth of Lodgepole was a great area of flat, grassy land. It was a beautiful place for camp.

CHAPTER XIX

COMING up from Cottonwood Springs I had a very good
chance to study the Pawnees. Up as far as Jack Morrow's
they kept huddled together, but after we passed that place
they began to spread around over the prairies. The Pawnees
were one of the capable tribes, and this battalion was the
pick of the whole. Major North was a brave, industrious
officer, and did his best to keep his Indians in some sort
of order and style, but it was almost like trying to command
a flock of blackbirds. At Fort Kearney there had been issued
to each of these Indians a hat, blouse, and pair of trousers.
All the balance they furnished themselves. They rode their
own horses, with Indian saddles and bridles. These saddles
were shaped like sawbucks, and on the forks were hung
their lariats and belongings. They did not care much for
hats, and by the time we reached Julesburg there were not
many hats left, and most of those were on the tops of their
ponies' heads, with holes cut in the top for the ponies' ears
to stick out through, and fastened to the bridle. In scouring
over the prairie they would race their horses, and if a hat
blew off the Indian paid no more attention to it than a bird
would in flight, shedding a feather. They were not used
to hats, and only those having some rank or authority
seemed to desire to hold onto them. In addition to this,
most of them from time to time took off their blouses
and tied them to their saddles, and above their trousers they
had on nothing but their naked, sunburned skin. The slang

expression for an Indian out there in those days was "abbri-goin." General Mitchell would watch them skirmishing around and would say, "What in [blankety-blank] do you think those abbri-goins are good for anyhow?" Before we got to Julesburg every Indian had cut the seat out of his cavalry pants, and they were in two sections, held up by an outside belt to the waist. Ever and anon squads of them would take off their two separate trouser-legs and tie them to the saddle, and then the Indian would ride along with nothing on but a breech-clout and moccasins, and he as a soldier was a sight to behold.

When we camped it was generally near the river, and Mr. Abbri-goin went in, not for the purpose of washing, or getting clean, but for the purpose of fun and cooling off. He generally came out as dirty as he went in. The Indian was kept as clean as he was accustomed to get, by abrasion. He wore off the surface dirt. It was attrition, not water, that kept him as clean as he got. The wild Indian if locked up in a room would soon kill himself with his own stench, were he not used to it. Horses could smell him half a mile to the windward, and civilized horses shied at him, sniffed and snorted at him, and tried to run away from him the same as from a buffalo or wild animal. The pioneers did not like the Indian, owing to the latter's unprintable manners and unspeakable habits. Our boys also would go into the river at the end of the day's trip, and although the Pawnees were as good in physique as any of the Indians and were picked men, they were not up to our men, who were not picked men. Our men were only the average Iowa farm boys, but in physical appearance they exceeded the Indian. They had heavier shoulders and thighs, and as they were around in the water with the Indians the superiority of the white soldier was manifest. Only one of the Indians was the superior of our company, and he was a very large young Indian about six and a half feet high; he was in fact the only really handsomely shaped Indian in the whole battalion. He resembled the "Big Mandan" of whom I have spoken, but he was an exception.

Besides all this, our men were the better horsemen, and as a class were better every way. The Indian as an individual was inferior, and as a race was inferior, to the Iowa farm boy, in whatever light it was desirable to consider it. There has been so much of fancy written about the Indian that the truth ought at times be told. The white man has done everything that an Indian can do, and I have seen things done during the Civil War that an Indian could not do, and dare not attempt to do. In physical strength, discipline and heroism the Indian does not compare and is not in the same class with the white man with whom the Indian came in contact. The Indian is not a soldier, and he cannot be made one. He has been tried and found wanting. He is spurty. He lacks the right kind of endurance, pertinacity, mind, and courage. We all got very much disgusted with Mr. Indian before we got through.

The Pawnee Indians are the favorite Indians of many writers of romance, and perhaps they deserve the celebrity. They had better tribal and village organization than most Indians. They held a wide extent of country, and along the Arkansas river on the south and along the Platte River on the north many places are pointed out as Pawnee battle-fields. One numerous band of them had a large village on a stream in northern Kansas. The village was called the "Pawnee Republic." It was visited by Major Zebulon Pike in October, 1806. This village gives to the river the name of the "Republican River," in Kansas; the county in Kansas is called "Republic County," and the modern city on its site is a flourishing county seat named "Republic." The Pawnees were taken, finally, and held, as in a vise, between civilization on one side and their bitter Indian foes on the other, and they had to fall as all other Indian nations before them had fallen. After the Smoky Hill route through Kansas to Denver was opened they never got south of it. They finally were crowded in by their foes, and were compelled to submit to being put onto a reservation. Thereupon the Sioux of the Ogallallah tribe, together with the southern Cheyennes, claimed to be the sole proprietors of the territory between the Platte and Arkansas rivers, and they objected to the Smoky Hill Route. This Route ran nearly between the two latter tribes, who had confederated, and with both tribes it was a demand that the Route should be abandoned. In both of General Mitchell's Indian councils it was demanded that it should be abandoned by the whites. The Smoky Hill Route did run through the best buffalo country, and its occupation was a vital menace to the Indians, although the whites did not fully appreciate the fact at the time. The Indians finally closed the Smoky Hill Route for a while by war and a concentration of hostilities, and afterwards the Government sent Lieutenant Fitch, a very capable officer, to reëxplore the route, improve its location and alignment, and make report. This was done. Lieutenant Fitch made his report and read it to me from his retained copy. I begged it from him, and still have it, and I make it a part of this narrative by attaching it as an appendix hereto.

On the morning of July 23, 1864, we left our camp at the mouth of Lodgepole Creek and started up the valley. It was one of the most beautiful mornings that ever was seen in what was then an empty and inhospitable country. The air was so pure and unvitiated that it was a delight to breathe it. It was a blessing to be alive, and be able to start with the cavalcade up Pole Creek valley. Our order of march was about as usual, except that Captain O'Brien rode ahead with the General and I stayed back with the company. We were never out of sight of thousands of antelope which played in vast droves as far as we could see. They were bounding about, and were enjoying the air and sun the same as we. Far off in the distances was an occasional wolf, lonesome and inquisitive, sitting on his haunches watching us closely. He might have been an Indian. Our Pawnee allies were acting like monkeys; they scattered out all over the country, bouncing on and off their horses, now in groups, now deployed out, as if in flight from some unseen foe behind them. They appeared to be examining tracks and trails, then appeared to be racing their horses, then they would all yell and run together in a bunch. Sometimes they would all be scattered out in front of us for a half-mile on each side, then they would all begin shouting and break and rally to our rear as if the devil was after them. We pushed on up the valley at a rate of about four miles an hour. The valley was quite wide—in places miles; it then rose up the slopes to the edge of the plateau, which at the top on both sides of us was as level as a floor, but which at places along the dry stream was broken into ragged and projecting bluffs. All the way up, far in the distance from these bluffs, smoke signals were seen, but we never saw a hostile Indian. This was what made our Indian allies act so; they were in the presence of the enemy. In vain did General Mitchell order Major North to keep his men in close column in the rear, and in vain did Major North try to execute the order; the Indians were nervous and ungovernable. They knew that there were Indians somewhere, not so very far off, and so did we, but they were frenzied over it. We did not care much how many there were, so that we could see them. We could have taken a position on the side of the Pole Creek arroyo and stood off a thousand Indians. We had an advance guard ride along the arroyo so that we would not be surprised. I constantly searched the horizon with my field-glass, but could not see a single Indian, although the smoke signals kept going up in front of us all day. Our Pawnees rode mostly as a lot of savages, which in fact they were, having on but little. The best dressed had on a breech-clout, moccasins, and two cavalry trouser-legs separately swung up with a whang to a rawhide belt, but the majority were only one-third as well dressed, and their sunburned skins were well greased and polished. All of them had Government carbines, all had butcher-knives; some had lances in addition, and some had bows and arrows. We had got tired of the antics of our allies before we reached Julesburg, but by the end of this day of July 23rd, after a march of from 35 to 40 miles we got positively weary.

We camped on the banks of Lodgepole, several miles above what appeared far off on our right to be the ruins of an old adobe hut. There was no visible water in the bed of the creek where we camped, but we found plenty of water by digging, and we were able to cook with the bunches of drift roots that the stream in its high career had dug up and floated down. We would find at places a wagon-load together of such fuel, dried and ready for use. We grazed our horses before night and put out our guards; we took our spades and dug rifle-pits for each guard. We put the Indians on the other side of the arroyo and told them to look out for themselves. We strung an inch-and-a-quarter picket-rope between our two company wagons near the bank of the arroyo, and tied our horses to the rope, one-half on each side. As night closed in and the smell of fried bacon and pancakes spread out upon the local atmosphere, the lamentations of what appeared to be a million wolves arose. Our stable guard said that the Pawnees did not appear to sleep much that night.

On the morning of July 24th we started over the ridge to the north. It was a long, tedious climb up to the top of the plateau, but the scene behind us was beautiful. We could see up and down the valley of the Lodgepole for many miles, until the rotundity of the earth hid the view. There was not a tree or a bush in sight. The valley was as smooth and polished as if it had been sand-papered and varnished. There was not a riding-switch that could be cut between us and Julesburg. It was simply an undulating expanse of short, struggling grass. Before we started out in the morning we gave our horses all the water they would drink, for it was said to be fully thirty-two miles across the ridge from water to water. This was the short line which Jules had laid out, so as to change the route and bring the pilgrim travel past his ranch. This particular strip of road was called "Jules Stretch." The road became considerably rocky as we ascended.

Late in the afternoon we reached the other side, at Mud Springs, eight miles east of Court House Rock. At these springs was the first water we got after coming over the Stretch. Up on the high land in the middle of the

Stretch, at what might be called the summit, the stage company, years before, thinking to adopt it as a line of road, had attempted to dig a well. Great quantities of dirt and rock were piled out, but the story went that they never could find a drop of water, and that they went down three hundred feet. I cannot say how deep it was, but it was a very deep well, for I crawled up to the edge of it, and dropped rocks down, and heard no splash, and knew by the time of descent that the well was a very deep one. In fact, I threw down several, and they went bounding down from side to side. I peered over the edge, because, owing to extreme heat and dryness of the atmosphere, the boys were very thirsty, and I wanted to get some water out of it, if by tying lariat-ropes together we could get it. But the well seemed to be dry all the way down.

Along the ridge we saw where several wagons had been burned, and knew by this that there had been Indian troubles along the line at some time. We also counted forty-seven dead oxen at various places along the road, all dried and torn. Many had probably perished from thirst, but two or three had old, broken arrows in them. Horse skeletons were also frequent, and there were old buffalo heads and horns scattered along the ridge, but we never saw buffalo between Cottonwood Springs and Fort Laramie. We were told that they were seldom seen between the forks of the Platte in July.

We went on past Mud Springs, after giving our horses plenty of water and a good rest, and camped on a little river east of Court House Rock. This river was composed of two streams, one called Punkin Creek and the other Lawrence Fork, but after the junction it was then called Lawrence Fork, and so on down to the North Platte.

We saw no Indian signals until we were descending from the summit of the Stretch. When we began to see hills and broken land far off in the distance, and began to approach to the Platte River bluffs again, the signals reappeared. I could see at great distances, with my glass, puffs of smoke, almost instantaneous but quite visible. The Pawnees also saw them and began again to act, as one of my sergeants put it, "like all-possessed." When we got to Mud Springs, after they had watered their ponies, the Pawnees spread out all over the country, following trails and tracks, or pretending to. They dashed around and yelled and charged back to camp, and charged out again; they were a sight to behold. Our guide, John Smith, said they were just showing off, and were trying to create the impression that they were warlike. It was much ado about nothing. General Mitchell had tried to stop it. They were wholly uncontrollable. We did not believe they would fight, and did not want to be bothered with them. Captain O'Brien and I expressed our views to the General and found that he agreed with us. He said, "The [blankety-blank] Abbri-goins, we will send them back." We all liked Major North, and felt what a disappointment it would be to him. But the General in the evening called the Major up and thanked him for his zealous services and had him call his Pawnees and get them in line. Then the General made a few remarks to them about their soldierly appearance and warlike spirit; and how pleased he was with their valorous services; and how he had taken them as far as was necessary; and that from now on it was safe for him and his escort; and that they could now go back to Fort Kearney and be mustered out and get their pay. The next morning, with long-continued yells and shrieks and "monkey business," as O'Brien called it, the Pawnees left us and were soon out of sight, much to our satisfaction. The Government has many a time tried to utilize the noble red man for a soldier but has always failed, just as we tried and failed; he is no good for anything.

These Pawnees went back and were reorganized at Fort Kearney during August, as scouts on the road. A new set of officers tried to do something with them, but finally had to give it up. The new Pawnee Company thus organized was 77 in number, and was under a Captain Joseph Mc-Fadden, with Frank J. North, of whom I have spoken, as Lieutenant. They served about forty days, until October 2, 1864, and were again and finally mustered out. I have in my possession a muster-roll of the Pawnee company, and as an exhibit hereto I insert on the following page a list of their Indian names, copied verbatim from the roll.

Major North afterwards made a great reputation as a partner of Buffalo Bill in the Wild West show.

As stated, we camped near Court House Rock. It was a very wonderful formation, very attractive and very beautiful. Captain O'Brien and I determined that we would go to the top of it, but gave it up for that particular evening because it seemed as if it might be too dangerous at that time of the day, but we agreed to get up early in the morning and climb the rock.

Names of the "Pawnee Scouts," 1864; Under Command of Major Frank J. North.

She-te-le-lah-we-tit.
Tuck-ta-shah-ki-rick.
Lah-roo-suck-hoo-la-shar.
La-re-roo-tah-ka-chicks-ooke.
She-te-le-lah-wis-sha-rit.
Lah-roo-rit-kah-hah-la-shar.
Ah-shah-wuck-ke.
Te-ah-kah-chicks-tus-peke.
Kah-kah-roo-re.
Too-ke-tah-we-he-ris-ah.
Tah-sah-hah-tah-he-ris-ah.
Koot-tah-we-koots-oo-te-lah-lah.
Te-lah-kah-ooh-ke.
Suck-koo-roo-te-wa-re.
Te-suck-koo-loo-le-wits.
See-te-kah-ricks-tah-hoo-re.
Kah-roo-re-ah-ris.
Tuck-ke-leh-re-wah-tucks.
We-tit-te-la-shah-ris-pe.
Kee-wuck-oo-te-lah-we.
Too-lah-we-oo-roo.
Ke-wuck-oo-roo-re.
Ke-wuck-oo-la-shar.
Koot-tah-we-coots-oo-kah-lah.
Koot-tah-we-coots-oo-rooh-kah.
Roo-kit-tah-we-its-pah.
Koot-tah-we-coots-oo-let-kah-hah.
Lah-li-e-coots-ta-shah.
La-kit-tah-we-la-shah.
Te-lah-kah-we-rick.
Lah-he-ris-oo-rick.
La-shah-too-rou-tah-we.

La-shah-roo-te-wah-re.
La-shah-roo-pit-coo.
Tah-we-li-he-ris-shah.
Te-reh-re-kucks-shah.
To-rah-re-chi-e-tus.
Teck-ta-re-roo-hut.
Koot-tah-we-coots-oo-la-shar.
Kah-kah-lah-la-shar.
Tah-hoo-rah-routs.
Ke-wuck-oo-lah-li-e-coots.
Lah-we-teh-re-oots.
She-rer-re-hoo-le-tah-we.
Koot-tah-we-coots-oo-te-rer-reh.
Koot-tah-we-coots-oo-te-lah-we-la.
Pe-tah-war-ucks-tee.
Lah-hock-tah-we-la-shar.
La-shah-kip-pe-re.
Te-er-re-ta-cosh.
Le-re-ru-tah-kah.
Lah-we-li-ish.
Te-ah-ke-la-rick.
La-shah-roo-roo-te-lah-kah-ta-rick.
Lah-li-e-coots-ta-shah.
Lah-roo-wuck.
Te-ah-ke-wah-hoo-re-rick.
Co-rooks-te-cha-rick.
Ta-ker-re-rah-we-hoot.
Ta-lah-wih-kah-wah.
La-tock-kots-lock.
Cha-kah.
Roo-rah-rooh-kah-we.
Te-kah-ricks-tah-kah-lah-ta.

Tel-re-kit-tah-wa.

Tah-weet-too-re-kah.

Te-hus-tah-we-re-kah-wah.

Ah-roosh-ah-lah-kah-hoo-la-shar.

Lah-roots-chah-koo-re-hoo.

Kiel-e-kah-ris-oo-too-rouh-tah-we.

Ta-sah-hah-kah-roit.

La-tah-kots-too-ri-ha.

Koot-tah-we-coots-oo-rah-lah-ha.

Roo-lal-re-roo-che-lah.

Koot-tah-we-coots.

Lah-li-e-coots-kit-e-buts.

Kah-wa-hoo-roo.

CHAPTER XX

ON JULY 25, 1864, the Captain and I got up early, and with a couple of lariat-ropes started out to ascend Court House Rock. We both succeeded in getting on top of the precipice. It had a covering of stone, not very hard, on which there were several names carved; we took a few minutes to add our names to the number. It was a good deal of a task to get to the top and one equally difficult and dangerous to get down. We rejoined our column, which had started on its march, and we camped in the afternoon at a deserted old place where it looked as if nobody had lived for a generation. It was called "Ficklin's," and was situated on the river sixty-seven miles east of Fort Laramie. It was named before the war, from one of the officers of the Overland Stage Company. We had marched that day about forty miles from Mud Springs. From Mud Springs the weather had been cloudy and misty, and we did not get a chance to see the beauties of the route; this was so for several days, but on our return we had delightful weather, and I will wait until then to describe what we really saw.

On July 26, 1864, we left Ficklin's and went up the North Platte River. We kept on the south side, and camped at what was called the "Agency." The weather was hot and dusty; the clouds seemed to fill the valley, which was entirely unusual. The guides said they had never seen anything like it before, and I must add that I myself never did afterwards. Antelopes appeared without number, and the hills where seen seemed to be alive with deer.

There was water in the river all along the line. We passed Scott's Bluff, fifty-eight miles east of Fort Laramie. We also passed Alcohol Butte and the celebrated Chimney Rock. The Agency where we camped was called the Woc-co-pom'-any agency. It was the place where the Sioux Indians of the north came down to get their annuity goods. There was a large, long, one-story rambling stone house on the place, but there was not a soul there. In fact, there was nobody then living along the river at that time, from the Forks of the Platte River down at Jack Morrow's up nearly to Fort Laramie, over 250 miles, except near the Fort, at Julesburg.

The next day, July 27, 1864, we camped north of Fort Laramie, and I went down to the Fort. Major Wood of our regiment was placed in command of the post by General Mitchell, and I was detailed as post adjutant. There were three companies of the Eleventh Ohio Cavalry then at the Fort; at least, the Fort was the headquarters of three companies, but they were out scouting and guarding trains, all in command of Major Underhill of that regiment. The Captains were named Shuman, Koehne, and Marshall; and there were eight Lieutenants. Five miles down the river from Fort Laramie was the ranch of a Frenchman by the name of Beauvais, and five miles still farther down was the ranch of Bordeaux. These two Frenchmen had Indian wives and children, and Indian herders, drivers, etc., etc., making quite a retinue, and they did all they could to keep the Indians from being hostile, and breaking out in war. These two traders were rich. They had made a great deal of money, had very large stocks of goods, and were reported to own considerable property; but, trade was at a standstill, there being no emigration. A very interesting acquaintance opened while I was at the Fort, under the following circumstances:

The ranchman, Bordeaux, had sent up word that there was a large band of Indians back in the hills; that he was afraid they might make a break on him; and he thought if the Government would send a few soldiers down for a demonstration, that the Indians would go away. The post commander, Major Wood, told me about four o'clock in the afternoon to take ten men and go down there and see what there was to it; stay all night, and come back in the morning. I got down to Bordeaux' before sundown, and he seemed very glad to see me, and he gave my soldiers a camping-place in his "pilgrim quarters," and we put our horses in the corral. I put the Sergeant in charge, and told him to keep a good lookout. The soldiers had their own rations, but Bordeaux insisted on being my host. After supper with him we went into his store. It was a large, rambling log building, with sod end to it, and additions and outbuildings attached to it, so that it was a sort of wandering, straggling cara-vansary and store combined. He got to showing me what he had, and then he went into the front of the store-building, where he had some cigars. The doors were all bolted and barred. He got to telling me about his visit to France. The floor in this part of the building was made out of pine logs brought down to a grade with an adz. It happened that I could read his French language, and I expressed myself very much interested, and he told me all about his recent trip to "La Belle France"; and he had a new variety of bitters known as Red Jacket Bitters, of which he was par-taking freely. We talked about Indians and Indian mat-ters and Indian habits and Indian customs, and he said that the Indians that had been back of his house had gone off. But I was very much interested in his description of Indian manners and his adventures among them, until it got to be along about one o'clock in the morning. And Mr. Bordeaux again got off onto the subject of his visit to "La Belle France," and he seemed to be very much pleased with the bitters he had and the attention with which I listened to his story. He was a much older man than I, and I was, in-deed, very much delighted to hear him talk. All at once he disappeared through the floor, by turning up a plank or puncheon, and the first thing I knew he came back from down below somewhere with two large, musty quart bottles of champagne, and sticking one down in front of me said, "We will drink to La Belle France." I was as much surprised as if the man had dug up a statue of Daniel Webster. The idea of a quart bottle of champagne in that dry, arid, heathen country almost paralyzed me, but I finally said to him that a quart bottle was more than my size, and that I would drink half of one of the bottles with him. I suggested that we split, and each drink half of the same bottle. Thereupon he got two tin cups, and with a hatchet knocked off the head. There in the stillness of night in that country we drank to the health of "La Belle France." I have never seen Mr. Bordeaux since then, but have retained a delicious memory of him and the occasion. In the morning we were up early, and at eight o'clock were back at Fort Laramie.

My duties as Post Adjutant were very light. I had to superintend guard-mount at nine o'clock in the morning, and act in dress parade every evening at six. The old regular army traditions of the post had been kept up, and everything was done exactly as it had been done before the war. Every little matter of detail had been handed down, and was perpetuated with nicety and zest. The post sutler was a man by the name of Ward. His manager was named Bullock, the most courteous old-school gentleman I ever saw. He was as dignified as a Major-General. Ward gave no personal attention to the sutler store, but he was making a great deal of money out of it. He had an enormous stock of goods, and as he had no competitors and as his prices were fixed by the post administration, he got the price, and sold enormous quantities. Bullock told stories of all the generals of the war. One afternoon he took about an hour and a half in explaining to me, and instructing me in making, a whisky toddy. It was with him a work of art. I never could see anything about his toddies that was anything more than normal, but somehow he had a reputation that none might hope to equal. In addition to this he had a mint-bed in a secluded place which was carefully watered every day, and more attention given to it than almost anything else around the post.

Off on one side in a low piece of land in a sheltered place, where the refuse of the cavalry stables had been hauled for years, a garden had been organized, and from a little irrigation-ditch water could be drawn with buckets, and the vegetables watered. The place, which I would say was a hundred feet wide and maybe three hundred feet long, had some vegetation on it.

Up above the fort about a mile among the bushes was what was called the "Squaw Camp." It was a place where Indians during peaceful times could come, and pitch their tents, and trade. There were always a number of squaws there in their tents, and a lot of half-white Indian papooses running around. Once in a while an Indian would come in with some beaver-skins and furs, and trade, and go out again; and old pioneers and trappers had their Indian wives there. And all together it was a jolly, careless, laughing, shouting lot of Indians, of whom nobody seemed to have much knowledge. It was said hostile Indians would occasionally run in, and secrete themselves there, and get all the knowledge they could as spies, and go back again.

While we were there a flight of grasshoppers came, such as in after years on several occasions devastated the vegetation of the Western States. During August the air became filled with these insects, and they took the little garden of which I spoke and ate it up almost instantly. One of the officers of the Eleventh Ohio came to me to go out with him and take a look at that garden. The grasshoppers were bunched together in swarms like bees. I remember seeing upon a handle of a spade a bunch of interwoven grasshoppers as big as a man's hat. The Indian women at the squaw camp were catching these grasshoppers, roasting them, drying them, and pounding them up into meal to make bread of during the winter. The Indians seemed to be anxious to utilize all the grasshoppers they could catch, and they made up a great many hundred pounds of them. There was also a berry which grew on the bushes along the broken lands which was called the "buffalo-berry," not unlike a cherry; these the Indian women usually gathered, and put into parfleches. These berries had a sort of tart flavor something like a cranberry. The Indian women gathered these berries and put them away for winter by the thousand pounds, and it was said that the berries were taken out as good as when they were put in. They did not become dry. I was told that they also mixed with them in the parfleches the fat from deer, antelope and buffalo, and ate the combined fat and berries during the winter. A parfleche was a half-tanned hide of some animal, with the hair all taken off and the inside scoured or scraped down smooth.

There was also at the Post, all the time I was there, Major Bridger, the celebrated scout and guide; also a hunter, trapper and guide named Jules Coffey. At least, that is the way they pronounced his name, although I imagine it might have been the French name of Ecoffe, because I heard one of them pronounce it Acoffay. He seemed to be very prosperous, and to have a great deal of money, and he loved to play poker wonderfully. He had, as all of those who fall into Indian life have, strange and intense superstitions. One of his superstitions was that "jacks" in playing cards was his good luck, and he always bet his hand for more than it was worth when he had jacks in it. It was a matter of much ridicule among those at the post, where there were poker games going from morning to night. There was also a celebrated pioneer and guide by the name of Charles Elston. Elston said that he was a Virginian, but he had been out forty years then among the Sioux. He knew the Sioux language, and the Sioux country, and Indian manners and customs by heart. He knew them with even more intelligence than an Indian knew them. As a white man is smarter than an Indian in civilization, so he is smarter than an Indian when it comes to competing in Indian matters and things. Elston was a most charming man. It was said that he had two Indian wives among the Sioux, and one among the Cheyennes, but he was a sort of high-toned fellow, and his wives were never seen at the squaw camp near the fort. He seemed to like pioneering and the frontier, and told many stories of his adventures. On one occasion he told a strange story of trying to take a load of furs down the

Platte river in a bull-boat, that is, in a boat made of bull-hide, with wooden ribs. He lost everything he had, and barely escaped with his life, while trying to navigate a Platte river freshet.

Another of these guides and pioneers was Leo Palladie. He was a pure Frenchman, but of the blue-eyed type. He had curly hair, and the happiest disposition of any frontiersman. He was a reader of books and newspapers, and yet he was a thoroughgoing mountaineer. He spoke all the Indian languages in the neighborhood, was an adept at their sign language, was always good-natured, telling stories and having fun. He was sunny-hearted from morning until night. He told me a funny event about when the post commander up at Fort Benton, on the Missouri river, heard that the Indians were plotting to destroy the frontier and had mapped out among other things, a campaign against Fort Laramie. That was perhaps about 1861 or 1862. The post commander of Fort Benton determined to send a messenger across the country during the winter for the purpose of notifying the commanding officers at Fort Laramie, because he thought the latter post could not stand in the dead of winter a heavy siege from the combined Indian nations. The mountaineer who was selected to go wanted a companion; a half-breed Indian was sent with him. This white courier was sent off with a letter which started out by saying: "I send you Mr. So-and-so, accompanied by a half-breed, So-and-so, to convey you the following important information." The letter was presented to Fort Laramie by the courier to the post commander, and he, after reading the opening portion of it, said, "Where is your comrade?" and the courier said, "I eat him." They had floundered through the snow and the mountains, and the mountaineer had to eat the other man in order to carry the message through in safety. Leo Palladie would tell this story, and laugh and shriek every time he told it. It always seemed new and interesting to him. I never could find anybody who ever heard the name of the messenger that was sent, and I often used to think Palladie was telling the story of one of his own personal experiences.

Of all these guides, Bridger was the most interesting. We left Fort Laramie on the 31st of August, and it is probably better to speak of Bridger once for all as of the time that we were there. Every night he was out in front of the sutler store sitting on the benches, and telling stories of his adventures. He was quite talkative, readily responded to questions, and would talk as long as he was talked with. I heard a funny story about Bridger soon after I arrived in camp. The largest building in camp was called Bedlam. It was the two-story large hospital building fronting on the parade-ground, and the upper part of it was used for theatricals at times. There were always some soldiers who were good at private theatricals, and occasionally there was one who had been an actor. So, during the long and tiresome winter evenings there were theatrical entertainments frequently. They were generally of some light, witty, flashy kind, with an occasional heavy piece from Shakespeare. Bridger had seen a couple of Shakespeare's pieces well played at the post, and concluded he would like to have somebody read Shakespeare to him. So, he had the sutler, Mr. Ward, send and get him a copy of Shakespeare, and Bridger got a man, a soldier, to start reading it to him. One evening while sitting in front of the adobe fireplace reading Shakespeare the soldier got to reading in the play where the eyes of the two boy princes were put out. After it had been read Bridger says, "Did he do that?" and when the reader said, "Yes," Bridger pulled the book from him and said, "By thunder, that is what I think of *him*," and threw the book into the fire, blazing in the fireplace, and that was all of Shakespeare he ever wanted to hear.

Bridger was a celebrity. Some time after my stay at Fort Laramie I met down on the Platte a man named Morgan, on the preliminary survey of the Union Pacific. He had run a trial line up past Laramie, but Bridger told him that the Cheyenne Pass at the head of Lodgepole was a lower pass than Morgan would find. Morgan said that he then went and ran that trial line, and found that it was, indeed, much lower than any other. But how it was that Bridger, traveling over it without a barometer, could know the fact was something which was very puzzling; but it was part of Bridger's wonderful powers of observation. Traveling through the country, over scopes of great distances, he instinctively fixed the grades and elevation as well as other points of the landscape, and that which he had once seen he forever remembered. It was to this wonderful gift that his great reputation was to be attributed. He knew exactly what would be found, and what was the lay of the country, the distances, the peculiarities; all these came within the scope of his observation. For instance, he would start and tell of an unmapped country over which he had been, and he would describe it mile by mile,—trees, rocks, grades, streams, everything. It seemed as if he made a moving panorama of the route as he rode through the country. In addition to this, he knew everything that an Indian knew. He could do anything that an Indian could do. He knew how Indians felt, and what to expect from them. And he apparently could do anything that a white man could do while in the country. One of the difficulties with him was that he would occasionally tell some wonderful story to a pilgrim, and would try to interest a new-comer with a lot of statements which were ludicrous, sometimes greatly exaggerated, and sometimes imaginary. For instance, one evening he told me that Court House Rock had grown up from a stone which he threw at a jackrabbit. This he did not give in response to a question, but he was on a philosophic and scientific strain of thought, and was saying that rocks grew the same as trees and animals grow, only they grew larger and for a longer time. He used to state that the mountains were considerably larger and higher than when he first came, and it was on one of his philosophical discourses that he told me with the utmost gravity the above story of the origin of Court House Rock. Laramie Peak was visible, although it was a considerable distance from the post. Bridger said that the peak showed up lots larger and plainer than it used to. In those days there was a vast amount of country that was unexplored, and Yellowstone Lake was not on the map nor was it known by white men to exist, and there were great scopes of country through which a white man had never yet gone. I often sat out with him on the bench to talk with him, and I became a good deal of a favorite with him. One time while talking with him I asked him about the country north of the California route which went west to South Pass. He said he had been hunting and trapping through it, and had seen a great deal of it; that he made a trip up through there once, dodging the Indians, and traveling principally at night, and he found a very rocky and romantic country. He told me that there was a large lake up there which he had seen that was so big he couldn't see across it in places, and that it was fresh water. He had told this story to others, but nobody believed him. He was somewhat indefinite as to its location, because he had taken a roundabout road, and was going through the country all alone, sort of scouting it, and dodging the Indians.

No doubt but that he had seen Yellowstone Lake, but nobody believed it. I can recite accurately only one of his stories, because I took time to put it down, as follows. He said: "That is the greatest country that I ever see. I was up there riding around, and I didn't dare to fire a gun only at long intervals, and then I got right out of the country where I fired it as soon as possible. I would bring down a deer, and cut it up and carry it, and move out. One time I was up among some pines, sort of hid in the side-hill along the stream that had a pretty wide valley, and I saw a couple of Injuns coming along down through the grass on their ponies on the other side of the creek. I wanted to watch and wait until they got out of sight, so I kept my eye on them for a long while. I saw them coming for nearly an hour, and they took their time at it, and I was afraid they would cross over, and might run onto some of my tracks. But they didn't, and they went down the valley on the opposite side from where I was. They hadn't gone very far before the crust of the earth gave way under them, and they and their ponies went down out of sight, and up came a great powerful lot of flame and smoke. I bet hell was not very far from that place." This story I never could account for, unless he had seen some Indians drop through the ground in some part of the hot-spring or geyser country.

One time I asked him what kind of a country it was west of the place where he saw the big lake, and he told me it was a very rocky country. Then he said: "Up there is one of the strangest mountains that I ever did see. It is a diamond mountain, shaped something like a cone. I saw it in the sun for two days before I got to it, and then at night I camped right near it. I hadn't more than got my horse lariated out—it was a little dusky—when I saw a camp-fire and some Injuns right through the mountain on the other side. So I didn't build any fire, but I could see them just as plain as if there hadn't been anything but air. In the morning I noticed the Injuns were gone, and I thought I would like to see the other side of the mountain. So, I rode around to the other side and it took me half a day." I said to him, "Might not that have been a mountain of salt?" I put this query to him because the country was entirely unknown, and I wanted to cross-examine him, but he said: "Oh, no. I went up and knocked off a corner of it, a piece of rock as big as my arm, a big, long piece of diamond, and brought it out, and afterwards gave it to a man, and he said it was a diamond all right." These were samples of Bridger's stories. He wasn't the egotistic liar that we so often find. He never in my presence vaunted himself about his own personal actions. He never told about how brave he was, nor how many Indians he had killed. His stories always had reference to some outdoor matter or circumstance. He never went on any scouts while we were there, but simply contented himself with telling the officers of the expeditions, or the scout who was going with them, just exactly where to go and what they would find.

CHAPTER XXI

ONE day a large detachment from the post had been
out scouting through the hills, and around, for three days.
They had been in separate details in different directions,
but were all to be back at noon of a certain day. Their
object was to find out whether there were any hostile Indians lurking anywhere around within twenty-five miles
of the post. They all reported on their return, that nothing could be found; they had seen a few pony-tracks,
they said, but probably from stray ponies; the scouting
parties were disbanded upon the parade-ground about noon.
The parade-ground was level and sandy, and the officers
thought it would be the best place for the horses to roll.
So the boys were ordered to take off the saddles and bridles,
and take these to the stables, but to leave the horses standing in the sun, and let them roll and rest awhile; then they
could be taken to the stables. The horses on being unsaddled began to romp around on the parade-ground, and
roll in the sand. Their backs were all more or less chafed
with the saddle, and it was a pleasure for them to roll.
They were on the parade-ground enjoying themselves rolling and cavorting, when all at once we heard a wild war-
whoop, and through post and parade-ground rushed a
body of wild Indians waving buffalo-robes, shooting firearms, and making a lot of noise. There could not have
been to exceed thirty of them. They came so quickly
and went through so fast, that there was hardly a shot

fired at them, and they stampeded every horse on the parade-ground, and off they went with them. I got a look at them, and I thought that this raid was one of the most ridiculous things I ever saw. The Indians did not stop to shoot anybody, although they did fire some arrows at some of the groups of soldiers and officers that were on the side. But there was plenty of open way for them to go, and the horses went in front of them, and they after them. They made a dash for the north, and before anybody knew what was taking place the horses and the Indians were scurrying afar off. But the Indians did not get all of our horses. "Boots and saddles" was immediately sounded, and those who got ready first started off first. It took time, however, to get out of the stables and saddle the remaining horses; get the ammunition, get together rations for the trip, and some corn for our horses to be carried, some on each, and some on pack-mules. About a hundred of us got started after these Indians, but we were at least an hour behind. It was useless to go out without corn, without rations, and without ability to stay with them. Major Wood, the post commander, was the maddest man I ever saw. He started out the command; it was in charge of one of the Eleventh Ohio captains; but my Captain O'Brien was one of the leaders of the expedition. We didn't know what we were bound to run into, and although we started with a mountain howitzer we soon sent it back because it couldn't keep up with the procession.

The Indians held together, and kept going steadily north. We chased them all night, but they had plenty of relays of horses, and each Injun could catch up a fresh horse from time to time. Although we went at as fast pace as our animals could endure, we did not seem to overtake them. We rode until morning, but during the night we could only follow a trail. We could not see the Indians. The next day we still kept after them, as the trail was plain. The next night the Indians scattered, and went every-which-way. The trail pronged out so that we could only follow part of the Indians. We had to keep together, as

we feared ambuscade, and didn't know but a large body
of Indians might at any time appear. We followed the
trail all night again. In the morning as the sun rose we
came down into one of the most beautiful valleys I ever
saw. We rode down through it in the rising sun. We
had been floundering among the mountains all night. We
had been doing our best to see what we could find. About
a dozen of the captured horses were recovered, having been
found along the trail, but they were all bunged up, and not
worth bothering with. Some had been killed with arrows;
others had just simply been abandoned because they were
worn out, and ruined. Our own horses were about at the
end of their usefulness. The beautiful valley lay in front
of us, made charming by the rising sun. No Indian was
in sight. There was only a light trail where perhaps a
half-dozen had passed. It was useless, and practically
impossible, for us to go farther. We camped and grazed
our horses in the beautiful valley, each man holding on to
his horse's halter lest some Indian should rise up out of
the grass and stampede the herd. We were so tired and
sleepy that we could hardly graze our horses. We had been
up two days and two nights, and the last night had been
very hard on us. We rested and let our horses graze until
about noon. They got a good feed of grass; they had eaten
up every grain of corn we had. Slowly and sorrowfully
we wended our way back by another route.

Our guide and scout had been Charles Elston. He
seemed to know the country fairly well, but we were out
of the usual Indian routes, and were in a country just
as it had come from the primeval hand of nature. There
was always something beautiful in the Rocky Mountain
country when we got into those places where no ax had
ever been. We had ridden about one hundred miles. Going
back, the boys went slowly, slept on their horses some of
the time, and walked and led their horses some of the time,
so as to lighten their load and diminish their pain, for
they were all suffering from the trip. In addition, we sort
of explored the country, and made rough sketches or maps

as we went. When we got back it was nearly a week from the time we started. All of the horses which the Indians drove off that were of any value, were lost, and the episode was freely commented on as showing how difficult it was to know whether or not there were any Indians around the post. It put the post upon the guard to keep a steady lookout, night and day, and was an additional illustration of the fact that it was cheaper to feed the Indians than to fight them.

Major Underhill had said to General Mitchell, who was telling about how the Pawnee scouts acted on our trip up Lodgepole: "They were afraid because they knew the danger they were in,—you did not; there were enough hostile Indians always around you, though not in sight, to have eaten you all up blood-raw." At this time while we were in Fort Laramie, immigration had entirely stopped. No stages had been running up past Laramie for months; and no trains were passing. The road from Julesburg to Laramie had practically been sealed up. There was a telegraph line which was kept running, from repairs constantly made by details of soldiers.

A very strange thing happened one evening at the sutler quarters. Along about sundown several squaws very finely dressed in mackinaw blankets came up to the sutler store with an old gentleman whose hair, long, white and curly, hung down over his shoulders, and down his back. He had a very venerable white beard and moustache. His beard had been trimmed with scissors so that it was rather long, but pointed, Van Dyke fashion, below the chin. He was dressed thoroughly as an Indian. He wore nothing on his head, and had on a pair of beaded moccasins. He sat on one of the benches in front of the sutler store, having in his hand a cane, staff fashion, about six feet long. Some of the officers were discussing Grant's Vicksburg campaign, and about the dangerous character of his trip around and below Vicksburg, and they were analyzing it as a military feat. After listening a little while this old fellow got up, and got out several feet in front of the talkers, and said: "Grant did just what Napoleon did." Then, taking his staff, he began marking in the sand, and said, "At Borodino, Napoleon started out from here, and he marched around to here," and so on. The old gentleman went all through the Napoleonic campaign and then went through the Grant campaign, with all of us looking on silently and listening. He finished the demonstration at great length, talked very sensibly, and everybody, whether they knew him or not, paid attention to what he said. After a while the party broke up, and I asked several present who the person was; they said they didn't know. Finally I met a man who told me that this man belonged to a very fine Eastern family. That he was educated in West Point, had been a Major in the regular army, and made up his mind years before to become an Indian, and live with the Sioux. That his name was Major Twiss; was married into the Sioux tribe; came down to Fort Laramie occasionally, and went back up into the unexplored Indian country, nobody knew where. The next day I inquired about him further, because I wanted to see him again, but he had gone out to the squaw camp, and from there he and his squaws disappeared to the north.

It now appeared that the condition of the country as to Indian troubles was that the Indians as tribes would not participate in the war, and that the whole Indian strength was not in the war; but that a large amount of trouble was made by individual young bucks who were bent on mischief, and on having what they considered fun; which was, the scalping of white men and women, and the getting of horses and plunder.

General Mitchell had sent out for the chiefs to come in, and have a conference at Fort Laramie. Sometime in the latter part of the month there suddenly appeared a number of Indians, and their squaws, perhaps about thirty Indians and twenty squaws. They came into camp in the daytime, and were told to camp out at the squaw camp. The convention was a failure. There did not enough appear to make it of any force, and those who did come, very few of them, were of much importance. Shan-tag-a-lisk was said to be near the post, but was doubtful as to whether he should come in or not.

General Mitchell ordered an issuance of rations to these visible Indians, and directed me to superintend the issue. He told me what stuff was to be issued,—so many sacks of flour, so many pounds of bacon, and other things. The Indian women of the squaw camp intruded themselves in on the party, so that about fifty Indian women sat around in a ring to get rations as distributed. The men stood off with great dignity, and would have nothing to do with it, because it was woman's work. I had the stuff brought inside of the ring. There was one young Indian woman who did not get into the ring, and I ordered her in, but she stood up on the outside. All of the other Indian women were sitting in a ring around the rations, which in boxes and barrels stood in the center. Finally I told that woman to get into the ring and told the interpreter to tell her that if she didn't get into the ring she wouldn't get any of the rations. She talked back, and upon my inquiring of the interpreter she said: "I am the daughter of Shan-tag-a-lisk. I have plenty to eat." Elsewhere I will speak more fully of this young lady; she was the one who wanted to marry a "Capitan." I wrote her up and published her story under the title of "The Daughter of Shan-tag-a-lisk" in a Kansas magazine, now defunct. I insert the story herein as an appendix. Shan-tag-a-lisk was afterwards killed, Aug. 1881, by a chief named "Crow Dog," over a woman.

The Indians slipped in stealthily, until the first thing we knew the squaw camp was largely populated. At night new tepees were put up, and the post commander one afternoon sent me up to look them over, count them, and see how many bucks I could see loafing around. I have forgotten how many I reported, but I would say, lying around in the sun, were about twenty lazy Sioux "Injuns" smoking and taking their ease. All this occasioned some apprehension, and the guards around the post were doubled. We were in a peculiar position. We did not want to make any enemies among the Indians, because we were trying to make peace, and we were afraid all the time that they would run in some bad Indians on us, and make us a lot of trouble; so everything was well looked after. In fact, a picket-guard was stuck up near the squaw camp, to keep an eye upon the camp at night, but the Indians were not painted up, and made no war demonstrations. General Mitchell ordered that they should leave the reservation, and go away before the next full moon.

I discovered in the course of my observation that two of the officers of the Ohio regiment had bought Indian wives, and had them stationed at the squaw camp. The Sioux were exceedingly technical in regard to the marriage relations. A marriage had to be preceded by the gift of a horse to the parent. This was an absolute requisite, and the acceptance of the horse by the parent was equivalent to consent to the marriage. If a parent did not want a certain young buck for a son-in-law, the young buck might come and keep offering horses until he had tied a dozen before the wished-for father-in-law's tepee, but the father-in-law would not receive them, while if some other buck tied one horse there he would get the girl. Two officers of our command bought squaws, but in one case the father ran off with the horse and the young squaw disappeared, and the officer was out his horse. The matter was well known to the entire command, for it immediately got out through the interpreters, and the officer was very much ridiculed, and he was afterwards killed in battle by his Indian brother-in-law. Another one of our officers bought a wife for two horses, and the Indian girl fought and scratched him up in a most ridiculous way, so that he was in his quarters pretending to be sick for some time until he healed up. The Indian girl was a fighter and a perfect tigress, and broke through the door to the rear of the officers' quarters, and went to the squaw camp, and quickly disappeared. These matters became known, and resulted in hurting the reputation of these officers very much. The latter officer was pushed out of the service quite a while before the regiment was mustered out as a regiment. Elston, the scout, used to say that the Sioux Indians, that is, the women portion of them, were the most virtuous people on earth. Finally the squaw camp was very much decimated by order of General Mitchell, who took pains to reprove all improper relations; he asked his officers to be examples to their men, and I think, although I do not know, that three discharges of officers came about by General Mitchell's recommendations. No charges were made against the officers, but they were simply ordered mustered out upon some pretext or another.

About the last evening that I was at the Post I had my farewell visit with Major Bridger. Major Bridger was a regular old Roman in actions and appearance, and he told stories in such a solemn and firm, convincing way that a person would be liable to believe him. I had received a letter from an officer down at Fort Kearney wanting me, when I came back, to bring him a cinnamon bear-skin. The cinnamon bear, so called from the color of the hair, was a favorite fur, and the Indian women at the squaw camp tanned them, and the skins were exposed for sale at the sutler store. On the evening to which I referred, Bridger was sitting out in front of the sutler store, and I sat down with him, and got to asking him about bears. He told me a bear story which I afterwards heard was quite a noted bear story, and gave rise to an expression of "only just sitting around." Bears were very plenty. The woods at that time had so many that it was not difficult to get sight of a bear.

Bridger's story was that he was up on La Bonta Creek, where there were trees scattered all around, and he was in a nook cooking his breakfast, when he happened to look up, and under the trees around him in a great circle were about two hundred and fifty separate bears sitting down and watching him. They had smelt the frying of the meat, and had come in as near as they dared to come; each one was sitting down under a tree, and Bridger knew nothing of them until he looked up and saw them. His idea was to impress me with the plentiful supply of bear in the country. I said to him, "Well, what did you do?" and he replied, "Oh! didn't do nothing." "Well, what did the bears do?" "Oh, they did nothing, only they just sot around." So the expression grew, that, as to the officers and others there at the post, like Bridger's bears, they "only just sot around."

As orders had been given that we should return, and as we were going back by Pole Creek, I asked Bridger about Pole Creek, how long it was, and what there was up at the head of it. He described it to me with great detail, and the pass through the mountains at the head of it. After he got through he told me that when he first came to the country, Lodgepole Creek, which was then only a valley in the plateau, used to be an awfully deep canyon, "one of the deepest, worst canyons in the whole country, deeper than Thunder Canyon," and yet since he had been in the country it had filled up from the winds and the wash of the mountains. As Lodgepole was only a depression in the clay which composed the plateau, this story was evidently impossible. I asked him why we had seen no herds of buffalo coming all the way up from Cottonwood Canyon, although on the divide at Jules Stretch there were many old buffalo-heads, worn by the weather, which showed that forty years before they might have been in great quantities. He said that the buffalo had quit running so near the mountains, and that they were ranging farther east down through Nebraska and Kansas. He said that down below Cottonwood Springs, on the Platte, one time there was the biggest herd of buffalo he ever saw. His party was camped in a train on the south side of the river; they saw the buffalo coming from the north, and corralled their wagons and animals to keep from being "tromped" (trampled). The big herd came plunging into the river one over the other in enormous droves, miring down, and walking over each other's backs. They dammed the river so that the water rose to overflow the flat where the wagons were, and the water went plumb up to the axles, and it would not have taken but a little more to have all been washed away and drowned. I was afterwards told that this was one of Bridger's favorite stories, and was called his "buffalo dam story." Bridger at this time was sixty years of age, and had been in the mountain country over forty years.

As there was no traffic upon the line of road, and no

pilgrims coming or going, and the Indian scare all-prevailing, General Mitchell determined to make some military posts along the line of the road; also to put up a fort at what was then called Julesburg. He ordered Captain Shuman of the Eleventh Ohio to build a fort at or near Scott's Bluffs; he also ordered a little fortified post to be put up at the ruins which were called "Ficklin"; and another at Mud Springs, which was at the north end of Jules Stretch. He ordered our company to go to Julesburg, and immediately begin the erection of a fort there, each place to have a telegraph operator and an assistant; he further ordered the road patrolled. Captain Shuman left Fort Laramie before we did, and the details referred to were also sent to Ficklin, and to Mud Springs. There was a sort of sub-district consisting of a territory from Mud Springs to South Pass organized, and this was put in charge of Lieut.-Colonel Collins, of the Eleventh Ohio Cavalry. This Colonel Collins had a son, Lieutenant Collins, who was continually scouting through the country with details of men under orders from his father. The Lieutenant's first name was Caspar, and he generally went by the name of Lieutenant Caspar. The Indians were getting bad west of Laramie, destroying trains, killing pilgrims and carrying off women. Far down in the east they were making violent incursions upon the road between Cottonwood Springs and Fort Kearney, so that there was a condition of war between Cottonwood Springs and Fort Kearney and between Fort Laramie and South Pass. The territory between Cottonwood Springs and Fort Laramie was comparatively quiet, but the fear was that the Indians from the north and south would begin to harass that territory. There was a fort built and named Fort Caspar after Lieutenant Collins, and afterwards a Fort Collins built. Lieutenant Caspar was killed by the Indians not very far west of Fort Laramie, but it was after we had left Fort Laramie, which we did August 31st, 1864. The country south of Laramie had been scouted down a considerable distance, and Fort Collins had been recently established.

Lieutenant Caspar (Collins) was a good deal of a favorite.

He was a young man, full of life and energy, exceedingly brave, exceedingly reckless, and almost without ballast. He seemed to dash into things without much premeditation, played a strong and magnificent game of poker, took one drink too much, once in a while, but was apparently a young man entirely devoid of fear and with an ambition to have military success and renown; his characteristics finally led to the necessary result: he was killed in an engagement with Indians which he ought to have avoided.

August 30th was a delightful day, and with my red silk sash, and imposing uniform, I mounted guard for the last time in due and ancient style, with the garrison, as usual, standing and looking on. In the evening we had our dress parade with all the style that could be displayed. It was my last one. Every soldier that could be got out was in line. The post commander was to issue a lot of orders which were to be read on dress parade. I marched up from the line; saluted the post commander with the customary formula, "Sir, the parade is formed"; walked around to his left and rear with the customary angular steps, and he drilled the post command for quite a while. We were cavalrymen on foot at the parade. Our parades were always on foot, and the men were put through the saber drill. Then he gave me a lot of orders in which my company were ordered to one place, and others ordered to others, indicating that a permanent separation was about to take place, which made us all have a sort of depressed feeling. When the parade was closed, I went to my company and gave it a very careful inspection, and also carefully inspected the horses. That was by order of Captain O'Brien, who had been in charge of the company while I was post adjutant.

In order to get a good start, for General Mitchell was a prompt marcher, we had bugle sounded at 2 o'clock in the morning, and hastily getting our breakfast we filed out on horseback at 3 A. M. and started down the road.

CHAPTER XXII

Departure from Laramie · Points on the Road ·
Camp Shuman · Shad-blow · Chimney Rock ·
Court House Rock · Table of Distances · Mud
Springs · Camp on Lodgepole · September 4,
1864 · Julesburg · The Indian Situation

I WILL give a better description of the country over which we marched on our return than on our march up, because on the march up it was cloudy and we were very tired and fagged out; but we started down with our horses well shod, rested, and well fed, and everything in good condition for a rapid march.

That day we marched thirty-seven miles, passing the ranch of Beauvais, five miles from Fort Laramie; Bordeaux ranch, ten miles from Fort Laramie; the "First Ruins," so called, eighteen miles; and the Woc-a-pom-any agency, twenty-eight miles. We camped at the mouth of Horse Creek, which was thirty-seven miles from Fort Laramie. This Horse Creek was the scene of a celebrated ancient treaty with the Indians, but which was no longer observed or recognized. But there had been heretofore many provisions in it which were referred to as the provisions of the "Horse Creek Treaty."

The ruins, first and second, were ruins of stone stations which had been put up by ranchmen for the overland express company running through to Salt Lake; but the express company, for the time being, was knocked out of existence, so that there was at the time of which I speak no mail, stage or express carried over the road except by soldiers. There was also a pile of stone about two feet high and ten feet square, where the celebrated Gratton massacre had taken place. This has been written of so often that I will not refer to it, except to say that a lieutenant with a few men was sent to deal with some Indians, several years before, and make them surrender some property, and having a piece of artillery, the Indians being obstinate, he fired over the heads of the Indians to scare them, and the Indians immediately massacred the whole detachment.

The Woc-a-pom-any Agency was a little grassy flat consisting of several acres of land on the Platte river, susceptible of irrigation. In fact, there were old ruins of the irrigation ditch. The Indian agent at the time for that agency was named John Loree, so I was told, but he did not stay around the agency, and confined his time and services, as was said, to keeping in a safe place, and drawing his salary.

The road from Fort Laramie to Horse Creek, almost the entire distance, was sandhills and deep dust. The dust was almost insufferable. There was but little air stirring, and the long line of horsemen kept the dust in the air so that it was very difficult to breathe. Horse Creek, when we reached it, was absolutely dry, although there was said to be plenty of water up ten miles, and the guide said that forty miles farther up it was a very rapid and beautiful stream. But the stream sinks down in the sand, and in dry weather disappears. We were very much disappointed to get no water at the Horse Creek crossing, and tried to dig for it with our sabers, but could not make much headway, although we went down a couple of feet. We then went down to the Platte River and camped on its banks, where there was no wood, and where we ate a dry supper of bacon sandwiches made up of sliced raw bacon between pieces of hard-tack.

We got up September 1, 1864, at four o'clock, but did not get started until half-past five. On our road down we passed Camp Shuman. The men were busy building sod quarters with adobe trimmings on the North Platte River bank, south side, three miles west of the gap of Scott's Bluffs. Captain Shuman had just received a box marked "Saint Croix Rum Punch," and he opened a bottle in our honor. He introduced us to his First Lieutenant, named

Ellsworth, and showed us the outline of the proposed walls which they were hurrying to build before cold weather set in. While there I noticed a young man who appeared to be the busy man of the occasion. He was ordering the men around, and keeping them at work. All at once he recognized me. He was First Sergeant, afterwards Lieutenant, of the company. We had a most fraternal meeting, because two years before that we had parted down in Arkansas, both being members of an Iowa cavalry regiment. I didn't know what his real name was when we met this time, because in the army the enlisted men all had "army names," and this young man's army name was "Shad-blow." I ought to stop to tell how this happened.

Shad-blow was the chief bugler of a battalion of Iowa cavalry in the invading army under General Curtis, who was marching down through Arkansas from the Pea Ridge battle-ground to Helena. We had reached Batesville. I at that time, as Sergeant, had been detailed as forage master of the brigade, and being out with a large number of wagons, and a detail of cavalry, had scouted up Black River, Arkansas, and not finding forage enough, and supposing that we were going to fortify at Batesville, I had loaded in the balance of the wagons with slaves. They said that they could live on corn, and they were not adverse to going with us to camp. This was early in July, 1862, and I came stringing in on that day with four hundred husky negro slaves, cotton-growers, almost all of them grown men, and a few old negro mammies among them. I dumped them down alongside of the river (White River) and dumped out a wagon-load of corn to begin on, expecting the quartermaster to do the rest. Major-General Curtis's headquarters were not far from there, and his Adjutant came over to protest. He said I ought not to have brought those people in, and I said they were just what we wanted. We had been coming down through the mountain country where there were no slaves; we had been in favor of abolishing slavery from the beginning of the war, and that was the first time the occasion had come up in Arkansas. The negroes had some banjoes along, and the boys got some boards and doors and end-gates, and started a lot of them dancing, and "patting juba." In the evening, about as the dancing was over, this sergeant, Marsh, came down to see the fun and look at the colony. He was a nice trim fellow with a bright uniform, and with a burnished bugle, which hung over his shoulder with a yellow cord. He was a very conspicuous-looking young man. He was so tall and lean that the army name had been given to him of "Shad," and we all called him "Shad." He had been called that about a year. The darkies clustered around him with great admiration, and not knowing but what he was a brigadier-general, they asked him a lot of questions, and among them some one asked him what his rank was. Several of the men of our regiment were down there. Marsh, in order to bring his rank within the understanding and conception of the bystanders, said, "I's the chief blow-man of the regiment." The soldiers all laughed, but the darkies all stared with wonder. The remark of Marsh was evasive. The chief blow-man might be the man who gave the command to the army through the bugle, and they looked at him with much awe and admiration. The boys afterwards told this story, and Houghton, the Sergeant Major, treasured it up in his mind. The boys began to call Marsh "Chief Blowman," and finally, "Mr. Blowman," but Houghton with great sagacity combined the two names, and called him "Shad-blow," which tickled everybody, and Marsh always afterwards went by the name of "Shad-blow." When by order of the War Department there were mustered out all non-commissioned staffs of cavalry battalions, Marsh was mustered out, and went back to his father's home in Ohio and reënlisted. So it was that we parted at Helena, Arkansas, and less than two years afterward met at Scott's Bluffs, in Idaho Territory, as it was then called. We hugged each other. He could only remember my army name, which was "Link," abbreviated from Lincoln, which I was formerly called, not by way of compliment, but because I was tall and lean. The customary nickname for one who was tall and lean in those days was "Shanghai," which was abbreviated to "Shang," but as we had one Shang in the company I was called Lincoln, abbreviated to "Link." So that when Marsh and I met, and hugged each other there at Camp Shuman, he called me "Link" and I called him "Shad-blow"; then we explained what our real names were, and got back onto a true personal and military basis.

Leaving Camp Shuman, we passed through the gaps of Scott's Bluffs, halting at Ficklin, where a detachment of the Eleventh Ohio was stationed, and reported by telegraph our whereabouts to Major Woods in command at

ALCOHOL BUTTE, ON THE NORTH PLATTE.

Fort Laramie. The marching down along the Platte River was indescribably beautiful. The days were tranquil, and ahead of us there seemed to be old castles, ruined cities, and vast cathedrals strung along the route. The plateau of the country, formed of what the pioneers called "joint clay," seemed to stand up in columns, joined closely together. The wind and storms of centuries had worn the plateau in places in to the most beautiful and fantastic shapes, and we could see everything depicted in the outlines of these hills and bluffs that could be seen along the Rhine or amid the ruins of Europe. The weather was most delightful. A haze hung over the whole country, the mirage was in front of us, and ever surrounding the foot of these worn ruins were lakes and moats of water. We saw wild sheep sporting on Scott's Bluffs. We saw a lot of deer on Alcohol Butte, which was separate from the Bluffs at no great distance. We camped three miles east of Ficklin's, on the river, and in front of Alcohol Butte. We were apparently near the base of Chimney Rock, but were in fact some distance from it. We had marched this day about forty miles. The story about Alcohol Butte was that some half-breeds had "cached" some alcohol there to be used in making up "pilgrim whisky," and that the wolves dug it out.

Upon September 2, 1864, we got up as usual at about 3 o'clock, and started at 4:15. The names of all the hills and objects along the river had been named long before by the army officers, pioneers and trappers, and Charles Elston, our guide upon this occasion, told us the names as

CHIMNEY ROCK, ON THE NORTH PLATTE.

we passed by. Most of the names had some tradition connected with them. When we started in the morning Chimney Rock was apparently quite near us, but we were two and a half hours reaching it. The air was so clear that the distance was very deceptive. Off to the south we saw lots of deer, and great droves of antelopes, and an occasional wolf. Our dogs jumped up rabbits from time to time near the highway, but we kept on without stopping for anything, General Mitchell being in a hurry. He was going down with us.

Of Chimney Rock we talked considerable, and it was the general opinion of all at that time, making the best calculations we could make, because we could not climb it, that Chimney Rock was three hundred feet above the bed of the river. We estimated the height of the chimney itself to be eighty-five feet. Elston said that it was the belief of the trappers that during the last fifteen years it had crumbled down from the top about thirty-five feet. The chimney was of a square appearance, and we estimated it to be thirty by fifty feet through. It is situated three miles from the river and a third of a mile from the main bluff. The grand plateau back of it was projected out into a peninsula, which threw a bold headland towards the river. A vertical view of this headland from above it would make it look something like a written letter I, and the Chimney Rock was the dot above the "I" like this:

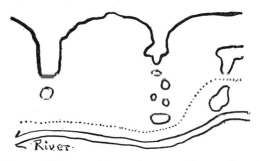

OUTLINE OF BLUFF, CHIMNEY ROCK; ALCOHOL BUTTE; SCOTT'S BLUFFS.
The road is marked by dotted line, and on the right of the picture runs through the gap in Scott's Bluffs. Next is Alcohol Butte.

Chimney Rock had at one time been the terminus of this projected headland, but had been worn away from it so that it stood out alone as a conspicuous feature of the landscape. It is nothing but clay, but it can be seen plainly from Scott's Bluffs, coming east. It is visible fully twenty miles, and when first seen it emerges from the atmosphere which has shrouded it. The trappers said that it could be faintly seen several miles west of Scott's Bluffs, coming east, which would make it visible twenty-four or twenty-five miles. It is first seen going west, from the summit of the hill a mile and a half southeast of Mud Springs.

Court House Rock is first seen from the west five miles west of Chimney Rock, being twenty-three miles distant. As that country down the valley is quite level, to make an object visible at twenty-three miles it must be nearly three hundred and fifty feet high. We marched on down, and halted at Punkin Creek, two miles from Court House Rock. I have already described Court House Rock. I do not remember of a march that was so thrilling and entertaining as the march down from Laramie. Everything was so absolutely wild. There was nothing there but nature as originally created. The scenery was the handiwork of the Almighty, and a man as he rode along knew that he, the man, was the master of the situation, and that the whole business belonged to the Almighty and him. The men in the ranks enjoyed it as much as anyone. They thought they were leaving it for good, and they drank in the scenery and the

COURT HOUSE ROCK, ON THE NORTH PLATTE.

situation as if it were champagne. Any private citizen could then, if he wanted to, come and settle where he pleased, could fence up all the land he pleased, take everything which he saw in sight, and be a king, providing some wild beast or wild Indian or wild white man did not seek to kill him, which they probably would in short order. But these hostile forces were nowhere to be seen. I asked General Mitchell what he would give for ten miles square amid that beautiful scenery, and he said: "All I could do would be to look at it. I have now looked at it. I would not give a dollar for a hundred square miles of it. It is of no use to anybody but animals and Indians, and no white man can live here unless he becomes both an animal and an Indian." There was no help from concurring in his views as we looked over the scenery. It was good for nothing but to look at. None of us ever dreamed that it could ever be cultivated or settled up, or become the home of white people, and made up into townships and counties and organized society. The very idea would have seemed preposterous. We were from humid lands, and here everything was a beautiful desert. Near Ficklin was a large cold spring. There were occasional cold springs in the country, but to us they were only phenomena. They prophesied nothing of the hereafter.

A short distance up from Court House Rock along the river stood a round-top butte which was called "Rankin's Dome Rock." It is about the same size of Court House Rock, which is about four hundred feet above the river. Shortly back of the Dome Rock come the outlines of the bluffs through which the river runs. Both Court House Rock and the Dome Rock are in slight bends of the river. Eight miles east of Chimney Rock is the junction where the old California Crossing road through Ash Hollow comes up the Platte. This was the route of travel until Jules, as stated, wanted to start a new and profitable ranch at Julesburg, and being an old mountaineer laid out the Pole Creek road and cut-off, taking the road past his ranch and within two miles of Court House Rock.

It is eight miles from Court House Rock easterly to Mud Springs. Half-way between is Punkin Creek, a prong of Lawrence Fork, which was dry where we crossed it, but it had plenty of water higher up, also some splendid grazing bottom-land where large herds of deer, elk and antelope could always be found. Mud Springs was a splendid watering-place, but without good grazing near it. Here was where another telegraph station had been planted. Lieutenant Ellsworth of Co. H of Eleventh Ohio, above referred to, had been made superintendent of telegraph lines, and he came down with us to this point. He was the one who told us that Captain Shuman posted pickets on Scott's Bluffs, and kept a picket stationed there always alert, and from that picket station on Scott's Bluffs Laramie Peak, over one hundred and twenty miles distant in the west, could be plainly seen.

The table of distances which Elston gave, at that time,

was as follows: Fort Laramie to Horse Creek, forty-two miles; Laramie to Scott's Bluffs, fifty-eight miles; Scott's Bluffs to Ficklin, nine miles; Scott's Bluffs to Chimney Rock, twenty miles; Scott's Bluffs to Court House Rock, thirty-eight miles; Scott's Bluffs to Mud Springs, forty-six

SCOTT'S BLUFFS,
As seen at a distance of 25 miles.

miles. Lieutenant Ellsworth gave the telegraph distances, that is by the wire, as follows: Laramie to Ficklin, sixty-five miles; Ficklin to Mud Springs, forty miles, making a distance of one hundred and five miles, while by the road given by Elston it was one hundred and four miles. These distances were the approximations of various methods of measurement. Elston said that the difference arose in this way: that from Laramie to Ficklin the telegraph line was a little shorter than the highway, but that from Ficklin to Mud Springs it was longer.

At Mud Springs we reported by wire to Major Wood. On this day we marched from three miles east of Ficklin to Mud Springs, being thirty-seven miles. On September 3, 1864, we started early in the morning, and ascended the Bluffs to make the trip across to Pole Creek over "Jules Stretch." The sight northwest was as beautiful as ever. Court House Rock, over twenty-six miles distant, seemed close at hand, and Scott's Bluffs, over forty-six miles distant, were plainly in view. We had watered our horses all they would drink, before we started across. When we reached Pole Creek our horses were very thirsty; the men were not so much so, because they had filled their canteens, and most of the soldiers on the road poured water from their canteens into their hats and gave the horses drink, dividing water with them.

The horses would drink every drop of water out of the bottom of the hat, and then lick the inside of the hat. We reached Pole Creek, and that night camped seven miles below the crossing, which made twenty-eight miles from Julesburg. Antelope were seen by thousands upon thousands in the Lodgepole valley. The plains were literally alive with them. Upon the evening of September 4th we arrived at Julesburg. On the whole trip from Laramie to Julesburg we had not seen a single Indian. Our guide, Elston, and I myself with my field-glass, kept a constant lookout. We saw two or three smoke signals on each side of the Platte, but coming down Lodgepole there was never a signal of any kind; and at night no fire-arrows went up,—so we came to the conclusion that the Cheyennes were all far south, and the Sioux had all gone far to the north. Yet, nevertheless, we never met a traveler nor a team nor a train on the entire march from Laramie down to Julesburg, a distance of 175 miles, which we made in five days, averaging 35 miles per day. The country was absolutely deserted by both Indians and white men.

We camped near the river at Julesburg station, and the men put up their "pup tents," as they were called, and slept under them. We had no regular tents, but only the little canvas sheet that had been invented during the war, and was called a "shelter tent." It was just long enough for a man, and wide enough for two, and stood from eighteen inches to two feet high according to the way the soldier put it up. We stretched our picket-rope between our company wagons, and the boys spread their pup tents wherever they wanted to, without any order or regularity, and, quite tired from the long and rapid ride, they went to sleep and rest. We found quite a collection of people at Julesburg station. They had fortified, and the road was being patrolled by soldiers from both ways. The Colorado soldiers patrolled down to Julesburg and our regiment patrolled from the east up the river that far, and brought through little trains consisting of rapid traveling horses or mule wagons, and stages; but there was no traveling either way on the road, owing to the lateness of the season, by "bull trains." It was too late for oxen to come up from the Missouri River, and it was too late for them to have started back, so that the road was practically clear of the usual freighting trains; but horse trains and mule trains going rapidly under escort were passing almost daily to Denver.

While we had been up at Fort Laramie, there had been great inroads made upon the ranches along the line between Kearney and Cottonwood. Many ranchmen and freighters had been killed, several ranches destroyed, many horses and cattle run off, and a great deal of destruction done in the Platte valley, but it was all east of us, none of it along the line where we then were, but everybody was prepared to resist Indians. Nobody was particularly afraid of them when in a ranch or doby house, or wherever gathered together in squads of armed men. But, nevertheless, there were no white men going out to trade with the Indians, nor were they hunting out in the hills or trapping along the rivers and streams. On the contrary, they were all bunched together in little nuclei along the river, and going from place to place, when they went anywhere, with an escort. But around Julesburg at that time there had been no indications of Indians, and it was believed that the Indians who had inhabited that portion of the country were far off, either to the north or south, and either afraid or without a desire to make any attack in the neighborhood of Julesburg. But this all changed.

CHAPTER XXIII

Julesburg · Wood · Ash Hollow · September 7, 1864 · Wolf and Bacon · The Shooting Star · Bancroft Ranch · Building-sod · Paid Off · Doctor Nosely · Thrown from Horse · Bugler

AT THIS time the telegraph station at Julesburg was in good working order, and there were two operators. General Mitchell had gone down the road, and was inspecting different points with a view to the distribution of cavalry troops. We were told to scout the country around Julesburg, and keep advised as to the presence of Indians. So details were made that went out daily in different directions to the south, from which at that time the trouble was apprehended. The Cheyennes were singing war-songs in their camps, and were "making medicine" as it was called; that is to say, getting ready for a military campaign. It was difficult for us to get information, but we got it from time to time through half-breed Indians. We had the guide Charley Elston with us. We were told that we would have to stay at Julesburg over the winter, and that some arrangement would have to be made for winter quarters.

The first thing we had to do was to get some wood for cooking. We had been using "bull-chips," and the boys had not had much cooked food. Captain O'Brien directed me to take the company wagons and an escort, and go for wood. There were no cedar canyons, and no trees anywhere in the neighborhood of Julesburg. The nearest point at which there was anything like a tree was over at Ash Hollow, and that was a day's march to the northeast, on the North Platte. The Captain was a little fearful that Indians might be found over in that neighborhood, and he suggested that I should take the two company wagons and a couple of idle freight wagons that were at the Julesburg station. These were mule teams, and he directed that I take along one of the twelve-pound howitzers, and an escort of thirty men.

Ash Hollow was a very rough piece of land; it was a wide gulch with a dry arroyo running from the south nearly north, into the North Platte River. The distance in a straight line was about thirty miles from Julesburg to the North Platte at Ash Hollow, but it was some little of a detour to get up onto the plateau, and down again to the North Platte, making the road about thirty-five miles. There were no roads in the country, and Elston, the guide, gave me the best of his information in regard to the direction, and very accurate, too, it was. He said that the mouth of Ash Hollow was ten miles east, and about twenty-five miles north; and he stood facing the north, and pointed the direction in which he believed it was, and I may say he pointed it out exactly as it was.

Bright and early in the morning of September 7, 1864, I started, and with four teams, picket-rope, howitzer, and provisions, taking the boxes off the wagons, and driving with only the running-gear, I started as nearly as I could direct in the line, crossing South Platte, going a little up the east valley of Pole Creek, and bearing off to the right so as to go through the hills. There was a sort of knob on the east side at the junction of the two valleys of Pole Creek and South Platte. We went around to north and west of this mound. It occurred to me that I would ride up to the top of this knob, which was a very conspicuous lookout, and see what sort of a place it was. When I got up there I found the top of it covered with water-washed gravel, some of it very large pebbles, and others smaller, as if at one time the river or the creek had washed over it, and it had been a stream-bed. I found a pile of "chips," and little light stuff that had been used in the making of a fire, and I found indications that the Indians had been there recently. This gave me an impression, for I saw that it was a signal station for the Indians, with preparations for use.

From there I struck out in a straight line for Ash Hollow.

There was hardly an object upon which I could fix my course, but with a little attention I made the line practically straight. When I was well over on the plateau I came across a depression in which there were several acres of mud and a little water, and all around it were horse-tracks; some of them were recent. Shortly afterwards, not knowing but what these might be signs of Indians, I sent one of the boys on ahead, and he said that he saw at a great distance a horse without a rider. Afterwards I was told by Elston that this shallow pond was a place where the wild horses congregated, and I think that must have been the truth, although we saw no wild horses. There were also tracks of wolves and antelope and rabbits, in the mud.

We had gotten a good early start. We stopped at one place and let the horses rest, and pick up what they could of the dried buffalo-grass, and then pushed ahead. We struck the upper breaks of Ash Hollow, and the sun was nearly setting. We went down upon an old piece of trail which was badly washed out, and saw trees scattered on both sides of the Hollow—an excellent place for ambuscades. We drove the wagons two abreast, and the men were deployed all out to the right and left, so that we might not run into an ambush. I went with a bugler in the advance, and we finally emerged out on the plain of the North Platte with a great deal of relief, and went clear out far from the hills, so that we could not be troubled.

We had cut some branches to be used for wood, and, putting the wagons together in a quadrangle, stretched the picket-ropes around on the inside, and were about ready to start to cook supper when one of the boys said he saw a fire-arrow go up from the bluff on the north side of the river. This worried us, and I was not sure that we ought to build a fire; it was best not to attract attention. But finally we dug a pit down in a little washed-out hollow, and by spreading blankets around, and making a sort of canopy, we made a fire and cooked some coffee. We always carried a pick and spade for the purpose of making our road, if needed, and we got our supper cooked without having a visible fire, but we

had camped some little distance off upon a flat that had no
deep ditches or arroyos near it. Then the men, leading their
horses, grazed them around for a couple of hours, then fed
them a quart of corn apiece which we had brought along,
and got the horses all inside of the quadrangle after dark.
We then put out four pickets extended from the corners,
with instructions not to fire under any circumstances unless
in self-defense, but to come in on the first apprehension. I
was only a little over twenty-three years of age, and felt
the responsibility heavily.

Coming down Ash Hollow we saw a great number of
deer, and in the valley were a great number of antelope,
and wolves without limit. As each wolf can make as much
noise as ten wolves ought to make, the chorus, after dark,
began. It must have been after ten o'clock before we rolled
up in our blankets. Each man had his saddle-blanket and
accouterments all in a pile by itself, and the horses were
on the inside of our extemporized corral. We fixed it so
that each man would know where he was to go in case
of an alarm, and we went to sleep pretty close to each
other. I slept on the outer line, about twenty feet from
my men.

About the time that we were going to sleep, one of the
boys who happened to look in a certain direction, thought
he saw a fire-arrow go up on the south side of the river,
which was the side we were on. None of the others had seen
it, but it was something that we could not take chances
on, so I ordered the men all to get up and saddle their
horses, but not to buckle the girths very tight, so that if
we had time we could tighten them, and put on the bridles
in case we needed our horses. Each man was to sleep with
his bridle and his carbine under his head. I also saddled
my own horse. In order to get a pillow, not having a saddle,
I went and got a sack of bacon. The bacon had been cut
in slabs about eight inches wide, two of them put together,
and covered with gunny-sacking. I made up my mind
that I would not sleep very heavily, and told the sentinels
to come in and notify me of anything which might appear

suspicious. So I put my head on this sack of bacon with my blanket over me, and put in my time looking at the stars and listening to the wolves. They kept up the wildest chorus that I ever heard. It seemed as if there were a million around us. I tried to see if I could ascertain whether any of the voices were Indians instead of wolves. The men had all gone to sleep, and I was studying up all the various things I might do or could do, or ought to do, in case an attack came from this side or that side, and indeed I was working my brain very actively, when all at once out from under my head went the bacon. I jumped up in a second. There was a wolf backing over the grass, pulling that sack of bacon, and making a sort of low growl. I did not dare to shoot him, and he was making small headway with the bacon. But I got my saber out, and made a pass at him without hitting him. He finally let go of the bacon, and lapsed back into the darkness. I then saw that the wolves were very hungry, and that the pillow which I had was not a very secure one. I went to the wagons, and put this bacon upon the rear running-gear of the wagon, and got part of a sack of corn. I was afraid that the wolves would make an attack on the mules and horses. Every once in a while a sort of dusky blur would whisk past the wagons, and as I wanted to keep awake anyhow so as to give the men a good sleep, for they had a big day's work to do, I from time to time, with my drawn saber, walked around the wagons, so as to be sure that the gang of wolves did not pitch onto some animal and have a feast. When morning came I was very tired and sleepy, but felt better after I had drank a quart of hot coffee.

We then drove the wagons up Ash Hollow, put out pickets, and started cutting and loading the wood. It was a kind of cedar. I really don't now remember whether it was the piñon pine or whether it was cedar. The trunks were thick at the base, short and bushy, and hard to cut. But the men worked hard, and reinforced each other, and the pickets came in, and were relieved, and took turns, and in the afternoon about three o'clock we had as much on the wagons as could be safely loaded to get out of the gulch with. We then left them standing, and took all the mules and horses and everything down to the river, grazed the horses, cooked supper, and went back so as to get out of the gulch before it was too dark. Along in the afternoon a smoke signal was plainly seen to go up from the bluffs on the North Platte. We came from the river, hitched up the teams, and started to get out of the gulch. We deployed in a sort of circle. We went slowly, for the teams had to keep together. In some places we had to unhitch the animals from one wagon, and double team, to get up steep grades. But we kept at work with it, and by ten o'clock at night we were up on the plateau; but the men were very tired.

We parked the wagons together in quadrangular shape, took the saddles off from the horses because we now had wagon-loads of wood to fight behind if necessary, and we were not in any wise afraid that we could be taken in. We put out four sentinels at a considerable distance from the wagons, and one of them came in, saying he had seen a fire-arrow go up southwest of us. This was in the direction of Julesburg. It happened this time that I was looking in that direction; it was the apprehension of the soldier; what he really saw was a shooting star. The next morning we followed our road back, gave the horses a little of the dirty water that we could find at what we called Horse Lake, and got into Julesburg late that night. The boys chopped up the wood, saving every little splinter of it, dug holes in the ground, cooked coffee and bacon, and got a good square meal, which was the first one that they had had for a long while. In fact, the boys had not had a good square meal since we had left Laramie on the evening of August 31st, and it was now about the 10th of September. I told Captain O'Brien the wolf story; he just hooted at it, and I had to bring up one of the boys to prove it to him.

About a mile west of Julesburg station, and almost exactly south of the mouth of Lodgepole, a man had started a ranch which had been almost completed during peaceful times. He had an adobe house one story high, an adobe store-room, and a sod corral not entirely finished. The man's name was Samuel D. Bancroft. A fine well had been dug in front, and was curbed up; it yielded very good water. The road led straight past the house. There was also a stock well in the rear. We were ordered by telegraph to make a fortification, and prepare to hold the place at any odds. The weather was getting chilly, and we came to the conclusion that we could not get a fort built in time for the cold weather, and by aid of the telegraph, we got permission to negotiate for Bancroft's ranch. Captain O'Brien carried on the negotiations; we got a provisional agreement, and went immediately to work on the ranch to enlarge and strengthen everything. There was a large sod-plow at the station, which had been much used. Our blacksmith took the share of the plow, drew it out wide and thin, and proceeded to harden it very hard all through. We put the company mules onto this plow, and, going down into the bottoms where the sod was tough and fibrous, we began to plow it in slices twelve inches wide. The tangled grass-roots that had been forming for centuries were tough as felt, and we had to plow at least six inches deep in many places to get under them. The way we worked was systematized as follows: A soldier rode the front team of mules to the plow. We had about five spans of mules. Another man held the plow, and another with a gad kept the mules almost on the trot. The furrows were long, and the slices were thrown up overlappingly. Men came behind with broadaxes, and, guessing at a three-foot length, chopped down through with a blow onto the furrow-slices. Men and teams followed, who hauled this sod up to the Bancroft Ranch, and others there laid it up as fast as it came, while others were puddling mud to make a mortar junction. The sod was laid up, breaking joints, and there were alternate running and cross layers, and it was rammed down as fast as laid. There was lots to do, and everybody worked well. Bancroft continued to occupy one of the houses, and let us go ahead and build, but he would not surrender complete possession until he got a Government voucher. Captain O'Brien and I went into one of the houses, and Bancroft in the other.

By telegraph we got a lot of cedar poles cut down at Cottonwood Canyon, and the post wagons there brought us up a lot under escort. There was nothing growing along the Platte of much consequence. The statement used to be that one could not get a riding-switch for seventy miles on each side of Julesburg along the Platte. It was thirty miles south of Julesburg to what was called the White Man's Fork of the Republican River, but it was seventy miles, nearly, to the Republican River. Pioneers had said that there was nothing on White Man's Fork and nothing until we went seventy miles to the Republican, and there only cottonwoods.

Inside of the corral we started to build our stables, and company quarters; the rear of the company quarters was the sod wall around the outside of the place. These we divided into rooms. On following page is a plan of the post as we established it.

Bancroft, during the summer, had cut down a great quantity of grass, on the north side of the river, and raked it up for the purpose of selling to the pilgrims, but he had been disturbed, and could with difficulty get assistance. He still had the grass, and was fearful that a prairie-fire at any time would sweep the country. We hauled up and piled the hay on the inside of our inclosure, and we set the mowing-machine at work upon the grass that now remained. There was plenty of it, but it was somewhat frosted, and dry. We continued however, to cut that grass so as to carry us through the winter, and it was brought up and stacked inside of our fort.

Down at Julesburg station was a great quantity of shelled corn. There had been an intention of trying to put the stages to running on the Salt Lake trail, in which event a large amount of shelled corn would be necessary. So there were stored at Julesburg station many thousand bushels of shelled corn. As the stage line on the Salt Lake trail was not yet restored, via Fort Laramie, we confiscated and took what we wanted, giving vouchers for it, which were honored and paid by the Government; so that we had hay and corn for our horses.

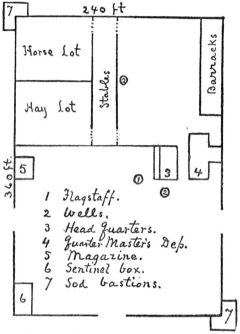

ORIGINAL PLAN OF FORT SEDGWICK,
AT JULESBURG, COLORADO.
The top of the map is north.

On the 15th of September, 1864, we were busy at work, as busy as bees, when, under an escort, along came Major Fillmore of the army, and paid us off. We had not been paid since back in the spring sometime, and there was no money left in the company. The boys were in the habit of lending to each other, so that the members of the company always went broke about the same time. Now that Major Fillmore had paid us up the boys felt better, but there was nothing they could buy. All that they could do with their money was to play cards for it, or send

it home. Those who wanted to send home money notified us, and the money was all put in separate envelopes
and duly sealed, for we had plenty of sealing-wax, and I
wrote my name across the back of the envelopes as a witness to the amount which was put in. After all the money
which the boys desired to send home had been fixed up,
Lieutenant Brewer waited until a train and escort were
going down, and he took the money down as far as Fort
Kearney, where it could be safely turned over to a responsible express company.

It is interesting to note, as illustrating the conditions
of the times, that there were issued to us, as a company,
so many quills for pens, and so much red sealing-wax, and
so much tape, as stationery supplies for the company. No
mucilage was issued, because that had not yet become a
matter of scientific manufacture, but the druggist sold gum-
arabic in the cities; and as for us, we made boiled paste
from flour. Our muster-rolls used to come in sections, and
we boiled the flour, pasted them together, and then with
some smooth piece of hot iron, would iron down the junction
smooth; we had no difficulty.

There was but very little sickness in our company. There
were sick civilians from time to time who needed attention,
and our application for a post surgeon was granted.

There was sent to our post a doctor named Wisely. My
recollection is that he came down from Denver to us, but the
first thing I knew of him he appeared at the post, and went
directly to work on some of the sick who were there, and he
was a very satisfactory doctor. His title was Acting Assistant
Surgeon. He was thoroughly and loyally devoted to his pro-
fession, didn't know anything or talk anything but medicine
and surgery, stayed with the boys carefully and attentively,
drank no whisky, played no cards, and was in fact as satisfactory an army surgeon as I ever saw. He had a peculiar
face. His nose was the most grotesque and disproportionate
nose that I ever saw on a man. It was more than a nose—
it was a combination of beak and snout. The boys, quickly
catching onto these things, started to speak of him as Dr.

Snout; but Dr. Wisely would have received no permanent nickname had not one of the boys one day called him Dr. Nosely. This appellation stuck. The Doctor received it good-naturedly, and we always after that called Dr. Wisely, "Dr. Nosely."

Our dogs here were a great benefit to us, and much society. Captain O'Brien ever and anon would direct me to go over into the hills with my field-glass, and see what I could see. The Captain was wide awake, and always on the alert. His natural mental and physical activity were so reinforced by nature that he had to be doing something or saying something at all times, and this made him so exceedingly valuable as an army officer. The Captain desired himself to get acquainted with all the lay of the country south of us, and desired that I also should; so I frequently, after the work of the day was almost over, say a couple of hours before dark, would whistle up the dogs and run my horse over into the hills. I could make a good deal of a reconnoissance in a couple of hours. The wolves were exceedingly plenty, and we could always find one. These reconnoissances were generally accompanied by a wolf-hunt; that is, the dogs would go after a wolf, and if they went in anywhere near the direction I desired to go, I followed them a reasonable distance. The ground rolled considerably, and the plateau was a good deal broken.

On one of these occasions after I had got about four miles south of the post, seeing nothing and starting west, the dogs jumped up a wolf which I kept up with, my horse going at full speed. Going down an incline at a rapid gait, my horse stepped into something where there had been an old hole. He was going as fast as he could run. He about turned a somersault, and when I gathered myself up I felt as if I were all broken to pieces. I was stunned. In a few minutes I was able to sit up. My horse was much strained, and stood still. I began to feel of myself all over to see whether I had broken any bones. I could with difficulty get my breath, and things were in a good deal of a whirl. I sat there as much as ten minutes, collecting myself together. I saw the fresh-made dirt where the horse had stepped. I finally made up my mind that although I had bounded and rolled considerably, I was still intact. I marked the place where I was sitting, and got up and with some degree of pain and effort, was able to walk to my horse, and I made an examination of him. In the meantime the dogs and wolf were out of sight. I walked around and led the horse, and came to the conclusion that he was pretty badly shaken up, but had no broken bones. I then measured the distance from where I had landed, back to the hole. It was thirty-two feet. I walked slowly, leading my horse back towards the post. He limped some little, and I finally succeeded in mounting him and we went back to the post slowly, leaving the dogs to take care of themselves. I was a week getting over it. The prairie-dogs would dig holes; then the badgers would dig down and eat the prairie-dogs; and then the wolves would dig out the badgers, and leave dangerous holes.

The Captain, when he made his explorations, generally killed a wolf, and he often got an antelope. We could get an antelope with our dogs almost any day if we took the time. In the breaks among the hills we often lost a wolf on account of the fact that a wolf would disappear over a ridge, and by making a flank movement would get out of sight, and stay out of sight of the dogs. We acquired a tramp dog that some one had lost. He was a genuine Virginia stag-hound. He ran by smell and not by sight, and he would go along the trail yelping at every jump. We called him "Bugler No. 2." We had lost "Bugler No. 1." The greyhounds ran by sight, and when the wolf eluded their sight they stopped, and were unable to proceed in the right direction. They could outrun Bugler, so he followed in the rear yelping, and if at any time the dogs were puzzled Bugler would follow right off on the trail, and lead the other dogs to the point where they could see the wolf. Then they would dash on ahead, and if they could keep sight of the wolf they could catch him; and if they lost him again Bugler would find him again, so that "Bugler No. 2" became as valuable an addition to our pack as was his predecessor.

CHAPTER XXIV

The Hermitage · "Old Bill" · Elder Sharpe · Colonel Shoup · The Devil's Dive · Attleboro Jewelry · Lieutenant Williams · Trip to Laramie · The Head Wind · Bridger · The Glee Club · Albert Sidney Johnston

WHILE I was pretty well bunged up over the fall from my horse, above mentioned, General Mitchell was going up and down the road with an escort making reconnoissances and plans for the reëstablishment of trade and travel. Captain O'Brien sent me down to Beauvais ranch with a communication and a report concerning things at our post. While there I met the Lieutenant Talbot who shot at the telegraph poles down at Fort Kearney, as before described. Also there was with him Major Armstrong, the chief inspector of the cavalry of the Western army; also Lieutenant Rankin, Aide-de-Camp. Beauvais ranch was about 25 miles east of Julesburg and about 15 miles south of Ash Hollow, and was at what was called the "Old California Crossing."

I concluded that I wanted another horse, and Rankin had a nice large horse, jet black all over, with curly mane and tail. Rankin told the history of this horse briefly as follows: When Rankin was in the army invading Kentucky and Tennessee, they had made a raid upon Andrew Jackson's old Hermitage farm, and had taken away all the stock that was there, and this horse, captured there, was turned over to the Government. As it was customary then, horses were appraised by the quartermaster and sold. The purchasers at these sales generally were officers who needed a remount, and Rankin had bought this horse, and had kept it as one of his horses all of the time. A pretty good horse could be bought for $100, and a very fine horse could be bought for $200. I asked Rankin to sell me this black horse. Rankin, being at headquarters, had no scouting to do; the horse had been having no more work than was necessary to promote its health, mere exercise, and was plump and full of life. He was an exceedingly showy animal, and a very large one, and a very strong one. Rankin did not very much like to sell the horse, but as I had been recently paid off, he consented to let me have it for $300, and I believe that it was the best horse that I ever rode or ever saw in the cavalry service. I called him "Old Bill," and had him all through the balance of my time, took him into civil life, and finally buried him, many years after the war, with pomp and ceremony, and planted a grape-vine over his grave. He was the most intelligent horse I ever saw, and he got so he would come when I called him, and understood every duty which he was called upon to perform. I did not like him at first as well as I did later on. He was a horse that seemed to be wanting to keep his mind active. When he was tied up by a halter-strap, he immediately began to pick the knot, and it was almost impossible to tie him with a knot which he could not untie, if he were given a little time. He was in some respects a fighting, vicious animal. When turned out with other horses he soon made them all know that he was king. He loved to chase wolves and antelope as much as rider or dogs did, and for durability he had no superior.

On September 25, 1864, we noticed a train coming down Lodgepole. There were about a half-dozen wagons; it was a Mormon train. General Mitchell had ordered us, at the Julesburg post, to let no train go east to Fort Kearney that did not have a hundred armed men in it, because the Indians had been seen around Cottonwood Springs, and had been doing great depredations east of there. So we held up this Mormon train. In it was an Elder named W. H. Sharpe. He was a very bright, quick-witted, companionable sort of man. We directed him where to camp down by the river; he came on up and got into conversation, and finally invited Captain O'Brien and me to go down and take supper with him. As a matter of curiosity we went, and were introduced to the other members of his party. We had no more than become acquainted than he began to talk Mormonism to us, and started missionary work. He told a great deal about the beliefs of the Mormons, and explained how they were sent to reclaim the lost tribes of Israel, which, as he stated, were the Indians of North America, and he gave me a copy of the old, original Mormon Bible, and desired me to read it, which I promised to do when I had time.

Several small trains under escort came down to Julesburg from Denver. It was several days before we could send them through solidly with a hundred armed men. One evening I took Elder Sharpe out, together with one of our sergeants, and had a jack-rabbit and antelope chase in which he participated with great pleasure. While we were riding out over the arid desert watching the dogs, I asked him what he was going to go back at this time of the year for. He said: "My first and original wife is a most estimable woman, and lives in Baltimore. I joined the Mormon faith, and married a second wife; my first wife would not go to Salt Lake with me, so I go back to Baltimore every fall to see her." He says: "I have business for the church which takes me back, and I use the occasion to go and see her, and see if I cannot get her finally to come out to Salt Lake." He spoke of her in the very highest terms, and said that she was misguided in her views, and influenced by her relatives; that they both thought a great deal of each other, and he hoped to finally persuade her to live in Salt Lake City. He was a very nice gentleman to all appearances. He refused cigars, and drank no liquor of any kind.

Finally a train with a hundred armed citizens was organized, and strung out on the road. Captain O'Brien gave them a very rigid inspection, gave them a speech as to what to do when Indians appeared, and how to march, and off they went. Sharpe was with us five days. I have never seen him since, nor have I ever heard of him, but in spite of his foolish creed, I took a good deal of a fancy to him.

While he was there Colonel Shoup of the Third Colorado Cavalry came on down escorting some travelers, who afterwards went into the train of which I have just spoken.

Colonel Shoup was a rollicking gentleman. One evening he had a fine silk buffalo-robe which I offered to buy. He said that he would play "freeze-out poker" for it. He valued it at $50, and would take one-fifth of the chips; so Captain O'Brien and I and two civilians took hold. Captain O'Brien won the buffalo-robe. Then one of the civilians, who thought he was a very fine poker-player, put out a $25 silver watch, as watches then sold, and put it up, and we took $5 apiece in it, and I won the watch. This watch made me a supernumerary watch; I sold the new one to one of the sergeants in the company at what the poker game had cost me, $15. The next time I met Colonel Shoup he was Senator from Idaho, but it was many years afterwards. Since that time his marble statue has been placed in the Hall of Fame in the rotunda of the National Capitol in Washington.

The train of which I spoke, started out on September 29th with more than a hundred armed men. They were a jolly lot. Elston and a detachment were sent down ahead of the train to where it would pass a very bad piece of road, a few miles east of Julesburg; there was at this point a very bad arroyo coming in from the south, and the hills of the plateau protruded north to the river-bed, obliterating the valley at that point. This place at the arroyo went by the name of "The Devil's Dive." When the train had passed that, it reached open country, and could see where it was going. These scouts of ours who went ahead, ran onto some questionable characters who were camped alongside of the river. One of them was an Indian who was called Shah-ka, another was a half-breed by the name of Frank Solway, and another half-breed by the name of Joe Jewett, of whom I have spoken before. These were arrested, and turned over to this train to be taken down to Omaha. Such matters as these, of which I have spoken, were merely diversions; the work went on steadily all the time at the post, and the sod was being piled up and winter quarters were being established. We had no doors or windows yet for the company quarters, and the men hung up blankets. To our repeated calls for clothing we got no response. October came, and the men were wearing their July and August uniforms, now quite ragged, and the nights chilly.

At last, about October 10, 1864, in a train which was being escorted west, there were some mule trains that stopped at our post and left us a hundred uniforms, rations enough to last until the next summer, a lot of bridles and repairs, a lot of ammunition, half a dozen good tents, a few pistols and carbines, and a good supply of howitzer ammunition. But in this whole supply there was only one barrel of whisky. The men had not had any for a very long time, and as the Irishman said, "What is a quart of whisky among one?" The first thing we did was to have that barrel of whisky rolled into the place where Captain O'Brien and I were bunking, and we issued to the men a good jigger all around, and got everything braced up. We were now ready to spend the winter as soon as we could get some doors and windows for our quarters. Through the efforts of General Mitchell the stages began to run again with light escorts, two or three and sometimes as many as six together, so that the stage service was again on its feet, and they went past crowded full, going to Denver and the west; but they were not permitted to go separately, nor up Lodgepole. The stages always stopped at our post. We knew most of the drivers, and we generally took an inventory of the passengers by name, and their destination, and where from, and this the passengers were always ready to give. Through this means I met a good many people whom I afterwards met again, and I made many acquaintanceships which were preserved for years. Among others was a man and his wife and daughter who had been out in the mountains. He was from Attleboro, Massachusetts, and was engaged in making what was then called, "Attleboro jewelry." This Attleboro jewelry was plated in a way that the stuff looked very fine, but the gold was so thin that it soon wore off. In fact, it used to be said that the wind would wear the gold off from Attleboro jewelry. I asked this man how it was he could put the gold on so thin, and this is the way he explained it. He said they took a piece of brass, as soft as it could be made, and say three inches wide, six inches long, and an inch thick; upon this brass there was a film of adhering precipitated gold. Then this block was run through a machine, and rolled down and continually rolled until it was quite thin, and from this rolled plate the jewelry was made.

On October 13, 1864, there appeared at our post quite a train of mule teams going through to Denver, and in that party was Lieutenant Williams, the Provost Marshal General of the department. Mr. Williams was a very brave young Lieutenant of about twenty-seven. He had with him an orderly with an extra horse, and he also had a very fine ambulance. He was going up to Fort Laramie for the purpose of making some arrests, with the directions that when he got through with that he should inspect the military posts on his return. On his arrival at Julesburg he had an order from headquarters directing me to take a sergeant and eight men, and escort him to Fort Laramie, a distance of 175 miles and back. We were exceedingly busy at the time that Lieutenant Williams came, and we persuaded him to wait for several days. We sent him out on a wolf-hunt, and he remained with us until the noon of October 18th. We had to get the men fitted with their new clothing, and get equipment in order, and have the horses shod that were to go on the trip. I did not like to make the trip; it was too small a number of men to go through so dangerous a country. The weather was not good; the trip was a long one of 350 miles, and we were busy getting winter quarters; but I said nothing and got ready. We did not get off until noon of the 18th.

I had just drawn a heavy new woolen undershirt from the supplies that had arrived, and when I put the undershirt on it was very harsh and prickly, and I determined to take it off and have it well washed. Our laundress, "Linty," had rejoined us with Lieutenant Brewer from Cottonwood Springs. The Lieutenant had been down to take the boys' money home, as stated. I gave this shirt to Linty and told her to give it a good washing, and to wash the starch and stuff out of it. When it came time to start with Lieutenant Williams, the shirt was hanging up trying to dry, but it was still quite damp. It was almost damp enough that water could be wrung out of it, and the question with me was whether to wear the shirt or not. I concluded to take my chances with the damp shirt, so I put it on, and we started for Laramie, and I with the nine men went up Lodgepole, eighteen miles, and camped beside Lodgepole at a place where there was some ruined work indicating that somebody had started in to make a habitation. The report was that the stage company had begun to erect stables there, but had not completed them. At supper-time my shirt was still not dry, and we laid down and slept in the open air. During the night a strong wind came up from the northwest that was quite cold, and I slept in a shiver about all night. In the morning we went up Lodgepole to the crossing, seventeen miles farther, and started across Jules Stretch.

All day long that head wind blew, increasing in violence until the air was filled with sand and pebbles. It seemed almost impossible to stem the wind. We started early in the morning. It was cold, and as we rode on our horses, we wrapped the capes of our overcoats around our faces, and only exposed one eye at a time, and most of the time we had our eyes shut, and leaned forward to give the horses the advantage of the wind. We could not see a hundred feet ahead of us. Two men kept the road, and we told them to keep a mile ahead of us, if possible, so that we might not run into any Indians. The Indians could not see us any better than we could see them. Every half-hour we stopped and gave our horses a rest. It was a snail's pace. We had on our horses five days of cooked rations, which consisted of boiled beef, raw and fried bacon, and hardbread. I never experienced a day of misery that impressed itself more upon my mind than that day. The horses could hardly be made to face the gale, and every once in a while would turn as a particularly swift wave came, and they would go milling around among themselves, and we had to straighten out the cavalcade and start again. The men in the ambulance, Rulo and Lynch, of Co. D, Eleventh Ohio Cavalry, suffered as much as we. The mules were continually leaving the track, and it was impossible for a person to hold his eyes unprotected against the wind, and the wind grew colder and colder. I made the following comment in my diary in regard to that wind: "Awful headwind; never suffered so much in my life from cold. Made fifty miles this day. Camped at Mud Springs."

We did not get into Mud Springs until long after dark. I had got my woolen shirt dry by this time, but I had a cold that was about as severe as anything I ever had. I coughed and rolled and tossed all night, and only got to sleep at some time towards morning. The next morning everything was clear and pleasant. The wind had subsided, and the beautiful castellated landscape charmed me again as it had before. I never mentioned my feelings, and tried to pretend that I was all right, and I commenced the procession, and rode at its head all day. We made forty miles, and camped that night at Ficklin ranch. That night I was aching all over. The men themselves were all used up. I asked Lieutenant Williams to make a short march, but he had got to riding in the ambulance and dozing as he went along, and consequently was not tired. I regret to say that he marched us, or rather he insisted on our marching, and we rode on that day, October 20, 1864, fifty-six miles. I then told Lieutenant Williams what I thought about his way of doing things; that while he had the right to set the pace, and command the squad, that he ought to be cashiered, and I told him that my men should have a rest even if he had to go on alone. He got up in the morning bright and fresh, and ordered me to follow him. My men were complaining considerably, and I was feeling used up myself, and I told him that I was going to rest my men until noon. He told me that he was going to report me to the General for disobedience of orders, and I told him that I was going to report him to the General for not understanding his business. The result was that he started out on horseback and with the ambulance alone, and I let the men get all the sleep they wanted in the morning, and a good hearty breakfast, and let them rest their horses, and after dinner I rode them into Fort Laramie, a distance of ten miles from Bordeaux Ranch. When I got into Laramie I got good quarters for my men, saw them all well established, and they started in eating and sleeping, and getting rested. I went around to the doctor and he took my case. He began feeding me with quinine and whisky, and cured my cold, from which I fully recovered in a couple of days, although I was up and around all of the time. I put in most of my time at headquarters with Major Woods (afterwards of Ottumwa, Iowa), who was still commander of the post, and in the evening we all gathered at the sutler store. Williams told me that he would go back with me in less than a week.

While at Fort Laramie I ran across my new friend Bridger, and in conversation with him there we talked a great deal about the country, and the Indians, and he told me over again his Buffalo Dam story, and his Diamond Mountain story, and I recognized the fact that he told them verbatim as he told them before. That is to say, that he had told each story so often that he had got it into language form, and told it literally alike. He had probably told them so often that he got to believing them himself.

There were among the soldiers at Fort Laramie several very fine voices, and they had organized a glee club who were accompanied by musicians. And they were in the habit of going around and serenading various officers, and places, and among others the sutler store. There was an old ordnance sergeant at the post who was a sort of permanent detail. He was one of those who had been left over from the regular army, a perfect martinet, knew everything which there was to be known about the details of post service, and he looked after the ordnance and ordnance stores. I recognized a piece which I had heard sung two or three times before, and when I heard it this last time the old ordnance sergeant asked me if I knew what that was; when I told him, No, he said that it was the favorite piece of General Albert Sidney Johnston. He said that on the Salt Lake campaign, before the Civil War, Albert Sidney Johnston had a headquarters brass band, and that he used to ask them every night to play that piece of music. It was a rather nice piece, pleasant and easy to learn, and the refrain to it when sung, at least all I remember of the refrain, was:

"Ever through life's campaign
I'll be a soldier still."

The ordnance sergeant used to describe Albert Sidney Johnston in very kind terms as a melancholy man of great genius and ability, apparently cramped by his jurisdiction and command, bigger than the flower-pot in which he was growing, devoted to duty, and, in matters outside of duty, very orderly and very kindly. He arrived at considerable distinction in the Confederate army, and had been killed in battle at the time when the sergeant had told me of this, his favorite piece of music. I had heard that piece of music down at Fort Kearney. I have never heard it since I left Fort Laramie.

CHAPTER XXV

Jules Coffey and the Jacks · Snake Fight · Indian Fight · October 29, 1864 · Sam Dion · The Indian Baby · Camp Shuman · The "Simple Instance" · 53-mile Ride · The Snow-storm · The Mormon Train · The Black-tailed Deer · Sergeant Lippincott · Stephenson and the Wolf · Venison · Arrival at Lodgepole

ON THIS visit to Laramie was the last I ever heard or saw of Jules Coffey. As stated before, Jules had a great deal of superstition about holding jacks while playing cards. He thought they were his lucky card. Happening in the back room of the sutler store where an almost continuous game of poker was going on, I saw Jules betting ferociously upon a poker hand. He said he would never lay it down, but he finally did. It consisted of three jacks, and Jules was beaten. His superstition had, in the language of the place, "busted him."

There were a couple of civilians in the employ of the Government, or who had dropped in the post some time before, who were gathering snakes for the Smithsonian Institution. There was a great deal said about the great quantity of snakes that could be found around in the rocky ledges of that country. A great many stories were told about the Indians eating them, and about the scientific way of capturing them. It seems that the Indian women would go out and hunt for them, but had to be very careful in capturing the snake so that the snake would not bite itself, and poison its own meat. The Indian women with a long forked stick would try to pin the snake down close to its head so that it could not bite itself. The trappers said that a rattlesnake was good to eat, and worth catching, providing it did not bite itself. One evening one of these men in the snake

252

business asked me to go around and look at some snakes he had in a box. He had got a musket-box which was made long, to hold a musket, but was not of very much interior capacity, and was heavily built. On one of these boxes they had fixed a heavy double glass top, and the snakes had been fastened in so that it wasn't expected that they could be fed or taken care of. The man said the snakes didn't need it. In this box were coiled, one at each end, two monstrous rattlesnakes, each one as long as the musket-box, and they were there motionless, looking at each other. The next day I was called to go and see the box again. The two snakes had coiled themselves around each other like strands of a rope from head to tail, except that the heads and necks were free. These were bent around looking at each other, and formed a picture not unlike the medical symbol of a caduceus. Just before I left Fort Laramie I was called again to look into the box. One of the snakes was dead, and the other was coiled loosely up in the end of the box, drooping as if hardly alive. The whole thing left me a most ghastly memory; one had strangled and killed the other.

While at Laramie on this trip a beef was killed, and the Indian women came and carried off all of the entrails. There was one sight which attracted my attention: an old Indian woman with two or three children around her was feeding them the raw stuff. She took the smaller entrails, stripped out their contents and cut them up into mouthfuls, then punctured the gall-duct, and, dipping the point of the knife into it, put a drop of gall onto each mouthful as if it were Worcestershire sauce. It was raw, with a flavor of the bitter. The children seemed to enjoy it very much; it was Charlotte Russe for them. I was told that the Indians ate up all of the entrails of the beeves that were killed there at Laramie, at least during the time when there were many Indians at the squaw camp. I should have considered this revolting if it had not been for the happy, cheerful way in which the little Indians devoured this stuff, and shouted for more. And the old Indian woman seemed to be proud and happy to feed the little creatures so well.

During my comments upon this in a talk with Bridger, he said: "It's all right. They like it, and it's all right. I have cleaned up that kind of stuff and eaten it myself, when I had to. The Injuns haven't got the same kind of tasting apparatus we have; their 'taster' is different from a white man's. Now, here is a band of Injuns that want to go off on a horse-stealing expedition, each one of them riding a spare pony. They whistle up their dogs, and start off. The dogs can keep up with the horses, and when they camp, the horses can eat grass, and the Injuns eat the dogs. That is the reason they don't have to have any commissary wagons. They don't have to have any corn for their horses, nor any bacon and hard-tack, and that is the reason that they can always run away from our people, and we never can chase them down on one of these raids, and catch them, unless we can travel like they do. They will swap horses every hour or so, and ride all the time. If they did not have women and children to look after, they would never be caught. But when you go to chasing them with their women and children, the women and children die off pretty fast, and after a while you come up with them; they are at your mercy."

Bridger also said that the Indians believed that like parts of the animal nourished like parts of the man, hence they ate all there was of the animal. When any organ of an Indian was sick he would eat the corresponding organs of animals and game for a cure. He told many revolting stories concerning this belief.[1]

While at Fort Laramie Lieutenant Williams was constantly engaged in taking affidavits of enlisted men and citizens as to some facts concerning which I never found out. Williams was very secretive. Rumor had it that there had been some misconduct on the part of quartermasters and commissaries at the post, and that Williams, as Provost Marshal of the district, had made up his mind to investigate. He swore all of the witnesses, when he got through,

[1] NOTE.—Since the foregoing was set in type an article has appeared concerning Bridger, in a Kansas City newspaper, which I will copy as an appendix hereto.

never to divulge what they had testified to until called upon by the court; so it was not very easy to know what he was at, although Williams about a year afterward incidentally remarked that his trip up to Fort Laramie resulted in the cashiering of several officers. I had a very pleasant visit again with Colonel Collins of the Eleventh Ohio Cavalry, and he again expressed his wish to lose me out on the desert prairie with nothing but a little salt and see how I would get along. This was one of his favorite remarks.

There came word at the post that an empty Mormon train with quite a lot of extra men, and seventeen wagons drawn by mules, was coming down, bound for Omaha, to load up with goods to be brought back in the spring. These Mormons traveled through the Indian country more safely than if they had been Indians themselves. I suggested that as the Mormon train was traveling light, they be impressed into service, and that I be permitted to load them near Court House Rock with pine timber for building purposes at Julesburg. This seemed to meet approval, and Colonel Collins took it up over the telegraph with General Mitchell, commanding at Fort Kearney, who approved the plan. The train came along; we equipped it with axes, a few picks and shovels to make roads with, a small supply of provisions, and passing through Fort Laramie it went on down the road. I expected to overtake them on the route, which I did at Mud Springs. Lieutenant Williams wanted to start October 29th in the afternoon, and so we went on down with him ten miles to Bordeaux Ranch and camped there, so as to get a good start the next morning. At Bordeaux Ranch I met with a frontiersman whom I had heard considerable of, and whom I had met once before, by the name of Sam Dion. He was one of the pioneer Frenchmen of the period, a jolly, royal, generous fellow who cared for nothing particularly, was happy everywhere, and whom the very fact of existence filled with exuberance and joy. He gave me a beautiful Indian-tanned beaver-skin, one of the largest and prettiest I ever had seen. A beaver-skin has two classes of hair. One is a coarse hair which sheds water, and the other is a fine hair which is intended for warmth. Dion had a way of taking a sharp razor, running it over a beaver-skin, and cutting out the coarse hair without at all injuring the fine hair, so that the skin which he gave me was as beautiful a piece of fur as I ever saw. I afterwards made it into a collar and cape for my big blue military overcoat, and wore it all through the service and long afterward. At Bordeaux we met Captain Shuman and First Sergeant George Marsh, going up to Fort Laramie for supplies with a small escort. I was glad to meet "Shad-blow" again, and we sat up talking over the invasion of Arkansas.

There rode with us from Fort Laramie an officer of the Eleventh Ohio, whose name I will not here mention, as he afterwards rose to considerable distinction in civil life. He had been stationed at Fort Laramie, and had been ordered to Leavenworth. Coming on down to Bordeaux Ranch he every once in a while took a nip from his canteen, and said that he felt bad, and hated to go from Fort Laramie and hated to stay there; that he had received a very excellent detail from the general commanding the department, and was going away from Fort Laramie, never to see it again. He went on in a somewhat melancholy strain all the way down, and took but little observation of the scenery on the route. After we had got down to Bordeaux Ranch, and had supper, he took me one side and told me his story. He said: "I came away from Fort Laramie and I did not act right. I have got an Indian baby up in that squaw camp, and I have got to go back and tell the baby's mother that I am never going to see her again, and it is going to raise Cain. I dreaded it, and I was too cowardly to go and tell her before I left. Now I will never see her again, nor will I ever see the baby again. I am going to get onto my horse and ride back there, and then I will be here in the morning ready to go on with you down the road." I told him that he was taking a good deal of a chance to be riding at night along that road, not knowing whom he would meet, and he said that he did not care; that he could get back there to Fort Laramie, kiss the baby good-by, and be on hand in the morn-

ing. He quickly saddled up, and off he went through the
darkness as swift as his horse could carry him. The next
morning when we were ready to start he turned up all right,
and we went on down. I asked him if he had much trouble
on the trip, and he said that he had a whole lot of it. He said
it was a heart-breaking sort of thing, but that it was now
over; that he had made up his mind to it, and he would
never be back again, and that the whole thing was now
ended. He kept taking nips from his canteen all day, but
never became talkative or effusive, and although I was with
him off and on for quite a while after that, he never again
referred to the circumstance.

We left Bordeaux ranch at six o'clock on the morning
of October 30, 1864, and rode forty-three miles to Camp
Shuman, now called "Camp Mitchell," near Scott's Bluffs,
as before stated. Captain Shuman had named it after General Mitchell. We all slept on the dirt floor in the headquarters room at Camp Mitchell that night. Lieutenant
Williams never drank anything. He was one of the few
officers I ever saw who were total abstainers. He and I
slept under the same blanket on the floor. The room was
about fifteen feet square, and Lieutenant Boyd, who was
the Second Lieutenant, slept on the floor near us. Captain
Shuman, as stated, had gone to Fort Laramie. Lieutenant
Ellsworth commanded the post, and Lieutenant Boyd the
company. This was a technical arrangement. There must
always be a post commander although there is only a company present at the post, so that Lieutenant Boyd commanded all the men at the post as "Company Commander,"
and Lieutenant Ellsworth commanded all the men at the
post as "Post Commander." While we were lying on the
floor Boyd every once in a while got up and went to the
corner of the room. We ascertained in a little while that he
was going into Captain Shuman's box of "St. Croix Rum
Punch." After a while Boyd got gloriously drunk, all by his
lone self. He never offered us anything, but just filled up.
Finally he got us up and wanted to tell us a "simple instance." What he meant was "a *simple incident*," but he

was so full that he could not get his words straight, and he would pull at us and at the blankets over us and have us listen to his "simple instance." His "simple instance" was how he and Captain Shuman had recently had a fight, and he had "knocked Captain Shuman just twenty feet." It was not an inch more or less. He had measured and it was just even twenty feet; and after he had told it all over and we had dropped off into a doze he would wake us up again to relate this "simple instance," and tell it all over again. By one o'clock in the morning Lieutenant Williams got a little bit tired of the "simple instance," and finally Boyd dropped off to sleep. The next morning Lieutenant Williams took some affidavits at the post, and among others the affidavit of Lieutenant Boyd about his "simple instance," and the result was that Boyd got dismissed from service for striking a superior officer and for drunkenness, and my old acquaintance "Shad-blow" got to be Second Lieutenant.

The ride of forty-three miles the day before had very much quieted down our horses; in the morning a storm came up, and the wind, blowing from the northeast, began to beat the snow into our faces. It was a very unpleasant day, and after a while it became positively distressing. Williams crept into the ambulance, and in its secure shelter ordered the driver to whip up, and then ordered me to keep up with the escort. The result was that we made fifty-three miles that day against the storm, and the men and horses were nearly used up.

At Mud Springs, on the evening of October 31, 1864, we found the Mormon train camped, together with eight wagons drawn by nineteen yoke of oxen belonging to Alexander Noble, who had come down a little while before with an escort, having hauled some stuff up to Fort Laramie. Noble's wagons were in bad condition, and so were his oxen. I pressed them all in; two of the Mormon wagons had to be loaded up with blankets and stuff which the train was carrying, and one of Noble's wagons was too weak to hold up a load of logs. It had snowed and hailed all day, the wind was blowing hard, skits of snow were coming all night, and the weather was growing colder. On the morning of November 1st we made a road and got the wagons and stock several miles up to where the trees were, and as we had plenty of help we cut the trees as long as the wagons could hold them, loaded them up as far as we dared, then put the wagon-boxes and all on top of the load of logs, tied down or chained them on, and let the wagons start down to Mud Springs. We cut only small, straight trees that were easily handled. No sign of Indians was seen anywhere. On November 2, 1864, we finished the loading of the wagons and sent them all, except a weak one, on down to Mud Springs. My squad of men was camped up on the north side of Lawrence's Fork, in a very nice little grove that stood about forty feet above the stream and formed a sort of shelf, above which, back of us, rose the high ragged edges of the plateau. It was a beautiful little camping-place, and was up three or four miles above Court House Rock. All this time it had been snowing. And as the snow fell upon the plateau the wind blew it down onto our camp, and it began to get deeper and deeper. We had run out of provisions and had borrowed some from the Mormon train, that really did not have much to spare; we had divided with the men on Noble's train because they had only enough to get them to Julesburg. The result was that we were short of provisions all around.

The snow kept falling and kept drifting all during the day of the 1st and 2nd, and all of the wagons had been loaded and got down to Mud Springs except one, and I determined that I would stay in camp over-night where I was, because there was plenty of wood for fires and we on horseback would overtake the train in the morning. Along in the evening of the 2nd the snow came furiously. We already had a couple of feet of it, and had dug paths around our little camp from the ground of shelter-tents to the fire. But during the night the snow fell so furiously that we got up and kept clearing the ground so as not to be entirely buried. The horse-feed and shovels were in the weak wagon then in camp with us. The snow fell on the plateau and the wind swept it all over onto the ravine, so that we were not contending with the snow that fell from above us, but with all the snow that fell upon the plateau for miles. The horses were tied to the trees, and they kept tramping the snow under them until they stood two or three feet above the ground. In the morning the snow around us was from ten to twenty feet deep. On the wind-swept plateau there was hardly any. Along about nine o'clock in the morning it cleared off cold. We dug out with shovels the places where the horses were standing and where our tents were and where our camp-fires were. We did not see any good way of getting out of camp. It was entirely a new experience for all of us, and we debated what to do. The snow all around us was deeper than a man on horseback was high. The worst of it was our shortage of provisions. While we were there undetermined what to do, Corporal Lippincott saw, up on the edge of the plateau, off about a mile, a black-tailed deer standing on a point and looking down into the valley; probably looking for water. It seemed to be absolutely necessary that we should get that deer. I had a fine target rifle, Smith & Wesson, caliber .44, which I always carried as if it were a carbine. There were several good shots in our party, but Corporal Lippincott was as good as any, and claimed the right to go after the deer because he had first seen it. The deer seemed to stand motionless for quite a while, and then it would disappear and then it would come up again to the edge of the rim of the plateau. The snow was rather hard and sleety, and Lippincott floundered through it slowly and patiently. We all stayed in camp and watched what his success would be. Up along the edge of the declivity of the plateau the snow was shallower, and Lippincott after going from the back part of our camp up towards the plateau floundered out of the deepest snow and got into snow that was about four feet deep. He then slowly progressed up until we saw him stop. The deer, if it was the same one, came up to the edge again, standing motionless for a few minutes, when, crack went the rifle, and the deer sprang tumbling over the crest and down into the snow below. This must have taken place about ten o'clock in the morning. We all started out to get the deer into camp, using shovels and lariat-ropes; we got the deer into camp along about four o'clock P. M. While out on this trip bringing in the deer, Sheldon, one of the men of the party, saw an antelope come up to the edge of the bluff between us and the camp, and while the antelope was looking with curiosity at the strange scene going on, Sheldon killed the antelope, and we succeeded in getting that also into camp. We built rousing pine-log fires and ate roasted deer and antelope, and we parched corn from the horse-feed. Roasted antelope hearts are fine.

We had felled some large trees, and the brush part of them stuck up in places above the snow along near which our roads had been dug out. As the snow was over we went to uncovering places so that we could get around and give our horses places to stand. W melted snow for water because we could not get down to the river; the snow was too deep. Both men and horses had suffered a good deal from cold and snow. We cut pine boughs and piled them up pretty well, and over them made our pup-tents, which were the only tents we had and which we carried on our saddles. But we had great fires burning, and did not suffer any more than we could help. During the night, about one or two o'clock in the morning, I heard a noise and some shouting, and jumped up with great anxiety; it proved to be a strange scene. One of the men, a brave little fellow by the name of Stephenson, who was afterwards made corporal, was in a fight with a big gray wolf; and a strange fight it was. The wolf had a trap on one of its hind legs. Where it got the trap we of course never could be able to tell, unless it had been set out by some of the detail camp at Mud Springs. It was profitable to set out traps and to poison wolves, and this was one of the occupations at every frontier post. The wolf with this trap on was unable to catch game, and was hungry. Being attracted by the fire and smell of meat at our camp, it had crawled through the snow and had got hold of the hide of the black-tailed deer, which Corporal Lippincott had thrown over the pine brush right on the edge of our clearing. The wolf when I got there was muttering and growling and pulling on that hide, and Stephenson was holding onto the other end of the hide, trying to scare the wolf off and pull the hide away from him. Stephenson had his carbine in his right hand and tried to shoot, but the cartridge would not go off. He snapped it twice at the wolf, and just as I came up Stephenson with more bravery than good judgment went after the wolf with his carbine as a club. He struck the wolf over the head and stunned it, and bent the barrel of his carbine at almost a right angle. All of the boys were up and saw the blow with the carbine; one of the boys then put an end to the wolf with a revolver. Thereupon Stephenson skinned the wolf. It was as interesting a little encounter as I ever saw. Of course if the wolf had not had a big trap on its hind leg it would not have lost its life as it did. But it was very hungry, and was weak with hunger, and with running through the deep snow trying to catch game.

The next morning we had nothing for breakfast but venison and antelope. We each ate a hearty breakfast of it and cooked pieces to take along with us, and going up towards the bluffs upon the path we had already made, we circumnavigated along and got up onto the plateau, and finally got into territory where the snow was not deep, and arrived at Mud Springs; but we had to leave the wagon because we could not take it with us, and in fact we were very glad to get out of the place as well as we did. It took us until noon to go the short distance that it was to Mud Springs.

On arrival at Mud Springs I found a telegram directing me to wait on my way home at Lodgepole, where a re- connoissance for an exploring expedition had been sent to look for Indians up Lodgepole, and who would be back about the time I got there. The log wagons had well strung out, and were en route for Julesburg over the ridge; the snow was blown from the road. After dinner we started and crossed Jules Stretch, and arrived in the evening at the crossing of Lodgepole and went into camp to await the appearance of the reconnoitering party that had gone up Lodgepole. We passed en route the log train as we crossed over the Stretch.

CHAPTER XXVI

Description of Lodgepole Creek · The Deserted Wagons · No Clue to Ownership · The Election · The Political Situation · Trip to Ash Hollow · Adventure of Lieutenant Williams · Cannon's Puzzle · The Stables Finished · The Indian Scare Over

OUR camp at Pole Creek the night of November 4, 1864, was very bleak and dreary. Pole Creek was a vast trough in the plateau. It had a bed wide enough for the Mississippi River at St. Louis. Through this bed the arroyo of the stream ran, a bed of beautiful tawny sand about a hundred yards wide, and cut down from ten to fifteen feet. Sometimes the arroyo was wider, and sometimes narrower, but from Julesburg to the crossing, thirty-five miles, there was nothing, as before stated, in the shape of a tree or bush. It was absolutely devoid of any vegetation except the grass. And above the arroyo the "flood plain" of the stream, if it could be so called, was as level as a floor for distances out of sight. Occasionally in the arroyo there were little clumps of drift roots and brush, sometimes a small, dead, drifted pine. Lodgepole Creek was said to have a well-defined bed for two hundred miles, and to head at the Cheyenne Pass, in the Rocky Mountains.

Above the crossing, which, as stated, was thirty-five miles up from Julesburg, there was no traveled roadway up Lodgepole. The only road from the crossing turned north across Jules Stretch; but, for a hundred miles up-stream from the crossing, the smooth bed of Lodgepole was said to furnish a most excellent route west to the mountains. The stream seemed to have no tributary of any consequence. A few miles above the crossing there was another

264

arroyo coming in from the south, but hunters said there were no running streams whatever entering the creek. On November, 1864, the date of which I am speaking, there was not a drop of water in the creek-bed, nor did I ever in fact see a drop of water in it. We could get water by digging, but we had to dig down two or more feet, and the supply seemed at this time to be scanty.

On the morning of November 5, 1864, we stayed in camp, the men got some drifted brush and roots out of the creek-bed, and were able in sheltered spots to make a little fire. I thought I would wait for the expedition which had been sent from Julesburg up Lodgepole during my absence, to which I have heretofore referred.

About nine o'clock A. M. I started up Lodgepole to see if I could discover any trace of them. We had seen no Indian signs of any kind anywhere. Soon I saw a horseman approaching me, and with my glass I discovered he was a soldier, and when he came up I found that he had been sent down to get in touch with me. He said they had made a find up Lodgepole, and would like to have me come up there, take a look at it, and pass an opinion on it. So, taking one of my men with me, I started up Lodgepole with the messenger. In the mean time the log train had got down to the crossing, and I ordered it to go into park and stay there until I got back.

Going up Lodgepole about fifteen miles, we came onto a strange condition. Out towards the bluffs were sixteen emigrant wagons. They were all deserted, and yet everything outwardly appeared to be orderly. They were arranged as if they had gone into camp for the night, and were in a sort of circle, in manner and form as was then the custom of parking horse and mule wagons. They were arranged so that the right front wheel of one wagon was against the left hind wheel of another, all curved in so as to throw the tongues inside of the circle, which sort of locked them together. On the tongues of each of these wagons, propped up with the neck-yokes, were the harness of four mules or four horses. Everything seemed to be in order except that the wagon-covers were all torn by the winds, and inside of the wagons everything was in disorder. The grass was growing up around the felloes of the wheels. The winds and storms had eliminated all appearances of newness; the camp might have been ten years old, or it might have been two years old; we couldn't tell. The parties had driven up in the grass and camped. There were appearances in several places on the wagons of bullet-marks, as we believed. There were from one to three trunks in each wagon, all of them with the tops open or torn off. There were no provisions nor any blankets, but there were dilapidated, worn, cotton-filled bedquilts. There was nothing in the shape of guns and ammunition, nor was there any camp equipage. It was one of the most puzzling sights I ever saw. We tried our best to see if we could solve it; we were greatly mystified. The wagons were old-looking, as if sand-storms and prairie weather had beaten them up considerably. I finally made up my mind that the Indians had been the cause of it, years before, although I was not really sure. Indians would, of course, take away everything in the way of cooking apparatus, blankets, food, and ammunition. The other stuff they would not take; as, for instance, in one of the open trunks was a real nice little writing-desk with a very fine little ornamental inkstand, and a nice ivory penholder, and pens. On the other hand, these parties might have been swamped in a storm, lost the greater part of their horses, and had been able to arrange a couple of teams loaded up with what they wanted, and get away. But these wagons were off from any known road, or any line of travel which anybody then knew of or heard of.

There were in our detachment a dozen cavalry soldiers; so I brought them up, picked out four of these wagons, the best ones, four sets of harness, hitched up, and started down Lodgepole. The harness was dilapidated and rotten, but by selecting from the various sets and by using some of our own stuff we managed to get enough for eight horses that worked reasonably well. We also took articles from the wagons: for instance, there were two sheet-iron wash-tubs in one of the wagons, also a couple of sheet-iron stoves. There were several good pine boxes with hinges on their covers, several articles of underwear. In short, we took about what there was that was of any value, and came down fifteen miles to the crossing.

Strange as it may appear, we searched everywhere to find something that would give us some clue to the owner-ship of the wagons, but not a thing could be found. Every-thing in the shape of letters had been carried off. This is one reason why we believed that it was an abandoned camp. But guides to whom we afterwards spoke, said that the Indians would have taken off or destroyed any letters or books which they might find. But this did not seem reasonable, because why should not the Indians have carried off the harness and burned the wagons? We gave the utmost publicity to this strange find, and had it pub-lished in the Denver and the Omaha papers, but never did anything occur which gave us any knowledge of the facts, or any clue to the ownership of the property.

We got down to the crossing, and the log train had pulled out for Julesburg. The next morning, the 6th, the men all rode down to Julesburg in the wagons, and took turns riding and leading the bunch of horses which went in front. We got into Julesburg the evening of the 6th of November.

The next day we had a muster of the company, be-cause the National and State election was to come off on the 8th. Lincoln was candidate for the second term and McClellan was the candidate back in the States of all the Copperheads, rebels, thieves, deserters, bounty-jumpers, and other branches of the then so-called Democratic party. The fight made on Lincoln was incredibly bitter. Mc-Clellan the "ever unready," ambitious, and incompetent, was the idol of every man who did not want to see the Union saved. A vast amount of Copperhead literature had been sent to the soldiers to get them to become dis-loyal. From time to time the wagons that carried the mail had delivered, at our post direct to our soldiers, barrels of mail. Some of it was from Prairie du Chien, Wisconsin, edited by Brick Pomeroy, who wanted to see Lincoln in hell, as he said, playing poker with red-hot sheet-iron cards. When this mail came, which was about every two weeks as the mail went through to Denver, Captain O'Brien and I went into the barracks, gathered up this literature, talked to the men about it, and burned it. Very much to my surprise, I found the company largely impregnated with McClellan doctrine. Captain O'Brien made a speech to the men that was brief, sharp and pithy, and he had the advantage in doing it, because, as his name was O'Brien, he had an opportunity to put the Irish handle on McClellan's name, and to denounce him as an unworthy Irish-American citizen.

When the time came for voting, a great number of the soldiers, fully one-half, declined to vote one way or the other, and when the vote was taken it was twenty-six for Lincoln and fourteen for McClellan. This shows in what a dangerous condition, and how perilous a crisis, the nation was in. It is a great wonder and a great mystery that the Union was saved, as I look at it now; although I was in the middle of it all, I cannot understand it. It seemed that from year to year, in one great crisis after another, we were just merely able in each crisis to save it, and that was all; time after time it was saved almost by a scratch. The Union managed to just get through, and that was all. Lincoln thought for a while that he was beaten.

At the time of which I speak, Price had raided up through Missouri as far as Kansas City, and we were dismally disappointed with the news. From time to time it seemed as if he were going to take Fort Leavenworth, turn the tide of war west of the Mississippi, and break the United States in two. However, Price was defeated, but scarcely anything more, and our side just did manage, and that is about all, to get him started back. I was feeling very despondent after our election, as I did up the returns, and handed them to Captain O'Brien to be forwarded to the Governor of Iowa.

We unloaded the logs at headquarters, and Captain O'Brien thought I had better go over again to Ash Hollow, and get some more wood. In the mean time the Government had furnished us, through their quartermaster at Fort Kearney, a few more tents suitable for campaigning in winter, if we had to make a winter campaign. We pressed in some of the wagons that we had freighted down Lodgepole, and with our company wagons, all together making a train of ten wagons, I started for Ash Hollow.

I may perhaps be permitted to go back, and say that on the entire road from Fort Laramie we had seen no Indians, and no Indian signs. Charley Elston said that the Indians had gone up into winter quarters, except the young bucks, who had gone off farther down the Platte. These young bucks were only in detached squads, and there was nothing for them to get on the Platte River west of Cottonwood; so that the Indian scare appeared to be over. I found that the ranches were being reoccupied. Gillett's ranch, about nine or ten miles west of Julesburg, had been filled up, and a large lot of cattle had been brought in. And the ranches east of Julesburg clear down to Cottonwood Springs had been filled up again. People had fortified the ranches, and the stages had started running regularly up the South Platte. The old stage-drivers said there was no difficulty, and although troops were stationed about every twenty-five miles along the road, there seemed to be no work for them to do except to escort the mail and the stages, and the caravans of teams which occasionally went by.

Lieutenant Williams had gone on down the road. He told us the story of his adventures between Fort Kearney and Cottonwood Springs, coming up. He and an officer named Hancock were riding west in the stage, and there was a man sitting up on the box with the driver. It was a bright moonlight night. It was a four-horse stage. After they had got well out of Plum Creek coming west, and were out on the broad plains, all at once about a dozen shots came from the Indians, and they killed the two horses that were in the lead, and these two horses dropped in their tracks. This was part of the Indian plan, and then they commenced shooting into the stage. Williams and Hancock with Smith & Wesson carbines, and the other two with Sharps' rifles, got down flat on the ground and kept up a fire with the Indians, who besieged them all night. The two dead horses kept the stage from being run away with, and the Indians soon killed the other two. As the Indians skirmished around, the men lay on the ground or got in between the horses, and when morning came they had fired off a greater part of their ammunition, and had succeeded in getting two or three Indians, but were themselves unharmed. They were reinforced in the morning by a party who had been warned by some one who had heard the firing. This was hardly to be called a night attack, for there was a bright full moon.

West of Cottonwood Springs everything seemed to be perfectly safe. The Cheyennes had met with some rough treatment down in Kansas, and along the Arkansas river, and had got over their war fever somewhat. But every once in a while some of the young bucks got out, and succeeded in capturing some emigrant wagons, or some frontier house, and killing somebody. It got to the point that everybody said that the only safety was to exterminate the Cheyenne Indians, but nothing had happened around our post to show an Indian present, nor had we seen any fire-arrows or smoke-signals for quite a while. And in my last trip from Fort Laramie, as stated, nothing of the kind was in view.

On the 9th of November, 1864, we got all ready to go to Ash Hollow, and I determined to make the trip in the night, so as to get there after sunrise, deeming it the safer. The several days of rest my horse had got made him almost unmanageable. I mean my Hermitage horse, "Old Bill." He seemed to be determined to run, and he started off on his hind legs, pawing the air, going on the tips of his toes, and frisking so that I found that I was in danger of having a runaway horse, or one which would be uncontrollable in case of danger. So, in order to get him down to business, I got him down in the Pole Creek arroyo, where the sand was about up to his knees, and I ran him a mile up the creek as hard as he could go, and a mile back. That was a very severe test. I made him go his best. This took the wire edge off of him, and for the balance of the trip he went along like a good, sensible horse.

We got to Ash Hollow, kept well on the lookout, worked hard most of the day, and filled our wagons, then went into camp, parking everything up as if for a fight. All at once, on the other side of the river, went up a smoke signal. We saw it answered up the river as far as a field-glass could spy. In the evening in the earliest dark a fire-arrow went up. I then concluded that trouble would begin in the morning; so we had the mules all hitched up, and the men all mounted, and we started up the road leading out of Ash Hollow, and finally got up on top of the plateau. The men were very tired, and I was very tired, for I had been at work as much as the men. I got them all together and told them that nobody could tell what there was behind us; that we could park upon the plateau, and go in by daylight, but that the Indians wouldn't tackle us by night, in all probability, and that we could go across to Julesburg three teams abreast, and in solid order, but that I was not going to make the order to march if they thought they were too tired or worn out to make it. They all spoke up that they were not very tired, and would be willing to make the trip. So, deploying out the men who were on horseback as scouts, and putting a white wagon-cover on the man who was to follow the trail and go in advance, so that we could keep line on him, we started across. About eleven o'clock a fire arrow went up far in front of us along the line of our probable trail, and a little after that an arrow went up behind us. Deeming it unwise to go any farther in the night, we parked our wagons, and waited for daylight. The starlight was very bright, and we could see considerably well. The wolves howled most fearfully, and as to some of it we could not tell whether the howling was wolves or Indians; so we got the log-wagons in such a position that we were within the circle of them, and we waited for daylight to come. The men dozed off alternately, and we each got two or three hours of sleep. As soon as it became dawn, we started on.

During this trip I rode, for a while, with the soldier Cannon, of whom I have heretofore spoken. When Cannon had no whisky in him, he was a very reliable soldier. That is to say, he had had good experience, and was sensible. Riding along, he told me that he was with Captain Pope, afterwards Major-General Pope, of the Civil War, when Pope was marking out the "Staked Plains" of Texas. That was a route for a future road projected by the Government over the wild and unending plains of northwestern Texas. Where this road was laid out it was called the "Staked Plains," but went down on the map under the name "Llano Estacado." He said he heard Captain Pope ask a question of another officer, and he always wanted to hear the answer to it. He said Pope asked this officer as follows:

"Supposing the Staked Plains are a thousand feet above the level of the sea, and on the first day of June a man gets up in the morning on horseback, and starts out following his shadow from sunrise to sunset at a rate of four miles an hour, where would he be at night, and what would be the shape of his course?"

This particular problem was very interesting. I had at that time a pocket diary showing the moon's phases, and the time of the rising and setting of the sun every day, for different latitudes. At first I could not grasp the puzzle, but before I got to Julesburg, I had it solved in an offhand way, and I told him the nature of the course. He would be at night twenty-eight and one-half miles north of the place where he started, and about a quarter of a mile east of it. This is not really accurate, but is as nearly so as a person could work it out on horseback with the aid of a pocket almanac.

When I got back from Ash Hollow, I found the men had all got into the new adobe post quarters, with battened doors made from lumber hauled down from Denver, and with some square glass windows. The boys had about finished the stables. The stables were 140 feet long, and 30 feet wide. There was a ten-foot door at each end and on one side. The sod was put up eight feet high; eight feet from each side we put up two rows of upright poles on the inside, marking each double stall. We put light logs across each of these, then split posts on top of the logs close together. The boys had waded around in the Platte River and cleaned off all the willows up and down the islands and banks. These had been put down on top of the roof-rails, and then on the willows was spread some spoiled hay, and it was well tramped down; then the whole was leveled off with dirt. When the dirt was all leveled we plowed more sod, and tightly sodded the top of the whole stable. It was fire-proof, cold-proof, and bomb-proof. It was one of the best stables I ever saw, and by all means the cheapest, considering the quality, I ever saw.

Confidence along the road seemed to be restored. There was always a surging impulse to go ahead and take chances. The East demanded an outlet West, and a reflex tide much weaker was always seeking the East. An open road between the Missouri River and the Pacific Ocean was a constant necessity. Although one Indian raid followed another, the tide flowed on between-times. And although the current was at times dammed up, it broke loose again with an increasing volume. No attention was seemingly paid to Indian hostilities; they were looked upon in the same light as a bad spell of weather: the hostilities would, like the weather, change from time to time, but no one made calculation about them or took them much into account. People relied on the Government and the soldiers and themselves, and their own good-fortune. Thus, when anybody wanted to cross the plains they just started and trusted to luck and their ability to go through. More than this, the great majority of the pilgrims and whackers rather enjoyed the prospect of having a little skirmish with the Indians, at some point, so as to have something to enliven the trip and something to tell when they got back to the "States." But it was all hard work for the soldiers along the line. Besides all this, the Civil War was loosening up whole blocks of society and giving them an impulse to the West. The war was on; in strong Union communities, if situated anywhere near the lines of the combatants or within the sphere of their influence, they made it hot for the secesh or for people who had relatives in the Confederate army. In places where Rebel sympathizers prevailed the Union men were hung, or driven out; hence in both such cases the minority party in groups sold out and moved away. The Union men went to the open lands of the North and the Northwest, and the secesh to the mountains, the West and the Pacific Coast, away from the theatre of possible strife, as if trying to forget it. These conditions, coupled with the growing demands of legitimate business, gave a constantly increasing impetus to the vast travel westward and eastward along the Platte River. This travel could finally be accommodated only by a railroad.

The Indian policy of the government was necessarily crude. The Indians were powerful, quite free, and fond of devilment; yet between them there was not much coherence, owing to rivalries and feuds. They were divided into bands under the control and leadership of favorite chiefs, who often envied and hated each other. Hence it was that we could not mistreat any Indian without taking the chances of making trouble; thus, if an Indian would suddenly appear at our post we could not kill him or imprison him or treat him as an enemy, because the particular Indian had done nothing that we could prove as an overt act. As far as the Sioux were concerned we had to keep on the defensive, because some of the Sioux chiefs were trying their best to keep their bands and young men from acts of war. It was cheaper to feed the Indians than to fight them, and the constant efforts of the commanding officers were to make treaties of peace; which resulted practically in our buying privileges and immunities from them. The demands of the Civil War which was straining the nation's resources added much to the difficulties of the occasion. So we were in an attitude all the time of about half war and half peace with the Indian tribes. We could not punish them adequately for what they did, nor could they drive us off from the Platte Valley. We let them alone if they kept out of our way, and they let us alone when the danger seemed too great. Of all the Indians in our territory, the Cheyennes seemed to have the least sense. They lacked judgment, and were entirely unreliable; the pioneers placed the Arapahoes next; for respecting treaty obligations, the pioneers placed the Brulé Sioux at the head of all the northwestern Indians.

CHAPTER XXVII

November 10, 1864 · Jimmie Cannon · The Sobriety Drill · The Stagedriver's Arrow · The Wagon Train Fine · The Quality of the Emigration · Commissary Measurements · The Ration · Desiccated Vegetables · Prickly-pear Sauce · Denver and the Cheyennes · The Wood Train · The Englishman · The Bets · The Trial

With the returning confidence of the public, and our orders to let no train go by except such as had one hundred armed men, and with the necessary continuous work upon the improvement of our fort and barracks, and on account of the necessity of keeping up our target practice, the men were quite busy. They had been free from annoyances, had been well fed and clothed, and whisky, except as we issued it sparingly to those doing extra duty, had disappeared from the camp. But with the return of trains and confidence, great numbers came down from Denver bound to the East, and the men began to get whisky again, and at times wild and violent occasions took place.

On November 10th, Cannon, who had a large white horse that was very frisky, got intoxicated, and while he was endeavoring to show off how the horse would follow him around like a dog, the horse took it into his head to go off frantically across the plains, canter around in a circle, and come back to the post. I was out in front of what we called our parade-ground when the horse came up, and Cannon ran up to try to stop him. The horse playfully wheeled, and kicked up its heels at Cannon. And Cannon grabbing his revolver from the holster, took it by the barrel and threw it at the horse. The revolver struck the ground right in front of me, and went off, and a bullet went so close to my head that I felt a little irritated. I grabbed Cannon by the collar, called on the sergeant to bring a lariat-rope, and tied Cannon up to a piece of artillery which was near.

About a dozen of the men suddenly appeared to be nearly as full of whisky as Cannon. I told the sergeant to immediately go to the barracks, get all their names, tell them all that they were detailed on a scout, and in fifteen minutes I had them all on horseback headed towards the hills, under command of a corporal, to get the whisky trotted out of them. I told the Corporal privately to take his men around, scare them a little bit if he could, and work them until they were all sober. This the Corporal did, and the trouble for that day was ended.

The stage-drivers had got to be very confident and reckless, and got so that they would drive off, and run away from their escorts who were on horseback, and were all pretending not to fear anything. Many of them were new, and affected to despise the soldiers. Some of them had been in the Confederate service, and really did.

On the evening of November 11th a stage-driver with a stage coming from Cottonwood Springs, drove up shortly after dusk. He came lashing his horses as if all of the imps were behind him, and well he might, because down a little way below the post, just as he was going along the plains where nothing appeared but clumps of cactus, an Indian rose quite near and shot an arrow at him. It was splendidly aimed. It went through his coat collar at the back of his neck, and the iron head of the arrow whipped around and hit him on the face, and he started his horses on a run. He said that all he saw was this one lone Indian. The Indian had refrained from firing a gun for fear of alarming the post. The stage-driver got off from the coach with the arrow in his coat collar, balanced about half-and-half on each side. Those in the stage coach did not know the full extent of the matter until the driver had driven quite a little distance, and seeing that he was not followed, the driver stopped and told the passengers, two of whom had seen the Indian, but were not aware of what had been done. The stage-driver was very proud of that arrow in his coat collar, and wore it there for a long while.

Seventeen miles east of Julesburg was a ranch that was owned by Dick Cleve. He had at one time abandoned it, but was now back again. An Atchison firm by the name of Byram & Howes had a train, and were coming from Denver en route home; they went on down with the caravan, and stopped at Cleve's. There were a good many in the caravan, and the particular wagon-master of said train got to be domineering, smart, and overbearing, and proceeded to help himself to things generally, and made up his mind that he was the boss of the track.

Cleve came up to our post and made complaint. I happened to be in command of the post that day, Captain O'Brien having gone down the road on orders from General Mitchell. So it was my duty as post commander to act as judge. Cleve said the wagon-master was a dangerous man; would shoot, and had a lot of roughs and toughs who would like to take a hand in the shooting, and that if I expected to get the man I had better send down about fifty men. I concluded a corporal with eight men was enough. I told them to go down, present my order to the wagon-master, and bring him in; and if he wouldn't come voluntarily, to bring him anyway; and if he offered resistance, to be sure that he didn't get away. And that if anybody else took a hand, to bring him also.

The corporal went down, stopped the whole caravan, and delivered my order. The wagon-master refused to come; the Corporal put a revolver under his ear, and made him mount his horse, and come. Two or three rough-neck bull-whackers wanted to take a hand in the matter, and there was quite a display of firearms, which resulted in the Corporal saddling up some of their horses and bringing the wagon-master and three of his party to the post. Cleve came along.

Cleve presented his bill for $162.50, told the story of what had been done, and the wagon-master did not dispute what had been done, nor what he had taken; simply made a defense that the stuff he had destroyed or taken was not worth as much as Cleve said it was.

I thereupon rendered judgment upon the fellow in favor of Cleve for $162.50. The wagon-master then said he would not pay it. I told him then he would go into the guard-house. He then said he would have General Mitchell order him out, and would have me cashiered. Thereupon, I put the whole bunch of them in the guard-house, and kept them over-night. The next morning the wagon-master said he would pay Cleve with a draft on his house. Cleve didn't know whether it would be honored or not; I told the wagon-master that he would have to stay in the guard-house until he paid that money in cash. Thereupon, after consultation with his mates, he paid Cleve the money, out of a big wad of other money he had.

I then detailed ten soldiers to go back with Cleve, escort the wagon train ten miles east of Cleve's ranch, and then tell them that I said if I caught any of them back on the road I would put them in confinement. The Corporal saw the outfit go down past Beauvais', which was twenty-five miles east of us, and that is the last we ever heard of them.

This was about as bad a trouble as I had, and was perhaps the most insubordinate. Almost every day appeals were made to the post for the settlement of disputes, quarrels and bets. We did the best we could, came as near to doing justice in each case as we knew how, and let the matter go at that. It was the only court that could enforce its decrees. I always thought the people had confidence in it, and that it was a good thing, because there were many disputes over matters that people did not want to kill each other for. Shortly after that there was a killing in a wagon train going down from Denver. One man shot another about fifteen miles west of our post. We arrested and held the man up, and finally sent him down to Fort Kearney, in confinement.

On November 17, 1864, news reached us that Lincoln was elected, and that Sherman had swung loose into the Confederacy. I thought it the occasion for jollification, and so as temporary post commander I fired off several shots from our mountain howitzers. I desired target practice with the howitzers, and combined that with the celebration of the political victory, and the action of Sherman. If McClellan had been elected, Sherman would have been called home. There was on that day quite an assemblage of pilgrims at our post, going either one way or the other, and held up for consolidation into trains, but they did not seem to me to have very much enthusiasm over national benefits and victories. They did not seem interested. I have heretofore spoken about the Loyal League. It was my custom to make signals often to those who were coming to Julesburg on the trains, or traveling in the stages, for the purpose of seeing how many of them belonged to the League. It was rare to find one, not one in a hundred; and the reason was that the people out in that part of the country were of the Democratic party faith. They included bounty-jumpers, secesh, deserters, people fleeing from the draft, or those who did not care one way or the other how the war turned out.

While we were at Julesburg we had been told from time to time of trains which had displayed on the road below us secesh flags, but nothing of the kind was ever visible from our post, or was ever seen in the neighborhood of Julesburg by any detachment of our company. The Colorado cavalry had been down in New Mexico, fought a good fight, and saved that Territory, and they were vindictively loyal, and were inclined to shoot. It was not good form for secesh to run up against any of the Colorado soldier-boys, because none of them had gone into the service except those who meant business, and were trying to save the Union.

But about this time there were a good many who were going west, through the country, toward the latter part of November, in trains of mule wagons. They were going rapidly, and always got escorts when needed. The report was that Price's invasion of Missouri having turned out disastrously, a great number of secesh citizens, seeing that they could not be rescued from the Union, and a great many deserters from Price's army, feeling that their secesh war was about over, had started for the mountains. The final re-

pulse of Price from Missouri had reawakened very strong
Union sentiments there, and the Union men were in favor
of cleaning out all those remaining citizens who were dis-
loyal. Hence it was that there appeared during the latter
part of November, and through December, a perfect hegira
of emigrants and mule teams, mostly from Missouri. Many
of these trains came through loaded with nothing but corn;
many were loaded with nothing but nails. They were loaded
lightly, and went as fast as the animals could be driven.

In the crisp November air, everybody at the post
seemed to improve. The duty was quite heavy. There was
much to do in taking care of the horses, watering and feeding and exercising them; there was continual work upon
the barracks, and sod walls and fortifications, if they could
be called fortifications.

Our family of dogs by gift had been increased until we had
five of the finest greyhounds that were ever found in any
place. They were named Fannie, Fly, Nellie, Kearney, and
Lady. Lady was jet black, and the best of all. Nellie was a
large white one, and was next best. With these dogs and
Bugler no antelope or wolf could get away unless it had
the start by a very long distance. Quite often we would take
the men, by turns in squads, out into the hills, and show
them a chase, and the men enjoyed it very much. Thereafter some of the men got some strychnine from some of the
ranchmen, and proceeded to poison wolves by baiting the
wolves with poisoned beef-livers. About fifty wolves were
poisoned, and all of the men of our company thus obtained
heavy fur collars and fur mittens. But one day on a chase
our best dog, Lady, happened to strike some poisoned meat,
and was killed by it. After that the poisoning of wolves was
discontinued.

We killed our own beef at the Post, and the cattle
were selected from time to time from a herd that was kept
in a corral down near the river. The method of measuring
meat was different out in the Western country from what it
was down South in the army. I never heard of the method
pursued until we were at Cottonwood Springs. Army beef

was to be heavy beef so far as it could be obtained, and was to be well cleaned and trimmed, and to contain as much net meat as possible. The way they measured was this: They put a line around the beef, back of the fore legs, and allowed a hundred pounds for every foot of circumference. That is to say, if an animal were eight feet around he would net, for army ration purposes, eight hundred pounds, although the animal might be live weight twice as heavy. If he measured seven and one-half feet around, it was called seven hundred and fifty pounds. The Quartermaster used to say that as cattle ran, the above method was exact enough. As to hay, the measurement was, after the prairie hay had been stacked ninety days,—seven feet cube represented a ton, the whole stack being taken into consideration. So our meat and hay were bought and figured by the above rules.

We never had any fresh vegetables at Julesburg; they could not be got to us. But there were issued to us what were called "desiccated vegetables." In the true pronunciation of the word the second syllable is long, but it was called by the boys as if it were dessy-kated, with accent on the third syllable. It was made of onions, cabbages, beets, turnips, carrots and peppers, steamed, pressed and dried. They were almost in the form of leaves pressed together. They were pressed, after they were dry, into cakes twelve inches square, and an inch thick. They were pressed so hard that they weighed about as much as wood, and came sealed up in tin cans about a foot square. They were intended to be put into the soups, and were largely used by us for that purpose. They were very nutritious, and it was convenient, when we went on scouts, for the boys to break off a piece and put it in a saddle-pocket. The boys would nibble at it as they were riding along; it was a kind of leguminous bread, and they ate about as much of it dry as they did by putting it into soups. But we had been so long without vegetables that indications of scurvy began to make themselves noticeable. Along in November, the first thing we knew one of our men was suddenly taken ill; black spots formed over him, which very much worried Dr. Wisely, and the soldier was immediately sent east on one of the trains to Fort Kearney. Other of the boys complained of the symptoms.

One day Dr. Wisely came to me, and told me that he had made a discovery that he thought of great value. He asked me to send out and have about a bushel of the "hands" of the prickly-pear gathered from the plains, and brought in. I ordered the quartermaster sergeant to attend to it, which he did. And Dr. Wisely, taking these prickly-pear hands, the common, coarse, ordinary opuntia, scraped the bristles and prickles off from it, cut it up and boiled it with sugar, and made a variety of apple-sauce which was quite new, and not altogether undesirable. Those men who were afflicted with symptoms were immediately cured, and the Doctor continued to use the remedy all of the winter, and as long as we stayed at the post. I have never heard of such a food, before or since, but think from the experiments of Dr. Wisely it must have much of merit in it.

All of this time we kept busy laying sod. There was always improvement to be planned, and more things to be built. There had been some little cold snaps, and some little snow, but as yet there had been no such weather as to freeze up the sod, and prevent us from plowing it.

On November 25, 1864, being in command of the post, I ordered the First Sergeant, Milo Lacey, to take the wagon-master, Donley, and all of the teams that he could get, and go over to Ash Hollow for another supply of wood. The trail was well laid out now to Ash Hollow and all the non-commissioned officers knew where to go, and how to handle the business.

We had no Indian scare for some time. It was reported that the Cheyennes had sent a delegation to Denver asking that a definite treaty of peace be made between the Cheyennes and the people of Denver, and that the Indians be permitted to come in near Denver below the town where there was plenty of wood, and go into winter quarters. As these Cheyennes had been ravaging Colorado and Kansas, killing men and murdering women and children, and driving in all the frontier settlements, and as the Colorado people were very much wrought up about it, a conference is reported to have been had in Denver, and to have given back word that the Cheyenne chiefs could not control their men, or would not if they could; that now the summer was over, and the raiding season past, they could not entertain the Cheyennes in that sort of way. They further said that they believed they would not make peace with the Cheyennes until they had given them a good whipping. And it was reported that the Indian delegation retired from Denver in very sullen anger.

The wood train, after four days, did not turn up on the evening of the 28th as was expected. It did not turn up on the 29th. There was not a sliver of wood at the post, nor was there anywhere anything that would burn except the hay, and that could not be burned to any advantage. We had received a lot of sheet-iron from Fort Kearney, out of which our company blacksmith had made several stoves and some pipe. The stovepipes ran up through the roof. These stoves were economical heaters, and we burned splinters and bull-chips in them. On the 30th we burned some wisps of hay in the forenoon; we were getting cold, and I concluded to go out and see if I could get word of the train. One of the boys said that he had seen a smoke signal go up from the Lodgepole Lookout, which I have heretofore described as on the northeast corner of the junction of Lodgepole and the Platte.

Going over onto the plateau, I saw the train coming, quite near. They had seen Indian signals from time to time, and had felt constrained to march closely and well packed, but no attack had been made upon them. We were delighted to receive the wood train and get warm again.

While the wood train was over at Ash Hollow, a very ridiculous circumstance occurred. An Englishman, who claimed to be of some degree of nobility, turned up at the post with two four-mule wagons, a camping outfit, some dogs and servants, and said that he had come to the Western country to kill game. He wanted to get bear, buffalo, black-tail deer, and everything else which ran on four legs. He was a man of about thirty-five to forty years. He considered himself the smartest man that ever crossed the plains. He was always talking about English manners, and English etiquette. He was a scamp with a lot of money.

He came up, as he said, to pay his respects to the post commander. I soon saw that he was a rich, unprincipled scalawag. His egotism was enormous. He was talking about himself and his family most of the time; his idea of good morals was confined to the impression that a man should not eat with a knife. That seemed to be the sum total of his views of morality and good form. He was vulgar, indecent, loud, and a general nuisance in every respect; but he didn't eat with his knife.

He spoke of his traveling in America, and how he had been entertained by some of the best families of the land, and he had actually seen people eat with the knife. There was nothing else coarse enough or vulgar enough to attract his attention. I got tired of him in a short time, and launched him back onto the prairie with my kind regards, and he went to his wagons down at the station. Among his dogs was a very nice thoroughbred greyhound. The frontiersmen, who were all smart enough for anybody, and could read the new-comers like books, immediately began to make this Englishman their prey.

In the first place they got some green coffee, boiled it until it was tender, then soaked it in strychnine. The Englishman wanted to bet on everything, and was so all-wise that nobody could offer a bet that he did not take, either one side or the other of it. Some of the pioneers got into a conversation with this Englishman, and asked him if he had ever traveled in Java. Of course, the Englishman had traveled in Java, and knew all about it, and then one of these pioneers suggested that he had heard that green coffee was one of the most fatal poisons to swallow; that while it would not hurt a cat or a horse or a human being, that five grains swallowed by a dog were fatal. The Englishman sneered at the idea. Then one of the bystanders said that he had heard the same thing, and would bet a hundred dollars that it was true, because his old friend A. B. C. had told him so. The Englishman immediately took up the bet, and thereupon they slid down the dog's throat the five grains of green coffee, well prepared, and in a short time this beautiful dog was *in articulo mortis,* and the Englishman had lost his $100 and his dog.

At the ranch there was a man who sold, among other things, beans, the common navy beans, out of a sack, having a sack holding about a bushel, dipping them out with a quart cup. One of these fellows took a quart of the beans somewhere to the rear, and spent a sufficient time to count how many beans there were in the quart, and then he came around to where the Englishman and the beans were. One of the pioneers made a bet with another pioneer in regard to how many beans there were in a quart. After they had guessed wildly and at random, from three thousand to twenty-four thousand, the Englishman got into the game, and they took him for another $100.

It would have been all right, and would have ended here if the joke had not been too good, and some one told the Englishman of the tricks that had been played upon him. He came to our post to have the "bloody scoundrels" arrested for robbery.

The whole story was told by the Englishman, and vouched for by one of his servants, and the confession of one of the parties was related. There were at our post headquarters, and standing out alongside of the door, about forty men, as tickled a lot as I ever saw; soldiers and all seemed to enjoy it immensely. After I had heard the evidence I asked the Englishman why he made the bet. He said he supposed it was an honest bet. I then asked him if he had won, what he would have done with the money. He said he would have put it in his pocket. I then told him that out in the Western country people got their experience in the manner that he had got his. That people paid for it, and therefore came by it honestly; and that I considered the matter as only a little question of propriety between man and man, except as to the killing of the dog. The man was in the room who had given the dog the strychnine coffee. I told the Englishman that he had lost his money, and deserved to lose it, and I would not order it paid back to him. But that any man who would kill a good dog ought to be imprisoned. I told the Englishman he had no right to risk the life of his dog by betting on it. I ordered the sergeant to take the poisoner to the guard-house and lock him up; I ordered the proceedings adjourned, and told all the civilians to get off the reservation. They all went off, enjoying the discomfiture of the Englishman very much.

As to my prisoner, I ordered him to be kept until he paid a fine of $200 into the post fund. I also had him put at work currying horses. This post fund was for the purpose of general post benefits, extra things for the sick boys, and such matters as were needed, and which the Government did not issue. The post fund was really the company fund of our company. The man was kept working in the stables about two weeks. He finally proved to me that he was a worthless scamp, without any resources, and couldn't pay anything. Afterwards there was a train going down the road; I let him go and told him not to appear on the Platte again, and I never saw him afterwards.

The arrival of Lacey and Donley from Ash Hollow with the wood put us all in good spirits, and we entered the month of December with but little apprehension for the future.

Upon the first of December Captain O'Brien returned from Cottonwood Springs, and assumed command of the post. Our First Lieutenant, Brewer, was made Quartermaster of the post, and that left me the only officer to command the company, and on December first I took personal command of the company.

CHAPTER XXVIII

*The Unfriendly Dinner · Apostle Cannon · Joe
Smith · The Mormon Doctrine · Alkali Station ·
The Mormon Train · The River Crossing · Cham-
pagne with Bancroft · Elston's Prophecy*

SHORTLY after the Captain reassumed command of the
Post, he and I were invited to the stage station, one
day, for dinner. There was a long table with about ten on
each side. They were the drivers of the stage line, about as
rough and jolly a lot of men as I ever saw. They were talking
about the Indian scare, and the probabilities of an Indian
outbreak, and how General P. Edward Connor was coming
through from Salt Lake to take charge. And the whole
dinner was a loud and uproarious occasion. The profanity
was pyrotechnic.

One of the stage-drivers who was pretty loud, got to talking about the dangers that would follow an Indian outbreak.
Every man at the table had on a revolver; some of them
two. This loud-talking and vivacious stage-driver said he
believed that the Cheyenne Indians could come and take
the post. Captain O'Brien asked him what made him think
so. He made some sort of a flippant reply which brought
on a controversy, and this stage-driver pretended to take
offense at what the Captain said, and told the Captain that
he, the stage-driver, had a notion to go across the table
and break him in two.

Thereupon the Captain quickly arose with his hand on his
revolver and told him that he must not talk that way, and
if he wanted to do any shooting that he could always get
satisfaction; that he, the Captain, would shoot toe to toe,
or across the table, or across the corral, or across the prairie,
or across the river. The fellow was inclined to be ugly, but

as he looked at the Captain he did not think it wise to say much more.

I do not know how many of those present had their hands on their revolvers, but I guess everyone around the table. I had mine ready. The Captain said he believed he did not care to eat any more dinner where such discourtesy was shown, and he withdrew from the table with his hand on his revolver, passing out of the door, and keeping his eye upon those present; I did the same. We went out, got on our horses, and went up to the post.

It was without doubt a put-up job to get us down there at dinner and have some fun with us. Some of them had been Confederate soldiers. Of course we never knew whether there was a design to be gay with us, but we took good care not to get into such a situation again. Some of the stage-drivers we knew personally; some we did not know, but had generally regarded them all as good fellows, and, singly and personally, they were; but, in bulk they were not very desirable acquaintances for officers in blue uniform.

One day, early in December, I was up on top of our stable gazing around with my field-glass, as I often used to do, to see if anything suspicious could be seen on the horizon, or up on the hills, when I noticed a dark speck up Lodgepole Creek. It was so much enveloped in haze that I could not make it out for a long time. Finally I saw that it was a covered wagon. I had a corporal and five men immediately go over to where it was, for fear that some Indian might rise up out of the grass and kill the traveler.

When he arrived at the post the occupant of the vehicle introduced himself to me as Mr. Cannon. He had a driver and a large, fine four-mule light-running wagon with rubber cover. I told Mr. Cannon that he would have to stay until a hundred armed men were going East. He very much opposed this, and did his utmost to persuade me to disobey my orders in such cases. He told me that he was one of the twelve apostles of the Mormon Church, and he was going East to meet an appointment, and if he were long delayed it would be very unfortunate. He told me, as every other

Mormon did, that he was not afraid of the Indians, and that no Indian ever killed a Mormon. But I was compelled to hold him; told him that I could not permit the orders to be violated; would have a train ready for him as soon as possible, and that there were already quite a number of wagons in corral near the post.

Cannon was a very fine, dignified-looking gentleman, and very much inclined to talk. And when I found he was a Mormon apostle, I was very desirous of hearing what he had to say, having already had the advantage of desultory conversations with his predecessor, Elder Sharpe, of whom I have spoken. As an evangelist and lecturer on the Mormon faith, Cannon was very much superior to Sharpe. Cannon saw the dogs, and wanted to see a wolf-hunt; so I with ten men went out on horseback with him. While on the hunt he got to telling me about the Mormon faith, and its introduction by Joe Smith. There came between us a series of very interesting colloquies. I would now be unable to depict these, except that I not only made full notes of them at the time, but I also wrote them out fully in letters to my Mother, upon whose death I found them all preserved. I am able, therefore, to go into the matter with more detail than I otherwise would, but will have to condense them very much here.

I asked him how he knew that the Indians were the lost tribes of Israel. He then went on to tell me how the lost tribes of Israel wandered from their country, came to the United States, and how they increased and spread out, and prospered. Then he gave me a long history of the wars that took place between them. He told me of the battles which were fought, one after another. At the place where Cincinnati now stands a great battle had been fought. There were pursuits by one tribe of another. One tribe endeavored to annihilate another. There was a great battle where Charleston, South Carolina, now stands, and there were secretaries who acted as historians to keep run of the vicissitudes of these wide and bloody wars.

Then he told about how finally the record was made which

Joe Smith found. He described to me the size of the gold plates upon which the characters containing these records were engraved. These gold plates contained it all, and had been placed in a stone box, and hidden in a hill in New York. He kept using scriptural quotations continually. He told how Joe Smith had found these plates, and had translated them. I asked him what kind of characters were on these plates. He said that he had not seen them, but he had had them described to him. He said they were not like the Roman letters, nor the Greek letters, nor the Chinese, nor the Hebrew, but they were written in a sort of elegant, cursive hand, something not unlike Pitman shorthand, smoothly, but with an entirely different character and meaning. He said nobody could read the characters without they had the tools to read them with. I asked him what he meant. He said that with these plates in the stone box there were placed two transparent pebbles, one for each eye to look through. These pebbles were rights and lefts, and must be held up before the eye, each pebble for the proper eye, and that when looking through those pebbles anybody could read the writing; that the pebbles themselves illuminated the mind of the reader, so that the reader, so long as he was looking through the pebbles, could read and understand the script, no matter what his native language was, but that he could not understand anything by simply looking at the plates with his unaided eyes.

I asked him why it was that as an apostle he had never seen these plates. He said that he did not dare to look at them. I asked him where they were. He said they were in a vault in Salt Lake; that they were sewed up in a heavy buckskin bag. He had hefted the bag, and it weighed about 25 pounds. He said that he had felt of them, and could perceive the size and thickness of the plates in the buckskin bag, but if anyone should look at those plates with unaided eyes, and without the urim and thummim they would be stricken dead. (The pebbles were named "urim" and "thummim.")

I asked him if the Mormons had any proof of immortality

that any other of the religious denominations had not. He said that they had, but that the proof only came individually to those who belonged to the church, and had been consecrated. In response to further questions he gave the Mormon theory of birth and life.

He said that every person upon the earth came to the earth from heaven; that everybody was born in heaven; that in heaven the person was simply a celestial spirit without a body, and had to come to the earth to get a body, and that having come to the earth and obtained a body, that is, having been born, then they on death became angels, capable of having children; but that the children born in heaven were celestial angels, who themselves had to come down to the earth to get bodies so that they in turn might be parents of other celestial angels. He said the object is, on this earth, to furnish bodies for as many celestial angels as possible, and thereby do good, because there are great numbers of celestial angels who need and want bodies, and who are waiting to be born on this earth so as to get them. And hence the father and mother of the most children did the most good, and it was for that reason that polygamy was advocated, and so much esteemed. He said the object of polygamy is to give bodies, as many as possible, to the celestial angels who are ready to inhabit them, and therefore the more children one has on earth the higher his standing in heaven.

I said, how did it come, if that were the case, how did it come that the human race was planted here on this earth? He said that the Lord was constantly making planets, and places for human abodes. It is work that is going on all of the time. When the earth was created, and became ready for human habitation, it was a question as to who should be sent to populate it. There were three archangels in heaven, and they all wanted the privilege of starting the human race on the earth. They were Lucifer, Michael, and Adam. Lucifer claimed the right because he was the senior archangel, and had a pride to be the originator of the race on this planet. Michael advocated no particular claim, and Adam in a humble way said, "The Lord's will be done." On account of the meekness and modesty of Adam, the Lord delegated him to come to the earth, and inaugurate the new system. These archangels had their own hosts of friends, followers and retainers in heaven, as well as individual territorial jurisdiction, and when Adam was sent down to the earth, Lucifer revolted, and his cohorts stayed with him and there was war in heaven, and Lucifer was finally expelled. And then Apostle Cannon with a delightful gesture said, "And then, in the language of holy writ, he drew one-third of the stars from heaven with him."

After I got over being somewhat stunned by this new theory, I said to him. "Well, then, you said I was born in heaven?" "Yes," replied Mr. Cannon. "And came down from there?" "Yes." "Well, then, if I was in heaven, I was in that war." "Yes," said Mr. Cannon. "Well, now," I said to him, "why is it that I don't remember that war?" He said, "You are not expected to while you are in your corporal form here on earth, but you were in that war and you helped fight Lucifer," and as he said this he patted me on the shoulder as we rode along. "In that war I have no doubt that you fought bravely and well, because you are an officer in command of a company here now." This knocked me entirely out of the box, and was the end of the propaganda. I said, "Oh, rats!" and we changed the subject.

Cannon was a very delightful and companionable gentleman. I remembered him always as he appeared then. In a short time he went down the road with a caravan. Many years afterwards, in 1892, at the National Republican Presidential Convention at Minneapolis, Mr. Cannon's son was there as a delegate from Utah with a contested seat. I was one of the delegates to the National Convention. I went in, took a look at young Mr. Cannon, liked his appearance, told him that I knew and remembered his father, and that I would assist him in getting a seat in the convention. I worked for him in the caucus, listened with pleasure to his speech to the delegates, and voted for him. He was admitted.

Apostle Cannon left on December 7th, 1864, just as a storm of unexampled severity came with a hurricane from the northwest, and lasted for three days. We could not get outside of the post. Water was carried to the horses in buckets from the well, and everybody stayed indoors. But we were very snug in our quarters. They were thick, and heavily built with a heavy roof, which was about two feet thick, covered over with well-laid, nicely joined layers of sod. We did nothing but tell stories, and play cards, cook and eat. In fact, there was nothing else to do. The weather stayed cold for quite a while.

Company "A" of our regiment had been sent up to occupy a place about twenty-five miles east of us, called Alkali station, and Captain O'Brien went down there with Lieutenant Brewer. Going down, they passed a large Mormon train, consisting almost entirely of freight wagons, but all drawn by horses and mules. There were no ox teams, because at this season of the year there was no green pasturage. The train was laden principally with supplies coming west, and was going as rapidly as possible. They wanted to get through to Laramie before they made a halt. The Platte river at Julesburg was frozen over from shore to shore. Captain O'Brien telegraphed me from Alkali, and told me to use every exertion to speed the train; that it was liable to be caught and ruined by the weather before it got to Laramie; that at Laramie they could take care of the animals in the Black Hills near there, and could push on farther when ready. The Captain also sent me a letter in charge of the wagon-master, requesting me to do my level best to get them across the river as speedily as possible, for their hurry and their danger were great. I was very much worried over the order. I hardly knew what to do, but I made up my mind as to one thing, that a route across the river ought to be quickly chopped out of the ice. The ice was not heavy enough to hold up the teams. It was in some places, but in the shoal places, where the water was only two or three inches deep, the wagon would cut through, and down in, and the only way to do was to cut them a channel clear across the river. So I went above the post to the Mormon crossing, and by chopping holes, and testing the river, I selected what I thought was the best and firmest route. I then went back to the post and detailed fifty men to go up with me to chop out the ice. We had a large number of axes and picks at the post, and I laid out a route about twelve feet wide, marked it on the ice, and set the boys to chopping so as to break the ice. This was accomplished in one day satisfactorily, but the weather was quite cold. We started in again the next day to get the ice out of the proposed wagon channel. We did not get to work until about ten o'clock, and with pitchforks and shovels we tried to do some of it, but we did not accomplish much before dinner. We all went back, after dinner, about two o'clock in the afternoon, to work on the river. The weather had become quite cold, and it became necessary to get the ice out as soon as possible, as it was said that the head of the train could be seen coming from the east. There appeared no way that was convenient or effective to get the ice out of that gap. It was difficult to push it down under the ice on top, and it was very difficult to lift it out with any appliances we had. In some places the water was quite shallow, and the deepest was about four feet. The deepest of the water was the nearest to us on the south side. I ordered the men to jump into the water, and begin lifting out the ice with their hands. The men did not seem to take kindly to it, and did not seem desirous of obeying the order. It was a pretty severe order, there in freezing weather, to get men into the water, and lift ice, and get all wet. So in order to get my commands enforced, I jumped in and had the orderly sergeant jump in near me, and we commenced raising the ice and tumbling it over onto the down-stream side. In a very short time I was soaked, and the water was quite cold. And the men, seeing how the thing was going, all jumped in, and we went across the river throwing the ice out until we got the channel cleared.

Then I got the men all out on the bank, gave the command of "double-quick," and we all started to run to the post. We went to the post in good shape, and got pretty well limbered, and the men got into the barracks and took off their clothes, and dried off. I got on some dry clothes just as the train was going by, and I went out to it and took charge of the matter of crossing; I stationed the fellows along the line of the channel with the whips which the drivers generally carried, and started them all in, and before dark the Mormon train was across the river on the other side. There were about thirty wagons of them, and as the channel was narrow, and the mules confined to the road, it was one of the best crossings I ever saw made on the Platte river.

After the train had all gone I found that I had got pretty thoroughly wet again in seeing them across, and carrying out the orders given me. Mr. Bancroft, the man from whom we bought the ranch from which we made our post, was on the bank watching the proceedings. He had a little, light, covered wagon, and where he was going to or coming from I do not remember. Maybe he did not tell me, but he said to me: "That was the finest crossing I ever saw made, and I heard that you fellows got right into the water and lifted the ice out with your hands." I said, "Yes, that is the way we did it." He said: "I want to tell you that is mighty satisfactory work as viewed by an outsider, and I have got some champagne in this wagon, and I think you ought to drink a quart of it." I said, "I am capable of drinking a quart right quick." So he brought out two quart bottles of champagne, and on the windward side of the wagon I drank one of them in about two minutes by the watch, and he drank one of them. I never saw him again until at least twenty years afterward, when I happened to meet him down in southwestern Missouri, where he said he was carrying on a flour mill. Mr. Bancroft had undoubtedly got from the Government the money for his ranch, and was engaged in high living, when I met him on the bank with the champagne.

Charley Elston, the scout, was nominally attached to our post, but as there was no particular work for him, he divided his time between us and Cottonwood Springs. But he kept all the time saying that we were going to catch it from the Indians before we got through. He would take rides out into the country off the road, and there were stories of how he found tracks of Indian lookouts along the line. He also told us of many rumors which were brought through by the pilgrims on the trains, and he kept constantly advising us to always be on the lookout, because "the first thing you know," he would say, "they will be onto your post here with their war paint on."

ON DECEMBER 20, 1864, the report came that Thomas had whipped Hood down in Tennessee; so we had a celebration again, in which we fired off our cannon at a target, and thus gained experience in target exercise as well as venting our enthusiasm.

In the course of the proceedings, the work, the scouting and the escort duty, we had lost the use of ten or a dozen of our horses, and there had been sent to Cottonwood Springs a lot of horses for the cavalry service. They had been placed there in the corral subject to assignment by the Quartermaster. So, after we had a big Christmas celebration, the Captain went down to Cottonwood to see if he couldn't get horses enough for a full remount. Our Christmas at Julesburg was quite an affair. We had dress parade, fired off the howitzers at a target, cooked the best beef we could find in the herd, and everybody wrote letters home. But some of the men got boisterously drunk, and on inspection I found out the cause of it.

A man had come in, and about a mile below Julesburg, which itself was a mile below our post, had repaired up and rebuilt and put in shape a two-room sod house, and he had been running a whisky establishment patronized by pilgrims in the first room, and a poker establishment in the rear room. He had been afraid to sell any whisky to the soldiers, and he had not been discovered. But shortly before Christmas he had been joined by another bandit, and they had begun selling whisky to the soldiers, and cheating them out of their money playing poker in the back room. This went on for two or three days, until the first thing that I knew there had been a lot of my men down there, having a row with a lot of pilgrims, and having a shooting-match with these two proprietors, who needed killing as badly as any two men on the Platte river.

The next thing that I heard was that these two bandits had attempted to kill and rob one of my men, had cheated a lot of them out of their money, and that there was a posse of my company going down to kill them both. I could hardly believe the stories that were told me privately by the non-commissioned officers, and by some of the men who knew all about the proposed plan. It was given to me one afternoon between Christmas and New Year's that some of the boys in the company were going to go down and lynch those two ranchmen (as they called themselves). Finally, I heard that it was to be the night of the 29th. Captain O'Brien and First Lieutenant Brewer, the Quartermaster, had both gone to Cottonwood Springs as stated, to make requisition and receipt for horses, and I was left all alone, and I was told that night they were going to lynch those two men, sure, and that both of them were Rebel deserters.

Nobody seemed to understand the extent of the plot, nor how many there were in it, but from what I could learn, all the toughest characters in my company had, by a sort of Masonic secrecy, planned to work together. That evening at roll-call, while the men were all drawn up in line, I told them that there had been rumors that some of them were going out of the camp that night, and were going to commit some depredations. I told them that if that should take place, and any citizen would be killed, that it would result in my being dismissed from the service as being unable to command my company; that I did not intend to be dismissed from the service; that I did not intend to let anybody go down the road, and commit any impropriety. And I told them that in view of the fact I would change the guard somewhat tonight, and there would be a little stronger detail than before.

After the company disbanded the orderly sergeant came to me, and told me that he believed the whole matter had been abandoned, and that there would be no trouble. But I was fearful of it, and while I did not think that there should be any real reason why I should prevent the two bandits being lynched, I knew that I could never explain it, and that it was my military duty to see that it did not happen.

I selected particular camp guards for that night, and put them outside of the post, one on each of the four sides. Before the guards were set, I called them into my headquarters and told them that I expected that there would be some men start out to commit some devilment that night below the station. I told them that I wanted them to keep close guard that the men did not run past in bulk or did not slip out one by one, and join themselves together down the road. I also told the corporal of the guard that I wanted him to report to me every thirty minutes. Along about eleven o'clock the corporal of the guard came to me and told me that two men certainly had slipped out during the night, and had been seen. I immediately called my orderly, and had him saddle up my black pony, of which I will speak more hereafter. I immediately went into the barracks to see how many of the men were on hand, and I found ten of them gone. I had the pony tied up in front of the office while I got my carbine and revolver loaded with some cartridges, and a pocketful of crackers to eat.

Just as I had got about ready to start, the corporal of the guard came in, and said that there was about a dozen more of the boys that had run the guards. So I got onto my pony, and not desiring to give them any clue to my coming, I rode out in a big circle on the prairie as fast as I could go, so as to get ahead of them. It was a long ride. Coming down to about a hundred yards of Julesburg station, I got down to the ground, and in the darkness I heard and dimly saw a large squad of the men walking on down at a route step towards me. I had got in ahead of them in the dark.

I rode up towards them until I got within about two hundred feet of them, and I cried "Halt!" and dismounted from my pony, and raised my carbine. They huddled together, and came more slowly. Finally I again ordered them to halt, and told them that I wanted them to stay halted until they heard what I had to say. They halted in silence. I told them that I knew what they were after; that it was a crime which they proposed to commit; that they had no right to kill Rebels that way; that if I permitted it I would be unfit to command the company; that I didn't propose to let them go any farther; that I would shoot the first man that got up near enough for me to draw a bead on him; that if they started to run around me, I would get as many of them as I could with my carbine; that I wanted them to stay together; that I wanted them to turn about right face and march back to the post. They remained still, and commenced whispering to each other. I then threw the bridle-rein around my pony's neck, gave him a kick, and off he started back to the post. I then told them that I was going to march them back to the post. I heard a revolver click, and then I clicked my carbine, brought it up to my eye, pointed it in the midst; they were about forty feet from me. I said, "You cannot shoot so quickly that I cannot get one of you. Now make up your minds to go back, because there is where you are going. There is no hurry about it; take plenty of time, but decide it right. You are not going a foot farther down the river tonight." I held the carbine up to my eye; I pointed at the group, and I kept holding it. It seemed a long while. I knew the men could make a rush, but they could not keep me from shooting at least one of them, and as I had two revolvers in my belt, both of them cocked, I knew that I was as safe as any of them. I knew that if they had time they would come to the right conclusion. They did not want to hurt me. Finally, after a very long pause, I heard one of them say, "Well, let's go back," and they began turning around, and starting back. I followed them, and I said, "Quick time—march," and the speed became more rapid. Finally I said, after we had gone a while, "Double-quick—march," and they all started off on the run. And they ran away from me for the reason, which I did not think of, that they wanted to get up into the post, and perhaps far enough ahead of me to evade indentification. I was weighted down so with lunch, overcoat, revolvers, carbine and ammunition, that I could not keep up, and they got ahead of me. The sentinel ordered them to stop, but they ran right over him, and he, disinclined to kill any of his comrades, let them go. My pony had come back to the post.

It was between one and two o'clock in the morning, and as bleak a December midnight as I ever saw. I sat up in my headquarters, not knowing whether they would attempt anything further or not, but determined to stay wide awake until morning.

After about an hour, say about three o'clock, one of the sergeants came in to me and said, "Those men who came back agreed among themselves, that they would come back, that then they would start out again, so you are liable to have a repetition before morning." I went out to the barracks, and I found them all awake. Everybody was sitting up, and the performances of the evening were being discussed. And I went in with my two revolvers buckled on, and told them that if anybody now started out to commit any depredation that they would know that I ordered them to stay in the barracks, and if anything was done I would have the offender court-martialed, and shot; that I thought I would have sufficient influence with the General commanding to have a man who would willfully disobey an order of that kind, shot, providing I couldn't do it myself, and that I would stay around until morning to see that no depredations were committed. I further said that I expected the support of all the honest and loyal soldiers in the company; that whisky was at the bottom of it all, and I thought perhaps by this time the effects of it had been worn off, and that

I wanted all the members of the company to return to their duties and obligations; that we were soon going to have an Indian campaign, and I wanted my company to distinguish itself, and I did not want them to have a reputation in advance which would not commend it to the good wishes of the commanding officers of the district.

Matters finally sort of died down, but I went out to talk with the sentinels myself every thirty minutes, and when morning came the thing was a memory. But the occasion and circumstance of my being out on that wild prairie that black night has always been a weird recollection. Before thirty days were over many of the men were in their graves. The two ranchmen disappeared. I tried to get them, but failed by reason of their timely flight.

A word here in extenuation of the conduct of my men. The two ranchmen ought to have been killed. I tried to get them next morning so as to put them under guard, and do something with them, but they had fled. My men under the influence of such vile whisky felt like doing anything. The men only got into those conditions spasmodically and at long intervals. They always meant well and never dodged work, exposure, or danger. As a whole they were a likeable lot, and their transgressions were as few as their service was hard, lonesome and bitter. I pretended never to know who were in this trouble and I never had any with the company afterwards. It grieved me at the time, but I soon got over it, and forgot it.

Having told about my pony on the evening alluded to, it occurs to me that I ought to say something about that pony. Sometime during November the young man, a citizen, whom I had been employing to take care of my horses, and whose position was that of an "orderly," as it was called, desired to go back to the "States." While waiting for a train and a proper occasion, he communicated his intention to me, and a young fellow about nineteen came and applied for his job. He did not have much to say. I asked him if he was acquainted with the care of horses, and he said that he was. Then I asked him if he could stand the climate, and the disagreeable conditions of military service, and he said he thought he could; and I employed him. The Government issued rations to an orderly and the two horses that a lieutenant had. I paid an orderly $20 a month, and he got his rations from the Government, and all he had to do was to provide his own clothes and do the work.

I always rode my black horse "Old Bill," and I turned over to my new orderly the other one, which had got into bad condition, and told him to bring the horse up to a better efficiency. My orderly went to work, and was a very satisfactory boy, quite taciturn, saying nothing, but keeping busy all the time, and I formed a good opinion of him, and so did those around me. He never said anything, however, to me, and was very silent, and lonesome. One day when there was quite a congregation of pilgrims going down the road he came to me and told me that he could trade my sorrel horse for a mighty good Indian pony, provided I could pay a little to boot, and I concluded to see what the trade might be. I told him to bring the man in, and he came. He was a strange-looking, impudent fellow, with a mustache like a cat's. He had about six bristles on each side that stuck out straight. He said that he wanted to go back to the "States," and he wanted a horse to ride, and he wanted $25 to pay his expenses. He said that he had been trading with the Arapahoe Indians, and that the pony which he offered to trade to me was the best war pony in the Arapahoe nation. He had got the pony, trained it, and it could run well and trot well, and could endure any amount of trial and tribulation that might be required of it. I took a look at the pony. It was jet black all over, with a roached mane. As it compared exactly in color with "Old Bill," I concluded to swap horses, and pay the man $25, and he went off on down the road.

At the same time that my orderly was employed, a young man named Pierce joined the company. I will speak of him further on. He and my orderly seemed to have been sort of chums at the time.

Concerning the black pony, I may say that it turned

out to be one of the finest animals I ever saw. It was as fleet as the wind. It could run all day, and was the most useful little animal imaginable. It had always been a pet, and had a disposition like a Newfoundland dog. I became very much attached to it, and it would follow me around, come at call, was very bridle-wise, and never got ugly. I may anticipate my story a little bit by saying that I kept him until after I got to Fort Leavenworth, and an officer of the regular army got attached to him, and persuaded me to let him have the pony for $400.

Returning to my new "orderly," who afterwards turned out pretty bad, as we will see, and whose name I will withhold, I found him one day talking Sioux to Elston, the guide. I asked Elston if the boy was talking Indian, and Elston said, "Yes, and he talks it just like an Injun." I thereupon called the boy up, and asked him if he spoke Indian, and he said, yes; and I asked him how that came. And he said that when he was a boy between eight and nine, his parents, who were from Blandinsville, Illinois, were crossing the plains with a party and were murdered. And that he was carried off by the Indians and was raised among them, and had been with them about ten years. I then asked him how it came that he turned up in our camp. And he said that he had got acquainted with the two white women, Mrs. Kelly and Mrs. Larimer, who were captured by the Sioux shortly before we went up to Fort Laramie, and that one of them had advised him to run away and get back to the white people. And that, being out with a party of Indians, he had run away from them, and had come into the camp at Laramie, and had come down with some people to Julesburg, and was going on, when he heard about a place as orderly, with the soldiers, and he thought he would be safe, have a better time, and that was how he came with me. His story was probably true.

Upon inquiry he told us all about the two ladies above referred to, and about his own wanderings among the Sioux, and he answered questions frankly, and to the best of his ability. But the reason that he was so taciturn was that he had about forgotten his own language, and could only express himself with difficulty, but he picked it up again very rapidly, so that by the time he had been with us a few months he had got a good deal of it back. The real reason why he had been so taciturn was that he couldn't talk. He afterwards had a great deal to say about the Indians, and their habits. He had been adopted into the tribe, and had an inclination to stay, but one of the ladies referred to had told him that he was likely at any time to be killed, and after some reluctance he had made up his mind to leave the tribe. He was very tanned and sunburned, and in a blanket would have about passed for an Indian in color.

During December I got a pair of cavalry boots which I ordered from Omaha. It shows something in regard to the deterioration of money, and the price of things, when I say that those boots cost me $18. In normal times, on gold basis, they would have cost $5.

I also bought from one of the traveling outfits going west a twenty-pound keg of butter for $20 and a twenty-pound can of lard for $10, the prices being $1 and $0.50, respectively, per pound.

Concerning the relative location of Julesburg, there was some little difficulty as to the question whether Julesburg was in Nebraska or Colorado. For a while we called it Nebraska, but afterwards we were addressed as Julesburg, Colorado, and the post was deemed definitely located in Colorado, which was the correct place. But Fort Laramie *was Idaho Territory*. It is now in the eastern part of Wyoming, but that part of the country was then called Idaho Territory.

CHAPTER XXX

Ben Halladay · Gold Gambling · Summary of Conditions · December 31, 1864 · Colonel Chivington · His Battle with Cheyennes · P. Edward Connor · Territorial Divisions · Troops Employed · Location of Posts · The Escort Lines

DURING December, as stated, Ben Holladay went through going west in a stage-coach, with a man named Leland, who was a great hotel man in New York City. The coach was a sort of Pullman conveyance. They had a mattress on the floor of the coach, and they slept in the coach, and when they rode, they rode with the driver, and on a seat on the top. They had another coach, in which there were servants, a cook, and supplies. Each of these coaches was drawn by six horses, and went as fast as the fastest. Holladay put in his time as long as he was at the post in receiving and sending off dispatches to the Gold Board in New York. They had in New York a speculative board which was gambling on the nation's good and bad luck, and the price of gold went up and down, governed by every little skirmish and battle of the war. It seemed to have had little reference to the actual amount of gold on hand. Holladay had a way of gambling on the gold market, and when he lost he delivered the actual gold, having a location on the Pacific coast in the gold-bearing country. Holladay's son, who went along the road shortly afterwards, said that his father, when going from the Pacific coast to New York, played the gold markets the whole way, and made $40,000 on the trip of about three weeks.

Taking the end of the year 1864, it is perhaps best for me to state what was the actual condition of things at that time. In the first place, the Indians between Cottonwood and Fort Kearney had committed depredations, the value of which was very great. They had harassed the frontiers in Minnesota, Iowa, Nebraska, Kansas, and Colorado. As stated, there was a squaw camp at Fort Laramie, where a lot of them were being fed. In the forts in southeastern Colorado, other Indians were being fed. The Arapahoes and Cheyennes, after committing all kinds of depredations, had pretended to surrender, and to come in and want peace. At Fort Lyon, down on the Arkansas river, the persons surrendered consisted of women and children and old men, who brought in a lot of worn-out horses used up in the raids of the frontiers; and they brought in some old guns that had become unserviceable. The young bucks, however, were on the war-path, and from these very Indian refugees at Fort Lyons occasional parties would go out, and rob a train and steal a lot of stock. There was no confidence to be placed in any of these Indians. They were a bad lot. They all needed killing, and the more they were fed and taken care of the worse they became. The condition was such in Colorado that a hundred-days regiment was raised, called the Third Colorado. The First Colorado, a brave and historic regiment, had a Colonel by the name of Chivington, and he had been drawn from the war to protect his own State against the ravages of these combined Cheyenne and Arapahoe Indians. The Government had sent in, as has been stated before, the Eleventh Ohio Cavalry, also our complete cavalry regiment of twelve companies, and then had drawn the First Nebraska from the front, down South, to help guard Nebraska, and had also raised a provisional home battalion to assist in the protection of the Nebraska frontier. The Government had deployed other regiments out on the Arkansas river, and along the Santa Fé trail, for the purpose of protecting that route, over a long strip of country.

I have stated that some of these Indians went to Denver, and wanted to make a treaty of some kind. The Indian idea was to have the Government feed the old people, women and children, while the bucks would ravage the country. As I have stated, the embassy to Denver was a failure, because the Denver people understood the Indian quite fully. After the Denver embassy the murdering and plundering along the frontier and line became so great that Colonel Chivington made up his mind to take the field, and hunt up the Indian villages and punish them. While he was getting ready, the refugee Indians who were being fed at Fort Lyons went out and plundered some trains and killed some women and children, and carried their scalps to the Cheyenne villages up on Sand Creek.

There came a great fall of snow in the latter part of November, about two feet deep, and Colonel Chivington, taking advantage of that fact, and knowing that the Indians could not travel in deep snow as the whites could, started out, and after a three-days march, day and night, he came onto one of the Cheyenne villages, and is reported to have killed about five hundred of them, captured a large lot of horses, and scattered the band; although he lost nine killed and forty wounded, because the Indians put up a pretty good fight. That fight occurred on November 29th, 1864. Among the humanitarians of Boston it was called the "Chivington Massacre," but there was never anything more deserved than that massacre. The only difficulty was that there were about fifteen hundred Indian warriors that didn't get killed. But they were scattered over the country, and started supposedly east on the Republican and Solomon rivers. They were in this scattered condition when the end of the year arrived. Nobody exactly knew where they were, but it was said that there were scalp-dances in all of the Cheyenne bands, and that scalps were carried up into the Sioux villages and into the northern Cheyenne villages for the purpose of making medicine, and getting up a war spirit, north of the Platte.

I will try to give a glance now as to the condition of the commands and their situation. At this time the Indian country was in a department which had had several names, but which at that time was called the "Department of Kansas and the Territories." Major-General Samuel R. Curtis was commander at Fort Leavenworth. The District of Nebraska comprised the line that went from Omaha to Laramie, and west of Laramie to Great South Pass. That was one long line of road, and was the great northern route that was to be guarded. This territory was divided into two sub-districts, one running from Omaha up to and including Julesburg. That was called the eastern sub-district, and was in command of Colonel R. R. Livingston of the First Nebraska Cavalry, with headquarters at Fort Kearney. The western district began west of Julesburg, with its first post at Mud Springs, and extended along the route to South Pass. This western sub-district was commanded by Lieutenant-Colonel William O. Collins, of the Eleventh Ohio, of whom I have spoken. The road from Julesburg to Denver was the northern district of Colorado, and was commanded by Colonel J. M. Chivington, of the First Colorado. Brigadier-General R. B. Mitchell was in command from Omaha through to South Pass, covering the two sub-districts of which I have spoken. Brigadier-General P. Edward Connor commanded at Salt Lake City. Neither Colonel Chivington nor General Connor was under the command of General Mitchell.

General Connor had the reputation of being the greatest Indian-fighter on the continent, and he had been requested to look over the situation by General Curtis, commanding the department, and pass his opinion as to what ought to be done with the Cheyennes and Arapahoes, and how best to do it. General Connor passed on down the road, it was stated, along in December, past our fort, incognito.

In my memorandum I have the following as being the companies and posts of each of these districts and sub-districts as they existed on the 31st of December, 1864, as shown by the general orders of that period.

On December 31, 1864, the organization of troops was as follows:

DEPARTMENT OF KANSAS.

Commanded by Major-General Samuel R. Curtis. Headquarters at Fort Leavenworth, Kansas.

The Department was composed of the following districts:

District of South Kansas, Headquarters at Paola, Kansas.

District of North Kansas, Headquarters at Fort Leavenworth, Kansas.

District of the Upper Arkansas, Headquarters at Fort Riley, Kansas.

District of Nebraska, Headquarters at Omaha, Nebraska.

District of Colorado, Headquarters at Denver, Colorado.

The District of South Kansas was commanded by Major-General James G. Blunt, with 42 officers and 998 men.

The District of North Kansas was commanded by Brigadier-General Thomas A. Davies, with 30 officers and 530 men.

The District of the Upper Arkansas was commanded by Colonel James H. Ford, with 24 officers and 803 men.

The District of Nebraska was commanded by Brigadier-General Robert B. Mitchell, with 54 officers and 1,201 men.

The District of Colorado was commanded by Colonel John M. Chivington, with 19 officers and 297 men.

The foregoing does not represent the total number of each command, but represents the number present, able for duty, and *in the saddle on December 31, 1864.* Of course there were many not "in the saddle."

The District of Nebraska was divided as follows:

East Sub-District, commanded by Colonel Robert R. Livingston. Headquarters, Fort Kearney, Nebraska.

In this sub-district were the following posts and garrisons:

Fort Kearney: Five companies 1st Nebraska Cavalry.

Plum Creek: Three companies 1st Nebraska Cavalry.

Cottonwood Springs: Two companies 7th Iowa Cavalry and one company 1st Nebraska Cavalry.

Columbus: One company 7th Iowa Cavalry.

Little Blue Station: One company 1st Nebraska Militia.

Mullala Station: One company 1st Nebraska Cavalry.

Dan Smith's Ranch: One company 7th Iowa Cavalry.

Gilman's Station: One company 1st Nebraska Cavalry.

O'Fallon's Bluffs: One company 7th Iowa Cavalry.

Alkali Station: One company 7th Iowa Cavalry.

Beauvais Station: One company 1st Nebraska Cavalry.

Julesburg: One company 7th Iowa Cavalry.

West sub-district, commanded by Lieutenant-Colonel William O. Collins, with headquarters at Fort Laramie, Idaho Territory. In this sub-district were the following posts and garrisons:

Fort Laramie: Four companies 11th Ohio Cavalry; one company 7th Iowa Cavalry.

Camp Collins: Two companies 11th Ohio Cavalry.

Fremont's Orchard: One company 11th Ohio Cavalry.

Fort Halleck: One company 11th Ohio Cavalry.

Camp Marshall: One company 11th Ohio Cavalry.

Camp Mitchell: One company 11th Ohio Cavalry.

Platte Bridge: One company 11th Ohio Cavalry.

In the District of Colorado there were the following posts and garrisons:

Denver: One company 1st Colorado Cavalry; one company 3rd Colorado Cavalry.

Camp Fillmore: One company 1st Colorado Cavalry.

Fort Garland: One company 1st Colorado Cavalry.

Junction Station: One company 3rd Colorado Cavalry.

Valley Station: One company 3rd Colorado Cavalry.

In the District of the Upper Arkansas were the following posts and garrisons:

Fort Riley: Eight companies 2nd Colorado Cavalry; one section 9th Wisconsin Battery.

Fort Lyon: Eight companies 1st Colorado Cavalry; one company 1st New Mexico Cavalry.

Fort Larned: At post and en route—Two companies 2nd Colorado Cavalry; one company 12th Kansas Cavalry; one company 11th Kansas Cavalry; one section 9th Wisconsin Battery.

Fort Zarah: One company 3rd Wisconsin Cavalry.

Fort Ellsworth: One company 7th Iowa Cavalry.

Salina: One company 7th Iowa Cavalry.

The foregoing applies only to *our theatre of war*. There were nine posts in Dakota Territory, garrisoned by 22 companies of Cavalry and two of Infantry. There were four frontier posts of Iowa, garrisoned by six companies of Cavalry; also six posts in Minnesota, garrisoned by 13 companies of Cavalry and three companies of Infantry. All of this in excess of the Artillery, which was stationed at some of the posts, amounting in the aggregate to 26 guns.

The soldiers engaged were all or parts of the following regiments:

1st Colorado Cavalry.	1st New Mexico Cavalry.
2nd Colorado Cavalry.	3rd Wisconsin Cavalry.
3rd Colorado Cavalry.	1st Dakota Cavalry.
6th Iowa Cavalry.	2nd Minnesota Cavalry.
7th Iowa Cavalry.	Two Battalions Minnesota
1st Nebraska Cavalry.	Cavalry Volunteers.
1st Nebraska Militia.	1st Connecticut Cavalry.
11th Ohio Cavalry.	30th Wisconsin Infantry.
5th Kansas Cavalry.	1st United States Volunteers.
11th Kansas Cavalry.	9th Wisconsin Battery.
12th Kansas Cavalry.	McClain's Colorado Battery.
15th Kansas Cavalry.	3rd Minnesota Battery.
16th Kansas Cavalry.	

These desultory facts may not be interesting, but are inserted here as due to history.

The road from Omaha to South Pass was guarded by the First Nebraska Cavalry, the Seventh Iowa Cavalry, and the Eleventh Ohio Cavalry—being three regiments of cavalry with about twelve pieces of artillery strung along the road. The road from Julesburg to Denver was under the command of Colonel Chivington, and was guarded and patrolled by the First and Third Colorado Cavalry, but principally by the Third Colorado under charge of Major Samuel M. Logan, who occasionally visited us at Julesburg. Yet we, on occasions, sent escorts up as far as Pawnee, over 30 miles west, on the Denver road; northwest to Camp Mitchell near Scott's Bluffs, 117 miles; and east to O'Fallon's Bluffs, 50 miles. Our company had the hardest work to do of any company in or on the line, and suffered more in losses than any other company, both in killed and wounded and in accident. Our escort line was about 150 miles long.

ON THE first day of January, 1865, I received a telegraphic
order to proceed immediately to Cottonwood Springs and
not wait for anything; to be there to receive instructions
by wire at noon on the third. In a little while afterwards I
received a specific telegram to be in Cottonwood Springs
at 12 o'clock, noon, January 3rd, with the addendum to it,
"This order is peremptory."

I saw that it would not be possible to make it in the winter
on horseback without great inconvenience, and I went down
to the stage station to see if I could get a stage with four
horses, to run me through, night and day; which would
bring me in in good time. There was an old driver there, a
reckless fellow, the man who got the arrow through his coat
collar, of whom I have spoken. He said that he would hitch
up as soon as he could have a couple of horses shod, and he
would start off with me. I told him I would have ten men
detailed as an escort. He said, "What in thunder do we
want of an escort? I'll drive you through all right." I said,
"Suppose some Injun shoots you off from the box?" He said:
"Well, if they get me they get you; but I'll take you
through all right. The Injun won't trouble us at night, and
I can get you through to O'Fallon's Bluffs before morning;
then if you want an escort at O'Fallon's Bluffs we can get
it there."

Of course, it would never do for me to appear scared, if a stage-driver wasn't scared. I would have eternally lost my reputation if I had said anything more about an escort. If my men should ever hear that I had wanted an escort when the stage-driver didn't, they would have probably called upon me to resign. I thought it very unsafe, but still I told him that if he didn't want an escort I didn't, so I put up the "bluff" that all I wanted of an escort was for his benefit; that I could take care of myself. This seemed to please him.

About nine o'clock on that evening, all by our lone selves, on the stage, we started for Cottonwood Springs. There was no snow on the ground anywhere to be seen. It had all gone. The whole landscape was slate-gray as far as could be seen; there was no moonlight—just a bright starlight.

The stage-driver told me to get inside, which I did, with a little bundle of blankets and paraphernalia done up in a strap; a Smith & Wesson carbine, two revolvers strapped on, a box of ammunition, a field-glass, a big heavy overcoat, and two buffalo-robes. The driver primed himself with ranch whisky before we started, and asked me to keep the windows of the coach down so that I could fire out on either side, and be ready to get out whenever he shouted.

So we started, I with a revolver on the seat on each side of me, and with the carbine across my lap. The wind whistled in with a strong December chill through the open sides of the coach door, and it was anything but pleasant and comfortable. We heard wolves yelping from time to time, and I kept on the lookout for fire signals. On and on went the coach at a mad rate. Every once in a while the driver would shout back to me, "Do you see anything?" or "Do you hear anything?" or "How are you getting on?"

At about broad daylight I woke up. I had been asleep. The stage was stopped. It took me a little while to gather myself together. I looked out, and saw that we were right close to the hills. From the other side I saw we were two or three miles from the river, and the horses had their heads down to the ground, nipping the dried grass. It im-

mediately occurred to me that the driver had been killed
on the box. The next thing occurred to me was that there
were some Indians around; so I began to peer cautiously
around the sides from one side to the other, and I could see
the driver's foot sticking out on one side above me. I spoke
to him, then again and again, louder and louder, and got no
response. I soon, by gazing around, was satisfied that there
was no Indian around the coach nor under it, and I got out.
And there lay the driver extended out on the box. The horses
were nipping along, and the reins were tangled up with the
horses' heels of the rear span. I got up and shook the driver,
and saw no blood, but I did smell a good deal of whisky, and
saw the cork end of the bottle sticking out of his overcoat
pocket. I pulled it out, and it was empty. I then shook
him some more. He stupidly aroused himself up, and I saw
that he had got drunk on the box. I got the lines up as fast
as I could from the horses amid the tangle, and, unaccus-
tomed to driving a stage, I managed to get the horses twisted
around, and started back to the road. I got them back there
as fast as I could. I expected every minute to see some
Indian rise up somewhere or come over the hill. In a little
while the stage-driver began to come to, after I had got the
horses into the road. They were galloping down, and I with
my foot on the brake was trying to keep the stage in the
road, and right side up. The driver came to—slowly and
painfully, but he came to. Come to find out, we had not
made much progress. He had got primed up high, and in a
little while the coach had slowed down; I, with the carbine
across my lap, had gone to sleep, and we had been camping
out a couple of miles off from the road all night. And when
we got back to the road we found that we had come only
about twenty miles.

We finally got down to O'Fallon's Bluffs. We got breakfast, and I sent a telegram to my orderly to come down
with the next train that came to Cottonwood Springs, and
bring my stuff and the two horses with him. At O'Fallon's
Bluffs a regular stage-coach pretty full of passengers over-

took us, under escort. I preferred to let my stage-driver go back, and I got aboard the crowded stage, and went on down to Cottonwood Springs, where I arrived about nine o'clock in the morning.

The object of my mission and the order for me to go to Cottonwood, was this: Recruiting officers in Iowa had forwarded to Omaha a lot of recruits for our regiment, and they were to arrive, one hundred and sixteen of them, that day from Fort Kearney, whence they had been brought in six mule wagons. I was to take command, and immediately organize them into a company, and go to work drilling them as rapidly as possible. I was told privately that an Indian expedition had been organized to go down and drive the Indians out of eastern Colorado and northwestern Kansas. That the object was to keep the Indians on the go; that an Indian expedition for that purpose had been arranged, and that these new recruits had to be drilled, so that when they were divided up and put into the companies they would be able to know what to do. I was authorized to appoint corporals and sergeants, was told to drill the company on foot in all the cavalry movements, and to instruct the non-commissioned officers in their duties, so that by the time the horses would get there, which they thought would be in a week, the men could go to work drilling on horseback. I was further told to drill them all they would stand, clear to the point of exhaustion. Of course, this meant exhausting myself as well. When I found out what I was detailed to do I did not like the job.

I received the men, drew them up into line on their arrival, told them that they were a company, and that we would call it Company "I." (The real Company "I" of the regiment was many miles off, up at Sioux City, Iowa.) I told them that they had just come in time to get in a glorious Indian campaign, and would all be covered with glory; that I wanted them to be drilled in shape before they went, and wanted their hearty coöperation, for I would drill with them and do just as much as they. I then went and telegraphed my arrival and the assuming of the command, and that I had begun work, and suggested that some one be sent to relieve me, as my own company demanded all of my services. My telegram received no response.

The weather turned off blusteringly cold. The poor young recruits dressed in their overcoats were got out for a drill right after breakfast, and I drilled them all over the country until noon. Then I gave them an hour in which to get dinner, and an hour to play poker, and then I drilled them until supper-time. After supper-time I opened at the post headquarters a school of instruction. With wrapping-paper and charcoal I made a wall blackboard, and demonstrated to them the calls, and the movements. The boys took hold of it all in a strenuous way. There was no grumbling; they were tired out every day, but learned quite rapidly. They learned it theoretically at night by the lectures I gave them, and in daytime by the drill.

On the morning of January 6th, I received a telegram from General Mitchell, commanding the district at Omaha, asking me if I would act as his personal aide-de-camp; and, if so, for me to proceed immediately to Omaha. I wired him that I would be glad to serve as aide-de-camp, and that I would start early the next morning. In the mean time my orderly and two horses had arrived, and I was all ready to proceed to Omaha. Owing to the crowded condition of the post, I was sleeping on the floor which was temporarily used by the adjutant of the regiment, Mr. Sheffield, who had moved his headquarters to Cottonwood Springs. Cottonwood Springs had become in point of strength and equipment the largest and most important post at that time from Fort Kearney to Denver, but in point of importance and danger Julesburg, or, as we called it then, "Fort Sedgwick," was of the most consequence. The post had been named "Fort Sedgwick" from Major-General Sedgwick, who served in the Civil War. On the forenoon of the 6th of January a band of Indians made a dash on a train near Julesburg, killed four men, and retreated. It could not be ascertained what tribe they were of, or whither they went.

That evening I went to sleep rolled up in a blanket, and lying upon a buffalo-robe stretched upon the dirt floor. I had all my equipment and worldly possessions right there, and the next forenoon was going to start according to orders with my orderly and an escort for Fort Kearney. I was tired, had eaten a hearty supper, and during the night I had a very strange sort of nightmare. It is not unusual for soldiers to grow superstitious, but I think that I had gained as little of it as anyone. But in the night I was awakened by something like a great man-frog jumping upon me, with knees and feet, and weighing about a ton, and saying to me in a stern and threatening tone, "You will never see Omaha." I woke up, making an effort as if to throw off the incubus which was heavy on top of me, and in a little while went again to sleep. After having slept soundly for a while, this incubus was weighing me down again with its knees on my chest, and its hands on my shoulders, looking me in the face, and saying, "You will never see Omaha." I knocked him off again, and after lying awake, and thinking of what I had had for supper, and imagining my nerves were a little bit unstrung at my very sudden and unaccounted for promotion to being aide-de-camp for the General, I went again to sleep. And in less than an hour the whole thing was done over again; this frightful object which was holding me down, told me again, "You will never see Omaha." This third time scared me. It seemed so natural, vivid and real, that I couldn't sleep. I floundered around a little, started a chip fire in the sheet-iron stove, got up and smoked some pipefuls of tobacco, and began to philosophize on the whole business, and think of all the strange things I had heard in regard to spiritualistic manifestations and premonitions. I remembered how in another regiment an old Mexican war soldier had always said that the initial of a man's name was on the bullet which killed him, and that people always had premonitions about these things. During the war the newspapers were full of premonitions, most of them written up by imaginative novelists. As dawn came I rolled up and got a little bit of a nap, and was called for breakfast. Here is a copy of my order.

Head Quarters District of Nebraska,
OMAHA, N. T., January 6th, 1865.

GENERAL ORDERS
No. 2.

2nd Lieut. EUGENE F. WARE, Co. F, 7th Iowa Cav. is hereby detailed and announced, as Aide de Camp upon the staff of the General Commanding, and will be obeyed and respected accordingly.

By order of

BRIG. GENL. ROBT. B. MITCHELL.
JNO. PRATT,
A. A. G.

Official.

A. A. G.

As I had a march of several hundred miles to make on horseback, I started to have my horses shod with great heavy shoes. I counted and inventoried the ordnance stores, pistols, and everything which my company had been drilling with, and took a receipt from the post commander. I also turned over all the stuff which I had received in shape of quartermaster stores for the company, and by the time I had got through getting receipts for the public property, and got ready to go, in the forenoon, a telegram came that the Indians were besieging Fort Sedgwick, and that my company had lost several men, killed, and wanted help. I immediately received an order from General Mitchell by telegram to take a detachment of forty men, and a piece of artillery, and proceed to Julesburg; and before I got started the commander at O'Fallon's Bluffs telegraphed that the Indians had run all around his post, and had halted a train and killed several persons. It was difficult to organize the new detachment quickly, and word came that the Indians had been seen around Gilmans' ranch east of us, at which place a company of Nebraska cavalry had been stationed. The Post Commander at Cottonwood did not want to give me more than ten men, but I finally succeeded in getting twelve mounted men, a twelve-pound mountain howitzer, and thirty-two of Company "I." The latter were armed and put into covered wagons with three drivers, making twelve cavalrymen and thirty-two infantrymen, and four drivers. I determined also to throw a wagon-sheet over the artillery, so as to make it look like a wagon. This would lead the Indians to believe that twelve mounted men were escorting four wagons loaded with supplies, and might induce them to pitch onto the train, and try to take it. The men on the inside all had their guns and ammunition, and the wagons were filled with hay as forage for the horses, and shelter for the men.

We started out, and rode all night against a northwest wind, making good time. We saw a fire-arrow go up from the "Sioux Lookout" near Jack Morrow's ranch, and we saw a fire-arrow go up in the air ahead of us, farther on. We stopped at O'Fallon's Bluffs, and were told that a train had been wrecked and burned within three miles of there by the Indians, the horses all lost, but none of the white people killed. They had all got to the post.

The ride had been very hard upon my twelve cavalrymen, and the drivers of the howitzer and wagons. It was about 40 miles. Some of the men in the wagons had frosted their feet, or thought they had, and had suffered a great deal from cold. They had been obliged to get out in little detachments, and hold on to the end-gates of the wagons and run, to keep up their circulation.

At O'Fallon's Bluffs I received a telegraphic order to come back with the detachment immediately to Cottonwood Springs. In fact, this order had got to O'Fallon's Bluffs before I got there. We stopped to cook a meal, and give the men some sleep before starting back, when all at once the order was countermanded, and I was ordered to proceed on immediately to Alkali Station, which was being threatened by Indians, and to lose no time. Thereupon all the men were waked up, and, amid a great deal of grumbling, we started out for Alkali Station, getting in there late in the afternoon. I then said to myself: "I see now what the pre-monition meant. I was ordered to go back to Omaha, and here now I am under orders going west. It was a very wise and sensible premonition that knew what was going on. I may never see Omaha."

When I got to Alkali I wired my arrival, and told them that there was news that the Indians were dancing around Julesburg, said to be Arapahoes and Cheyennes, and that Alkali Station was all right. I thought I had better be per-mitted to go on to my destination. The word was that quite a battle had taken place at Julesburg, but the telegraph line was so occupied that I could not get into it. As soon as I had reported my arrival at Alkali I was immediately ordered to send back the men and artillery to Cottonwood Springs. Hearing of the trouble my company was having at Julesburg, I did not obey the order, and protested to Colonel Livingston, commanding the sub-district, asking him to rescind it, and let me go to the relief of my company. At 10 A.M. on January 10, 1865, Colonel Livingston sent me a very cross and peremptory order, telling me to send back the whole detachment immediately. I construed the words "send back the detachment" to mean that I need not go back myself, but that it could go back under any proper commander so it got back. So I sent the detachment back in the charge of a sergeant, and I remained at Alkali to get into communication with Captain O'Brien, and ascertain what the trouble was at Julesburg. Finally I heard from Captain O'Brien the full reports of the battle.

I quickly received a peremptory order to return to Cotton-wood Springs. I rode that night all by my lone self down to O'Fallon's Bluffs on my horse "Old Bill." I knew no Indian could catch me as long as I rode him. At O'Fallon's Bluffs a caravan going east had been halted for some little time, and with ten men belonging to Captain Wilcox's company, that was stationed at O'Fallon's Bluffs, we started late in the afternoon, marched all night, and arrived in the morning of the 13th of January at Cottonwood Springs, and there I found General Mitchell, and to him I reported for duty.

This riding all night up and down the dreary, arid wastes of Nebraska in winter was no fun. The General detailed me as Acting Assistant Adjutant-General of the district, and told me that an Indian expeditionary command would march on the second day, January 15, 1865.

All this time companies of cavalry were arriving from the East. The Indians had disappeared, having committed great depredations all along the route from within fifty miles of Denver to Cottonwood Springs. Almost every ranch had been besieged or had had a fight with the Indians. The Indians had captured a number of horses, killed a lot of people, and had disappeared, going south. And while this was going on on the Platte, they had raided the Arkansas River, and had done great damage. They had burned trains, and great quantities of stores and supplies. Newspapers said that a million dollars of damage had been done on the Platte, and another million had been done on the Arkansas River. I think it must have been overdrawn considerably, but yet much damage had been done. The Indians had had a fight wherever they had appeared. They had either struck frontiersmen, pioneers or soldiers, and they made no movement without they had a fight. The country was all ready for a fight, and every man in it expected to fight. I will stop now here to tell of the fight at Julesburg, in which my company was engaged. It was a matter of great regret that I was not with my company at the time it happened, but it was all unexpected at Julesburg. I will make it the subject of the next chapter.

at least, he used to talk about the Mississippi River and about Illinois people. I swore him in verbally and issued him horse, arms and clothing. In short, he was a soldier and a member of our company, but we had no blank enlistment papers, and we had to wait until we could get some from Omaha. His muster-in would have dated November 25, 1864. The young man had been out in the Western country two or three years, as I would suppose, and he was full of fight. He seemed to understand Indians. He dashed in among the Indians as bravely as anyone on that unfortunate day of January 7th, and lost his life. We never had an inquiry afterwards from any friend or relative of his, and he has ever remained practically unidentified. He was an excellent young soldier, with great pride in doing his duty well. He was cheerful, companionable, and well liked, and was ever afterwards missed; but who he was and whether his name was "Pierce" was always a mystery. Hence it was that our company lost killed in battle first and last with Indians, sixteen men—much more than any other company lost in any other of the regiments that I have named. The loss of these men and non-commissioned officers was a great misfortune to the company, but it was war, and was the only way the country could be made habitable, or possible for settlement. Whether or not this battle should have been fought is a question that may arise in the reader's mind; but, Captain O'Brien was full of fight and was devoted to duty, and the fight had to be.

The number of Indians killed and vouched for was fifty-six. That may or may not be correct. At any rate, the Indians held most of the battle-field; the fighting was not far from the post; within the range of the artillery the Indians did not come, on that occasion. Some of our men were killed in the territory of their control, and were scalped. The Indians carried off their dead, and disappeared. As soon as they disappeared, reconnoitering parties were sent out on horseback from the post, and the next day the whole country around the post was scouted, and not an Indian was to be seen. It was reported that they had all gone down in the country southeast of Julesburg, heading for the Republican River, in southwestern Nebraska. On the evening of the 8th of January, Captain O'Brien had reported that the Indians had entirely left his part of the country, and that was the reason why I was ordered with my detachment back to Cottonwood Springs, because it was supposed that the body of the Indians going south of there might try to take the post at Cottonwood Springs. It was fortunate for me that they stayed off from the main traveled road while I was going.

Upon the 10th, Captain O'Brien was ordered to put the post of Julesburg in charge of the invalids and dismounted men; to garrison the post from the caravans that might come, and from the people who were already there, and proceed with all available force to join General Mitchell at Cottonwood Springs for an Indian campaign.

The Julesburg fight was considered by the Indians as an exceedingly bitter and unexpected resistance on the part of the white men. The Indians were repulsed and injured so that they did not try to take or capture the stage station and the stores and supplies a mile down the river. In fact, it was believed that the Indians were endeavoring to cross the river above our post, and go up Lodgepole, and off into the northern country; that their object was to capture and kill what they could and get through the lines north, and hence the resistance which they met from the soldiers turned them from their purpose, and although they were quite numerous, it started them back again into the great wilderness of country which lay south between the two rivers.

Of the events of the fight many strange stories were told. The Indians were all well armed, and in one sense better armed than our soldiers. They had firearms, and they also had bows, and quivers full of arrows. A bow-and-arrow is a much more dangerous and effective weapon than a revolver in the hands of an Indian. While a revolver could shoot six times quickly, as then made, it could not be loaded on horseback on a run with somebody pursuing, but the Indian could shoot six arrows that were as good as six shots from a revolver at close range, and then he could shoot twenty-four more in rapid succession. And so, when a soldier had shot out all his cartridges, he was a prey to an Indian with a bow-and-arrow who followed him. In addition to this, the Indians carried lances, which they used to good purpose. Our boys had sabers; an Indian could not hit a soldier with a lance if the soldier had a saber, nor could a soldier saber an Indian if the Indian had a lance.

All during this fight an Indian upon a hill nearest the post handled his red troops by signal, using at times a looking-glass, and at other times a buffalo-robe. He swung his men around in very good style. Our soldiers were deployed during part of the fight, and the Indians had a drill not very much unlike it. During the fight James Cannon had a cartridge in his carbine, which would not explode; after snapping it once or twice, while the soldiers and Indians were cavorting around among each other, Cannon took his carbine by the muzzle, and, using it as a club, started in, and finally got to chasing an Indian. As the Indian was about to get away from him, Cannon threw his carbine at the Indian and struck him in the back with it. Cannon said the Indian "howled like a tomcat," but of course Cannon couldn't hear anything or make any observations at that time. He got out of the mêlée without injury. Several of the boys were slightly wounded, in addition to those killed. Several of the horses were wounded, and some died of their injuries.

One of our boys was shot with a frying-pan handle. It struck him in the rear part of the hip. The frying-pans of that day as used on the plains were little, light steel utensils, with slender, heavy hoop-steel handles with a ring in the end. The Indian had a large arrow, and about nine inches of this frying-pan handle sharpened on both sides, and pointed, was fixed into it. This arrow went in several inches, and through the pelvic bone. Although the soldier got out of the fight alive, he could not pull the arrow out. He succeeded in getting back to the post. Then one of the soldiers got the company blacksmith's pinchers, and, laying the wounded man down on his face, he stood on top of him, got hold of the arrow-head with the pinchers, and finally succeeded in working and wrenching it out. The poor fellow was in great

pain, but subsequently recovered all right. We had no anes-
thetics in the army in those days.

All of the stage-drivers and civilians around Julesburg
flocked into the fort, and made up their minds to hold it
against all odds that should come. All the available men of
my company, about fifty in number, turned up at Cottonwood Springs, ready to march with General Mitchell, on the
evening of January 14, 1865, about a week after the battle.

On the 15th of January, 1865, the command was drawn up
in line, and consisted of 640 cavalrymen. This was in addition to about 100 mule-wagons lightly loaded with rations,
corn, tents, and supplies. There was also a herd of about fifty
extra horses that were fastened together close at the bit, and
driven by fours. There were also four twelve-pound mountain howitzers, and two light three-inch Parrott guns. Captain
O'Brien was made chief of artillery under General Mitchell.
Colonel Livingston was the next in rank to General Mitchell,
and to him was confided the looking after, and taking charge
of, the line of march. On the evening of the 15th of January
we went up the river to within three miles of Jack Morrow's,
and spent a cold, unpleasant January night on the flat plains,
without any fires, but we had tents which furnished us a
good deal of shelter.

At Jack Morrow's ranch General Mitchell drew up and
handed to me a paper which read as follows:

"HEADQUARTERS, EXPEDITIONARY FORCES IN THE FIELD,
January 15, 1865

SPECIAL FIELD ORDER No. 1

"PAR. 1. Lieutenant E. F. Ware, A. D. C., is assigned to duty
as Acting Assistant Adjutant-General during the Expedition now
in the field, and will be obeyed and respected accordingly.

"PAR. 2. Captain O'Brien, Co. 'F,' 7th Iowa Cavalry, is hereby
assigned to the command of the artillery in the field. All detachments in charge of artillery ordered to the field will report to him
immediately for orders, with such officers as have been detailed
for the artillery service.

"PAR. 3. Colonel R. R. Livingston will have the immediate
command of the troops in the field, and all orders issued from

these headquarters, for record, will be transmitted through his headquarters to regiments and detachments.

"PAR. 4. Lieutenant Thompson, First Nebraska Vet. Vol. Cavalry, will act during the expedition as Acting Assistant Quartermaster and Acting Commissary of Subsistence, and will be obeyed and respected accordingly.

ROBERT B. MITCHELL, Brig.-General,

Comdg. District and Expedition."

That evening I told General Mitchell about my visitation and premonitions, and how the frog-man got down on me, and told me thrice that I would "never see Omaha." We had quite a talk in regard to it at headquarters. I had made a memorandum of the circumstance in my itinerary, as I wanted to put it down and have proof in black and white, so that, in case anything should happen to me, the premonition would stand in writing as of the proper date and show something definite as to what had occurred. But in the discussion that evening with General Mitchell, in which Captain O'Brien took part, the doctrine of premonition was pretty thoroughly riddled. Said Captain O'Brien, who had about him no savor of cowardice, or superstition: "These premonitions and prophecies are all bogus. Now," he said, "if any spirit, seen or unseen, any ghost or any angel, knows anything, why in thunder don't he tell it and tell it straight? Why does he give it to you in such a dark and veiled manner? If he knows you are going to be killed or die on such a day or hour, why doesn't he say so, tell it plainly, and leave the thing open to positive proof? No," said Captain O'Brien, "that isn't the way it is done. These things are always put into some sort of equivocal, double-dealing shape. Now, in your case, the message is, 'You won't see Omaha.' That doesn't mean that you are going to be killed, nor that your death is going to take place. You may never see Omaha, you may never see the North Pole, and may yet live a hundred years. Supposing, for instance, we should march on down to Fort Leavenworth, and didn't have to go to Omaha. Now that would be an every-day, unromantic fact, and entirely unimportant. And it would be just the same as if you were never going to see Davenport, Iowa. There are lots of places you are not going to see again. Now to pay attention to any such things as these is cowardice."

Then said General Mitchell: "These things are always double-barrel and meaningless in one sense, and very full of meaning in another. It looks as if somebody was guessing, and waiting for the guess to turn true. Take all the oracles of which classic language speaks: they were always put into such shape that nobody could understand them when given, and if they didn't turn out, no notice was taken of them; but afterwards something happened, and some deep and new hidden meaning was found in it. It's so with the prophecies of the Old Testament. If the prophecies of the Old Testament are read in a plain, sensible, straightforward way, then you will find they are not prophecies at all. The prophetic part of them was studied out long after the thing had happened; as a lawyer might say, 'It was a prophecy after the fact.' Now," said General Mitchell, "I don't suppose there is anybody that ever lived who hadn't had a lot of these premonitory experiences, but sensible men never pay any attention to them. If it should happen that you never do see Omaha, and should be mustered out and go home, you would always think there was something in the nature of prophecy to this nightmare of yours,—that it was a revelation. Now, I think you ought to see Omaha anyhow, and I think I'll have you down there alive and well inside of thirty days."

I said: "I have no confidence in premonitions, and I'll go to Omaha anyhow, just as soon as we make this raid down on the Republican River. If I get killed in it, well, then it can be said there was something to the premonition."

This ended for the evening the discussion of that subject. But there were some of the officers who were superstitious, who had heard the conversation, and had heard my statement of the fact. They said, "Now, there may be something in it, and you better go mighty careful. What's the use to go to Omaha anyhow?" Said one, "My advice to you is to resign as aide-de-camp and go back to your company." Another said, "Be on your guard all the time, and it may be that the premonition is intended only to put you on your guard."

In the morning of January 16, 1865, we started early, and took the road up Morrow's Canyon. We took what was known as the "Trader's Trail." Our troops were composed of the Seventh Iowa Cavalry, the First Nebraska Veteran Volunteer Cavalry, and Companies "B" and "C," First Nebraska Militia (mounted). The First Nebraska was an excellent regiment; it had been in the service for a long time. It had been down in Arkansas doing duty, had got pretty well cut up there, but had been filled with recruits. As I had been with the invading army in Arkansas, it was a great pleasure for me to talk with the officers of the First Nebraska. We had been over the same trail. I told one of them about bringing in the negroes at Batesville down on White River, as hereinbefore related, and that I got a lot of them from a large plantation owned by a named Le Neve.

"Yes," said one of the officers of the regiment, "the Le Neves were ruined by the war, and Mrs. Le Neve and daughter came into Batesville to be under protection, and we had to issue them rations as 'needy persons.' They were on our ration-list all the time we were at Batesville, Arkansas." This officer said: "I well remember a young lady riding up to the post quartermaster, and saying, as she whipped her dress with her riding-whip, 'Please, Captain, can Mamma have a little coffee this morning? She is not feeling very well.' Coffee was high-priced and difficult to get, and was not included in the rations which were issued to refugees. My recollections of the Le Neve plantation were that it was one of the finest in that country. I heard one of the negroes say that they were raising that summer, four hundred acres of corn for the Rebel army. This was in addition to a large quantity of cotton. The Le Neve home was a very fine one, with a village of negro quarters and smoke-houses situated near it."

The First Nebraska Cavalry had "veteran volunteered," as it was called. After a person had served in the field eight-

een months, then he could "veteranize," as it was said, and
enlist for three years longer and get a bounty of $300, so
that soldiers and sometimes regiments "veteranized." The
First Nebraska was a regiment in which the men had veteranized to such an extent that it was reorganized as a veteran
regiment, and bore the name of veteran volunteer in the title
of the regiment. The incursions of the Indians, and the vast
damages which they had done in Nebraska, raised such an
outcry that the Government had to send Nebraska troops
home for the protection of Nebraska, the same as a portion
of our regiment was stationed in Iowa. And so it happened
that the "First Nebraska Veteran Volunteer Cavalry" was
drawn from the field, and the Confederacy, and sent out to
fight Indians in the Northwest. The Seventh Iowa and the
First Nebraska got along together very well.

The Nebraska MILITIA were frontiersmen who furnished
their own horses and arms. They were, as soldiers, first-class
in every respect. The companies were small but efficient.

As stated, on January 16, 1865, we went up the Trader's
Trail seven miles. There was a small canyon on the left, very
full of cedar. We crossed a basin up at the head of the canyon about two and one-half miles in diameter, and turned
to the right after crossing it, striking southwest. We passed
at the base of a butte, which from one scraggly tree being
in sight, was called "Lone Tree Butte." It was a sand butte,
scooped out and ragged by the action of the wind. This butte
is about ten miles from where we turned off after having
crossed the basin referred to. Thence our course was southwest by south a few miles, then we turned around the base
of another sandhill, and went southwest by west, and passed
a tree with an eagle's nest on it, on our left about one mile.
We marched then about southwest and struck the Medicine
Creek ten miles from its source. The Indian name for this
stream was Wau-kah Woc-ca-pella. Woc-ca-pella in the Sioux
language meant "stream."

In the crossing of the Medicine we were obliged to get
out the picks and shovels and make a crossing, because the
stream was sunk down so far below the level of the prairie.

We made the crossing at what appeared to us as the only available place for miles up and down. There were little cottonwoods, water, and a considerable grazing-spot, although the grass was dry and frosted. Nevertheless, we led our horses around, and let them eat what they would of it, and then fed them corn. The distance marched on that, our first day out, January 16, 1865, was thirty-three miles.

CHAPTER XXXIII

January 16, 1865 · Medicine River · The Red Willow · Indians in Distance · The Lo-ca-po · The Skull · Place for a Fort · The Big Timbers · The Scout into Kansas · The Ree Fork · The Boundary · The Split Hill · The Indian Dash at Night

WE WERE now on the west bank of the Medicine River. The stream as we viewed it from the northeast was the arc of a circle marked by a high line of ragged bluffs. The march that day had been a cold and severe one. Indian signals had been noticed during the night, and from time to time in the distance we saw smoke signals, and some of the scouts saw at a distance some straggling Indians. In fact, from long distances on both sides of us the Indians were viewing and sizing up our expedition. Of course, the more they saw of it the less they would want to tackle it. We were sort of groping our way through the country; but we wanted to get in west of the Indians and drive them east and cut them off from retreat to the mountains and the north.

The bugle called us at 5 o'clock, and we were all up and ready to start, January 17th, as soon as it was daylight. We crossed the ridge west of our camp, marched one mile southwest by west, came to a dry ravine filled with scattered trees, thence southeast a half-mile, when we struck a stream. The main canyon running west was narrow, with high banks in which was cottonwood timber. It was marked for about a mile with springs, which formed the stream; above them the canyon was dry. We moved up this canyon about two miles, where it forked into three prongs. We took the left one running southeast by south, followed it up three-quarters of a mile, and came upon the plateau by a gradual slope. Without much work we made a road through the ravine and canyon, that was good. This canyon would have made an excellent place to camp. Up on the plateau we marched about three miles east of south, then about two and a half miles west of south; then we marched southerly ten miles, gradually swinging around to the west until we struck the Red Willow. When we struck the Red Willow we were marching due west. We struck the stream at a place where there was a large clump of trees in a bend of the stream that made a reverse curve. The following is a diagram of it:

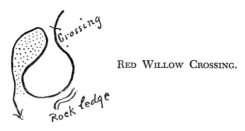

RED WILLOW CROSSING.

We found the old trail crossing two hundred fifty yards above where a ledge of rock jutted out over the stream, but it was too difficult to fix up and make passable, so we did not cross here. It was evidently an old buffalo trail, much traveled by the Indians, and all right for ponies, but it could not be utilized by our wagon train, so we went down the stream three miles farther. At this old trail-crossing was a clump of timber where an Indian camp had been, but which had been deserted a short time before. The guides said the camp could not be over a month old, and might be newer.

On this day's march, January 17, 1865, we saw observing Indians far in the distance, but we only got glimpses of them, and they disappeared so that we could not tell which way they were going. But as we went scouting through the country, several of us who had field-glasses and good horses, rode up on all the highlands in the neighborhood to scan the horizon with our glasses. This camp on Red Willow had been a large Indian camp, and the indications were that they had gone down the stream. The three miles which we went down the stream from the old trail-crossing were along deep buffalo trails, cut wide, and we followed these trails until they struck the stream. We utilized this buffalo trail across the stream, and in a short time with picks and shovels made an excellent crossing. In fact, if it had not been for these buffalo trails we would have had a great deal of trouble; the banks of the stream were very precipitous, and it would have delayed us much to have had to make wagon-roads across. But where the buffalo trails had worn down the banks, we made a good crossing without very much difficulty. Four miles down the stream from this crossing, on the other side, we camped.

From our camp down on the Red Willow as far as we could see, the cottonwood timber along the stream was very dense. The stream was sunk about four hundred feet below the level of the plateau, and along the stream were signs of great Indian camps. We had evidently got right into the country where the Indians lived, and where they had their permanent villages. We could see where they had been cutting down the limbs of the cottonwood trees for their ponies to browse on, and the grass was pretty well eaten off around in the neighborhood. There were many large cottonwood trees lying on the ground. The weather was very cold, and we chopped up these logs, and snaked them around with mule teams so as to get them in position, and we cooked supper and sat around discussing Indians until we crept into our tents at night. We had marched that day about 22 miles.

We emerged on the morning of the 18th from the canyon at the mouth of which we had camped, and went on southwest, leaving the river. There was an endless succession of sandhills. These hills had just enough clay in their composition to keep them from blowing entirely away; and they supported a slim lot of grass and weeds. On our left was a chain of ragged sand-bluffs. The road was rough on account of the many branches and ravines that struck it perpendicularly every quarter- or half-mile, many of them almost impassable. Our route was a succession of digging. We had to keep back as far as possible towards the sandhills, and we had to make a crossing at every ravine.

During this day's march three wagons broke down, showing the rough treatment which they had received in going
across these ravines. An army wagon for Indian service had
to be made out of the very best kind of stuff. It had to be
made from old, well-seasoned timber, which in turn had to
be kiln-dried before it was put into the wagons, otherwise,
out on the plains, during the dry and cold weather, woodwork would shrink. Once in a while a wagon had been made
of timber not sufficiently seasoned. This would be discovered
upon a march such as the one we were on, and then great

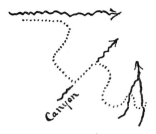

DOTTED LINE INDICATES ROUTE
TO BLACKWOOD CREEK.

trouble was occasioned by it, because the wheels had to be
taken off, and thrown in the stream overnight so as to soak
and swell up, and this occasioned work and delay. If the
wheels were not kept tight, the wagon was bound to collapse
under the hard usage which it had to sustain. As we were
eating up rations and horse-feed rapidly, the three broken
wagons were left as empties. The wheels and some of the
woodwork, however, were distributed through the train to
furnish repairs in case of trouble.

This day's progress was only ten miles in a straight direction, but our journey was fifteen miles; we made a good road
as we went. We crossed Blackwood Creek and a bad ravine
going in a very crooked southwesterly course. Camped on
the south side, where water was standing in pools.

The recent presence of large bands of Indians was noticeable, but there were none to be seen except an occasional
scout far distant. The day's march, with few exceptions, ran
on high ground.

On the morning of January 19, 1865, the cavalry started

out ahead of the train. We did not believe there were any Indians who would attack the train, and as a few of the men were badly mounted, their horses having shown signs of weariness, they were left back with the train and a piece of artillery. We made a dash across the plateau a little south of west, headed for the big timbers of the Republican River. A march of twelve miles, about ten miles in a straight line, brought us to the L'eau qui Peaue. That was a French phrase, and it was called briefly, "Lo-ca-po." The translation of it from the French name is borne on the modern maps as "Stinking Water," but the old name of Lo-ca-po should have been retained.

We struck this stream two or three miles above its junction with White Man's Fork, went down its east side, and crossed the "White Man" below the junction. At the time we struck the Lo-ca-po its volume of water was twenty-four feet wide by sixteen inches deep, with a velocity of three miles per hour. The main stream of White Man's Fork had a width of eighty feet, by two feet deep, with a velocity of three and a half miles an hour. The Indian name for White Man's Fork was Wah-Seecha Wocca-pella. A short distance below where we crossed, a stream came up from the south called Ten-Mile Creek, which was small and impassable. Along the "White Man" at this point there were high bluffs on the south side, and a short distance down the river below our crossing the rock jutted out of a bluff and the river ran up under it at its base. The name of the stream is from the Sioux language. In that language Wah-Seecha means "white man." "Seecha" means "bad," and "Wah" means medicine; therefore a white man was, in Indian parlance, "bad medicine."

We then came in a southerly direction up on top of the plateau from the bed of the stream, and after about five miles of travel came to the head canyon of Ten-Mile Creek bent around to the west. This we crossed, and kept on to the Republican, our course from White Man's Fork being west of south. I give all these names as they were then used by traders and guides. I do not know present names.

In going across the upland upon this march, the advance guard, with which I happened to be marching, right at the highest point came onto a skull. It was the skull of an Indian and was very much decayed. Skulls upon that high, dry, hilly country lasted for a great many years. This one looked very ancient. It might have been a hundred years old. The skull had an iron arrow-point penetrating it from the upper side, the parietal region, entering the skull about an inch and a half. The arrow on the outside was almost rusted away. No other bones were visible. It was probably the relic of an ancient combat. We struck the Republican five miles below the upper end of the "Big Timbers," near a stream, and camped one-half mile below. The distance from White Man's Fork to the Republican would be about twenty miles direct, but by our line of march it was twenty-five.

A short distance above where we camped was a most excellent place for a fort; the contour of the country and stream was as follows. I give it from the drawing I then made:

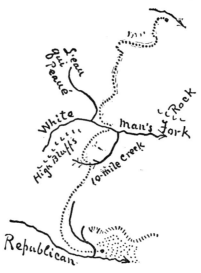

ROUTE TO THE REPUBLICAN RIVER.

The distance we marched that day, January 19, 1865, was thirty-seven miles, and the line of march was principally on high plateaus. We made splendid time, and it was fine scenery, and everywhere we saw signs of Indians. The trails were running in every direction. They seemed to be coming and going, backwards and forwards over the country, but nevertheless we saw none of the Indians except a few fugitive scouts.

General Mitchell directed me to prepare recommendations for the establishment of a fort at the place just above described. The details were as follows: On the bench of land above where we camped the stream came into the Republican, with a curve from the north. Up along the stream above the junction was a beautiful level table, with bluffs high and rough but well back. The streams were very heavily timbered with cottonwood, and the little one came down through a ravine filled with heavy cottonwood timber as far as we could see. This table was about a quarter of a mile wide, and ran up the river about two miles. The bluffs were about a mile from the edge of the Republican river, and a fort there would be fully thirty feet above high water, and surrounded on three sides with water and difficult, abrupt banks. It was stated by the guides that the "Big Timbers" at the Republican practically ceased five miles above this place. The big timbers were enormous cottonwood trees that were along the Republican in and around here. Above them there were only scattering trees on the river. These trees finally ran out into nothing, towards the west. Nine miles below this place the big timbers almost entirely ceased, so that this camp was in the very midst of the big timbers. These big timbers were therefore about fourteen miles long, and filled most of the bottom-lands. There were several springs coming in at this place, and on the edge and through the timbers were dense growths of grass. The guides told us that this camp was about thirty-five miles below the "Ree Fork" (that was the common expression for Arickaree) and thirty miles up from the mouth of "White Man," but

I think that this estimate of distance by the guides could be only guess-work. Above this camp five miles, and ten miles on the north side and ten miles on the south side, streams came in from the hills. These big timbers were all cottonwood trees averaging and exceeding two feet in diameter, and located on an average of about one to every fifty yards square, without a particle of underbrush, but a dense growth of high bottom-grass. Here was where the buffalo used to live, and here we found Indian signs everywhere prevalent. The location of the Big Timbers was as follows:

BIG TIMBERS ON THE UPPER REPUBLICAN RIVER,
Fourteen miles along the stream.

From this camp in the big timbers scouting parties were sent out to see if we could find the Indians. Very great numbers of them had been hibernating through the heavy timbers scattered along the river at this place, and the question was where had they gone.

Joe Jewitt had been brought along, and he was sent out in one direction to guide a party; Charley Elston was sent out in another direction; Leo Palladie was sent out in another.

The latter command consisted of most of my company, and I went with them. We were sent southwest to go across the plateau, and follow a tree line which ran up the south fork of the Republican River, and then go south to the head-waters of the Sappa rivers. There were then the North and South Sappa; now the north one appears on the map as Beaver Creek. Sappa, in Sioux, meant "black." These creeks were full of beavers then.

We started, and as we came near what is now the Kansas line, Leo Palladie, who was riding with me at the head of the company, looked up and surveyed the landscape, and said: "We are now in Kansas. We have crossed the line, and we are not very far from the northwest corner." As we rode up to the plateau he pointed to the west, and said: "There is Ree Fork. You see where it strikes that other stream? Well, that high ground on the other side is across the line. The northwest corner of Kansas is up near where those two streams come together." I asked him how he knew, and he said that one time he was going over the country with some Indians and a white man who knew about the survey, and the white man pointed out to him where the northwest corner stake of Kansas was driven. It was not far from the water-bed of Ree Fork.

We went up onto the plateau. The country was as poor and arid as it could be on the upland; there was grass growing on the bottoms. Looking some little distance ahead, I saw a hill which was split down from the top like a Bishop's mitre. I said, "What hill is that?" and he said, "That is a sandhill." As it was in our course we soon reached it, and there I found a large hill of sand, through the middle of the top of which the wind both ways (north and south) had excavated the same, and spread it over at least a half-mile square on the north and south sides of the hill. I asked Palladie how that could happen, and he said: "Well, it happened like this. Deer are very curious animals, and the old bucks do guard duty for the herd, and give signals of danger. These bucks will go up on the tops of the hills, and will wear out with their sharp hoofs, while stamping off flies, whatever coat of grass happens to be there. Perhaps a single file of buffalo have gone over the top of the hill, as they are prone to do. Then the winds come and get a start, and hollow it out." This hill was a very large mound, and the excavation which the wind had made was one in which vast quantities of sand had been carried away.

During the whole scout we had seen in the far distance from time to time, single isolated Indians. In one case, off at a distance of perhaps three miles, we saw a pony running with a lodge. The Indians place a lodge-pole on each side of a pony, allowing the ends to drag, and upon these ends place their tent and equipment, and it goes over the ground dragging as fast as the pony can go.

We got down into Kansas at what would now be called Sherman county, went into camp on a little stream, and the next day returned to the Republican river, making about 100 miles in two days. We found nothing in the nature of a large trail. The trails were all small, but very numerous, seeming to indicate that the Indians had scattered every-which-way, each one for himself. The difficulty of this condition of things was that we could not scatter out ourselves, and follow the individual trails. The Indians in all directions had scattered out like a fan. They probably had some place arranged for meeting again, but we could not follow those tactics. We had to keep together, and be ready for them upon all occasions. There was a large migration Indian trail coming from the southwest, but it appeared several months old.

One of the other scouting parties that went west had a different experience from ours. They were up amid a nest of timber, had taken a wagon along with tents, and at night went into camp, but with due precaution they had their horses tied up closely in camp all night. But a body of Indians, not large in number, ran through their camp at night, shooting off firearms, breaking tent-ropes and pulling up pegs, but doing no damage. No soldier was injured nor an Indian hurt, and they went off in the dark night as rapidly as they came. Although the soldiers had guards out, the guards could give no intelligent account of the matter.

CHAPTER XXXIV

January 21, 1865 · Back to Republican River ·
Zero Weather · General Mitchell's Opinion on In-
dians · A Terrible Night · Twenty Full Degrees
Below Zero · Lieutenant Talbot Kills a Buffalo ·
January 25th, Turned Back · Arrive at Cotton-
wood Springs · March of Forty-two Miles · The
Indian Courier to Fort Kearney · General Mitchell
Dislikes the Indian Service · Itinerary of the
March · Distances Marched · The General's Final
Order

THE weather was exceedingly cold when we returned to
the Republican River; we had not got a very good night's
sleep, but when we got back to the river on the evening of
January 21st, where the main command was, we felt more
at home. We were better able to cook our rations, and enjoy
more safety in the camp. That night was very cold; the
sky was covered with clouds; it was too cold to snow, and
ice was falling in little frozen pellets. General Mitchell had
among his camp equipment a thermometer, and that night
the thermometer went down below zero. We stayed up during the night alongside of the fires, to keep from freezing,
and dozed a little.

On the next day, January 22, 1865, we marched down
the river nine miles into the last bunch, down-stream, of
the big timbers; that was a hard day's march. During the
day we were joined by all the parties who had been sent out
scouting. They all found about the same conditions that we
found on our scout. The Indians were flying and separating
purposely so that it would distract pursuit, but they had
some place where they were going to rendezvous again; at
least that was a fact upon which all the guides agreed, and
the question was whether or not we should go back up the
Republican River. There was a great deal of discussion as to

where the Indians might go. It was agreed upon by all that the big timbers had been their great rendezvous, and that we had driven them out; but, where they had gone, or where they would meet again, was a problem. This matter of chasing the Indians was discussed a great deal over the camp-fires. General Mitchell's idea was that such terms of peace ought to be made with them as would put them upon reservations, and make them dependent, but yet would feed them well and clothe them well. General Mitchell's argument was something like this: "It is a well-known fact that it costs a million dollars a year to keep a cavalry regiment in the field. It takes in my district, from Omaha to South Pass, three regiments of cavalry; that is to say, three million dollars a year. This is outside of the loss of productive labor, and loss of men by death and disease." Then the General added: "I would put these Indians on reservations, dress them up in broadcloth, feed them on fried oysters, and furnish them money to play poker with, and all the tobacco and whisky they wanted, and then I will be a million dollars ahead of the game in my little district every year."

Along in the afternoon of this day the weather began to grow colder and colder. The wind came down from the northwest with the fury of a cyclone, and it blew the ashes from the fire so that, although we had large log-heaps, we could only stay on one side of them with the wind blowing on our backs; we could only get warm by hugging the fire. As the night grew on it became dangerous to go to sleep. The horses were taken into the most sheltered part of the woods, and fires were built in log-heaps some little distance from the horses to the windward, so that the warmth would blow down onto them. Nobody went to sleep that night. The guards were changed every thirty minutes, and the men brought in. Guard duty was exceedingly severe, but had to be maintained. At 3 o'clock in the morning, General Mitchell's thermometer showed twenty full degrees below zero. The night seemed an intensely long one. Everybody kept in motion, nobody dared to go to sleep, and although we had log-heaps blazing, it seemed almost impossible to keep from being frost-bitten. Finally the wind ceased in the morning as the sun rose, and it rose clear and still. What such a streak of weather would do for the Indian fleeing across the country we could well imagine. It carried out Bridger's theory of the death of the women and children if the chasing of the Indians continued during a winter campaign. An Indian campaign in the winter is anything but pleasant. There is absolutely no fun in it.

As there were but few trees up the river above the Big Timbers, and as the scouts all reported that the heaviest body of Indians seemed to have gone down the river, fleeing from our approach, we started the next morning, January 23, 1865, to march down the river. At headquarters a pail of water that had been brought up from the river to be used in cooking, but which had not been used, froze solid clear through that night. And that morning when we started out,

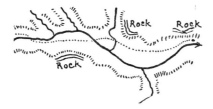

ROUTE DOWN THE REPUBLICAN.

our artillery crossed on the ice which had been frozen that night. The wagon-train also crossed to the south side on the ice. The men were in no condition to march, nor were the horses in very much better condition, but it was not possible to let up, and we were obliged to keep on the go; so down the river we went. A march of thirty-two miles brought us down below the mouth of White Man's Fork. Four miles down from the mouth of White Man's Fork was a stream called Black Wood Creek, before referred to, coming in from the north. The mouth of White Man's Fork was marked by five cottonwood trees. Up White Man's Fork clumps of scattered trees were seen for about eight miles. The mouth of Black Wood Creek was marked by an immense undergrowth, with trees on the side, probably all willow. Eight-Mile Creek, on the south side, had a dense undergrowth at its mouth, and a forest of large trees, probably cottonwoods, extending miles up its course to the south. The trappers said that Eight-Mile Creek was a great beaver creek. Below that a stream came in from the north with a few scattered willow bushes and cottonwoods on its banks. We crossed the river twice on the march, with our wagons and artillery, on the thick ice.

We went into camp under some rock bluffs where the course of the river deflected northerly, and went up near the bluffs. Our camping-line at this camp, January 23rd, ran

MAP OF CAMP,
JANUARY 23, 1865.

north and south. The rock bluff was limestone without fossils. There was a heavy growth of very large willows here, quite tall and some of them two feet in diameter, with very heavy underbrush of willows. From the mouth of White Man's Fork down to this camp was twenty miles, and the river-bend and the bottoms were about five miles wide, covered with high rank grass. We were in this camp about four miles up from the mouth of Red Willow. Some of the most splendid hay lands that we had seen in the western country were along the river. The roadway was very fine—no heavy pulls. Wood was not very plentiful, but sufficient for any amount of overland travel. Above I give a map as I drew it of the route down the river.

Lieutenant Talbot, a Nebraska man—I have spoken of him before—spied a lone buffalo, and killed it. As we came down, fire accidentally got out, and swept the bottoms smooth, and clear from bluff to bluff. The night of that camp was again very cold. In the heavy cold of the night before I had frosted two of my toes, and this night I frosted two of my fingers. We had plenty of wood. It was not as cold as before; fortunately it was still, and we dozed around the fire all night. The two fingers which I frosted were the two front fingers on my left hand. It annoyed me very much, but there was not a person in the command who was not

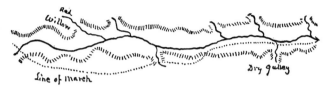

LINE OF MARCH DOWN THE REPUBLICAN RIVER.

more or less frosted. General Mitchell got his ears very seriously frosted.

But there was nothing for us to do except to push on; so, the next morning, January 24, 1865, over the burnt landscape down the river we went, a direct distance of thirty miles; but, by the route we traveled, thirty-five. We camped down the river a little distance east of Medicine Creek. It was sometimes called "Medicine Lake Creek," from a lake on the west prong. The bed of the river all day long was all about a uniform width of two and a half miles. The grass lands, although burned, showed plainly, down the river as far as we could see, a very fertile valley; and there was wood enough all the way. Our route was a little north of east. We marched on the south side of the river all day. Above is a line of the march as taken from my map made that evening.

As there was nothing to be found going east, we turned

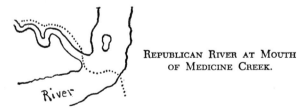

REPUBLICAN RIVER AT MOUTH
OF MEDICINE CREEK.

back January 25th. There was an island in the river just below the mouth of Medicine Creek, and avoiding the island we went across the Republican River on the ice, up Medicine Creek a little distance on the ice, and then came out on its east bank. We crossed the trains and artillery on the heavy ice. The stream was a very difficult one for us to march along, because its course curved backwards and forwards from bluff to bluff, and rock strata pointed out of the bluffs at several points. That day's march up Medicine Creek was twenty-four miles in a course north of northwest, and we went on bluffs or plateaus most of the way. The guides thought we would find Indians on the east of Medicine Creek.

All this time the wind blew clear and cold from the northwest, and the whole command led their horses until from time to time the command was given to mount, and then the horses would be run for a little while to get them warmed up, then the men would dismount and walk. And so we went, running our horses and then running on foot, all day. Riding against the wind was very unpleasant; all of us had our heads muffled up in the capes of our overcoats, and we kept our roadway by peering through openings in the folds of our capes. As we were riding against the wind we would look out through our capes with one eye. In a little while the tears of that eye would be frozen up, and vision entirely obscured; then we would shift our capes to the other eye while we warmed up with our hands and thawed the ice out from the other eye. We thus alternated all day, January 25th, and the result was that almost everyone frosted his eyelids. Mine got into bad condition, and every once in a while an officer would say to me as we rode along, "You will never see Omaha." In fact, whenever we got into any bad place some one was telling me that I would "never see Omaha."

We crossed the Medicine twenty miles from our morning camp, and camped that night farther up in a valley, in a clump of timber which the Indians had been occupying shortly before. It was a most beautiful valley, where we camped, capable of irrigation and cultivation, and a stream came in which we named Mitchell's Creek, after General

Mitchell. We made a total march that day of 26 miles, most of it in the face of a freezing wind. The place where the lake was is shown on the accompanying map. On this page I give the map exactly as I drew it that night.

Medicine River forked, and we went up the east fork. The next day, January 26, 1865, we marched up the east fork of Medicine Creek, and made our noon halt within two miles of the head of the stream, a distance of twenty-one miles; thence we went up the stream, thence seven miles over the divide to the head of Cottonwood Canyon, then down Cottonwood Canyon twelve miles, and arrived at Cottonwood Springs at four o'clock P. M. after a day's march of forty-two miles.

It appeared to me that this last march of forty-two miles

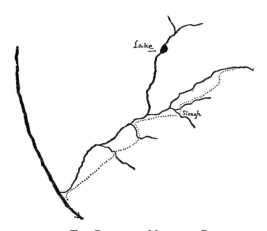

THE ROUTE ON MEDICINE CREEK.

was the longest march I ever made in my life. The keen northwest wind, the hard riding, the want of sleep, the inability to properly cook our food, and the fact that not a member of the command escaped being frost-bitten, contributed to make it a march long to be remembered.

An incident happened when we were camping on January 20th in the Big Timbers, which I ought not to overlook. We had been out six days on the expedition, and General Mitchell was afraid that he might be snowed up or frozen in somewhere, and thought it safe to have a train loaded with supplies of corn for the horses, and rations for the men, all ready at Fort Kearney so that it could start out for our relief on a moment's notice, on receiving word from a courier: the question was, how to get such a message back to Fort Kearney. There was a little red-mustached Irish sergeant, but from what command I do not know, who volunteered to make the trip if he could have a proper guide, and he would strike right out across the country to Fort Kearney. I think he belonged to one of the Nebraska Militia companies. There were a couple of Pawnees with us as guides, and one of these Pawnees offered to go across with the sergeant, and act as scout, and deliver him safely to Fort Kearney, provided that General Mitchell would give him a horse. The General promised to do this; the Indian had no horse; said he preferred to go on foot anyhow, and that he could keep up with the sergeant's horse all the way in to Fort Kearney. This was a sort of a funny proposition, and I remember looking at the long, gaunt, slim Pawnee, a young buck about twenty-three, and wondering whether he could keep up all day with the cavalry horse or not. Leo Palladie said that the Indian would hold onto the sergeant's stirrup-straps, and run alongside of the horse as fast as the horse could go, for a week. So the commissary issued them each four days' rations of bacon, hard-bread and stuff, and they were ordered to immediately get ready. They proceeded to cook up their rations; when they were cooked the Indian went to work and ate up every vestige of his four days' rations. He bolted down an enormous quantity of raw bacon, and he ate the other stuff as fast as it was cooked. The sergeant took an ordinary white man's dinner, and put the balance in his haversack swung onto his saddle, but as to the Indian, all he did was to buckle up his belt as tightly as he could get it, and start off on a trot alongside of the sergeant's horse and hold of the stirrup-strap. They started out after dark, and they both arrived at Fort Kearney, a distance of over a hundred miles in a straight line, on the afternoon of the second day.

General Mitchell was sorely disappointed that we had not been able to find out where the Indians had gone, and what they intended to do. We had not killed a hostile Indian, and probably not less than fifty soldiers had to be discharged on account of freezings and injuries received on the trip. In addition to that, we had ruined about a hundred horses, and six wagons had been broken down and abandoned. The General, as we rode down Cottonwood Canyon, on the end of the trip, was quite melancholy, and all he could say was: "Well, what more could we do? What more could we do?" and he seemed disconsolate over the fact that there was not an Indian less, and he keenly felt the distress which his men had suffered. He was constantly referring to the "poor fellows," and how bravely they had stood the weather, and how awfully cold it was, and what enormous marches had been made under such suffering conditions. And then the General would get moody; and say that, while the war was going on down South, here he was fighting Indians; that there was no glory in it, and when the war was over all he could pride himself on was his former service down in the Southern Confederacy. That when he would reflect as to what good he had been to his country, he would say that he hadn't been any good while he was out in the Indian country. He said that he would make an application to be sent down to fight where there was some glory, and if he couldn't get it he was going to resign; that he would not have any more Indian-fighting in his military history; that this trip had demonstrated to him that he was no Indian-fighter, and that there was no glory in it, and the Government was wasting money in paying him a salary for trying to look after the Indians. It was really distressing to hear the General talk. I rode with him in his ambulance down Cottonwood Canyon, and as I was his aide-de-camp he talked to me in a very free and kindly way. As I had seen him after he was carried off from the battle-field at Wilson Creek, wounded, and had referred to it, he said that he had lots rather go down South and be shot to death than to stay up North and fight Indians and be frozen to death. And that although his superiors might order him to make another Indian campaign for the purpose of keeping the Indians moving, he was going to have a command farther south or else leave the service. The General soon after sent in his request for a detail farther south in the theatre of the war, or else that his resignation be accepted.

A recapitulation of the trip is as follows: It had lasted from January 15, 1865, to January 26th, inclusive, being twelve days. The men of my company had marched, owing to the side-trip they took down into Kansas, more miles than the Expedition had marched, and more than any other company had marched. The record of my company was as follows:

January 15th,	10 miles.	January 21st,	50 miles.
" 16th,	33 "	" 22nd,	9 "
" 17th,	22 "	" 23rd,	32 "
" 18th,	15 "	" 24th,	35 "
" 19th,	37 "	" 25th,	26 "
" 20th,	50 "	" 26th,	42 "

Total 361 miles.

This was a total average of thirty miles per day during a cold winter period. As about one-sixth must be allowed for detours, the distance in straight lines would be three hundred miles. My distances are guess-work, but we became able to guess with considerable accuracy. On our return to Cottonwood the General wrote out and issued the following order:

"HEADQUARTERS EXPEDITIONARY FORCES,
IN THE FIELD, *January 26, 1865*
COTTONWOOD, NEBRASKA TERRITORY.
SPECIAL FIELD ORDER NO. 8.

PAR. 1. The General Commanding wishes to tender his thanks to the men of his command who were with him on his recent expedition against the Indians.

PAR. 2. Especial credit is due:

To Colonel R. R. Livingston, of the 1st Nebraska Vet. Vol. Cavalry, commanding.

To Captain T. J. Majors, commanding detachments of the 1st Nebraska Vet. Vol. Cavalry, and First Nebraska Militia.

To Captain N. J. O'Brien, commanding battery formed from artillery detachments.

To Captain E. B. Murphy, commanding detachments of 7th Iowa Cavalry and 1st Nebraska Vet. Vol. Cavalry, for valuable services rendered on the march.

PAR. 3. Although unsuccessful in meeting the enemy in battle, hardships were encountered which to overcome, required the highest order of soldierly qualities, patience and endurance. And during a march of over three hundred miles, over a wild and desolate country, in the midst of winter and during intense cold, not a word of impatience or complaint was heard.

PAR. 4. The General Commanding further wishes to call especial attention to the admirable conduct of Captain Wild's Company 'B,' and Captain White's Company 'C,' 1st Nebraska Militia; who, although poorly equipped and supplied and their term of service expired, excited admiration by their soldierly conduct and cheerful performance of duty.

This order will be read to each company that was on the expedition. By order of

ROBERT B. MITCHELL, Brig.-General,
Comdg. District and Expedition."

General Mitchell had been revolving in his mind, and for seven days planning, a big prairie-fire. He had determined that if he could not catch the Indians he could at least fire the whole country and make it a lean place for them. On the morning of January 27, 1865, the sky was bright and clear, with a keen wind blowing from the northwest. "Just the day I want," said the General. "I will give them ten thousand square miles of prairie-fire." He cleared the telegraph line early in the forenoon, and wired instructions up and down the river, and also requests to the officers in command of Colorado stations. The orders and requests were that fire details be sent up and down so as to connect, and that at sundown the prairies be simultaneously fired from Fort Kearney west to Denver. Instructions were sent to every ranch and post along the line. Each was to use its own method to accomplish the purpose, but the whole country was to be set in a blaze at sunset. The order was fully carried out. The country was fired for three hundred miles. At Julesburg the method used was to make light bales of hay, bound with chains and pulled, while blazing, over the prairie with a dragging lariat-rope. The bale would skip and set fire once in a while as the horses ran with it. The fire details had their horses loaded with hay, and each man had several boxes of matches. The wind took up the scattered beginnings; they were soon united, and they rolled as a vast confluent sheet of flame to the south. At Cottonwood Springs we rode out onto the plateau to see and watch it. The fire rolled on and on, leaving in its train only blackness and desolation. All night the sky was lighted up. The fire swept the country clean; three days afterwards it was burning along the banks of the Arkansas River, far to the south, over which river it passed in places and ran out down in the Panhandle of Texas. There were some islands of grass left in some places far apart, here and there, but not many. The Indians back-fired against it in places, and managed to save themselves, but the game was driven out of the country before the fire. It did much damage to some portions of the Kansas frontier, which was then far east of the middle of the State. Leo Palladie said, "Now, Mr. Indian has got to get north of the Platte River."

The raid of General Mitchell, driving the Indians out of the Big Timbers on the Republican, and the subsequent prairie-fire, had shown them that they were in great danger. It made clear to them that they were in between two fires; that an expedition could at any time be sent north from the Arkansas River and south from the Platte, and that they could not expect to be at war, or carry on prolonged hostilities, along the Republican or Smoky Hill rivers, without final extermination. It was forced upon them by the Mitchell expedition, that, as a strategic matter, if they wanted more war, they must go north across the Platte into the vast "Shallow-water" country. General Mitchell's actions and plans worked out much better than he expected, and instead of being failures they worked out as great successes, for they practically cleared the country between the two rivers, and thereafter it was only subject to sporadic raids. The Indians recognized the fact that the white soldiers could go at any time, to any place, and that the road was never so long or the cold so severe as to stop them. Hence, between the two rivers there was no place to which they could at any time go and say that they were safe from pursuit and attack. Nor could they live in an area of territory which had been burned over and cleared of game; nor could the game stay during the winter in a country that was burned over. General Mitchell showed them plainly that they were in great danger, and that if they did not make peace they must move. They could all go north and join their brethren; but they were assured they would have a fight on the Platte, going north, wherever they struck it; and a pursuit, perhaps. The Indians were called upon to act promptly, and they did. They determined to go north, although some of them went south across the Arkansas River. We will see how they planned to go north.

CHAPTER XXXV

WHEN we got back to Cottonwood on the 26th (January, 1865), we were told that war parties of Indians had appeared along the Arkansas River and on the Colorado frontier east of Denver, showing that they were on the wing. My company was immediately sent back, on the 27th, to Julesburg, but Captain O'Brien remained back at Cottonwood by order of General Mitchell, for the purpose of consultation as to some further movements. General Mitchell, the same as everybody else, took a great fancy to Captain O'Brien, and wanted to consult with him. Captain O'Brien always did his duty promptly and well, and his judgment was good. The company went up in charge of Lieutenant Brewer, who happened to be then at Cottonwood Springs. He was not on the recent expedition. A howitzer and ten men were left behind at Cottonwood as an escort for Captain O'Brien. I remained behind as aide-de-camp to General Mitchell. Lieutenant Brewer was ordered to push through as rapidly as possible to Julesburg. I was going now to Omaha with General Mitchell, and we were to start on the morning of the 29th. I said to myself, "Now I will see Omaha or know the reason why," but several officers said to me, "You will never see Omaha." In fact, it got to be a matter of interest to all of the officers of the different regiments and companies to see how the premonition was going to come out; they were all watching my movements, and several of them wanted me to write them if I did actually get into the city of Omaha.

Very strangely, on the evening of the 28th, General Mitchell was informed by wire that the Indians had been seen around Julesburg; that they had appeared at Gillette's ranch, nine miles west of Julesburg, in great numbers, and besieged it, but had been driven off; that they had also appeared east of Julesburg at Alkali station, and driven off some cattle in broad daylight; and that they had appeared at several other places. General Mitchell directed me to go up to Julesburg, and see what the condition of things there was, and report to him by wire. So, on the afternoon of the 29th Captain O'Brien and I, with the escort of the ten men of our own company who had remained behind to escort Captain O'Brien back, started up the Platte river with the howitzer; and as I went west, the officers in bidding me farewell said, several of them, "Good-by! You will never see Omaha."

This new trip of mine—starting back to Julesburg—connected with General Mitchell's announced intention of resigning, or going South, led me to immediately see that it was quite possible that the premonition which I had received might be correct. Nevertheless, I was beginning to feel a little bit skittish, but I argued to myself that I would be in Julesburg only a little while; that I was still aide-de-camp for the General; that he would go South, which he in fact, soon after did; that I would rejoin him, which I soon after did; and that through natural causes and in the proper order of things I would "never see Omaha."

Captain O'Brien and I started out with our escort, and that night we stopped at Jack Morrow's, which, as stated, was ten miles up the river. The place was fortified and garrisoned by a lot of cowboys, trappers, ranchmen, and squaw-men; enough to hold the place.

Captain O'Brien and I had a gay and festive time at "Jack's tepee," as it was called, on the night of January 29th. That night we ate antelope-hearts and beaver-tails, and listened to the old pioneers tell Indian stories. Jack Morrow insisted on opening a quart bottle of champagne each for Captain O'Brien and me, but the Captain and I had business on hand, and touched it very lightly; and Jack Morrow, who always loved champagne, drank all the balance of it, and became very full and talkative. Among other things he told about how much money he was making and how the Indian scare had diminished it, and how he was going to put in a claim against the Government for not keeping the Indians where they would not restrict trade. Jack's legal ideas upon this subject were quite hazy, but he easily found out how, through the negligence of the Government, he had "lost a million dollars."

In the morning we pushed on to Alkali, and there overtook a stage which had been driven in, and kept there. Alkali was a mere sod stage station with a sod corral, and with some sod works to fight the Indians from. Captain Murphy of Company "A" was there with his company, together with Tom Potter, my old friend. I had formerly belonged to Company "A," and I was glad to meet the boys at this time. The First Lieutenant of Company "A" was named Smith, and he had learned the Sioux war-song from a Sioux, and he got so that he could sing it as well as an Indian. That evening he lay in his bunk with his clothes on, for we never undressed in the Indian country, and he sang that war-song pretty near all night. In fact, I heard it so much that I was able to sing it myself, after a fashion, but none of us could come up to Lieutenant Smith in the tones, quavers and curlicues of the song. In the station was one of the agents of the stage company, going through to Denver, by the name of Andrew Hughes, a royal fellow, brave as could be, and pushing his way through to Denver, from post to post, seeking to reëstablish his stage line and then attend to the duties of his position. And with him was a man named Clift. They had a stage of their own.

We were furnished by Captain Murphy with an additional escort to go through on. Captain O'Brien and I had our piece of artillery and gun squad with us from

Cottonwood Springs, making in all ten men. One of the men was taken ill, and we were furnished with ten more, and started on to Beauvais's ranch, which was twenty-five miles east of Julesburg. This was on the last day of January —the 31st. The coach kept up with the procession, and in it were the two citizens referred to, and their camping outfit. They had two drivers on the box. Everybody was armed to the teeth. The provisions and bedding and baggage of the stage outfit were tied up on the rear of the stage on the trunk-rack. The stage had four horses. Our piece of artillery had only two, but they were large, strong horses.

We had hardly left Alkali in the morning before we saw smoke signals in the valley, and in a little while we saw Indians on the other side of the river in squads of two, seldom more or less. They seemed to be searching the other side of the river for cattle and horses which had been turned out to graze. We saw two Indians driving about fifteen head of horses. We went along the road as rapidly as possible, keeping our eye upon the Indians across the river, but passing them rapidly, and they were soon out of sight in the rear. But we noticed that when the Indians had a bunch of cattle they struck north through the hills, as if going to the North Platte. We had no guide with us, but we knew the route perfectly, and were enough familiar with the Indian manners and customs to be able to know that we were in danger. From time to time some Indian would rise up out of a swale or out of the grass on the other side of the river, and defiantly fire a gun or a pistol at us; but the distance was such that no good aim could be taken nor much danger experienced, except as showing the threatening conditions of the march. We camped at Beauvais's ranch, where there was a detachment of one of the companies, and where there was a telegraph operator. We sat up late at night, and told our superiors, by wire, how the Indians were acting along the river. Colonel Livingston, commanding the eastern sub-district, in the meantime had come to Cottonwood Springs, with some of the First Nebraska Veteran Volunteer Cavalry, owing to the rumors that were coming down the river in regard to the appearances of Indians along the line of route. Livingston ordered us to proceed immediately to Julesburg, and await his arrival; that he feared the Cheyenne Indians were to make another effort to cross the river, and go north and join their brother tribe, the Northern Cheyennes, which, at that time, was up in southern Dakota somewhere near the Deadwood country. The garrison at Beauvais was so small that we felt that we ought to leave some men there to help protect it. We were in entire ignorance of what was ahead of us, as we shall see; so we left six men there.

In the morning of February 2, 1865, we started out from Beauvais's ranch, and saw Indians from the very start. When we got to Dick Cleve's ranch, we saw some Indians rounding up his cattle on the other side of the river. There was quite a number of ranchmen gathered there, a sort of conglomeration left over from a train which, together with the garrison of a few soldiers, made a place which the Indians could not very well capture. But the Indians around Cleve's ranch were so numerous that we left them four men of our cavalry. They expected an attack, but we did not feel alarmed, because we had the piece of artillery, and our horses were the best.

From Dick Cleve's we started on, and Captain O'Brien and I with the coach, the piece of artillery and nine men, being the gun squad and four others; with the four civilians we were fifteen men. We had not gone far past Cleve's when we saw ten or fifteen Indians on the other side of the river. Having a very fine Smith & Wesson target rifle, I thought I would go down towards the river, and give them a trial shot. They were some little distance on the other side of the river, and after I had made my shot, an Indian arose out of the willows on the bank on the other side of the river, and, pulling a revolver, fired six shots, and then he pulled another and fired six shots more, and then he fired a gun at me. It was evidence that the Indian was better armed than I was, and as I stopped to reconnoiter, he began to fire a lot of good American words at me, and they were shot in such good English that I became satisfied that the Indian was not a Cheyenne or a Sioux, and I concluded he was one of the Confederate emissaries sent from the Indian territory. I was afterwards confirmed in this supposition.

As we got near to Julesburg, but not in sight of it, we saw large bunches of cattle over on the north side of the river, being driven. At one time on the other side of the river there were five little droves of from five to ten cattle each, being driven separately by two or three Indians each. They seemed to be heading diagonally northwest towards the bluffs. That is to say, they were going up the river and obliquely to the right so as to strike the valley of Lodgepole. They paid no attention to us, and never attempted to rally and come over and make an attack on us, nor did they appear at all alarmed. We also saw Indians peering up over the hills far to the south, but they did not appear to be in motion or active. They just stood and looked at us. They made no signals and did nothing to alarm us, knowing we were marching right into danger.

Our line of march was that the Captain and I marched at the head, then came eight men on horseback, then one man, the ninth, riding the near artillery horse, and behind them the coach. The captain and I had an anxious consultation as we went along. We determined to push forward, and get into the post at Julesburg as rapidly as we could, but we did not know what was ahead of us. East of Julesburg the plateau pushes a promontory north to the edge of the river, so that the view of the fort at Julesburg was shut off from us until we had got entirely around that plateau and promontory. On the other side was the arroyo of which I have spoken before, called the "Devil's Dive." As we got up to this promontory it was a little after noontime. We noticed a number of black specks far out on Lodgepole. They were Indians, but we could not see our fort, on account of the intervening bluff. We stopped there to reconnoiter a little as to the passage around this promontory. The ground was quite broken, and we did not wish to run into an ambuscade.

While we stopped there I inspected the artillery fully,

to see that everything was all ready for use; imagine my horror to find that the priming-wire had jolted out of its fastening and been lost. The priming-wire was an absolute necessity, because the cartridges were in thick flannel bags, and when rammed down they had to be opened, so that the friction primer would throw the fire down into the powder. This priming-wire had to be pushed down through the vent into the flannel or the charge could not be exploded. A feeling of great horror ran over me as I vainly searched in the chest of the howitzer. Near us ran the telegraph line. I told one of the boys to climb up a pole, swing out on that wire hand over hand, and pull it down to the ground. With the aid and assistance of several, we finally got the wire swung down nearly to the ground, but not near enough. Thereupon, with an artillery hatchet, we chopped down a telegraph pole so as to give the wire more sag. We then cut the wire, and tying one end of it to the rear of the coach we had the four horses pull on it until we got all the slack that could come from that direction. Then we pulled the other line and got all the slack that could come from the other, and we managed to get off two feet of wire, and then put the wire together, and make a new connection. This took us nearly half an hour, but we got a priming-wire made out of this telegraph wire which was all right. We pounded it to a point on the iron tire of the howitzer, and were then ready to go ahead.

When we had finished with this telegraph wire, Captain O'Brien observed a smoke over the promontory, and called my attention to it. He said: "What do you think that smoke can be? It is this side of the post, and yet beyond the hill. Go carefully up with your field-glass, and see what is the matter, and see what those black specks mean up the Lodgepole valley." I went up on horseback, looking in all directions, and could see no indications of Indians nor ambuscade, and finally peeped over the hill Indian fashion through a cactus bush. And lo, and behold! I could see Indians scattered everywhere in front of us; they were crossing the river, running around the stage station, blacksmith shop and telegraph office, which were burning. The haystacks of the stage station were also burning. Back on the hills west of the post was a large group of Indians, apparently motionless, while between us and the fort was a body of Indians running around and evidently shouting and yelling and having a good time, although they were so far off I could hear no noise. I came down to see the Captain, and told him what I had seen, and I said, "You go up there, and see what you think about the matter." He came down, and said, "There is a large body of Indians crossing on the ice north, and a large body at the stage station a mile this side."

The question then was what to do. What could 15 men do with a thousand Indians on the war-path in front, with no outlet for retreat and no place for defense?

There appeared in the present juncture only one thing to do that had any wisdom in it, and that was to make a bold dash for the fort; because if the whole gang of Indians got after us we could find no shelter and we could not hold them off. The Captain ordered the gun shotted with "canister." Canister was a large tin can fitting the calibre of the gun and filled with iron balls. The boys called it "canned trouble." The gun having been loaded, one of the soldiers carried a friction primer so as to be able to fire the gun quickly from horseback without dismounting. The Captain detailed me as an advance guard with my field-glass to go on ahead and feel the route along the cape of the promontory and to prevent an ambuscade.

We started on, and we went just as fast as we dared. We went around the point, carefully inspecting the road. I went ahead about two or three hundred yards, and we were visible to the Indians up at the post only for a short time as we rounded the cape, but were not recognized, on account of the film of smoke from the burning stage station. Then there was a little rise in the ground ahead of us, that kept us out of sight from the post, and by following around the rim of it outside of the road, we were able to go unseen a little nearer to the post. And so it happened that we got up within much less than two miles of the post, and there did not seem to be any alarm among the Indians. We then rushed our horses, and determined to make a bold dash for the post. As we came over the hill we deployed at intervals of about twenty yards, with our artillery and coach up in the center of the line. Some of the Indians began to see us; then we went a-howling and yelling towards the post. It did not take us long to pass the burning stage station. The Indians were rallying on both sides of us, and shooting at us from a distance; they did not know but what a regiment was coming behind us. Around the cape behind us then came a squad of Indians on the run.

When we got to the stage station it was a sight. A lot of the Indians were there before us, and they started away. We saw that a large number of Indians were carrying off corn from the stage station. There were so many of them that they had sanded a road across the ice of the river, and this road was about six feet wide. Their ponies being unshod, they could not carry the corn across without the road being sanded; it was too slippery. There were enough of them to sand the entire road, and there was a line of them all around the burning stage station. There were animals killed; a couple of horses; and a cow, that had been grazing around. Chickens were killed. It seemed as if the Indians thought it was a funny thing to shoot an arrow down through a chicken and pin the chicken to the ground. We saw chickens still fluttering that were thus pinned down to the ground.

We fired the canister at the Indians ahead of us. The post was still a mile off, and they had evidently seen us coming. There was no use of our trying to compete with the Indians, who were flocking in on both sides, in pistol-firing. Captain O'Brien ordered all the boys to draw sabers, and we started. After we had gone about two hundred yards a group of Indians were in front of us. Our men at the post had run the other howitzer out, and began firing shells directly at us, and we stopped long enough to fire a shell towards the post. The Indians in front of us got out of the way, and the post kept firing in our direction. The Indians did not understand the situation. Our appearance had been too sudden. They did not know it was a bluff. They did not know what was behind us, or what the smoke might conceal. They did not dare to charge us, but got out of our way and hovered on our flanks. We, all the time, were going as fast as our horses would carry us toward the post. We went through with the Indians firing and cavorting all over the prairie. Not a man in our party was injured. The Indians, like a hive of bees, showed great alarm, and were dashing around in groups. Andrew Hughes and his companion Clift, on the stages, kept up with the procession in fine style; they seemed to enjoy the occasion. They kept their horses on the run—yelled as much, and fired as often, as they could, kept the stages right side up, and seemed filled with hilarity. We made a royal bluff, and it won. I never felt so relieved in my life as I did when we got up nearer the post.

When we got to the Post we found, besides our diminished Company "F," about fifty citizens there, all armed, who had been driven in. We were told that fifteen hundred Indians had struck the post that forenoon, and had run all around it, had fired at the post, at everybody whose head appeared, and that their camp was right across the river above the mouth of Lodgepole. I never could account for why the Indians did not make an attack on us sooner. But the smoke from the burning hay, which we had seen miles before, obscured the atmosphere, and the wind was blowing gently from the northwest and spread the smoke over the ground, and the Indians, who were running all over the country, failed to distinguish us as soldiers until we got up within a couple of miles or nearer. And then the alarm could not be conveyed to the body of Indians any faster than we could go ourselves, so we kept up with the information, and it was not until we dashed past the burning buildings that the Indians got any comprehension of the situation, and they were unable to get us before we got in, owing to the coöperation of the fort.

A Colorado man, somewhat of an artist, happened to be among the citizens at the post on that eventful day, and many years afterwards I saw a picture that he had *drawn at the time* in commemoration of the event.

CHAPTER XXXVI

*Indians Around the Post · Duel at Long Range ·
Fight at Gillette's Ranch · The Big Haystack ·
Big Indian Camp-fire · Captain and I on Guard ·
The Fire-arrow · Jimmie O'Brien · The Indian
Dance · The Wild-fire · The Retreat · The In-
dian Herd · Colonel Livingston Coming · Gil-
lette's Ranch · The Trains of Machinery · The
Poisoned Whisky · The Wasted Flour · Diagram
of Post*

WE GOT into the Post about half-past three. The Indians in a very short time circled around the post, howling and yelling and shouting defiance, and later went across the river to the camp. The carrying of sack corn on ponies across the river did not cease, but we did not consider ourselves able to stop them, as it was a mile from the post.

A little while before sundown I noticed a motionless Indian on horseback over in the bottom across the river from the fort, and I thought I would go and see what effect I could make on him with my target rifle. I started to walk from the post down towards the river, the boys of the post being out, ready to furnish me any protection I might need. The Indian on the other bank of the river dismounted and left his horse, and started walking towards me. He finally stooped down in the grass, which was quite heavy, but I could plainly see him. By throwing up the sights of my target, I pulled on him, but the bullet fell short, as I could see by the dust which rose where it struck. I had scarcely fired my gun when the Indian fired and a bullet went whizzing over my head in a way so familiar that I knew it to be a Belgian rifle-musket. I had heard them often down South. I then made three quick shots, to see if I could reach the Indian, but my rifle would not carry to him. I began to march obliquely back to the post, going somewhat to the left, so as to change the Indian's line of fire, but he got in two shots on me before I got back to the post, to which I went in a leisurely but somewhat interested way. The Indian had a better gun than I had, that is to say, one that would shoot farther, and I knew that the gun was one which had been furnished from some military command. The Indians did not buy Belgian muskets. This man had been standing out there making a target of himself so as to get somebody to come out and fire at him, and I had done exactly what he wanted me to do, and he had got three good shots at me before I was through with him. And I had to thank my stars that it was no worse.

In talking with one of the citizens, I was told that these Indians were the Arapahoes and Cheyennes mixed, that had gathered together and come up from the southern country; and that they had struck the river some little distance above Julesburg, but that they wanted to go up Lodgepole Creek, cross over the divide, and go up the Bluewater River, called by the Indians, Minne-to-wocca-pella. The word "to" in Sioux language means blue. They always put the color adjective after the noun; for instance, Manka-to, "Earth blue."

These Indians coming down had driven everything before them, but at Gillette's ranch, nine or ten miles west of the fort, they had met a stubborn resistance. But during the night the occupants of Gillette's ranch had made a dash for the river, and had come down on the ice, going from island to island and defending themselves from time to time by rallies upon these little willow islands. On the outside of Gillette's ranch were eight large, heavy freight wagons that had been held up. These eight wagons were filled with bottled liquors for Denver, and the Indians the next morning had got these liquors, and had come down to visit Julesburg. They also had a large number of oxen which they had captured, and they had a large herd of beeves which they were driving down to Julesburg. There were those among them who knew how to hitch up oxen, and so the oxen and the wagons with the bottled liquors were driven on down in a herd along with the cattle. The wagons were zigzagging along the prairie according as the oxen were herded here and there on the route, and they had got the whole business across the river to their camp. They had cut down telegraph poles, and camped from time to time, and burned the telegraph poles for a long distance. They had cut them up and dragged them with ponies so that in the camp, which was now in plain sight of our post and on the north side of the river, they were having high jinks with fires made out of telegraph poles, drinking "S. T. 1860 X," "Plantation" and "Hostetter" Bitters, and all kinds of good stuff which they found in those wagons. This was the condition of things at sunset on the day that we got into the Julesburg Post, February 2, 1865.

The arrangement which we made for the evening was that the guards should go one hour on and two off. We got the civilians together, divided them into groups of three, and put a civilian in charge of each group, so that he could have his men ready, the object being to stay prepared for a rush on the fort, and to have one-third of the garrison, soldiers and civilians, ready and on guard to repel the first symptom of attack. As for Captain O'Brien and myself, we determined to stay up all night, except that we would take turns in dozing if everything was looking favorable.

The best point for observation was the haystack in the northwest corner of our Post. The stable was nearly as high, but was sort of in the center, so that a person upon it could not see well over the haystack. The haystack was a large, heavy, weighted-down stack of about eighty tons. Captain O'Brien and I got on top of it, and worked holes down in it so as to be somewhat protected from the weather, and yet to have a good observation. The stack was between thirty and forty feet long on the summit. It could be reached by getting up on the sod wall, which at that point was about eight feet high, and then getting up from that portion of the stack whence the hay was being used. Fearing that the Indians might come up and start to set fire to the stack, we had down on the ground several camp-kettles full of water with a quart tin cup floating in the top of each. The weather had very much moderated, and the afternoon of the day had been quite pleasant for a winter day, although freezing. The sun set gloriously, with a livid burst of red which held quite late. We could see a large smothered camp-fire, and could hear yells and shouting, and every once in a while some Indian shot off a gun. The Captain and I took a-plenty of ammunition and a lot of hard-tack to munch on, and as soon as dusk began to fall we got up into our holes on that haystack. Guards were also on the north end of the stable, and on the barracks, and on the headquarters building. Our fort, being made of sod, was incombustible, and we felt no real danger except as it might come to the hay, which, if it got on fire, might burn us all out. We had some of the men sheltered down under the sod wall on the inside at the end of the haystack, ready to take any action that might be required.

About the time that nightfall set in the big camp-fire of the Indians began to blaze up strongly, and we could see the cattle coming in in droves, both east and west, and also bands of American horses, not large in number, but they were prancing about. We could see with our glasses quite plainly. In a little while the fire grew larger, and the Indians began to caper around it in a war-dance. We could hear them shrieking and yelling, we could hear the tum-tum of a native drum, and we could hear a chorus shouting as if there were squaws there taking a part in the exercises. Then we could see them circling around the fire, then separately stamping the ground and making gestures. It seemed as if the fire grew larger and more scattered, and the ring grew larger and the yelling grew stronger, and finally it was a perfect pandemonium lit up with the wildfire of burning telegraph poles. We knew that the bottled liquors destined for Denver were beginning to get in their work and a perfect orgy was ensuing. It kept up constantly. It seemed as if exhausted Indians fell back and let fresh ones take hold, and around that fire they did jump and scream, and make motions with lance and tomahawk, and caper and cut up, in a wild and picturesque way.

It was a very thrilling scene, except that we knew if they had courage to make a dash on the post there would not be any of us left by daylight. Pioneers told us, however, that the Indians would not make a dash on us in that time, but that we might look for them at sun-up. In the mean time our telegraph line was down, from the burning of the station, and from the destruction of poles west of us, so that we had no way of sending out word of the post further than had already gone.

The Captain and I stood in our holes in the hay up about to our waists, with our target rifles on one side of us and our box of ammunition and crackers on the other side, and watching with the field-glass what might take place. We were suffering somewhat from anxiety. We had also a couple of dogs up with us in holes in the hay, and the dogs seemed just as earnest and as excited as anybody. As late as twelve o'clock there seemed to be no diminution of the orgy. It seemed to keep on just as strong as ever, and we saw ponies coming across the prairie dragging pieces of telegraph poles chopped down, and every once in a while the sparks would rise as a new piece was thrown on the fire.

Our dogs were muttering and grumbling all the time, but the ground was practically clear in front of us for quite a distance, with the exception of some little clumps of sage-brush and cactus, and these were scattering. We kept our eye, however, well upon the prairie in front of us, so that no skulking Indian might come up and pick us off. Some of the time we were crouched down so that we could just plainly see over the hay with our field-glasses.

All at once a spark came before our eyes. I could not understand it for a second. It seemed as if a star fell. It came in a curve, and fell into our hay. An Indian had crept up, in spite of us, back of a sage-brush, and had fired a fire-arrow right into our haystack. I was taken much by surprise, but by the time it struck the stack I knew what it was. Captain O'Brien happened to have his gun in his hands, and with great presence of mind he drew up and fired the best he could in the direction of the arrow. The hero of the occasion was Jimmie O'Brien. The arrow had scarcely struck the hay when it flashed. I struck the spot with my carbine, but Jimmie O'Brien grabbed a cup, jumped up on the wall, and with one dash he made a center shot with the tin cup and put the entire fire out with one effort. It was the prettiest thing I ever saw. The boys on detail all cheered, and Jimmie O'Brien never got over being complimented for his presence of mind and his steady nerve upon the occasion. But we saw no Indian arise from where the arrow came, and the Captain was almost an unerring shot. We all believed that the Captain killed the Indian, but we never got the Indian's body, because as a matter of fact, the Indians were skulking around the post that night and we never got a chance to see them or get a shot at them. What they did may be imagined from the fact that the next morning out on a telegraph pole within twenty feet of our sod fort the Captain's dog, "Kearney," was found with its throat cut, and tied hanging about six feet up on the telegraph pole. So that, if the Captain killed the Indian, they could have got him away that night, because towards morning it was cloudy and dark.

After the fire-arrow episode we kept a still closer lookout. Once in a while we would think we saw a moving form or something crawling on the ground, and we kept plugging away with our rifles at all such symptoms, so as not only to get an Indian if we could, but keep them on the *qui vive,* to let them know we were waiting for them. About one o'clock the orgy seemed to reach its height. The yells were the most blood-curdling and frantic I ever heard, and although we were a long distance off, perhaps a half-mile, we could hear them all upon the midnight air quite plainly. And we discussed among ourselves whether or not the bottled liquors would not get them finally worked up to a point that would lead them to besiege us. Suddenly the fire began to grow brighter, and greater, and the Indians circling around it seemed to form a larger ring. We soon saw that the fire had spread to the prairie-grass, and that the Indians were not trying to put it out. The night was perfectly still. There was no breeze of any kind, and the prairie-grass burned slowly, and the Indian ring kept growing larger and larger as the fire increased. And still the thing went on until the fire was an acre in extent, and still an undiminished ring of Indians were going around it shouting and yelling, and it kept growing in extent until there were at least four acres of this burning prairie in a ring, and still the Indians were shouting and prancing singly and in groups. Then we all began to think that the thing was going to break up with an attack. The fire finally spread and spread until it lit up the whole country, and all at once the Indians were not seen between us and the fire, and the smoke prevented us from seeing where they were.

We concluded they were all coming towards the post. The smoke began to hang sort of in a pall, not being borne in either direction. We got the bugler up, and had him sound the assembly. We got him up on top of the stable to blow bugle-calls. Everybody turned out, everybody was assigned to a duty. One of the howitzers we got on top of the stable, which was really heavy enough to hold a cannon. At the corners of the fort several sentinels were placed to watch carefully, and still we watched, and still the prairie-fire spread. It finally struck the river on the south, and stopped; then it struck up Lodgepole on the east, and stopped; and then it started up the river, going quite slowly, but still no Indians. We imagined a short time before daylight that we saw some Indians south of the post, and then we imagined that we saw some among the hills. It turned out, however, that they were simply reinforcements of Indians, few in number, coming with great speed. They passed west of the post, going towards the river.

Finally it became dawn, with us all on the watch. There were no Indians in sight. It was impossible for so great a number of Indians to be hidden, and Captain O'Brien and I determined that we would get on our good horses and make a survey of the condition of things; and we sent some men on down to the telegraph station, which had been burned, to repair the wire. We had a telegraph operator in the post by the name of Holcomb, who was one of the most capable young men I ever saw. After we had got the line up running east we had no instruments, nor any means of telegraphing. Yet this man Holcomb succeeded in sending off a message and in receiving one. First he chopped an ax into the ground, and taking hold of the wires with gloves, he alternately played the ends of the wires upon the iron poll of the ax in such a way as to telegraph, and then he put the wires in his mouth and read the dispatches. At least he said he did, and the message was: "Get ready to follow. Am coming. Livingston." But we could not send or receive any telegrams to or from Denver or Laramie.

The Captain and I got on our horses and rode over the river to the late Indian camp. There were places where the grass had been trodden down so that it was not burned near the camp-fire. We saw there the business cards of the manufacturers of various kinds of liquor, together with pamphlets, and advertisements, great quantities of broken bottles, and heads of one hundred and fifty-six cattle, that had been slaughtered. The fire had died down, and was only going up in a narrow streak on the west side of Lodgepole. The Indians had driven off a great quantity of beef cattle. It looked as if there were at least five thousand head. Along with the beef cattle that had been driven were the irregular and waving lines of the wagons drawn by oxen that went along with an undulating track because the draft oxen hitched to the wagons had been herded along with the balance of the cattle. The wheel-tracks were sunken, indicating that they had got the wagons loaded with something. They had gone up Lodgepole, and there were a great number of them. Elston believed that it was the whole Southern Cheyenne nation that was on the move, together with the Arapahoes and some Sioux.

As a matter of fact, we did not know it, but Colonel Livingston, with a large detachment, was within thirty miles of us that morning. The Indians knew it, and that was why they started off as they did. Their signals had told them a story which we did not know, or comprehend.

After having viewed the late Indian camp, and got the

telegraph line restored to the east, Captain O'Brien thought
we ought to scout the hills and see if there were any Indians
in hiding that might become dangerous to the post. So he
took a squad with a bugler to go south and east, and sent
me with a squad to go west. A signal to come in if necessary,
was a shot from the twelve-pound howitzer at the post.
Everything was to be done as fast as possible, and we all
started off on the gallop. I was told not, on any account, to
go west farther than Gillette's Ranch, which was nine miles.
The Captain started for the hills on a rush, and I started with
eight men for the west. At a point one-half mile west of the
post we found the telegraph wires all cut and the poles gone;
they had been used for cooking at the Indian barbecue
which I have described, across the river. The valley was
wide before us on our trip west; we saw no Indians in the
hills south of us, and we kept up the south bank of the river
and were soon at Gillette's Ranch. Most of the telegraph
poles all the way from Julesburg were gone. The posts were
up one-half mile west of Gillette's Ranch, but the wire was
down, how much farther we could not see. The grass around
Gillette's Ranch clear down to the river had been burned
off, evidently a month or two before. The whole country
looked black and desolate. Out on the plain were 24 large
freight wagons, not parked, but scattered out separately as
if they had been run in hastily and abandoned. They were
loaded principally with mining machinery, bar-iron and cast-
iron piping. Apparently no effort had been made by the
Indians to burn these wagons; in fact, there was nothing for
them to burn the wagons with; there was nothing inflam-
mable to use within a half-mile. On one of the wagons was
a large cast-iron wheel, with a wide, smooth rim which projected over the sides. On it was written in a large bold hand,
"Go to Hell." The words were freshly written in charcoal,
and had been done by some one among the Indians. I have
briefly stated that the vanguard of the Cheyenne incursion
first struck Gillette's Ranch, and that the people there made
a fight until dark, and in the cover of the night retreated to
the river and came on down to Julesburg. These fugitives

told of an Indian, with the attacking party, who wore a hat, blanket cape and high-top cavalry boots, and who shouted loud swear-words in English, and had a rifled musket of the new United States pattern. He was probably the man who wrote on the flywheel. He was probably an ambassador from the Southern Confederacy sent to keep the Indians fired up, and was an Indian from one of the "civilized" tribes of the Indian Territory. We heard of him several times and in several different ways. Off to one side a little east of Gillette's Ranch were several large wagons with a lot of whisky and liquor advertisements in. They had been in little burlap-covered bales, and had been ripped open and scattered.

Standing out on the prairie not far from the house was a barrel of whisky, all by itself, untouched. One of my men said that it was poisoned; that he had heard one of the men who came down from Gillette's Ranch say that they put a lot of strychnine in a barrel of whisky and stuck it up where the Indians could get it; that the Indians never touched it but helped themselves to other goods of the same kind, in the wagons. I shot out the bung and emptied the barrel. All over the prairie were large white spots leading down toward the river. These spots were in pairs, and quite many. Upon investigation I found that they were of flour, and it happened in this way: There was at the ranch quite a lot of flour, and it was 50-pound sacks in heavy paper and 100-pound sacks in muslin. The Indians threw these sacks across their ponies and started off; if the ponies got to trotting, or bucking, the sacks would break in two and fall on opposite sides of the pony, and maybe the Indian gathered up the flour and maybe not. There was a great waste of flour. We led our horses around and got them a good feed each of this flour, and then on a gallop started home, where we arrived at just about the time that Captain O'Brien did. We both reported no Indians seen, no smoke signals, or anything to indicate the presence of any Indians south of the Platte River. A party had been sent up Lodgepole composed of soldiers and citizens, to see what they could see. They came back reporting that the Indians were making the fastest time possible up Lodgepole; that the cattle were making lots of trouble for the Indians, who were hurrying them forward on the run; that the scouting party could hear the Indians yelling and shouting furiously in the distance; that the dust rose up in clouds; that the Indian line from front to rear was about five miles long; and that the tracks of the wagons were zigzagging all over the prairie. This party brought back more than 500 head of cattle which they had picked up from those that had escaped or bolted the herd. The Indians had no time to stop and round them up. We afterwards got a lot more. Our post was packed as full as it would hold of people and horses; when all of the scouting parties had got in and reported, and when it was found that there were no more Indians and no more danger, there was general rejoicing among the civilians, and some of them, by means of concealed supplies, got gloriously drunk, and had to be put into the guard house.

CHAPTER XXXVII

Arrival of Colonel Livingston · Poles Ordered from Cottonwood · "Chief of Artillery" · Nothing Impossible · Rebuilding the Telegraph Line · Buffalo Springs · Valley Station · The Shelled-corn Bastion · Germans and Oysters · Forty Hours' Work · Line Reëstablished · Return to Julesburg

ON THE evening of February 3rd, 1865, after dark, in came Colonel Livingston from the east, with fully four hundred cavalry, four pieces of light artillery, telegraph instruments taken from some station along the road; and also forty-six mule-wagons loaded with supplies of various kinds. The Colonel had organized on his own account a little dwarf Indian expedition to keep the Cheyennes in motion. The forces were composed of Seventh Iowa Cavalry and First Nebraska Veteran Volunteer Cavalry—about half-and-half each. The Iowa troops were in command of Captain Murphy, of Company "A," and the Nebraska troops were in command of a captain of that regiment, named Wetherwax, a very fine officer. The horses were in good condition and well shod; the men were tired, but full of zeal. The weather late in the afternoon turned quite cold; the tents were pitched on the windward of the post. The men crowded by invitation into the post and barracks. The Lieutenants and officers, several in number, together with Colonel Livingston, crowded into our headquarters room, where at night we all slept on the dirt floor. Our visitors were tired because they had been making forced marches to reach us for fear the Indians would capture our fort. The Indians knew of their coming. I reported promptly to Colonel Livingston on his arrival, and told him of the destruction of the telegraph to the west as I had seen it. I estimated for two hundred and fifty poles and a mile of wire. The Colonel, by telegraph to Cottonwood

Springs, ordered wagons to be taken or impressed, to be quickly loaded with the lightest poles, started as soon as possible and pushed through night and day to Julesburg, as fast as the animals could stand it. There were a lot of cedar poles cut and stacked at Cottonwood and Jack Morrow's, ready for repair work along the line.

Then the next thing that Colonel Livingston did was to issue a special order detailing me as "chief of artillery." I did not know what particular use he had for a "chief of artillery," and I told him that I was already an aide-de-camp on the staff of the General commanding, and was not subject to his detail; but he paid no attention to my objections, and told me to immediately proceed to get my artillery corps together and drill them, in view of a proposed Indian expedition to the north.

Four of the guns were twelve-pound mountain howitzers and two of them were light three-inch Parrott guns. On the morning of February 4, 1865, I got the gun squads all together and had everything hitched up, and we drove around and drilled so as to get the men acquainted with one another and their duties. I found that a large wrought-iron bolt was out from the trail of one of the Parrott guns, and that if the gun were fired it would probably break itself to pieces, or turn a somersault. I went to the blacksmith of the company and told him to fix it if he could. After running around a good deal, he came and reported to me that he didn't have anything that he could use to fix the gun with; so I reported the fact to Colonel Livingston, and he, without discussing the matter, said to me, "I want you to go and have that gun fixed and put in shape, and don't fail to report to me that you have done it." I went, but after exhausting all my resources and getting the blacksmith to exhaust all of his, I saw no possible way in which the gun could be fixed, unless we could get the iron to fix it with. As we could get nothing to fix it with, I finally with great regret, some hours afterwards, went to the Colonel, after I had about run my legs off, and told him that it was impossible to fix the gun; that we didn't have the material to do it with and couldn't find any. He turned to me in a gruff manner and said: "I want you to have that gun fixed, and don't you report back here without it is fixed. So now attend to it right away." This was a novel proposition, and after I got over being angry and feeling that the Colonel was much displeased and somewhat unreasonable, it occurred to me to take some of the men and go a mile down the road to where the buildings had been burned and see if anything could be found among the ashes. So we went down there and scratched over the ruins of the burnt buildings, and the ashes, with our saber scabbards, and just about dark I ran onto a piece of wrought-iron, among the ashes of the stage office, that seemed to me to be the thing to use. I galloped up to the post, got hold of the blacksmith and showed him the piece of burnt bar-iron. He said, "I think I can use it," and I said, "You go to work and do it right quick and fast." I stayed with him about an hour, and by the aid of the portable forge we fixed the iron so that it made a bolt that fitted the place, and by dark the piece of artillery was fixed.

With great pride I went up to the Colonel and saluted him with much ceremony, and said, "I have the honor to report that the piece of artillery is fixed." Thereupon he called me up, and he said: "Young man, anything can be done if a person goes to work at it intending to do it. Don't you ever, during your military career, report that a thing isn't done and can't be done. Nothing is impossible, sir, nothing. You have been taught a good lesson, sir. You ought to have been reprimanded for reporting in the first place that the gun couldn't be fixed. Let this be a lesson to you, sir,— let this be a lesson. Don't ever give up anything as impossible; people who give up things as impossible, sir, don't get anywhere, sir. In this case, sir, you are to be commended for your success, and I take great pleasure in complimenting you."

On the forenoon of February 5, 1865, Captain Murphy of Company "A," with about a hundred men, was ordered up on the Denver road and told to go on up until he had crossed the trail of the Cheyennes and had reached that portion of the telegraph line which was uninjured, so that messages could be sent to Denver. Holcomb, the expert young telegraph operator, was sent up with them.

At the same time, Captain Wetherwax, of the First Nebraska Veteran Volunteer Cavalry, with a like number, was sent up Lodgepole to see what there was to be seen of the Indians, but not to bring on any engagement with them. They both started out at a rapid gait. On the next day, the 6th, towards the evening, both of these parties came back. Captain Murphy reported that at a place about twenty-five miles west, the lines were uninjured to Denver, and that he had had a talk with the Denver office and was told that the people of Denver were in great anxiety and at great inconvenience on account of the destruction of the wire; that the people of Denver wanted the wire put up just as fast as possible, as a great quantity of messages needed transmission, and that being cut off wholly from the outside world, the people were despondent as to the situation and did not know what had happened or might happen.

Captain Wetherwax returned, bringing back a straggling herd of cattle which had gotten away from the Indians, and saying that the Indians were crossing Jules Stretch for the Platte River, and that they were taking their time and herding the cattle along more carefully and with less expectation of pursuit and attack.

For a couple of days small scouting parties were sent in every direction, towards the south and up and down the north bank of the river, among the hills, to see what the Indians were doing and where they were, if there were any. Colonel Livingston received a telegram to guard the road, open up trade, protect the posts and the stage lines, as a first matter of duty; and the overtaking and punishing of the Indians as a second, but cautioned him against too bold an attack against so large a party of Indians as appeared to be within striking distance of him, and which seemed so strong and warlike. In fact, it did not seem safe for any party of cavalry that we then had to attack the large Indian band which had gone north.

On February 6, 1865, a large party of freighters and travelers came up the road, under escort, and the stage lines were reëstablished from the east. Captain O'Brien was detailed to take the train on up the river towards Denver, together with such of the refugees at our post as had been stopped and held there. The Captain started out and delivered his valuable train, and its following, far up the river to a party of Colorado cavalry that were starting down with another large train and outfit, going through to "the States." This train Captain O'Brien brought down to Julesburg.

I was mostly engaged in drilling my new battery and exercising it in rapid flying movements and in target practice, although the supply of ammunition did not give much room for that. In Indian warfare, as in all other kinds, accuracy and rapidity are the chief things to acquire; so we drilled all of the variety known as "flying drills." In the mean time, the poles for the telegraph line had been started up the river towards us, with instructions to put the teams through night and day until they reached Julesburg. No communications could be had with Laramie, Salt Lake or the Pacific Coast, owing to the destruction of the telegraph line. Always before this time the Indians had respected the telegraph wire, for reasons hereinbefore stated, but at this time they had emissaries among them, civilized Indians from the Southern Confederacy, as we believed, who were not disturbed by any superstitions and who knew the value of telegraph lines to an enemy, and who did not neglect to destroy the communications whenever convenient. It was urged upon us that the lines of wire must be fixed up; that was imperative. The demand of the overland telegraph company was constantly and urgently reiterated. The restoration of the telegraph seemed to be the principal thing to be done, and to be paramount to any question of punishing the Indians or recovering property. Those were the days when there were no railroads and no rapid mail communications, and the telegraph wire was in very great demand, and as there was only one wire to do the business through on each route, it was busy every minute of the day, from the end of one month to the end of another; and so when the line was down, great interests suffered, as did also many private and personal matters.

On the evening of February 9, 1865, Colonel Livingston sent for Captain Murphy, who was a most active, industrious and enduring officer of our regiment, to form plans for the restoration of the line from Julesburg west, and ordered him to plan an active party to take charge of the work and restore the lines through to make communication with Denver, and telling him that he could have forty soldiers. Captain Murphy was to make the plans, consider them well, and submit them to Colonel Livingston; and was told that he might take along a piece of artillery. Captain Murphy came to me to talk the matter over, and said that he wanted me to go along with him, and that he wasn't satisfied with only forty men and one piece of artillery. He asked me if I couldn't take two pieces of artillery and go with him and assist him in the very arduous task which the order entailed, adding in a humorous way, "You will never see Omaha." I was not particularly attracted by the idea presented by Captain Murphy, and told him that I did not think that Colonel Livingston would permit his artillery to be divided up in that way; that I would go, of course, if I were ordered, but that if there was an expedition up to attack the Indians Colonel Livingston would probably want me along with him, and I would prefer to go on that expedition, instead of putting up telegraph poles. All this time I was an Aide-de-Camp for General Mitchell.

On the next morning, Captain Murphy went to the Colonel and told him his plan, and succeeded in getting me detailed with two pieces of artillery to go with his party. Colonel Livingston sent for me and told me about it, and I objected, saying that I desired to go with the expedition, if any were sent out; but the Colonel said that he was not certain as to any future movements, and thought I had better go with Captain Murphy. Thereupon, I went to see the Captain and told him that I was going with him and would take two twelve-pound mountain howitzers. We then together discussed the methods of doing the work, and what we would need to take along; got a lot of rations cooked up, tools and implements prepared, two wagons, and awaited the arrival of the telegraph poles.

In the mean time, Captain O'Brien had been down the road on escort duty, and, having struck the head of the telegraph-pole train, ordered it to push forward as rapidly as possible. The Captain was always pushing things. The result was that the pole train reached our fort about ten o'clock in the evening of February 11, 1865. As they were heralded as coming, Captain Murphy got his detail of men, which in fact amounted to 46 men, exclusive of him and me, and when the train arrived it was ordered that they should stop two hours, rest and feed and water the mules, and then push right on. The train was scattered and strung out for several miles down the road, and, as the teams kept coming up, the same order was given to each of them. Such a volley of oaths and protestations I hardly ever heard before. These men had been coming night and day and were all used up, and the profanity was terrible, especially that of the wagon-boss. His remarks had a sublimity that no unprofessional wagon-boss could hope to excel. He had a collection of compound adjectives that equalled anything I had ever heard. Nevertheless, at twelve o'clock at night the head of the wagon train and our squad of cavalry started west, and the teams fell in one by one, as they became fed, watered and hitched up, and we kept going until we came to where the first pole was out. As stated before, the whole matter being one of emergency, the lightest poles had been selected for transportation to Julesburg, and they were smaller in diameter than most of the poles which had been used on the line. We detailed the men by fours; "number four" held horses; numbers one and two had picks; and number three had a spade or shovel. Instead of digging holes to put the posts in, it was immediately discovered that the quickest way was to pull out the stump of the old pole and put the new pole in its place; so numbers one and two drove their picks into the stump at the ground, and number three put in his spade and they pried the stump out. Then the wagon came up and a telegraph pole was taken out, put into the vacancy, tamped down and filled in. In the mean time others of the company had moved on to the next stump, where four more were detailed, and so on, and in a short time the company was strung out a quarter of a mile "by fours" and as fast as a post was set, the order was, "Mount! Forward! Gallop! March!" and the four men went past all the other fours and seized on the first vacant stump. We had about six sets of fours running. We also had guards riding out. It was moonlight.

During all of this time the teams were going along until they finally overtook and passed the head of the column and dropped a pole at each stump. With the train was a light ambulance wagon with a lot of wire and insulators and telegraph instruments. We held the teams occasionally, so as to have them equally unloaded, and that the mules might share their burdens equally. From the telegraph wagon the wire was uncoiled and a climber went up and fixed the insulator and set the wire. From time to time the wire was fastened to the wagon and stretched tight by the pull of the mules. A rear guard of two men, an advance guard of two men and a flank patrol of two men were all that was needed. It was arranged so that every man was hard at work doing something. We loaded onto the wagons the stumps we pulled, to be used as firewood. When morning came we stopped and got breakfast (February 12th), and rested our horses and ourselves for two hours; then we started on and worked all day. It was a hard, severe task, but every man seemed to be animated by a desire to get the job through with and get back to the post at Julesburg, so as to get into the expedition north, if one started. We did not let the teams get very far ahead of us, and from time to time we coralled them, so that if any attack might occur or any danger might appear, we could rally on the wagons. The artillery went along in the center, among the wagons. We worked all day, got the poles all in, strung up the wire and established communications with Julesburg, showing that the line was open to Omaha. We were now about twenty-five miles west of Julesburg, at a place called Buffalo Springs, and Indians, for the last two or three miles, had been seen in the hills south of us.

From this place, Buffalo Springs, the telegraph line west was but little damaged, but still the line would not work to Denver. There was some fresh trouble. We got through with setting poles about 8 P. M., but there was a bright, beautiful moon. The day had been an exhausting one, because many of the pole-holes had to be deeply dug, and tamped down. The new poles in many instances were as big as the old one had been, and would not fit. We fried bacon and made hot slapjacks for supper, and every one ate heartily. We were a very tired lot of young men. Captain Murphy was the oldest man in the party. He had been quite active, and at night was thoroughly exhausted.

A stray steer was grazing on the river-bottom, and we killed and skinned it that night, and with the pole stumps we boiled beef all night, with the guards to watch it. The wolves howled around us that night as if there were a convention. The moonlight and the smell of the meat kept them going in concerts all night. We slept until 6 A. M. (February 13th), and at 8 A. M. we started west; occasionally a pole was down or out, and at places the wire was cut, but we made repairs with such rapidity that the train kept moving steadily on. We kept in constant touch by wire with Julesburg.

Finally we reached Valley Station, 52 miles west of Julesburg; at that place we found we could talk over the wire with Denver, and the telegraph wire was restored. There we found some teams that were coming down in a train from Denver. They had been held up by the appearance of Indians in the hills, and had got into a sod ranch and were holding themselves in readiness. It was about three o'clock in the afternoon when we got there. There was a large supply of corn in the stage station, in sacks. About twenty-five Indians made their appearance in the hills, and the position of the ranch was such that the artillery could not be used from the inside of it. Captain Murphy and I talked the matter over, and decided that the appearances were that the Indians were going to make an attack. We thereupon put every man to work and carried out the sacks of corn onto the prairie, where there was a good chance to put the artillery, and we made a large shelled-corn bastion. It would be bullet-proof as against the Indians, and we had two embrasures from which to fire the artillery. It did not take us over thirty minutes to put up this bastion. The Indians pranced around in the hills, but did not seem desirous of making an attack, and we stayed there until the sun had nearly set and our horses were rested, and then the question was, whether or not we had better go on down that night or wait until morning. Captain Murphy decided that we would go in the evening, as soon as our horses were rested; those civilians who were penned there determined to go with us.

Just as the sun was about sinking, the Indians disappeared, and I got up on the bastion with my field-glass to see if I could see anything, and casting my eyes down the river, I saw a black speck which to me looked like a moving team. After watching it for a while, it slowing emerged into view, and sure enough, there was coming up the river a lone wagon, with two dark-colored horses, and two men walking, one on each side of the wagon. Not knowing what it could be, Captain Murphy sent a corporal and four men out towards the team to tell them to hurry in. After a while they came into camp. I wanted to talk with them and find out how it was that they were traveling around all alone, through that kind of danger, when to my surprise, I found that they were two Germans who could not speak English. We finally got a man out of the company who could speak German, and strange was the story which the Germans told. They said that they had just arrived at Omaha from Germany and were going west to the mines; that they wanted to make some money, and had concluded to haul a wagon-load of fresh oysters to Denver. They had put the rectangular tin cans of oysters in their wagons at Omaha, poured in water and froze the whole wagon-load into one solid lump. They had got all that their two mules could possibly haul, and covering it all up, started for Denver. They had been so afraid that they might be seen and robbed, that after they got past Fort Kearney they had gone down and hid near the river and then traveled all night; they had never seen any trouble nor heard of any trouble. They had made good long travels every night, and had hidden down by the river every day; and supposing everything was safe where they now were, they had just started on their evening trip. They had been hidden alongside of the river, about three miles below the place where we then were. They said they were afraid to travel in trains for fear they would be robbed. This was all told in German; they couldn't speak any English, and hence had not been told anything which they could understand.

I thought I would see if they were telling the truth, so I dug into their ice-bank and found it as they had said, and I bought two quart cans of them for five dollars, one for Captain Murphy and one for myself. Several of the men bought cans. Sitting out on the corn bastion after sunset, Captain Murphy and I each ate a can of frozen oysters, as delightful and fresh as if they were just out of Chesapeake Bay. Under the circumstances, we did not feel like saying to those two Germans that they could not go any farther, and when we had our interpreters tell them about the Indians, they simply shook their heads, and said, "Es macht nichts aus" (it makes no difference). So on they went, and as they had each taken forty chances on their lives, I have always hoped that they sold their oysters for two dollars and a half a can, and if they did, they made a great deal of money.

There was much objection and protest on the part of the men toward starting back. We had in forty hours built eight miles of telegraph, strung up twenty-one miles of down and damaged wire, and marched fifty-two miles. This was a lot of work to do in so short a time. Captain Murphy concluded to rescind his order, and to camp all night where we were, at Valley Station. This made the civilians angry, and they protested. They wanted to get on down the road, but we stayed in camp, ate boiled beef, drank quarts of hot coffee, and enjoyed our rest. Captain Murphy was used up. He was too well along in years to stand so much; he was resolute, but he had to succumb. During the night he was quite ill. His trouble was principally over-work.

Many were the congratulations which we received for our quick work in putting up the line. The Denver papers and the Omaha papers gave us great commendations.

We started back at 8 A. M., just as a train under escort arrived from the west with a squad of soldiers who were trying to overtake us, they having by wire found out our whereabouts. The soldiers (I think, Third Colorado Cavalry) were ordered to stop and garrison Valley Station, and to hold it so that the stage line could be reëstablished. We started on down to Julesburg with a great retinue of travelers. Murphy was being hauled in a wagon. The command fell to me. We marched carefully, solidly and slowly. We saw no Indians, not even a smoke signal. The weather in the morning changed to bad, and the wind began to blow from the north terrifically. It blew so hard we could not see ahead of us, and we rode with our capes over our heads and faces. Twenty miles down, we struck Moore's ranch, and having the stumps of some of the telegraph poles in our wagons, we camped for the night, and made fires. The weather turned quite cold, and it was zero weather. We saw no Indians during the whole day's march of twenty miles, but we marched solidly and carefully all day. Twenty miles was the best we could do for that day. We were thirty-two miles west of Julesburg. I am not now sure about it, but I believe the place was called Lillian Springs.

The next morning when we got down to Buffalo Springs, which was twenty-five miles west of Julesburg, we were overtaken by another detachment of cavalry from the west, with a convoy of stage coaches from the west. The soldiers were ordered to garrison Buffalo Springs and turn the coaches over to us, for us to guard to Julesburg. This opened up and completed the stage line again from Denver to Omaha, and thereafter the stages ran regularly. It was a bitter day going down to Julesburg, but every one did his best to make it cheerful.

We arrived in Julesburg at 6 P. M., after a march of thirty-two miles. The wind blew hard all day and the weather was exceedingly disagreeable, and we went with our wagon-train and stages in a compact and solid column. When we got in I found a telegram for me to immediately come to Fort Kearney. I also found Colonel Livingston ready to start back to the east, and we were told of the proceedings which had taken place up on the North Platte while we were gone, which I will tell of in the next chapter.

CONCURRENTLY with our telegraph repair expedition which
went west under Captain Murphy, of which I have just
spoken, another expedition was organized to go north, repair
the line, open up communication with Salt Lake, and punish
the Indians. In addition to getting in touch with Laramie and
the garrisons on the "Salt Lake Trail," Colonel Livingston
had determined to go over on the North Platte and see if he
could get back some of the cattle from the Indians. When he
got up to the North Platte he found a very peculiar condition
of things. The Indians had got the cattle all across the river
by sanding a track on the ice, the river being frozen solidly
across. The Indians had to go slowly and it took a long time
to get the cattle over. The moment that Colonel Livingston
appeared in sight, the Indians, being on the north side, came
charging over the river on the sanded track. Colonel Livingston's command was not near enough to the river to be able
to command the track with his artillery, and the Indians
came on over before he could get near enough. When it was
seen that the Indians were going to come over and make a
fight, the first thing which the Colonel did was very properly
to corral his wagons and men and prepare to resist the attack,

because if the cavalry should be deployed out the Indians could defeat them in short order. The Colonel occupied a spot where he thought he could deliver a good fight, and the Indians surrounded him, lying on the ground and in the gullies and shooting under cover, so that the fight was a very difficult and desultory one. Our soldiers got scarcely any opportunity of firing the artillery, but the cannon was sufficient to scare off the Indians from a charge upon the command; the Colonel could see other Indians across the river driving the cattle off, until he watched them drive plumb out of sight in the hills to the northeast. Several of the soldiers were killed, also several of the horses, and several of the Indians. The soldiers understood Indian fighting as well as the Indians did themselves, and were able to hold them off.

During the night the Indians withdrew, and in the morning there was not an Indian to be seen; they had all gone up into the hills and struck northeast for the head of the Bluewater River, a most beautiful stream, the "Minne-to-wacca-pella"—"Water-blue-river." So the Colonel returned to Julesburg, but there was one big feature of his trip: about two hundred head of the wildest of the cattle had got away from the Indians, and not having time to bother with them, the Indians had let them go and our boys gathered them up and brought them in. Colonel Livingston got into Julesburg just about as I did, on the evening of the 15th, and he proceeded to communicate by wire with General Mitchell.

This was the last that I ever saw of Julesburg until more than forty years after. I visited the place in 1908, and tried to find where the post had been; nobody could tell me. I finally located it, and found a house standing on the site of the old stables. The house was occupied by renters who had no knowledge or tradition of the old post, although it was occupied by the regular army after we left it, and was one of the important posts of the frontier for a time. Thus does glory fade. Near it was a promising field of corn, growing well without irrigation, a thing impossible to conceive of when we were there. Across the river near Julesburg was a modern bridge.

Colonel Livingston told me to get ready immediately to start with him on horseback, together with a small detail of well-mounted cavalry, down the Platte, leaving the balance of the command to return to their respective posts. The roads were now all opened up both ways to Denver and Salt Lake, and the telegraph working both ways, and the post of Julesburg relieved from siege; so the Colonel got ready to start east. I was exceedingly tired from the work that I had been doing of late, and from riding all that day thirty-two miles in the wind, and I was a little surprised when the Colonel said that he would start promptly at eight o'clock that night on horseback; but I got ready, and off we rode. We rode all night, halting in the morning for breakfast; we then rode all day in a most terrible windstorm, and arrived at Cottonwood Springs, a distance of one hundred miles, late at night on Feb. 16th, 1865, making the trip in a little over twenty-four hours.

As this was also my last visit to Cottonwood Springs, until the year 1908, I will briefly describe what I found on the latter visit. Nobody could tell me where the old fort was. The whole country was peopled by foreigners. I located MacDonald's ranch in the midst of a fine corn-field. I located the well by a depression where it had caved in. Beside it I plucked an ear of corn that would have looked well at a county fair. Upon the site of the old post a field of wheat had been harvested and was being stacked. Of eleven men working in and around the field a few of them could not speak English, and none of them knew anything about the military post or had any tradition of its existence. Up in the cañon, several miles, was a large horse ranch, but nobody was at home. Not a cedar tree was in sight. On the old parade-ground, which I could pick out by its location with the hills, I found a few of the trees which we had planted. Such a field of wheat, grown without irrigation, would have been impossible in 1864. Not far off, in the junction of the Plattes, was the bright new city of "North Platte."

Between the old site of the post at Cottonwood and the spot where Jack Morrow's Ranch was, there is now a National Cemetery, of recent date. In it are buried all of my men who lost their lives on the plains. Their bones have all been taken up from their original resting-places and all placed together under the trees where the sun is shining and the birds of summer singing; guarded by the great nation they fought for; unknown heroes, the vanguard of their race, they did their share, and they loved their country. If they could rise from their graves they would do their work over again if it were necessary. I went up to where Jack Morrow's ranch stood; I found near its site a house in which people were living in much comfort, surrounded with trees and smiling gardens; they were Swedes, they had never heard of Jack Morrow, and had lived there 18 years. The entire valley of the river was a mass of fine farms, and about all I could recognize in the landscape was the Sioux-Lookout. Pardon the digression; I now return to February 16, 1865.

We slept four hours at Cottonwood. I met some of the officers of the post and they all said to me, "You will never see Omaha." I thought that was about true, as I was almost ready to drop from fatigue. After four hours of sleep, we started out before daylight, and rode all day and night until two o'clock A. M. of the 19th; making two hundred miles, in the dead of winter, through that country, which we had ridden from eight o'clock in the evening of the 15th to two o'clock in the morning of February 19th, 1865. Colonel Livingston was as nearly used up as we were and we got into Kearney without any of the soldiers that we started with. From time to time their horses had given out and we had left them at the various posts. I had my big black horse, "Old Bill," and my Indian pony, which I rode alternately, and we made the two-hundred-mile ride on a run about all the way. I had averaged sixty miles a day for four days after leaving Lillian Springs. My horses were tired but uninjured. As we arrived at 2 P. M., I wanted to smoke a cigar before I went to sleep. I saw a light in the sutler's store, went there to get the cigar, and found a party of officers, all of whom I knew, engaged in a poker game. I was most enthusiastically received, and was asked to sit in the game, or, to use the language of the period, to "take some of the chicken pie."

I do not like to tell these stories, but it is necessary to do so in order to depict the men and the times. It is due to history. Of course I sat in; it would not have done for me to do otherwise; an officer must never get tired, must never admit he is tired. He is judged and rated, and his usefulness considered, according to his durability. It was the best possible thing I could do, to raise myself in the esteem of those officers, to sit in the game. They knew the kind of work I had been on for a week, and not to be tired was a matter of admiration to them; under the circumstances I could not help "sitting in." I was, in fact, very tired, but I told them I felt gay and frisky and was just looking for a game. I would have given forty dollars for a chance to sleep, but I sat in, and when we quit at breakfast-time I had won $55.

Then I slipped away and slept all day. War furnishes a great outlet for a superabundant energy.

Returning now to the North Platte, I will briefly describe what took place. When the Cheyennes appeared before Julesburg on February 1st, and before the telegraph was destroyed, Laramie and the North Platte posts were all notified. The sudden destruction of the line caused them all alarm. Scouts came down from Mud Springs, saw what the trouble was, and, being unable to cope with the situation, returned and gave the alarm to the other posts. Soon afterwards, seeing an advanced scouting party of the Cheyennes, all the posts east of Scott's Bluffs retired west to Camp Mitchell at that place, and some cavalry from Laramie came down to Fort Mitchell to prevent it from being taken. When the Indians were crossing "Jules Stretch," the whole command from Camp Mitchell came down to oppose them, but were soon driven back with several killed; but this turned the Indians to the northeast, towards the head of the Bluewater river. These troops had been driven west before Colonel Livingston had come up with the Indians. Owing to loss of telegraph line they did not know of each other's movements, and could not make a junction. Between both parties, however, the telegraph line was finally restored through to Laramie and Salt Lake.

Here at Fort Kearney, for the first time, I began to do duty as an aide-de-camp; and, here for the first time in my journal, appears the name of General Grenville M. Dodge as commander of the Department. As stated heretofore, on December 31st, 1864, the Department had been in command of General Samuel R. Curtis, with whom I had served down South in the Invasion of Arkansas. Sometime between January 1, 1865, and the fifteenth of February, his place had been assigned to General Dodge. As I afterwards served as aide-de-camp for General Dodge, I will briefly refer to him. The General was born in Massachusetts, and was a graduate of a Vermont military academy at Norwich. He was at first Colonel of the Fourth Iowa Infantry. I had seen him being hauled away from the battle-field of Pea Ridge, all shot up. He recovered, was made Brigadier-General, and soon after on merit made a Major-General, and served with Sherman. He was one of the best and bravest, and in the Atlanta campaign was shot up again. He was one of the great generals of the war—prompt, efficient and capable. He was not yet 34 years of age when General Grant assigned to him, sometime in January or February, 1865, the command of the very difficult task of looking after the West, and the Indians of the vast country then called "Kansas and the Territories." His home was Council Bluffs, Iowa. He was afterwards Chief Engineer of the Union Pacific Railroad, and his civil career was as illustrious as was his military career. He was a member of Congress shortly after the war, and was the one who read on the floor of the house the letter which our Major had written to Jeff. Davis, seeking employment in the Southern Army, of which I have spoken in a former chapter. General Dodge, in his 80th year, is still living at the time of the publication of this book.

While I was at Fort Kearney my orderly turned up, the one who had been taking care of my horses theretofore, and I sent them by him down to Omaha, intending to go by the stage. General Mitchell was wiring me from time to time to make haste. I went down to Columbus on the stage and found the orderly—he being the one who had lived with the Indians—in a sad state of mind; he had gone on a spree, lost all of his own money and the money that I had given him to take care of the horses with, and he was tied up at a livery stable, unable to move. When the stage came down to Columbus, the Loup Fork was frozen over; there was a ford, but it looked quite dangerous. There were a couple of officers going down with me, and they were constantly telling me that I would "never see Omaha." The ford looked quite dangerous, and we all got out of the stage and walked on the ice, I saying to them that while I might not see Omaha, I did not want to get drowned under such unfavorable circumstances. When I got into Columbus, which was on the east side of the river, I got my horses and equipment all ready and determined to ride from there into Omaha. At Columbus I met my old regimental friend Lieut. E. K. Valentine, who was in later years Congressman from Nebraska.

That night at Columbus, the post got up a big dance, they said in my favor; everybody was invited, and it was a great occasion. I hadn't been to many dances lately, and we kept up the waltz and the cotillion until it was daylight, and, getting my breakfast, I mounted my horse to start for Omaha. Just as I got ready to start I got a telegram to go back immediately to Fort Kearney. This puzzled me very much, but I turned around and rode my horses back 110 miles to Fort Kearney. Again a sort of irresistible feeling came over me that I would "never see Omaha," and as the times increased in number in which I had started for Omaha and been called back, the more I began to doubt whether I was superstitious or not,—but back I went to Fort Kearney. I arrived in Fort Kearney on the 24th, and found General Mitchell there with Lieut.-Colonel Baumer, of the First Nebraska Veteran Volunteer Cavalry. The General was having a conversation as to what matters were necessary in view of an approaching change in the command. On the evening of the 25th, General Mitchell sent for me and told me that he was hurrying troops forward as fast as possible, and that the Sixteenth Kansas Cavalry, of which Mr. Plumb, afterwards United States Senator, was then in temporary command, had started for Kearney, but could not be found nor heard from. General Mitchell directed me to start out towards Leavenworth, and where the roads divided to cross over from one to the other and ascertain where the regiment was. There was no telegraph line on this road. It started to rain about the time that I got ready to go, and with a poncho I rode all over the country inquiring for the regiment, until I got down into southeastern Nebraska, where, at a place called Pawnee City, a place away off from the traveled road, I found the Sixteenth Regiment, stuck deeply in the mud and unable to move. It seems that in coming up they had encountered high waters and bad weather, and their horses were not well shod, and some of them had their hoofs so worn that they were disabled, and Colonel Plumb had been scouring the country for horse-shoes. He had finally gathered a lot in and made up his mind to stop at Pawnee City and shoe up his regiment. For that purpose he had got all the blacksmiths and horseshoers in the country and was busily engaged in this work. Having communicated to Colonel Plumb the orders of General Mitchell, urging him forward, I set out to return to Fort Kearney.

One incident I remember very plainly. I came to a place which was called Beatrice; there was one house there, and a blacksmith shop, and it was Sunday. I saw up on a post a board marked "Postoffice." Out of the house a family came and got into a large farm wagon, and, as I found out, were starting off somewhere to go to a church. I asked them if it was really a postoffice there, and they said it really was; so at my request they were courteous enough to wait until I could send a letter to my mother from that place, and I gave it to one of the people in the wagon, and it went through all right. It is the same town and place which now appears on the map as a very important city.

I had ridden twenty miles without seeing a house, to Beatrice, thence to Blue Springs, a distance of thirty miles. At Blue Springs I stopped with an old gentleman who had been ten years a soldier in the regular army; they called him "Old Pap Tyler." At Pawnee City I stopped with a

Mrs. Fry, and was told by her that they had a young and growing institution there, called "The Nemaha Valley Female Seminary." From Pawnee City I rode twenty-two miles south to Seneca, so as to get onto the traveled road again. Seneca was a mere hamlet, and there, for the first time, I saw patches of prairie-grass. Prairie-grass as we generally know it and as the early settlers found it, is in fact a domestic grass, moving steadily westward, and as I came into Seneca I saw patches of prairie-grass growing around among the buffalo-grass; but the solid sheet of prairie-grass was considerably east of Seneca. Its invasion west was told me to be about four miles a year.

From Seneca I started back to Fort Kearney, along with a captain and six lieutenants of the Third United States Volunteers. These "United States Volunteers," as they were called, were soldiers recruited from the military prison-pens at Chicago and Rock Island, and were made up of men taken from the Southern Confederacy who were willing to go West and swear allegiance to the United States on the condition that they would not be requested to go South and fight their own brethren. They wanted to get out of prison, were tired of the war, didn't want to go back into the service, did not want any more of the Southern Confederacy, did not want to be exchanged, and were willing to go into the United States service for the purpose of fighting the Indians. A detachment of these troops had gone up the road from Omaha, but I had not seen them. They were called "galvanized Yanks." These officers were all officers of undoubted courage and ability, who had been selected from among the capable sergeants of the State regiments, and I became much attached to this captain and six lieutenants before I got through to Fort Kearney, for I had served in the same army down South with some of them, though I had not known them. They were as intelligent and capable a lot of young men as you could hope to find; in fact, they were selected from the best, and averaged up much higher and better than the usual run of volunteer lieutenants.

This trip down into the country was a very interesting one to me, and it took considerable time, but there is nothing to it worth going into details about. It was March 26th when I got back to Fort Kearney. General Mitchell then said to me, "Now, you will see Omaha."

On arrival at Kearney, I found that troops were being hurried forward—several regiments—to the West. General P. Edward Conner was placed in command of the district. The application of General Mitchell to be sent South had been approved by President Lincoln, and he was ordered to turn over the district to his successor on arrival.

On March 30, 1865, General Conner assumed command of the district, and I was detailed as his aide-de-camp. This detail was without the consent of General Mitchell. I was in a good deal of a quandary; the premonition of which I have spoken so often, that I would "never see Omaha," had become a matter of interest and discussion to all the officers not only of my regiment, but along the line. It had been talked up so much for nearly three months, and discussed so freely, that everyone wanted to see how it would come out. I was beginning to feel a little bit superstitious myself, and now that General Conner had taken charge of the district and was said to be about to make his headquarters at Fort Laramie, it looked a good deal as if I might not see Omaha. In a discussion at headquarters in Fort Kearney on March 30th, 1865, I was asked what I was going to do. General Mitchell desired me to go with him. He was going down to take command at Fort Leavenworth, of the "District of Kansas," which extended south and took in the Indian Territory.

I had thought my dream over a good deal, and there was so much of "premonition" stuff in the papers and magazines that I thought I had better come to a conclusion and see what there was to it. Being now about to go to Omaha, it would be considered an act of cowardice to take any step that would postpone the situation. On the other hand, I didn't feel like having the thing hanging over me and its being continuously discussed, and with perhaps a final eventuality to it. So, after considerable thought, I made up my mind that the first thing for me to do was to see whether I would ever see Omaha. So I begged off from the detail on General Conner's staff, and started on March 31st with General Mitchell for Omaha. Our horses were all rested, and as we had some baggage, a new six-mule wagon was detailed to haul the headquarters stuff, which included a small office desk and valise for me, and light camping equipment for the headquarters. There was General Mitchell, his Adjutant-General, John Pratt (the handsomest man in the army), two aide-de-camps, Lieutenant Schenck and myself; a medical director by the name of McClelland, and a couple of officers of the First Nebraska. The day was raw and cold; the wind blew from the west; our horses were all well shod, and we started out on a run and kept it up about all day and the next. When we got to Columbus, General Mitchell's observation to me was to be very careful and not get drowned at that point, because that was the only serious difficulty on our way. I got across the river the same as the rest did, and on we went.

On the 4th of April, in the evening, we were arriving near Omaha, and the General said, "Now, nothing can happen to you except that your horse throws you off and breaks your neck." I said to him, "Things will have to happen now quite soon, and I will get onto my Indian pony and go on ahead and see what will take place." So on I went, pell-mell, ahead of the party. As the city appeared in sight I became more interested; I soon reached the city limits and I said, "I wonder if there is any technicality about this,— will the city limits fill the prophecy?" So on I went at a good round speed, and finally was dashing down through the middle of the street into the bottoms and past where we had been camped a year and a half before. Ahead of me, in the heart of the city, I saw a big sign labeled, "Saloon." The load was off from my mind; I had ridden right into the very heart of Omaha; the superstition was a thing of the past. In a little while, along came General Mitchell and his staff. They saw me there on the curb waiting for them, and General Mitchell said, "You made it all right." I said, "Yes, and I will never believe in premonitions again." Then the General gravely said: "There is nothing in them, absolutely nothing. If a man believes in them they will make him a coward. The future is a sealed book, and anybody that thinks he knows anything about it or can find out anything about is badly mistaken." So we all went in and took a drink on it, each a good old-fashioned American cocktail, and everyone in the party said he would never put any faith in premonitions thereafter. We had scarcely had time to reach headquarters that evening when cannon began to boom. Local companies were firing salutes to celebrate the news from Virginia. Lee had abandoned Richmond, and Grant was in full pursuit. *The War was ending.*

Here I ought to conclude my story, but I will briefly epitomize what followed. We waited for a steamboat, and after a few days we loaded up horses and baggage, and in an April snow-storm started down the river, and on the fifth day of our boat-ride arrived in Leavenworth, on April 13, 1865, amid thunders of artillery celebrating the final surrenders. Everybody, every man, woman and child, was "hurrahing." *The War was ended.*

The next day Lincoln was assassinated. The next day, by telegraph from the War Department, every officer was ordered to put crape on his sabre. The first officer I was introduced to on my arrival in Leavenworth was Lieutenant-Colonel Hoyt, who had been one of the attorneys defending John Brown at Harper's Ferry. I afterwards got well acquainted with him, and he told me all about Brown's trail.

Very soon troops were rushed to the West, and the following were on duty there:

Five regiments of "Galvanized Yanks," known as the First, Second, Third, Fifth, Sixth, United States Volunteer Infantry. Two regiments of Regular Infantry, viz.: The Thirteenth and the Eighteenth. Also, the Third California

Infantry, Twelfth Kansas Infantry, and the Forty-eighth Wisconsin Infantry, being a total of ten regiments of infantry.

Also the following cavalry regiments, viz.:

First and Second California.

First and Third Nebraska.

Twelfth, Thirteenth, and Fourteenth Missouri.

Fifth, Sixth, Ninth, Eleventh, Fifteenth, and Sixteenth Kansas.

First, Second, and Third Colorado.

Also the ten following named cavalry regiments: Second United States Cavalry, First Michigan, First Nevada, Seventh Iowa, Sixth West Virginia, Eleventh Ohio, Twenty-first New York, Seventeenth Illinois, Third Massachusetts, Third Wisconsin. In all representing twenty-six cavalry regiments. There were also the Fourth United States Artillery and the Ninth Wisconsin Battery, together with twenty-six other guns stationed at the posts.

Separate, and in addition to the foregoing, were the large number of troops south in the Indian Territory and north in Iowa, Minnesota and the Dakotas.

In addition to this was the vast Western emigration by the hundred thousand of the soldiers of both armies, thirsting for land, gold and adventure. The Indian had to get out of the way. The lines of travel were soon garrisoned and guarded; the stage lines ran uninterruptedly. Soon the Union Pacific Railroad was built, and the Indian problem was solved.

The Seventh Iowa Cavalry was continued in service, but our company never lost a man after the date of which I speak. Captain O'Brien resigned to get married, and I was commissioned Captain in his place.

Here I was detailed as confidential aide-de-camp for Major-General Dodge, who, as stated, had been one of Sherman's division commanders, and my subsequent experience need not be related here, as it does not pertain to the Indian Campaigns. I had ridden on horseback, as a soldier,

North and South, during the war, over ten thousand miles.

The condition of Leavenworth at this time is shown by a contemporary newspaper article, which is as follows:

"Russell, Majors & Waddell's transportation establishment, between the fort and the city, is the great feature of Leavenworth. Such acres of wagons! Such pyramids of extra axletrees! Such herds of oxen! Such regiments of drivers and other employés! No one who does not see can realize how vast a business this is, nor how immense are its outlays as well as its incomes! I presume this great firm has at this hour $2,000,000 invested in stock, mainly oxen, mules and wagons. (They last year employed 6,000 teamsters and worked 45,000 oxen.) Of course, they are capital fellows —so are those at the fort—but I protest against the doctrine that either army officers or army contractors, or both together, may have power to fasten slavery on a newly organized Territory (as has just been done in New Mexico) under the guise of letting the people of such Territories govern themselves. Yet this is just what 'Squatter Sovereignty,' unmodified by law, amounts to."

APPENDICES

APPENDIX A.

THE DAUGHTER OF SHAN-TAG-A-LISK
A PIECE OF WESTERN HISTORY.

[The following as a piece of truthful history was published several years ago in a magazine. That portion of it is omitted which has appeared in the preceding pages.]

When, like the red-man of Plato, the American Indian shall have become a myth, some future anthropologist will wonder what manner of man he was.

Those who have been thrown in contact with him do not love him. His treachery, his cruelty, his basest kind of ingratitude, his wild, half-maniac superstitions, make those who knew him wonder where all of the sentimentality about the "noble red-man" came from.

A true description of the aboriginal Indian dare not be put into print. The novelist and the dramatist of future times will give a character to the Indian which he never possessed, and he will be, like the Spanish Aldoran, knighted and put on horseback after he is dead. Yet, as Buddha says, "Amid the brambles and rubbish thrown over into the road, a lily may grow."

It is the object of this brief article to tell the true story of an Indian girl, and what happened to her. But in order that a comprehension may be had, by the reader, of the girl and her situation, it is necessary to go into some detail as to Sioux Indian life and history. It is also necessary to give some details of the Sioux nation as to its customs and geographical location, past and present; for without these facts the life and character of the Indian girl referred to cannot be understood.

Her name was Ah-ho-ap′pa, the Sioux name for wheaten flour. It was the whitest thing they knew. She had other names, as Indian women often have, but when the writer first saw her she was called Ah-ho-ap′pa. How she got the name is forgotten.

Her father's name, Shan-tag′-a-lisk, meant "Spotted Tail"; some of the Indians pronounced it "Than-tag-a-liska." He was one of the greatest chiefs the Sioux nation ever had. In order to explain him and what follows, it is best to give a brief description of the Indian question as relates to the Sioux nation at the time of the Civil War.

The great Rebellion broke out in 1861, after having been planned for years, and not only were the Northern arsenals emptied, the South armed, and the navy scattered, but the entire Indian population, consisting of several powerful Indian nations, were precipitated upon the frontiers of the North and West. The "civilized nations" of the Indian Territory formally joined the Confederacy, and helped to raise armies. The other Indians raided and ravished the borders from southern Kansas to the British Possessions, so that it was necessary to station troops in a long cordon, and build forts and transport military supplies in enormous quantities, often at great distances, in some cases a thousand miles from a railroad, and store and guard the supplies. This greatly hampered the General Government.

At the time the war closed there were in the Department of "Kansas and the Territories" nearly 60,000 troops. And long afterwards, when the clouds of the civil war had passed away, I find from a return in my possession that there were stationed along the line to protect Kansas, Nebraska and the overland line to Utah, 10,000 men and twenty-six pieces of artillery. This is exclusive of northern Iowa, Minnesota and the Dakotas, that required another army.

The time to which my narrative refers is between the summer of 1864 and the spring of 1866. After a long, hot march to reinforce Fort Laramie, which was then described as being in "Idaho Territory," we, a detachment of Iowa cavalry, arrived at the so-called fort in July, 1864. A regiment of Ohio cavalry had preceded us, and were building additional forts and were holding the passes in the mountains. Fort Laramie seemed, at that time, to the outside world, to be an echo from a vast, unknown, perilous interior. Soon after arrival the writer was detailed as adjutant of the post.

Let us now turn to a view of the Sioux nation of that day. The Sioux nation occupied a vast territory, and was subdivided into subordinate tribes which had been so remotely sundered that their languages differed and had run into dialects. Their traditions said that they had come from the salt water, but they could not tell when, for the time was so great. They had traditions of the East but not of the West. They claimed kinship with the Iowas, Missouris, Kansas, and Quapaws or Arkansas Indians.

I will repeat here that the tribes of the Sioux nation with which we had to deal were the Brulé, the Oga-llall'ahs, and the

Minne-con'-jous, pronounced Minne-kau'-zhous. The name of the first is the French interpretation of the Indian name, "The Burnt-thighs." The second, "Oga-llall'-ah," is a Sioux expression meaning "The Split-off Band," *i. e.,* "The Secessionists." The third, Minne-con'-jous," means the "Shallow-water people," they being residents of the country where the streams were all shallow and choked with sand. It was a vast territory, and was called "The shallow-water-land."

Shan-tag-a-lisk was one of the greatest of the Brulé leaders, with a commanding influence over the Minneconjous; which bands roamed through the vast country north, northeast, and east of Fort Laramie, but mostly north of the Platte.

Owa-see'-cha ("Bad-wound") was the chief of the Oga-llall-ahs, which roamed mostly south of the Platte, at the beginning of the time of which I speak. I have stated that Owa-see'-cha had suffered much at the hands of a Pawnee chief in a battle, hence the name.

Shan-tag'-a-lisk and Owa-see'-cha claimed to be able to bring into the field 26,000 Ar-ke'-chetas, or public soldiers. The Sioux nation then had what might be called a regular army. Not all of the men were soldiers; some were mere hunters or food-providers, but most of the strong and able-bodied were enrolled in a sort of military guild called Ar-ke-chetas, and were either out stealing horses, fighting and plundering, or else acting as policemen at home, and taking care of one another while drunk.

To rise among the Ar-ke-chetas the aspirant must "count coo," as it was called. The term "coo" was the French translation "coup" of the Sioux word *strike,* and the French term was the one always used by the interpreters, who were mostly French, and the various Indians came to adopt the word themselves. The relative importance of an Indian in his own estimation was the number of times he could count "coo," and the Indian never failed to advise his white listener as to the number. The Indian is a great deal of an Ananias. His native character is that of a vain-glorious braggart. He always claims to be a "heap-big-war-chief." He could fool the white man who knew nothing about it, but the Indians could not fool one another. They knew each other's methods and manners, and they had a way of regulating those things.

A "coo" meant the blow first given to an enemy by a Sioux with his hand or something in his hand.

The Indian idea was that anybody might shoot an enemy, but it was the man who touched him first that was entitled to the glory. It was not the man who killed an enemy, or who scalped an enemy, that took the glory, but the man who touched the enemy first. One Indian might shoot and instantly kill a foe, another Indian might rush and *strike* the fallen foe with a riding-whip, and a third might secure the scalp, but the glory went to the Indian who made the "strike."

There was much reason in it, for a wounded Indian, like a little learning, was a dangerous thing; and the really brave Indian was he who first struck an enemy with something held in the hand. Sometimes blows were so close together that disputes arose as to who was entitled to the "coo," but these matters were settled by evidence in council. No Indian could claim and take a "coo" that he could not prove. The warriors held their "coos" by a sort of judicial determination of the tribe, or public concession of known facts.

An Indian who made two or three "coos" was a hero. When he could claim half a dozen he was a war chief. He was generally killed before he got any more. Shan-tag-a-lisk was the greatest of the warriors of the Sioux nation, at that time, and counted more "coos" than any other one in the nation. He said, "I count twenty-six coos." He was a quick, nervy, feminine-looking Indian of only medium size and height, and about forty years of age.

The writer had met both Shan-tag-a-lisk and Owa-see-cha before making the said trip to Fort Laramie. It was at Cottonwood Springs where two peace conventions were had, ten miles below the forks of the Platte. The object was to pacify the Sioux nation so that our Government might draw off some of the troops on the frontier and send them to the front at Atlanta, Georgia, where Sherman, at that time, was busily engaged and needed all the troops he could get. But nothing came of our peace conventions. It was also desired that a free opening might be had to the west for the scattering, disorganized soldiers and citizens of the Confederacy, who were fleeing from the theatre of war and from places where the Rebel conscription was, in the language of Grant, "robbing the cradle and the grave." These travelers to the west, although they might not be loyal to the Government, could ably protect themselves from the savage; they formed an army of extermination, and were exceedingly valuable to the General Government for the services they could render in exploring and building up the country and getting the Indians upon reservations.

At Laramie half-breed runners were sent out to bring in the Sioux and have an adjustment of pending difficulties, but the raid upon the line west of Laramie and the warlike feeling of the young men of the Sioux made it a failure. Nevertheless, some of the Indians came in, and Shan-tag-a-lisk was said to be within a hundred miles of the Post with many lodges of his band. On consultation at the sutler's store it was considered best to issue provisions to all the Indians who came in, especially as Shan-tag-a-lisk was keeping his band and his young Indians out of the war. It was thought best to make some presents to the Indian women who came in, and the Post commander was instructed to do so from the post fund. The Indian women were presented with red blankets, bright calicoes, looking-glasses, etc., etc. The writer, as adjutant of the post, superintended by order of the post commander a distribution of provisions. All of the Indian women and children sat down in a circle on the parade-ground, into the middle of which were rolled barrels and boxes of flour, crackers, bacon, and coffee. Then from the few Indian men, two or three were selected who entered the ring and made the division with great solemnity; going around the ring repeatedly with small quantities of the several articles that were being divided. My instructions were to see that everything was fairly done and all the supplies equally divided.

As I came up to the ring, on the day of the first division, an Indian girl was standing outside of the ring, looking on. She was tall and well dressed, and about eighteen years of age, or perhaps twenty. As the distribution was about to begin I went to her and told her to get into the ring, and motioned to her where to go. She gave no sign of heed, looked at me as impassively as if she were a statue, and never moved a muscle. A few teamsters, soldiers and idlers were standing around and looking on from a respectful distance. I shouted to Smith, the interpreter, to come. He came, and I said to him, "Tell this squaw to get into the ring or she will lose her share." Smith addressed her, and she replied. Smith looked puzzled, sort of smiled, and spoke to her again; again she replied as before. "What does she say?" I asked of Smith. Smith replied, "Oh, she says she is the daughter of Shan-tag-a-lisk." "I don't care," said I, "whose daughter she is; tell her to get into the ring and get in quick." Again Smith talked to her, and impatiently gestured. She made a reply. "What did she say?" I asked. "Oh, she says that she don't go into the ring," said Smith. "Then tell her," I said, "that if she doesn't go into the ring she won't get anything to eat." Back from her, through Smith, came the answer: "I have plenty to eat; I am the daughter of Shan-tag-a-lisk." So I left her alone, and she stood and saw the division, and then went off to the Indian camp. Several times rations were distributed during the week, and she always came and stood outside of the ring alone. During the daytime she came to the sutler's store and sat on a bench outside, near the door, watching as if she were living on the sights she saw. She was particularly fond of witnessing guard-mount in the morning and dress-parade in the evening. Whoever officiated principally on these occasions put on a few extra touches for her special benefit, at the suggestion of Major Wood, the Post Commander. The Officer-of-the-guard always appeared in an eighteen-dollar red silk sash, ostrich plume, shoulder-straps, and about two hundred dollars' worth of astonishing raiment, such as, in the field, we boys used to look upon with loathing and contempt. We all knew her by sight, but she never spoke to any of us. Among ourselves we called her "the princess." She was looking, always looking, as if she were feeding upon what she saw. It was a week or ten days that Ah-ho-appa was around Fort Laramie. At last she went away with her band up to Powder River. Her manner of action was known to all, and she was frequently referred to as an Indian girl of great dignity. Some thought she was acting vain, and some thought that she did not know or comprehend her own manner. There was no silly curiosity in her demeanor. She saw everything, but asked no questions. She expressed no surprise, and exhibited not a particle of emotion. She only gazed intently.

One evening in the sutler store the officers of parts of three regiments were lounging, when Elston was asked if he knew Ah-ho-appa. "Very well indeed," he said; and then he proceeded to say:

"I knew her when she was a baby. She was here in the squaw-camp eight or nine years ago, and must have stayed with her relatives here two or three years. She is very much stuck up, especially in the last four or five years. She won't marry an Indian; she always said that. Her father has been offered two hundred ponies for her, but won't sell her. She says she won't marry anybody but a 'capitan',' and that idea sort of pleases her father for more reasons than one. Among the Indians every officer, big or little, with shoulder-straps on, is a 'capitan.' That's a Spanish word the Indians have adopted. Every white man that wears shoulder-straps is a capitan. With her it's a capitan or nobody. She always carries a knife, and is as strong as a mule. One day a Blackfoot soldier running with her father's band tried to carry her off, but she fought and cut him almost to pieces— like to have killed him; tickled her father nearly to death. The young bucks seem to think a good deal of her, but are all afraid to tackle her. The squaws all know about her idea of marrying a capitan; they think her head is level, but don't believe she will ever make it. She tried to learn to read and speak English once of a captured boy, but the boy escaped before she got it. She carries around with her a little bit of a red book, with a gold cross printed on it, that General Harney gave her mother many years ago. She's got it wrapped up in a parfleche [piece of dressed rawhide]. You ought to hear her talk when she is mad. She is a holy terror. She tells the Indians they are all fools for not living in houses, and making peace with the whites. One time she and her father went in to Jack Morrow's ranch and made a visit. She was treated in fine style, and ate a bushel of candy and sardines, but her father was insulted by some drunken fellow and went away boiling mad. When he got home to his tepee he said he never would go around any more where there were white men, except to kill them. She and her father got into a regular quarrel over it, and she pulled out her knife and began cutting herself across the arms and ribs, and in a minute she was bleeding in about forty places, and said that if he didn't say different she was going to kill herself. He knocked her down as cold as a wedge, and had her cuts fixed up by the squaws with pine pitch; and when she came to he promised her that she could go, whenever he did, to see the whites. And she went; you bet she went. She would dress just like a buck and carry a gun. White men would not know the difference. They can't get *her* to tan buckskin, or gather buffalo cherries. No, sir. There was a teamster down at Bardeaux ranch that wanted to talk marry to her, but his moustache was too white." (In the old folk-lore of the plains a man's liver was supposed to be of the color of his moustache. So the speaker meant that the teamster was white-livered, hence cowardly.)

Here ended Elston's story, and all of the officers listened, and some asked questions, until all knew Ah-ho-appa, who did not know her before; and when Mr. Bullock, the post sutler, brought in a gallon of his fine new whisky-toddy the subject changed to Petersburg and Richmond, and whether Sherman's artillery could carry shells over Hood's lines into Atlanta. All efforts for peace at Laramie were failures and hostilities raged along the line, but Shan-tag-a-lisk stayed out of it.

Here for a time we leave the daughter of Shan-tag-a-lisk. She has gone north to Powder River with her father's band. The writer was adjutant for only thirty days, and then was ordered east down the Platte. The Government was making every effort to end the war. Richmond was invested. Atlanta fell into our hands. Rebellion and disunion was being pressed to the wall. The blows were now redoubled and terrific. Fighting day and night, the Confederacy was doomed. Every man was called upon to do his best. Every man did his best, and then came Appomattox; and there was written into our national constitution, with the sword, an amendment that States could not secede from the Union. Then the disbanding armies poured out into the Western States and Territories to begin the making of homes and the building of railroads and cities. Then peace was proffered to the Indian tribes. A commission was sent from Washington and a convention of the "Civilized Tribes" held at Fort Smith, Arkansas. Judge Cooley, of Dubuque, on behalf of the United States, was spokesman. I was there, but still in the United States' service. Ross and Boudinot made speeches, and peace was established there ere frost fell in the autumn of 1865. Commissioners were selected to make treaties with the Western tribes. They were no longer stirred up by emissaries from the Indian Territory and the Confederacy.

Early in 1866 the Department of "The United States forces in Kansas and the Territories" was commanded by Major-General Grenville M. Dodge, who had commanded an army corps under Sherman. The writer had seen General Dodge being hauled off in an army wagon, badly wounded, at Pea Ridge, at which place was first invented the American battle theory of fighting three days without stopping, contrary to the traditions of the "Fifteen Decisive Battles of the World" which had theretofore happened, and which were generally fought in a few hours each.

General Dodge had placed Colonel H. E. Maynadier in charge of the sub-district at Laramie. The Indian troubles had slackened up, but there were at the post about six hundred men, including everybody there. A year and a half had elapsed, and the writer was still in the military volunteer service.

Let us now visit Powder River, far north of Laramie. It was a cold and dismal day in February, about the 23d, 1866. Ah-ho-appa was stricken with consumption, and was living in a chilly and lonesome tepee among the pines on the west bank of the river. She had not seen a white person since her visit to Laramie in August, 1864. During this time there had been a continuous state of war along the routes. Most of the Indians were involved in hostilities that seemed unlikely to ever end, except with the extermination of one party or the other. But Shan-tag-a-lisk kept out of it as much as he could. His camp had been moved backwards and forwards all over the Big Horn, Rose Bud, and Tongue River country, and was again on the Powder River not far from where the three hundred horses of the Seventh Iowa cavalry perished in a September snow-storm. Ah-ho-appa's heart was broken. She could not stand up against her surroundings. In vain her father had urged her to accept the conditions as they were, to be happy and contented and not worry about things out of her reach. But she could not. The object of her life was beyond her reach. She had an ambition,—a vague one; but her hopes were gone. Shortly before her death a runner from Laramie announced to the Indians on Powder River that commissioners would come with the grass, who would bring the words of the Great Father to his Indian children. Shan-tag-a-lisk was urged to send runners to all the bands south and west of the Missouri River, and to meet at Laramie as soon as their ponies could live on the grass. Ah-ho-appa heard the news, but it came too late. It did not revive her. She told her father that she wanted to go, but she would be dead; that it was her wish to be buried in the cemetery at Fort Laramie, where the soldiers were buried, up on the hill, near the grave of "Old Smoke," a distant relative and a great chief among the Sioux in former years. This her relatives promised her.

When her death took place, after great lamentations among the band, the skin of a deer freshly killed was held over the fire and thoroughly permeated and creosoted with smoke. Ah-ho-appa was wrapped in it and it was tightly bound around her with thongs so that she was temporarily embalmed. Shan-tag-a-lisk sent a runner to announce that he was coming, in advance of the commissioners, to bury his daughter at Laramie. *It was a distance of two hundred and sixty miles.*

The landscape was bleak and frozenly arid, the streams were covered with ice, and the hills speckled with snow. The trail was rough and mountainous. The two white ponies of Ah-ho-appa were tied together, side by side, and the body placed upon them. Shan-tag-a-lisk, with a party of his principal warriors and a number of the women, started off on the sad journey. When they camped at night the cottonwood and willow trees were cut down and the ponies browsed on the tops of the trees and gnawed the wood and bark. For nearly a week of the trip there was a continual sleet. The journey lasted for fifteen days, and was monotonous with lamentation.

When within fifteen miles of Fort Laramie at camp, a runner announced to Col. Maynadier the approach of the procession. Col. Maynadier was a natural prince, a good soldier, and a judge of Indian character. He was Colonel of the First U. S. Volunteers. The post commander was Major Geo. M. O'Brien, a graduate of Dublin University, afterwards brevetted to the rank of General. His honored grave is now in the beautiful cemetery at Omaha.

A consultation was held among the officers, and an ambulance dispatched, guarded by a company of cavalry in full uniform, followed by two twelve-pound mountain howitzers, with postilions in red chevrons. The body was placed in the ambulance, and behind it were led the girl's two white ponies.

When the cavalcade had reached the river, a couple of miles from the post, the garrison turned out, and with Col. Maynadier at the head, met and escorted them into the post, and the party were assigned quarters. The next day a scaffold was erected near the grave of "Old Smoke." It was made of tent-poles twelve feet long imbedded in the ground, and fastened with thongs, over which a buffalo-robe was laid, and on which the coffin was to be placed. To the poles of the scaffold were nailed the heads and tails of the two white ponies, so that Ah-ho-appa could ride through the fair hunting-grounds of the skies. A coffin was made and lavishly decorated. The body was not unbound from its deer-skin shroud, but was wrapped in a bright red blanket and placed in the coffin mounted on the wheels of an artillery caisson. After the coffin came a twelve-pound howitzer, and the whole was followed to the cemetery by the entire garrison in full uniform. The tempestuous and chilling weather moderated somewhat. The Rev. Mr. Wright, who was the post Chaplain, suggested an elaborate burial service. Shan-tag-a-lisk was consulted. He wanted his daughter buried Indian fashion, so that she would go not where the white people went, but where the red people went. Every request of Shan-tag-a-lisk was met by Colonel Maynadier with a hearty and satisfactory "Yes." Shan-tag-a-lisk was silent for a long while, then he gave to the Chaplain, Mr. Wright, the "parfleche" which contained the little book that General Harney had given to her mother many years before. It was a small Episcopal prayer-book, such as was used in the regular army. The mother could not read it, but considered it a talisman. Mr. Wright then deposited it in the coffin. Then Colonel Maynadier stepped forward and deposited a pair of white kid gauntlet cavalry gloves to keep her hands warm while she was making the journey. The soldiers formed a large hollow square, within which the Indians formed a large ring around the coffin. Within the Indian ring, and on the four sides of the coffin, stood Colonel Maynadier, Major O'Brien, Shan-tag-a-lisk, and the Chaplain. The Chaplain was at the foot, and read the burial service, while, on either side, Colonel Maynadier and Major O'Brien made responses. Shan-tag-a-lisk stood at the head, looking into the coffin, the personification of blank grief. When the reading service closed Major O'Brien placed in the coffin a new crisp one-dollar bill, so that Ah-ho-appa might buy what she wanted on the journey. Then each of the Indian women came up, one at a time, and talked to Ah-ho-appa: some of them whispered to her long and earnestly as if they were by her sending some hopeful message to a lost child. Each one put some little remembrance in the coffin; one put a little looking-glass, another a string of colored beads, another a pine cone with some sort of an embroidery of sinew in it. Then the lid was fastened on and the women took the coffin and raised it and placed it on the scaffold. The Indian men stood mutely and stolidly around looking on, and none of them moved a muscle or tendered any help. A fresh buffalo-skin was laid over the coffin and bound down to the sides of the scaffold with thongs. The scaffold was within the military square, as was also the twelve-pound howitzer. The sky was leaden and stormy, and it began to sleet and grow dark. At the word of command the soldiers faced outward and discharged three volleys in rapid succession. They and their visitors then marched back to their post. The howitzer squad remained and built a large fire of pine wood, and fired the gun every half-hour all night, through the sleet, until daybreak.

In the morning a conference was had at post headquarters, which was decorated with flags; speeches were made, and the evils and misfortunes of the last five years were gone over. Col. Maynadier told of the expected coming of the commissioners, and made a speech. He said: "There is room enough for all of us in this broad country." Pointing to the silk flag of the Eleventh Ohio Cavalry, hanging from the wall, Col. Maynadier said: "My Indian brother, look at those stripes. Some of them are red, and some of them are white. They remain peacefully side by side—the red and the white—for there is room for each."

After this there was a brief interval of peace. A full account of this funeral may be found in the St. Louis newspapers of March, 1866.

With the grass came the commissioners. Then came the Union Pacific Railroad. Then came Indian resistance. Then war again. Then the decadence of the Sioux nation.

The daughter of Shan-tag-a-lisk was an individual of a type found in all lands, at all times, and among all peoples: she was misplaced.

Her story is the story of the persistent melancholy of the human race; of kings born in hovels, and dying there; of geniuses born where genius is a crime; of heroes born before their age, and dying unsung; of beauty born where its gift was fatal; of mercy born among wolves, and fighting for life; of statesmen born to find society not yet ripe for their labors to begin, and bidding the world adieu from the scaffold.

We all of us know what it is to feel that at times we are out of tune with the world, but ever and anon we strike a node and come back into temporary harmony; but there are those who are never in tune. They are not alone the weak; they are the strong and the weak; they are the ambitious and as well also the loving, the tender, the true, and the merciful.

The daughter of Shan-tag-a-lisk wanted to find somebody to love worth loving. Her soul bled to death. Like an epidendrum, she was feeding upon the air.

When wealth and civilization shall have brought to the Rocky Mountains the culture and population which in time shall come, the daughter of Shan-tag-a-lisk should not be forgotten; it may be said of her, in the words of Buddha:

"Amid the brambles and rubbish thrown over into the road, a lily may grow."

APPENDIX B.

LIEUT. FITCH'S REPORT ON THE SMOKY HILL ROUTE.

FORT LEAVENWORTH, Sept. 25th, 1865.

MAJOR:

Sir—I have the honor to report that in compliance with Special Order No. 143, Hd. Qrs., Dept. of Missouri, dated Fort Leavenworth, June 9th, 1865, I left Fort Leavenworth on the 13th of June to accompany the Butterfield Surveying Expedition on the route to Denver City, via Smoky Hill River.

No assistance having been furnished me, and my instructions authorizing me to employ such as I might need, I employed Chas. H. Fitch as First assistant, and Daniel Clark as scout and Second assistant; and with my party fully equipped I took the old Fort Riley road, which I followed as far as Fort Riley.

At this point we were joined by Major Pritchard of the Second Colorado Cavalry, who was in command of the escort, which at this time consisted of two companies of the Third Wisconsin Cavalry, under Capt. Pond. From that point I proceeded on the Fort Larned road as far as Fort Ellsworth, on the Smoky Hill River, at which point I diverged from the old road and bore west up the river on the north side. Having been instructed to report all streams that should be bridged, and their depth and width, together with the estimated cost of such bridges, I commenced my observations on the old road, as I found that the only difficult part of the route, at a point fifty miles west of Fort Leavenworth, on the west side of Soldier River. The road enters upon the Pottawatomie Reserve, and through the entire reserve for a distance of thirty miles will be found innumerable small streams, most of which should be bridged. It being Indian land, private enterprise is not available, and the United States is now paying toll over no less than four bridges in a distance of thirty miles. All of these streams could be bridged for a sum not exceeding that now paid for toll in the course of a year. At present there is no bridge across Cross Creek, it having washed away while I was camped on its banks.

Between the Reserve and Fort Riley, a distance of thirty-five miles, the streams are good and need no bridges. Directly at Riley, on its west side running through the Reserve and by its junction with the Smoky Hill forming the Kansas River, is the Republican, the largest tributary of the Kansas with the exception of the Smoky Hill. At the crossing of this river on the Military Reserve is a ferry belonging to private parties, and the Government is paying toll daily for crossing its own teams on its own reserve. This stream should be spanned by a good, substantial structure, though its cost will be considerable owing to the size and nature of the stream. I did not make an estimate of the cost of bridging, as I supposed it had already been done by engineers stationed at Fort Riley.

Leaving Fort Riley, on the Fort Larned road passing through Junction City, at a distance of thirty-five miles, we crossed the Solomon's Ford of the Smoky Hill at Whittly's Ferry. The Solomon is a fine rapid stream, with high banks, and has a watercourse eighty feet in width; will require a span of two hundred feet, which can be put up there at a cost of $6,000. Should there be stone piers erected, it would cost considerable more, as the country is level and affords but little building-rock. The bridge could be built to advantage at this particular point, as there is a high island right in the middle of the stream that would afford a good foundation for a pier or bent to the bridge.

The country on this stream is the finest stretch of land in Kansas, having no bluffs, and a soil ranging from five to twenty feet in thickness, while all the streams in the neighborhood are very heavily timbered. The stream bears southeast into Smoky Hill, one mile below where we crossed it. After crossing we bear a little south of west, across a high level bottom between the Smoky Hill, the Solomon and the Saline, and at a distance of eight miles we cross the Saline at Woodward's Ferry; the upper ferry being impracticable on account of the road leading to it. The Saline is a fork of the Smoky Hill, similar to the Solomon, with the exception that the water is impregnated with salt, and it will require about the same bridge. Country is level and the timber fine. Two miles and a half west, we again touched the Smoky Hill, at Salina, the county seat of Dickson, on the eastern terminus of the great bend of the Smoky Hill, bearing south of west from Saline.

At a distance of thirty-two miles we reached Fort Ellsworth, on the western terminus of the great bend of Smoky Hill. Here we were joined by two companies of the Thirteenth Missouri Cavalry, under command of Capts. McMichael and Snell.

After resting a day and killing a few buffalo, which we now

found in considerable numbers, and diverging from the old road, we bore a little north of west upon the north side of the Smoky Hill River, near our old trail of 1860, which had at this time become entirely obliterated. Our road from this point lay over a broad stretch of level bench-land, covered with a luxuriant growth of buffalo-grass, intersected every three or five miles with fine streams of water. Our party at this time consisted of Col. Eaton and his party of constructionists, twenty-six in number; eleven of our mule-wagons loaded with tools, reapers, and everything necessary for putting the road in fine condition; Major Pritchard; two hundred and fifty cavalry as escort, and the Engineer Corps. On the 14th day of July, with everything looking fair and all in good spirits, we started on our work. I was accompanied by my wife and Capt. West by his.

Five miles west of Fort Ellsworth we were fairly in the buffalo range; for miles in every direction as far as the eye could see, the hills were black with those shaggy monsters of the prairie, grazing quietly upon the finest pasture in the world. Should I estimate the number of buffalo to be seen at one view at a million, it would be thought an exaggeration, but better authority than myself has estimated them at millions, or as being greater in number than all the domestic cattle in America.

Truly it has been well said, that the Smoky Hill is the garden-spot and hunting-ground of America.

Following along on the high level bench before spoken of, erecting mounds at every station, our route lay through a fine, rich and fertile country bountifully supplied with wood, water and grass, everything necessary to make a good wagon-road or railroad, finding fine springs as we traveled along. At thirty-four miles west of Fort Ellsworth, we found a coal-bed on what we named as Coal Creek.

Parties that accompanied us on our expedition and who were capable of judging, pronounced it as being a fine vein, and capable of yielding in sufficient quantities to pay for working it.

Twelve miles farther west we came to Big Creek, a large stream having a fine valley and heavy timber. Here we made a good rock ford, erected a large mound and stake for a home and cattle station. We camped here over Sunday and Monday, to rest and hunt.

On the morning of the 18th we left camp, bearing little south of west over the same character of country, close to the Smoky Hill, which at this time, owing to the rains, would have floated a large steamboat. At a distance of twenty-eight miles we came to a large spring, one of the largest and finest in the west. Fifteen miles farther, we bore away from the river and kept on high level land about three miles north of the river, which at this point makes a southerly bend.

On the south of the river, opposite this point, we discovered high bluffs covered with cedar. Twelve and a half miles farther west, we camped at the head springs of a stream emptying south three miles in the Smoky Hill. The water and grass at this point are unusually fine; we called the place Downer Station. Nine miles west we came to a basin of springs covering an area of one mile square, one of the finest spots on the route. We called it Rushton. Nine and one-quarter miles farther west, we crossed Rock Castle Creek, and camped two days to rest. The scenery here is really grand; one mile south is a lofty Calcasieu limestone bluff having the appearance of an old English castle, with pillars, and castellated towers, in every direction. We named it Castle Rock.

Leaving Rock Castle Creek we once more bore a little south of west into the divide between the Smoky Hill and the creek; keeping along the bench of Smoky, crossing streams at convenient distances for stations.

At a distance of about fifty miles we found the largest spring on the route, situated on Ogallallah Creek, in a valley one-half mile south of Smoky Hill. Eight miles farther on, we crossed the north fork and kept up the south fork. The great difficulty on what was known as the old P. P. road lay in the fact that emigration kept up the north fork and then bore across a divide eighty-five miles without water to the Sandy, lengthening their route. We followed the south fork, finding wood, water and grass all the way. Twenty-eight miles from the forks we came to a bottom extending to within two and a half miles of Big Cottonwood Grove, covered with grass six feet high, and containing some splendid springs. This we called the Meadows, and left a reaper in the grass.

Two and a half miles west of the Meadows, we camped at Big Cottonwood Grove. This is a grove of large cottonwood trees, and used to be a celebrated camping-ground for Indians. Sixteen and a half miles west, we reached the Cheyenne Well, at the head of Smoky Hill. This well was built by our party in 1860, and is one of the finest of wells, yielding sufficient water to supply a heavy emigration. At this point we left the Smoky Hill, bearing south 57° west, across the divide between Smoky Hill and the Sand branch of the Arkansas. At eleven miles erected a mound for a well to be dug, and at twenty-one miles came to Eureka Creek, at the junction with Sandy. Here we found a large living stream of water and good grass; we bore from this point north of west up the Sandy seventy miles, to its most northern bend, finding an abundance of water, grass, and some timber, though the latter is scarce. Fourteen miles east of this point we had our first view of the mountains, which we had been prevented from seeing on account of clouds. This morning the snow-capped mountains burst upon our view, looming far above the clouds. The long-expected view cheered our men and we pushed on with renewed vigor, now that our work seemed almost done and our goal appeared within our reach.

Leaving the Sandy at the bend before mentioned, we bore northwest across the divide, crossing Beaver at nine miles, then the Bijou and Kroway, also other well-watered streams, and struck the old Taos road at Cherry Creek, nine miles from Denver. This we followed into Denver, where we were received with congratulations.

Our trip lasted after leaving the old road twenty-four days, six of which we rested. We lost but one mule, and one pony that died of colic.

ADVANTAGES OF THE ROUTE.

The advantages of the Smoky Hill route over the Platte or the Arkansas must be apparent to anybody. In the first place, it is one hundred and sixteen miles shorter to Denver, making two hundred and thirty-two miles on the round trip, and emigration, like a ray of light, will not go around unless there are unsurmountable obstacles in the way. In this case the obstructions are altogether on the Platte and Arkansas. Aside from the difference in distance in favor of the new route, you will find no sand on the Smoky Hill route, whilst from Julesburg to Denver, a distance of two hundred miles, the emigrant or freighter has a dead pull of sand without a stick of timber or a drop of living water, save the Platte itself, which is from three to five miles from the road; and when it is taken into consideration that a loaded ox-train makes but from twelve to fourteen miles a day and never exceeds sixteen, it will not pay, and will double the distance to drive to the Platte, the only water in the country, for the purpose of camping; and all will admit that the Platte waters are so strongly impregnated with alkali as to render it dangerous to water stock from it. The carcasses now lining the road along the Platte bear evidence to its distinctive qualities, whilst on the new route not a particle of this bane can be found.

Another advantage of the new route is that on the Platte from the Junction to Denver, a distance of eighty-five miles, hardly a spear of grass can be found to help hide the sandy, desert-like appearance of the route, whilst on the new route, an abundance of fine buffalo and grama grass can be found all the way. The near approach to the mountains does not seem to affect it, as all kinds of grass can be found from one end of the route to the other.

On the new route we saw no sign of Indians, or in fact any signs later than last fall. This can be accounted for from the fact that the Platte and Arkansas routes being so heavily garrisoned, Indians, with their natural shrewdness, will not wedge themselves into a strip of country entirely surrounded by Government troops.

In addition to the advantages above enumerated, the new route is located through its entire length along and directly parallel to the Central Pacific R. R., which is now running daily trains as far as Lawrence, forty miles west of the Missouri River, and I have been confidently informed that the cars will be moving as far as Topeka, the State capital, this fall, which will shorten a stage route over the new line sixty miles, making the distance to be traveled by coach but five hundred and twenty-four miles, or one hundred and seventy-six miles less than by the Platte and two hundred and seventy-six miles shorter than by the Arkansas, as it is seven hundred miles from Leavenworth City or Atchison to Denver by the Platte route and eight hundred by the Arkansas.

Further, should emigration ever increase to such an extent as to cause a scarcity of timber, nature has bountifully supplied the Smoky Hill with an abundance of bois devache, which is always cheerfully chosen by the tried emigration in preference to cutting timber for a fire.

Having been instructed to suggest places suitable for Military Posts on the route, I would state that I deem but two necessary at present, and position can be found for those,—one at a point on Smoky Hill, seventy miles west of Fort Ellsworth, at the mouth of Turkey Creek, and one at the forks of Smoky Hill; at both of those places an abundance of water, wood and grass can be found convenient.

Having also been instructed to find an avenue through which the Santa Fé trade could be directed via the Smoky Hill, I desire to report that at a distance of three hundred and eighty-six miles west of Fort Leavenworth and one hundred and ninety miles west of Fort Ellsworth, a creek bearing northeast empties into Smoky Hill on the south side, which I deem available (from my own personal observation, and from information gained from the Indian tribes in that vicinity in 1860), by following it to its head and crossing the Big Sandy at a point northeast of Fort Lyon and intersecting the Arkansas road at Fort Lyon. Circumstances prevented me from fully testing this, though I think it could be done with advantage to the Government.

Accompanying this report, you will find a copy of my notes, and also a correct map, which I hope will show truly the relative positions of the two routes, as I have tried to describe them in this my report, fairly and impartially; and having first returned by coach over the Platte route, I think I am fully qualified to decide between the two.

I am, Sir,

Very respectfully,

Your Obt. Servant,

(Signed)   JULIAN R. FITCH,

Second Lt. Signal Corps.

To Major Geo. T. Robinson,

    Chief Engineer.

APPENDIX C.

[From Kansas City Star, Feb 24, 1911.]
JAMES BRIDGER—PIONEER

In Mount Washington Cemetery is the Grave of the Trapper.

In the *Missouri Republican* of March 20, 1822, appeared a notice advertising for "enterprising young men" who would engage to "ascend the Missouri River to its source, there to be employed for one, two or three years." Among the enterprising young men who responded to this advertisement—which emanated from the Missouri Fur Company—was a young blacksmith apprentice named James Bridger, whose unguessed destiny it was to become almost a legendary figure in the pioneer history of the new West. The bare facts of his story are thus summarized upon a monument to his memory in the Mount Washington Cemetery, Kansas City:

1804—JAMES BRIDGER—1881

Celebrated as a hunter, trapper, fur trader, and guide. Discovered Great Salt Lake, 1824; the South Pass, 1827. Visited Yellowstone Lake and Geysers, 1830. Founded Fort Bridger, 1843. Opened Overland Route by Bridger's Pass to Great Salt Lake. Was guide for United States exploring expeditions, Albert Sidney Johnston's Army in 1857, and G. M. Dodge in U. P. surveys and Indian campaigns, 1865–66.

Piquant glimpses of the man himself, however, are captured for us by Edwin L. Sabin, writing in *Recreation*, New York. From Mr. Sabin we learn that, while still a young man, Bridger's qualities won him the honorary appellation, "Old Jim"; that when he discovered Great Salt Lake and tasted its water, he concluded that it was an arm of the Pacific Ocean; and that while not the discoverer of the Yellowstone National Park, he and his companion, Joe Meek, were the first to explore that marvelous region. For a long time their accounts of the wonders of the Yellowstone were received incredulously as trappers' tales.

When the trade in beaver fur declined at the advent of the silk hat, "Old Jim" Bridger established a general trading-post known as "Bridger Fort," on a fork of the trails that led to Oregon and Salt Lake. Here he made the acquaintance of George Gore.

It was in 1854 that Sir George Gore, real Irish nobleman and thorough Irish sportsman, passed up the Missouri from St. Louis on the vastly executed hunting expedition which has been compared to the exploits of Gordon Cumming in Africa, and certainly surpasses the late feat of Mr. Roosevelt. Gore must have been one of those royal good fellows such as the Britisher so often proves when tried out, for he and Bridger became fast friends. The nobleman's custom was to lie abed until near noon, then to arise, bathe, eat and set out, by himself or with Bridger, upon a hunt.

Sir George Gore delighted to read aloud to him out of Shakespeare and Munchausen (who "war a durned liar"), and hear his comments. Bridger declared that "that thar Mr. Fullstuff [Falstaff] war a leetle too fond o' lager beer"; but Shakespeare, withal, so enthused him that he waylaid an emigrant train and bought a copy for a yoke of oxen. He hired a boy at forty dollars a month to read to him; only to quit in a rage at Richard III— he "wouldn't listen to any more talk of any man who war mean enough to kill his mother!" He has been called "the Daniel Boone of the West." And it pleases me to think it was something more than a coincidence that he should make his "last camp" (even though he did not remain) in the very same house in which that other great Virginian had passed over the range fifty years before. It pleases me to think that at least they were drawn there by a common impulse.

Quaint, honest old Bridger. Men today in their prime recall him with a smile and a word of praise. He lived to hear his Yellowstone yarns vindicated, to see a railroad using his particular pass and trail, and to realize that his mountain days had not been wasted. His post has crumbled into a shapeless mass; but over the mountain-man's dust, removed, after twenty years, by a friend, from the farm burial-place to the Kansas City cemetery, arises a noble granite monument, the deed of another friend; and Jim Bridger knows also, that he is not forgotten.—*Literary Digest.*

ABBREVIATED TITLES CITED IN THE NOTES

ABEL. Abel, Annie Heloise. *The American Indian as Participant in the Civil War*, vol. 2 of her *The Slave Holding Indians*, Cleveland: Arthur H. Clark, 1919.

ALTER. Alter, J. Cecil. *James Bridger, Trapper, Frontiersman, Scout and Guide: A Historical Narrative*. Salt Lake City: Shepard Book Company, 1925.

BANNING. Banning, William and George Hugh Banning. *Six Horses.* New York: Century Company, 1930.

BIOG. DIR. AM. CONG. *Biographical Directory of the American Congress, 1774–1927*. Washington: U.S. Government Printing Office, 1928.

BYERS. Byers, S. H. M. *Iowa in War Times.* Des Moines: W. D. Condit & Company, 1888.

CLARK. Clark, Charles M. *A Trip to Pike's Peak & Notes by the Way.* With editorial and biographical notes by Robert Greenwood. San Jose, Calif.: Talisman Press, 1958.

COLORADO GUIDE. Writers' Program of the Work Projects Administration. *Colorado: A Guide to the Highest State.* New York: Hastings House, 1941.

COLTON. Colton, Ray C. *The Civil War in the Western Territories: Arizona, Colorado, New Mexico, and Utah.* Norman: University of Oklahoma Press, 1959.

CUNNINGHAM. Cunningham, Frank. *General Stand Watie's Confederate Indians.* San Antonio: Naylor Company, 1959.

DAB. *Dictionary of American Biography.* New York: C. Scribner's Sons, 1928–1936.

DANGERS OF THE TRAIL. Young, Charles E. *Dangers of the Trail in 1865: A Narrative of Actual Events.* Geneva, N.Y.: Press of W. F. Humphrey, 1912.

FT. LARAMIE. Hafen, LeRoy R. and Francis Marion Young. *Fort Laramie and the Pageant of the West, 1834–1890.* Glendale, Calif.: Arthur H. Clark Company, 1938.

FREDERICK. Frederick, J. V. *Ben Holladay, The Stagecoach King: A Chapter in the Development of Transcontinental Transportation.* Glendale, Calif.: Arthur H. Clark Company, 1940.

GRINNELL. Grinnell, George Bird. *The Fighting Cheyennes.* Norman: University of Oklahoma Press, 1956.

HAFEN. Hafen, LeRoy R. *The Overland Mail, 1849–1869: Promoter of Settlement, Precursor of Railroads.* Cleveland: Arthur H. Clark Company, 1926.

HODGE. Hodge, Frederick Webb, editor. *Handbook of American Indians North of Mexico*. Smithsonian Institution, Bureau of American Ethnology, Bulletin 30. Washington: Government Printing Office, 1907–1910. 2 vols.

HOLLISTER. Hollister, Ovando J. *Boldly They Rode: A History of the First Colorado Regiment of Volunteers*. With an introduction by William MacLeod Raine. Lakewood, Colo.: Golden Press, 1949.

HYDE. Hyde, George E. *Red Cloud's Folk: A History of the Oglala Sioux Indians*. Norman: University of Oklahoma Press, 1937.

MATTES. Mattes, Merrill J. "The Sutler's Store at Fort Laramie," *Annals of Wyoming*, XVIII (July, 1946): 93–137.

MONAGHAN. Monaghan, Jay. *Civil War on the Western Border, 1854–1865*. Boston: Little, Brown & Company, 1955.

MORRIS. Morris, Maurice O'Connor. *Rambles in the Rocky Mountains: With a Visit to the Gold Fields of Colorado*. London: Smith, Elder & Company, 1864.

NEBRASKA GUIDE. Federal Writers' Project of the Works Progress Administration. *Nebraska: A Guide to the Cornhusker State*. New York: Viking Press, 1939.

OHLER. Oehler, C. M. *The Great Sioux Uprising*, New York: Oxford University Press, 1959.

O.R. *The War of the Rebellion: A Compilation of the Official Records of the Union and Confederate Armies* (Washington: Government Printing Office, 1880–1901).

PADEN. Paden, Irene D. *The Wake of the Prairie Schooner*. New York: Macmillan Company, 1943.

R & R. *Roster and Record of Iowa Soldiers in the War of the Rebellion*. . . . Des Moines: Emory H. English, State Printer, 1908–1911.

ROGERS. Rogers, Fred B. *Soldiers of the Overland: Being Some Account of the Services of General Patrick Edward Connor & His Volunteers in the Old West*. San Francisco: Grabhorn Press, 1938.

SPRING. Spring, Agnes Wright. *Caspar Collins: The Life and Exploits of an Indian Fighter of the Sixties*. New York: Columbia University Press, 1927.

STUART. Stuart, A. A. *Iowa Colonels and Regiments*. . . . Des Moines: Mills & Company, 1865.

VESTAL. Vestal, Stanley. *Jim Bridger, Mountain Man*. New York: William Morrow & Company, 1946.

WHITFORD. Whitford, William Clarke. *Colorado Volunteers in the Civil War: The New Mexico Campaign in 1862*. Denver: State Historical and Natural History Society, 1906.

YOUNG. Young, Francis C. *Across the Plains in '65: A Youngster's Journal from "Gotham" to "Pike's Peak."* Denver: Lanning Brothers, 1905.

NOTES

CHAPTER I

Page 1. The number of Confederates surrendered at Vicksburg was nearer 30,000 than 27,000, although the statistics (like all Civil War statistics) are contradictory and unreliable.

Page 2. Buchanan's Secretary of the Interior was Jacob Thompson of Mississippi. He resigned in 1861 to join the Confederate army, which he served as inspector general and special agent in Canada. Thompson is given credit for Confederate espionage in Canada and for raids across the border into the United States.

Albert Pike, born in Boston, became a well-to-do lawyer and newspaper man of Little Rock, Arkansas; at the time of the war was the Confederate Indian commissioner. He was well acquainted with Indians and their ways and was an excellent commissioner. He was able to negotiate treaties with the Choctaws and Chickasaws, tying them to the Confederacy; his efforts to have the Creeks and Seminoles secede were futile but almost threw those tribes into civil war. The Cherokees reluctantly signed a treaty in August, 1861. But Pike's efforts with the wild Indians bore no fruit; he was able to induce a few Comanches to sign a treaty, but it could not be enforced and was actually meaningless.

Pages 2–3. The Battle of Wilson's Creek was the biggest battle fought in Missouri during the war. The Confederates were led by Benjamin McCulloch and Sterling Price (James McIntosh was not the senior commander), the Union by Nathaniel Lyon.

In the Battle of Pea Ridge, Union troops were led by Samuel R. Curtis, and the Confederates by Earl Van Dorn; both Confederate Generals McIntosh and Benjamin McCulloch were killed. It is likely that Ware refers to McIntosh as the dead Confederate general.

Pages 2–3. There were Indian troops in both Confederate and Union service. At the Battle of Pea Ridge, Cherokees, Creeks, and Choctaws fought for the South, and some atrocities were committed, although the extent of the scalping—by Union soldiers as well as Indians—is still a matter of controversy. The Indians had no appreciable effect on the outcome of the battle and soon were out of the control of Confederate officers.

Pages 3–5. A number of writers mention the capture of eleven Confederate Indians at the Battle of Pea Ridge, the planned tour of the captives through the North, and their death, one by one, while "attempting to escape." Ware greatly exaggerates the effect the death of these captives had on other Indians.

See *Cunningham,* p. 36, and *Monaghan,* p. 249.

Page 6. The Gallagher carbine was patented July 17, 1860, by Mahlon J. Gallagher and was manufactured by Richardson and Overman of Philadelphia. It was 38 inches long, weighed 7½ pounds, and fired a .54 caliber projectile. It was operated by a finger level which cammed the barrel forward permitting the breech end to tip upward for loading the cartridge. Between August 1, 1861, and December 10, 1864, the War Department purchased 17,728 of these weapons.

The Gallagher carbine was designed so that the percussion cap nipple at the top of the barrel, and the firing vent leading from it to the cartridge, bored straight down, then reversed at right angles to the center of the chamber. The vent quickly became fouled after a few shots so that the fire from the exploded percussion cap would not ignite the powder in the cartridge. This malfunction was so common that the Gallagher carbine had (and certainly deserved) a bad reputation with the soldiers.

Page 7. Indians were frequently called "Lo" or "Mr. Lo," the allusion being to Alexander Pope's verse: "Lo, the poor Indian! whose untutor'd mind . . ."

Page 7. Brevet Major General Thomas Jefferson McKean attended the United States Military Academy, fought the Seminoles in Florida, and then resigned to enter civilian life. He rejoined the army for Mexican War service, and rallied to the flag once again in 1861, being commissioned brigadier general, November 21, 1861, and brevetted major general March 13, 1865, for gallant and meritorious service. He was mustered out that same year and died in 1870.

General McKean was commanding the District of Nebraska. This district was not officially called "Nebraska and the Plains"—although it may have been so called unofficially.

Page 7. The Herndon House, built in 1858, was located at Ninth and Farnum Streets. It was named for William Lewis Herndon, a naval officer who had led an expedition into the Amazon River Basin in 1851. His report, "Exploration of the Valley of the Amazon," published by the government (2 volumes, 1853–1854), helped open the river to merchant shipping.

Commander Herndon went down with his ship *George Law* in September, 1855, after heroic efforts to save its passengers. There is a monument to his memory at the Naval Academy at Annapolis.

Page 8. Both "Joe Bowers" and "Sweet Betsy from Pike" are well-known folk songs which were popular in the 1849 gold rush. A broadside in the Illinois State Historical Library gives these words for "Joe Bowers":

My name is Joe Bowers, I've got a brother Ike,
I came from old Missouri, all the way from Pike,
I'll tell you why I left thar, and why I came to roam,
And leave my poor old mammy, so far away from home.

I used to court a gal there, her name was Sallie Black;
I axed her if she'd marry me, she said it was a whack;
Says she to me: Joe Bowers, before we hitch for life,
You ought to get a little home to keep your little wife.

Oh! Sally, dearest Sally, Oh! Sally, for your sake,
I'll go to California and try to raise a stake;
Says she to me, Joe Bowers, you are the man to win,
Here's a kiss to bind the bargain, and she hove a dozen in.

When I got in that country, I hadn't "nary red,"
I had such wolfish feelings, I wished myself most dead;
But the thoughts of my dear Sally soon made them feelin's *git*
And whispered hopes to Bowers, I wish I had 'em *yit*.

At length I went to mining, put in my biggest licks,
Went down upon the boulders just like a thousand bricks,
I worked both late and early, in rain, in sun, in snow,
I was working for my Sally, 'twas all the same to Joe.

At length I got a letter from my dear brother Ike,
It came from old Missouri, all the way from Pike,
It brought to me the darndest news, that ever you did hear,
My heart is almost bustin', so pray excuse this tear.

It said that Sal was false to me, her love for me had fled,
She'd got married to a butcher, the butcher's hair was red,
And more than that the letter said, it's enough to make me swear,
That Sally had a baby, the baby had red hair.

Now, I've told you all I can about this sad affair,
'Bout Sally marrying a butcher, that butcher had red hair,
But whether 'twas a boy or gal child, the letter never said.
It only said that the baby's hair was *inclined to be red*.

   Like most folk songs, both of these have a number of variant verses. Carl Sandburg in *American Songbag* says that "Sweet Betsy" is "droll and don't care, bleary and leering, as slippery and lackadaisical as some of the comic characters of Shakespeare, or as trifling as the two murderers who are asked, 'How came you here?' and who answer, 'On our legs.' It was a good wagon song." Sandburg uses these words:

Oh don't you remember sweet Betsy from Pike,
   Who crossed the big mountains with her lover Ike,

With two yoke of cattle, a large yellow dog,
  A tall Shanghai rooster, and one spotted hog.

Refrain:

Saying goodbye, Pike County,
  Farewell for a while;
We'll come back again
  When we've panned out our pile.

One evening quite early, they camped on the Platte,
  'Twas near by the road on a green shady flat;
Where Betsy, quite tired, laid down to repose,
  While with wonder Ike gazed on his Pike County Rose.

Refrain:

They soon reached the desert, where Betsy gave out
  And down in the sand she lay rolling about;
While Ike in great tears looked on in surprise,
  Saying, "Betsy, get up, you'll get sand in your eyes."

Refrain:

Sweet Betsy got up in a great deal of pain,
  And declared she'd go back to Pike County again.
Then Ike heaved a sigh and they fondly embraced,
  And she traveled along with his arm 'round her waist.

Refrain:

The Shanghai ran off and the cattle all died,
  The last piece of bacon that morning was fried;
Poor Ike got discouraged, and Betsy got mad,
  The dog wagged his tail and looked wonderfully sad.

Refrain:

One morning they climbed up a very high hill,
  And with wonder looked down into old Placerville;
Ike shouted and said, as he cast his eyes down,
  "Sweet Betsy, my darling, we've got to Hangtown."

Refrain:

Long Ike and Sweet Betsy attended a dance,
  Where Ike wore a pair of his Pike County pants,
Sweet Betsy was covered with ribbons and rings,
  Quoth Ike, "You're an angel, but where are your wings?"

Refrain:

A miner said "Betsy, will you dance with me?"
  "I will, old hoss, if you don't make too free;
But don't dance me hard. Do you want to know why?
  Dog on ye, I'm chuck full of strong alkali."

Refrain:

Long Ike and Sweet Betsy got married, of course,
  But Ike getting jealous obtained a divorce;
And Betsy, well satisfied, said with a shout,
  "Goodbye, you big lummux, I'm glad you backed out."

Last Refrain:

Saying goodbye, dear Isaac,
  Farewell for a while.
But come back in time
  To replenish my pile.

Pages 9–10. The National Loyal Union League—the "Loyal League"—sprang up in the North to counter sentiments expressed by "Copperheads" and by those who voted the Democratic ticket. The first of these (and similar) leagues started in Pekin, Illinois, in 1862, and the movement spread rapidly through the North, culminating in a general consolidation into the Union League. This national organization published pamphlets, raised money, and held meetings to support Lincoln and Republican Party candidates. The Union League was an active political force through the reconstruction period, but its influence declined as war passions cooled; the Union League is known today more as a conservative club for socially prominent businessmen than as an active and forceful participant in political affairs.

Page 11. Captain Nicholas J. O'Brien, a younger brother of Major George M. O'Brien of the 7th Iowa Cavalry, was born in Ireland. He was twenty-five years old when he entered service at Dubuque, receiving an appointment as captain January 17, 1863. He resigned February 1, 1866.

Page 11. Herman H. Heath, whom Ware thoroughly detested, was a native of New York who was appointed captain of Company L, 1st Iowa Cavalry, September 24, 1861, while living in Dubuque. He was honorably discharged February 28, 1863, and mustered in as major of the 1st Battalion, 7th Iowa Cavalry, May 15, 1863. He was then thirty-nine years old. On May 3, 1865, he was promoted colonel. On March 13, 1865, he was brevetted lieutenant colonel, brigadier general, and major general of volunteers for meritorious service and gallantry during the war, particularly for service on the frontier while operating against hostile Indians. He was mustered out May 17, 1866, at Fort Leavenworth.

Ware repeats his charge of treason by Heath on pages 131–132, stating specifically that Heath had offered his services to Jefferson Davis as a brigadier general and that General Dodge found the letter and read it on the floor of Congress in 1866. As a result of Dodge's publicity, Heath "fled to Peru and died a pauper and tramp."

None of the biographies of Dodge mentions this letter, and Dodge was not a member of Congress in 1866. He served one term, March

4, 1867–March 3, 1869. A search of the *Congressional Globe* for these years failed to discover any mention of Heath by Dodge, or anyone else.

Further, Heath was appointed secretary of New Mexico Territory by President Johnson, taking office July 18, 1867. Heath treated this office as a matter of patronage due him as a successful defender of the Union, and his administration was not without controversy. In March, 1868, he organized the New Mexico Department of the G.A.R. It is interesting to note that Robert B. Mitchell, whom Heath served under during the war, was governor.

CHAPTER II

Page 12. Ware and Company F were following the old Mormon road from Omaha into the valley of the Platte River. They stayed on the north side of the river until they arrived at Columbus, Nebraska; from that point they proceeded up the Loup River to the Pawnee Indian agency in eastern Nance County, near Genoa, Nebraska. There they crossed to the south side of the Loup and marched south to the Platte River, crossing Prairie Creek en route. Apparently Ware stayed on the north side of the Platte at Grand Island, since he telegraphed from the O. K. Store. After telegraphing, he marched to Wood River and then crossed to the south bank the day after leaving the camp site on Wood River. On the south side of the Platte, Ware followed the rather well-defined overland trail to Cottonwood Springs, some ten miles east of the forks of the Platte.

Page 12. James Cannon was born in Ireland in 1830, joined the 7th Iowa Cavalry, December 27, 1863, and was not mustered out until May 17, 1866. He said, when he enlisted, that he was a resident of Cottonwood Springs, Nebraska—obviously preferring not to list his real place of residence or actually being, as Ware suggests later, an irresponsible vagabond.

Page 14. Major John S. Wood was born in Delaware. At age thirty-eight, he enlisted from Ottumwa, Iowa, as a captain, September 12, 1862. He commanded Company A of the 7th Iowa Cavalry until he was made major of the 3rd Battalion on July 8, 1863. Major Wood was mustered out January 31, 1865, at Omaha, Nebraska.

Page 15. Columbus, Nebraska, was founded in 1856, and named after Columbus, Ohio. The town developed as a supply point on the overland trail and as a stop on the Union Pacific Railroad.

Pages 15–16. The "white-haired, gray-whiskered, incapable man" was First Lieutenant John S. Brewer. Born in New York State, he entered the service from West Union, Iowa, when forty-four years old. He was appointed first lieutenant on April 21, 1863, and he served in this capacity until discharged, November 3, 1865.

Page 16. The "man named North" must have been Frank J. North, elder brother of Luther H. North; both men were famous frontiersmen who were later associated with William F. "Buffalo Bill" Cody. See George B. Grinnell, *Two Great Scouts and Their Pawnee Battalion* (Cleveland: Arthur H. Clark Company, 1928).

Pages 17–18. In October, 1863, Nebraska was not a part of the Department of the Northwest but a district in the Department of the Missouri. The districts within the department kept changing throughout the war. In October, 1863, the District of Nebraska had its headquarters at Omaha City, with subdistricts at Omaha City, Fort Kearney, Cottonwood Springs, and Dakota.

On January 1, 1864, this was all changed, and Nebraska became a part of the newly created Department of Kansas, which included Kansas, the territories of Nebraska and Colorado, and Indian Territory; headquarters were at Fort Leavenworth.

The District of the Plains was not created until after the Department of Kansas was abolished and the Department of the Missouri again given authority over the area. The District of the Plains was created early in 1865 but was abolished August 22 of that same year.

Page 17. This officer was probably First Lieutenant George P. Norris of Company E. A Canadian by birth, he was appointed first lieutenant March 1, 1863, from Ottumwa, Iowa. Norris, who was thirty-one when appointed, was promoted captain June 3, 1865, and mustered out May 17, 1866, at Fort Leavenworth.

Page 18. The Pawnee Agency was located in Nance County, Nebraska, in the Fullerton-Genoa area.

Pages 18–19. The Pawnees were the most northerly of the Caddo family of Indians, a family believed to have been founded by a relative to the ancestor of the Iroquois; the Iroquois and Pawnee languages have a common origin. The Pawnees were traditionally friendly with the white man and made excellent scouts and guides for the cavalry, serving the army from 1864 to 1885. The first treaty with the Pawnees was made in 1818. In 1833 they ceded their lands south of the Platte, and in 1857 they relinquished all their lands north of the Platte, except for a thirty-by-fifteen-mile strip on the Loup River. This area was ceded in 1876, and the tribe moved to Indian Territory; in 1892 they took their lands in severalty and became citizens.

The tribe once numbered 10,000 but had decreased to perhaps 3,500 at the time Ware saw them, in large part because of a cholera epidemic in 1849.

Pages 18–20. Benjamin F. Lushbaugh, the Pawnee agent, anticipated the North brothers in trying to organize the Pawnee warriors for army service. He went to Washington in 1862 for this purpose (and to get permission to raise a regiment of Nebraska volunteers), but on October 13, 1862, his request was turned down. In 1863 Agent Lushbaugh also held a lucrative mail contract.

Page 21. Brigadier General Isaac F. Quinby was an 1843 graduate of the Military Academy and a friend of General Grant's. An experienced soldier, Quinby had been colonel of the 13th New York, and was appointed brigadier general March 17, 1862. He commanded Columbus, Kentucky, and the 7th Division of the Army of the Tennessee around Vicksburg. Because of illness contracted in this campaign, he found it necessary to resign from the army on the last day of 1863. His illness, however, was not fatal; he lived until 1891.

CHAPTER III

Page 27. The O. K. Store, a telegraph station and immigrant supply house, was located at the eastern edge of the settlement on the south side of the Platte River which later was moved to the north side of the river to become the present city of Grand Island, Nebraska. During the Indian raids of 1864 in the settlement, a fortified log house called Fort Independence and the O. K. Store were points of safety for settlers and immigrants.

Page 28. The Omahas and Poncas are both members of the Lower Missouri division of the Siouan Indian family. Ware apparently did not know that Indians generally are less hirsute than whites and that they usually removed facial hairs by pulling them out, one by one.

CHAPTER IV

Pages 31–32. Fort Kearney was originally located on the Missouri River at the present Nebraska City but was relocated in June, 1848, on the south side of the Platte River, across from the present city of Kearney, Nebraska. First called Fort Child, it was renamed Kearney (usually so spelled) after General Stephen Watts Kearny.

The fort was established to help organize and protect the overland trail, and it was a military post of major importance until abandoned in 1871. Here the traveler found a post office, telegraph station; supplies could be purchased and advice about trail conditions was available. It was here that the emigrant really entered the true "plains," and it was between here and Fort Laramie that the Indians ravaged the overland trail in 1864 and 1865.

Dobytown (sometimes Dobeytown) was an unsavory place that catered to gamblers, traders, stage drivers, teamsters, and others of the floating population about the fort. *Paden* says that "the place was a grisly combination of delirium tremens, stale humanity, and dirt." It was certainly a dismal place, but it was in Dobytown that many officers were quartered during the Civil War.

A traveler in March, 1865, described Dobytown: ". . . at five o'clock pass through Ft. Kearney, and a half hour later reach Kearney City or 'Dobytown,' so nicknamed because of its houses being all built of adobe or sod, cut from the prairie. . . . This Kearney City is two

miles west of Ft. Kearney, & is mainly composed of boarding-houses
and quarters for the officers stationed at the Fort." *Young,* pp. 115–16.

A detailed study of Fort Kearney is by Albert Watkins, "History
of Fort Kearny," *Collections of the Nebraska State Historical Society,*
XVI (1911): 227–67.

Pages 34–35. If there was any such forty-mile buffer zone between
the western Indians and the Pawnees, it is not reflected in the treaties
which apply to 1863. The Pawnee reservation, some thirty by fifteen
miles in area, was to the east of Fort Kearney, near Fullerton and
Genoa. The Sioux, according to the Fort Laramie Treaty of 1851,
owned the land west of the forks of the Platte, but, while hunting,
were not confined to their own land.

Pages 35–36. Sir George Gore, a titled Irishman, visited the West in
1854–1855, traveling with luxurious equipment: 6 wagons, 21 carts,
112 horses, 14 dogs, and 40 servants were with him when he reached
Fort Laramie to spend much of the winter with Jim Bridger. The
Irish sportsman's name remains permanently in Colorado's Gore Range
and Gore Pass. While "hunting," Gore's party is supposed to have
provoked the Indians of Colorado by their wanton slaughter of more
than three thousand buffalo.

Page 38. The English traveler Maurice O'Connor Morris, traveling
the Overland Trail in 1863, described a typical "ranch":

"It must not be supposed that these ranches imply farming on any
scale whatever; they are simply business stations to meet the wants
of the emigrants and travelers westward, and therefore each mainly
consists of one room, which serves for store, grog-shop, and bedroom
by night. In the smaller ones, and they are far the most numerous, the
stock in hand may be set down as consisting of much pork and ham,
a few pounds of coffee, salt, pepper, vinegar, pear-ash, soda, flour,
butter, eggs, corn, dried apples, peaches in tins, and oysters also, with
a Falstaffian proportion of a vile compound of whiskey and I know
not what, which is popularly known as 'bust head,' or 'forty rod,'
because the unfortunate imbiber is seriously affected in either brain or
legs, or even in both, before he has gone the distance. . . . But one
of their great sources of wealth lay in 'trading' oxen. For this purpose
they begin with a few of their own, and when a man passes with a
foot-sore ox which can go no further, they sell the traveler a fresh one
at their own rate, while a dollar or two is considered the 'rule of
the road' for the faded ox: or rather was, for competition is beginning
to mar this golden age. Under these circumstances it will not be surprising that these rancheros make their 'pile' pretty quickly." *Morris,*
pp. 47–49.

CHAPTER V

Page 41. There were two assistant surgeons in the 7th Iowa
Cavalry, James W. LaForce of Agency, Iowa, who was mustered

June 2, 1863, and Stephen P. Yeomans of Sioux City, Iowa, who was mustered August 5, 1863. It is likely that Ware refers to LaForce, since he mentions him again on page 167, and never does mention Yeomans.

Page 41. Smith's ranch, run by Daniel L. Smith, was some seventy-five miles west of Fort Kearny. Clark, who passed there in 1860, commented: "Smith's Ranche is a small building constructed of logs, where licquor, preserved fruits, etc., are to be had. Why these buildings, or stations, are called ranches, is more than I can say. The proprietors do not cultivate the soil, nor do they raise stock, they have merely squatted along this line of travel, for purposes best known to themselves. These miscalled ranches throughout the Platte Valley are essentially, one and the same thing; sometimes differing in size and style of construction—some are of the adobe species, while others are constructed of rough logs and poles, and sometimes we meet with one built of square cedar posts, that looks very neat. The proprietors are generally rude specimens of humanity, in every sense of the word, and many of them dress in garments made from elk and deer skins, ornamented with long fringes of the same materials, up and down the seams; their hair and beard, in many cases, had been suffered to grow, giving them a ferocious look, and in fact, they are as primitive as the country they inhabit. In order to insure the respect and confidence of the Indians, many of them have squaw wives, who inhabit a lodge erected near by." *Clark,* p. 41.

CHAPTER VI

Many of the men Ware was to meet in and around Cottonwood Springs were the first settlers in Lincoln County, Nebraska. "Boyer," mentioned on page 46, was Isador P. Boyer, who, with one of the Roubidoux's, erected the first permanent building at the springs in 1858. The "man named Hindman" was Washington M. Hinman, who had come from Fort Laramie to the springs in 1860 to ranch and trade with emigrants. Charles McDonald had purchased the second building erected at the springs to stock with general merchandise, and in 1860 brought his wife out to live with him. She was the first white woman to settle in Lincoln County. Their son, W. H. McDonald, was the first white child born in the county. Jack A. Morrow, mentioned on page 59, had come to Lincoln County in 1860 to furnish supplies to overland trail travelers.

When the county (first called "Shorter") was organized in 1860, Cottonwood Springs was the county seat, and the county commissioners were Boyer, Morrow, and J. C. Gilman; the judge was Mc-Donald, and the treasurer was Hinman.

The Gilmans (page 61), Sam D. Fitchie (page 190) and Hugh Morgan (71) were all pioneer residents and were well known to travelers who stopped at their ranches.

The Daniel Freeman mentioned on page 65 ran a general store of a story and a half near present Lexington, Nebraska; travelers were accommodated on the second floor, where blanket partitions assured a measure of privacy. Mrs. Freeman sold bread and cheese (50¢ a loaf and 25¢ a pound in 1862) while her husband sold supplies and doubled as county clerk.

The Daniel L. Smith mentioned on page 65 met a tragic end in 1871 when he murdered his wife in a fit of jealousy and fled to the hills. He was hunted down by a party of soldiers and killed the next day; the place where he died is still called "Dan Smith Canyon."

Pages 49–50. In the election for governor in Iowa in the fall of 1863, the Republicans nominated Colonel William M. Stone, who had commanded the 3rd Iowa Infantry at Shiloh and had been captured; after his release he commanded the 22nd Iowa Infantry at Vicksburg and Port Gibson. He had been wounded at Vicksburg.

The Democrats nominated General James M. Tuttle, who had commanded the 2nd Iowa Infantry at Fort Donelson, a brigade at Shiloh (and Wallace's Division after Wallace's death); he commanded Cairo, Illinois, and then the 3rd Division of the 15th Corps at Jackson and Vicksburg.

Tuttle was attacked as a Copperhead and was reported to favor an immediate peace conference. Neither charge was true, for Tuttle was an ardent patriot who favored a vigorous prosecution of the war. The Iowa soldiers voted Stone, 16, 791—Tuttle, 2,904; the over-all vote was Stone, 86,122, and Tuttle, 47,948. (*Stuart,* pp. 7–15 and 51–58; *Byers,* pp. 259–73.)

Page 51. Gilman's ranch, fifteen miles west of Cottonwood Springs, was another of the well-known stopping points.

Clark stopped there to purchase wood in 1860; a chance remark made a ranch "hand" believe Clark's company might try to steal some wood, and he produced a pistol and a fight was narrowly averted. *Clark,* p. 44.

On April 2, 1865, *Young* commented that Gilman's was a military station of some importance, with soldiers occupying about a dozen log houses.

Page 53. Gold had been found in the mountain streams of Colorado by miners on their way to California in the 1840's. By 1858, accounts of Colorado gold had reached the East, but the rumors far exceeded the facts. In early 1859 the rush started to the Denver area, although no important strikes had yet been made. In January, 1859, George A. Jackson, an Indian trader and relative of Kit Carson, found a rich deposit of gold, the first major gold strike in Colorado, at the junction of Chicago Creek and the South Fork of Clear Creek, some thirty miles by modern highway west of Denver, close by the present town of Idaho Springs. This discovery precipitated the founding of Blackhawk and Central City and marked the real beginning of the mining industry in Colorado. *Colorado Guide,* pp. 39, 55, 257–76.

CHAPTER VII

Page 57. When the author says "Lodgepole," he means Lodgepole Creek, which empties into the South Platte at Julesburg, Colorado; the trail along Lodgepole Creek was one way to start toward Salt Lake City.

Page 57. Court House Rock, some five miles from Bridgeport, Nebraska, was supposedly named by early travelers who thought it resembled the county building in St. Louis. Another story suggests that the rock was named after a dozen outlaws who were shot at the top of the formation, following a hasty trial. The base is brule clay and the top is Gering sandstone; the custom of carving one's name in the "rock" is noted in many overland diaries. (See pages 269 and 311.)

Page 59. Jack Morrow's ranch, some ten miles west of Fort Mc-Pherson, was a large, well-known establishment. One traveler in 1860 commented: "Jack Morrow is a somewhat noted character, having lived in the country many years, and has been employed by government, to some extent, in carrying the mail through to Fort Laramie and other points. . . . He is a small, slim personage, rather below average stature, light complexion, wearing long auburn hair, his features small, but regular, no beard, and withal, a very social man. He had a squaw wife, and has had several. By some it was thought that he was connected with the organized band of thieves, for did anyone mention that they had lost animals, and he would offer to find them for a certain renumeration." *Clark,* p. 47.

Morris, who arrived here June 11, 1863, noted: "As usual in the better ranches, there was a good supply of ice here. . . . I could not help feeling intensely amused at the manners and customs of the labourers at these establishments. A man would go out—they were doing some building work—for some twenty or thirty minutes, then he would come to the bar, take a 'smile' of whiskey, followed by a gulp of water (the usual style of mixing grog in America), then he would cast his eye over a paper, and so on, *da capo.*"

Young, on April 7, 1865, was impressed by ". . . the handsome and extensive log building, filled to the roof with a general stock of Plains staples. There is no great variety, perhaps, but as for quantity, his shelves of canned goods look like the long courses of brick in a blank house wall: tier on tier of sardines, tomatoes and peaches— these seem to monopolize to a large extent the canning industry, or at least they appear to form the chief demand of the Plains trade of this class. . . ."

Pages 60–61. Colonel James Baker was a practicing attorney of Bloomfield, Iowa, who entered the army as the commanding officer of Company G, 2nd Iowa Infantry. He was promoted lieutenant colonel on November 2, 1861, and colonel on June 22, 1862. Baker's regiment took part in the operations around Corinth, and he was shot from his horse during a charge, dying in a military hospital November 7, 1862. He was the first Iowa colonel to fall in battle and, at the time of his death, was considered to be an officer of considerable promise. *Stuart,* pp. 59–64.

Page 61. The post, some two miles west of Cottonwood Springs, had been established as Cantonment Fort McKean, in honor of Major General Thomas J. McKean, who then commanded the area. It was redesignated the Post (or Fort) of Cottonwood in May, 1864, and on February 20, 1866, it was renamed Fort McPherson, in memory of General James B. McPherson, who was killed before Atlanta, July 22, 1864.

Pages 61–63. Ware was firing 12-pound mountain howitzers. According to the Ordnance Department's *Ranges of Guns, Howitzers, and Mortars* (1863), Lieutenant Ware's "schedule of distances and seconds" is precisely the same as the elevations, seconds, and distances the Ordnance Department recommended to artillery officers.

Pages 63–64. Major George M. O'Brien had been born in Ireland and at age thirty-five entered the army from Dubuque, being appointed major of the 2nd Battalion, 7th Iowa Cavalry on May 15, 1863; he was later transferred to the 1st Battalion. He was promoted by brevet to lieutenant colonel and brigadier general of United States Volunteers on March 13, 1865, and was mustered out at Fort Leavenworth, May 17, 1866.

Page 65. Thomas (Pat) Mullally's ranch.
Morris stopped here June 8, 1863, and commented: "Here we camped, and more rain fell. However, it ceased towards night, and with the aid of a roaring fire and a mighty brew of 'egg nogg' we contrived to be pretty comfortable."

Page 65. William Peniston and Andrew J. Miller operated a ranch —between Smith's and Mullally's—at Cold Water, about twenty-five miles west of Plum Creek. Peniston and Miller were the first citizens of North Platte and moved their store to that place in 1867. *Morris,* on June 9, 1863, commented: ". . . we came to Miller's ranche, where we dined. This house, like most about here, bore as its emblem a pair of stag or elk's horns fastened over the door. . . ."

CHAPTER VIII

Page 68. The first successful "transcontinental" stage route was the result of a mail contract awarded to John Butterfield and William G. Fargo. Their stages followed the southern route, from St. Louis and Memphis through Missouri, Arkansas, Oklahoma, Texas, New Mexico, and Arizona to California. The first western trip began September 15, 1858, at St. Louis and took 24 days and 18 hours; the first eastern trip left San Francisco on September 15, 1858, and required 23 days and 4 hours.

The Leavenworth and Pike's Peak Express, owned by William H. Russell and John S. Jones, began service May 17, 1859, between Leavenworth and Denver. This company bought a mail contract covering service to California on the central route through Salt Lake City and would have made a financial success of their routes (the route to Denver went through Fort Riley and along the Smoky Hill fork of the Kansas River to near Cherry Creek, to Denver, the "Smoky Hill route") except that the rush to the Colorado gold field diminished. Russell was able to avoid financial ruin only because he was also a partner in the firm of Russell, Majors and Waddell, which took over the Leavenworth and Pike's Peak line. But they abandoned the Smoky Hill route in favor of the Platte River trail.

In 1860 they rechartered their companies under the title Central Overland California and Pike's Peak Express Company. Meanwhile, Russell promoted the pony express mail over the central route, beginning April 3, 1860, at St. Joseph, Missouri. When the telegraph line was completed to California on October 25, 1861, there was no further use for the pony express, and it died a natural death.

When the Civil War began, the Butterfield route through Texas was discontinued and moved north, with a new contract which gave Butterfield the route from Salt Lake City west. The C.O.C. & P.P.E. was awarded the route from the Missouri to Salt Lake City. The "Overland" had been in financial trouble, and Russell, Majors and Waddell had been borrowing from Ben Holladay; the new contract seemed to offer a sure road to financial success.

But the Overland was not yet paying its way; Holladay loaned the company more money and took a mortgage on the line and its equipment. Finally, on March 21, 1862, he bought the firm at public auction for $100,000. The new owner would handle passengers on two divisions, Atchison, Kansas, to Denver and Denver to Salt Lake City. The company was now called the Holladay Overland Mail and Express Company.

During the war, Holliday had to contend with Indian raids that destroyed coaches, feed, buildings, and other equipment, with changes in routes and delays ordered by government action, and with property requisitions by troops that totaled $529,090.60 for the years 1862–1866. Although troops frequently guarded the stages and were sent to patrol the routes, running the stages during the war was a difficult task, but one to which Holladay was equal. He sold his lines to Wells, Fargo and Company on November 1, 1866.

For more detailed information, see *Hafen, Banning,* and *Frederick.*

Pages 74–76. The standard sources do not indicate that anyone by the name of Gardner was a Cheyenne Indian agent. There was a James Frank Gardner who was in charge of some volunteer soldiers at California ranch (now Franktown, Colorado) at this time. The agent for the Arapahoes and Cheyennes was Major Samuel G. Colley (or Colly), who was appointed from Colorado and stationed at Fort Lyon, Colorado.

CHAPTER IX

Page 85. Colonel Samuel W. Summers had been born in Virginia and was forty-three when he entered the service from Ottumwa, Iowa, and was commissioned colonel January 8, 1863. He was "a slender, spare man, of great activity, and weighing about one hundred and forty pounds. He does not have the appearance of vigorous health; and yet, he is one of the hardiest men of my acquaintance. I have never known him to be sick. He has a small, restless, black eye, sunk well in his head, and wearing, at will, a most unfriendly leer. You would know, to look at him, that he was a sharp, shrewd man. He is sociable and agreeable, and would be generous and liberal, if he loved money less. 'Keep what you get' is his motto. He will do anything to accommodate a friend, except to disembowel his wallet, or put his property in peril, by attaching his name to a note or recognizance." Colonel Summers was mustered out of the army at Omaha on January 31, 1865. *Stuart,* p. 638.

Pages 85–86. Wilham Hakel, born in Prussia, had enlisted from Marengo, Iowa, on April 20, 1863. He was then twenty-one years old. Ware must have been pleased with the outcome of the affair Hakel. The report of the Iowa Adjutant General for 1864 says that Hakel was "accidently killed at Cottonwood Springs, N.T., October 14, '63." The Iowa Adjutant General's report published January 1, 1865, says that Hakel was killed "accidentally while loading his revolver," and the official Iowa history of the Civil War, the *Roster and Record of Iowa Soldiers in the War of the Rebellion,* Vol. IV (1910), reports him "accidentally killed."

Pages 86–87. John Ryan, born in Indiana, enlisted from Dubuque, April 11, 1863. He was twenty-one years old. Originally assigned to Company C, he was transferred to Company F, July 16, 1863, and deserted June 15, 1864. Ware describes the circumstances of Ryan's desertion on pages 195–97.

Pages 87–88. Robert McFarland had been born in Ireland and claimed Rock Island, Illinois, as his residence when he enlisted on December 12, 1863. He was, according to the official records, twenty-five years old. The official Iowa records also show that he deserted June 15, 1864, while stationed at Cottonwood Springs, Nebraska.

Page 89. Joseph Cooper was born in England and came west from Madison, Wisconsin, enlisting in the 7th on January 19, 1864. He was forty-five years old when he enlisted. He deserted December 26, 1865, at Fort Laramie.

John Jackson was born in Tennessee; when he enlisted on January 19, 1864, he said his residence was Dakota City, Nebraska. He was twenty-seven years old when he joined the 7th. Jackson deserted June 15, 1864, at Cottonwood Springs.

Page 90. Milo Lacey was twenty-two when he enlisted from Clayton County, Iowa, March 5, 1864. He was promoted company commissary sergeant October 2, 1864; company quartermaster sergeant July 6, 1865; first sergeant April 10, 1866. He was mustered out a little more than a month later at Fort Leavenworth.

CHAPTER X

Page 93. Corporal Thomas Forbush, a native of Virginia, joined the army from Muscatine, Iowa, when he was twenty-nine years of age. He was promoted eighth corporal September 5, 1863, and by successive promotions reached second corporal May 29, 1864. "Our great big Corporal Forbush" was discharged "because of wounds" at Julesburg, Colorado, on March 30, 1865.

Pages 93–95. The "Plantation Bitters" may have been the first of the well-known bitters after "Stoughton," but Hostetter's was by far the most popular and successful.

The original formula for Hostetter's Celebrated Stomach Bitters was a prescription by Dr. Jacob Hostetter, of Lancaster County, Pennsylvania. The man who made "Hostetter's" a byword, however, was his son, David, who advertised the product widely and soon made a fortune. The fact that the bitters were 47 per cent alcohol may have had something to do with their popularity.

Charles E. Young, who crossed the Plains in 1865, when asked what his wagon contained, ". . . crawled in, struck a match, and found a case labeled Hostetters' Bitters. Its ingredients were one drop of Bitters and the remainder, poor liquor. I soon found a case that had been opened, pulled out a bottle and sampled it. The old story came to me about the Irish saloon-keeper and his bartender. I called my Chum and asked him if Murphy was good for a drink, he replied, 'Has he got it?' 'He has?' 'He is then!' and we all were." *Dangers of the Trail,* p. 51.

On April 7, 1865, *Young,* stopping at Jack Morrow's ranch, noted that ". . . you may buy stacks of the 'Log-cabin' bottles of Drake's Plantation Bitters! There seems to be a vast consumption of these— for while, fortunately for the mental rest of the weary pilgrim, there are no rocks or other available surfaces on the Plains on which to paint the cabalistic 'S. T.—1860-x.' with which Drake's advertising fiends have covered so many of the picturesque points of the dear old Hudson river we have found the curiously-shaped empty bottles in such quantities in places along the road as, in Western parlance, to fairly 'blaze the trail.' "

An entertaining account of the Hostetters may be found in Stewart H. Holcomb, *The Golden Age of Quackery* (New York: Macmillan, 1959), pp. 157–66.

Pages 94–95. Charles Farrar Browne, better known as "Artemus Ward," was a famous humorist who first used his pen name in the *Cleveland Plain Dealer,* February 3, 1858. He was later on the staff of *Vanity Fair* and was successful as a lecturer. His books were *Artemus Ward: His Book* (1862), *Artemus Ward: His Travels* (1865). Ward was an uncompromising Union man, and it is well known that Lincoln particularly enjoyed his "High Handed Outrage in Utica."

Ward had been lecturing and visiting in California, Nevada, Idaho, and Utah, and after a lecture in Salt Lake City ("the theatre was crowded, but receipts were light") left for Denver on his way east. After a short stay in Denver, he continued his trip, reaching Julesburg, March 1, 1864. He wrote:

"Meals which have hitherto been $1.00 each, are now 75 cents. Eggs appear on the table occasionally, and we hear of chickens further on. Nine miles from here we enter Nebraska territory. Here is occasionally a fenced farm, and the ranches have bar-rooms. Buffalo skins and buffalo tongues are for sale at most of the stations. We reach South Platte on the 2d, and Fort Kearney on the 3d. The 7th Iowa Cavalry are here, under the command of Major Wood. At Cottonwood, a day's ride back, we had taken aboard Major O'Brien, commanding the troops there, and a very jovial warrior he is, too.

"Meals are now down to 50 cents, and a great deal better than when they were $1.00." *Artemus Ward: His Travels,* pp. 207–8.

Pages 95–97. George W. Heath, aged twenty-three, was appointed second lieutenant of Company G (not Company F) July 21, 1863, from Dubuque, Iowa. Earlier, April 23, 1861, he had enlisted in Company I, 1st Iowa Infantry, and been mustered out on August 21. Then, on December 29, 1861, he enlisted in Company L, 1st Iowa Cavalry, and was discharged from that regiment to accept a lieutenant's commission in the 7th Iowa Cavalry.

According to the official Iowa records, Lieutenant Heath was accidentally killed at Cottonwood Springs on March 21, 1864. He was succeeded by Lieutenant Everton and then by Job S. Beals of Newton, Iowa. Beals enlisted March 2, 1863 (at the age of twenty-one), as fourth sergeant, was promoted third sergeant July 27, 1863, and second lieutenant September 29, 1863. He was mustered out May 17, 1866, at Fort Leavenworth, Kansas.

The captain of Company G was Elisha Hammer, also from Newton, Iowa. He was appointed captain March 20, 1863 (at the age of thirty-five), and was mustered out July 17, 1865.

The first lieutenant of Company G was Joseph Bone, a native of Ohio who entered service from Homer, Iowa. He was appointed first lieutenant April 27, 1863 (aged thirty-three), and resigned September 28, 1864. He was succeeded by Charles E. Everton of Keithsburg, Illinois, who, at the age of twenty-eight, enlisted as second sergeant May 7, 1863. Everton was promoted first sergeant July 27, 1863, second lieutenant March 22, 1864, and first lieutenant September 29,

1864. He was mustered out May 17, 1866, at Fort Leavenworth, Kansas.

Pages 98–99. John Dillon and his wife had appeared at the Montana Theatre in Central City, Colorado, in the summer of 1863, among a "new troupe of celebrities from Europe." In Central City they were "widely heralded [as] new additions to the cast."

Curiously enough, an article by Emily O'Brien (Captain Nicolas J. O'Brien's wife) titled "Army Life at Fort Sedgwick, Colorado," repeats Ware's description of Dillon's visit almost verbatim, although the time then was 1867. Mrs. O'Brien's article appeared in *The Colorado Magazine,* VI (Sept., 1929): 173–78.

Page 99. Thomas J. Potter, born in Ohio, enlisted at age twenty-three from Ottumwa, Iowa, October 17, 1862, as first sergeant of Company A of the 7th Iowa. He was promoted sergeant major September 4, 1863, and transferred to the regimental staff. He was promoted second lieutenant of Company A, March 11, 1865, and first lieutenant November 14, 1865. He was mustered out at Fort Leavenworth, May 17, 1866.

Ware was mistaken about Potter's being president of the Union Pacific Railroad. He was with the Chicago, Burlington and Quincy Railroad for many years, rising from agent to vice-president and general manager. In May, 1887, he left the Burlington to become vice-president and general manager of the Union Pacific, remaining in this capacity until his death March 9, 1888.

Page 100. Captain Samuel M. Logan, commanding officer of Company B, 1st Colorado Cavalry, achieved local fame when he pulled down a Confederate flag raised over the general merchandise store of Wallingford and Murphy in Denver on April 24, 1861. It was the 1st Colorado Cavalry that had been responsible for stopping the Confederate advance up the Rio Grande Valley. The decisive battle was that of Glorieta, or Pigeon's Ranch, March 28, 1862, when a Union column, led by Major John M. Chivington, destroyed the Confederate supply train. See *Whitford.*

Page 100. In 1863 Ovando J. Hollister wrote *History of the First Regiment of Colorado Volunteers,* a book which is now exceedingly rare. It was reissued in 1949 by the Golden Press, Lakewood, Colorado, with an introduction by William MacLeod Raine and a new title: *Boldly They Rode.*

Page 100. The 11th Ohio Volunteer Cavalry, one of the most interesting but least publicized regiments of the Civil War, never served together in one place. The regiment was split up into smaller units, guarding and patrolling the overland trail.

"Companies A, B, C, and D of this Regiment were organized as the Seventh Ohio Volunteer Cavalry, but were consolidated December 19, 1861, with the Sixth Ohio Volunteer Cavalry, forming the First Battalion of that Regiment, the whole being then rendezvoused at Camp Dennison, Ohio. March 13, 1862, the First Battalion, under command of Lieutenant Colonel William O. Collins, was detached from the Sixth Ohio Volunteer Cavalry and ordered to report to General Halleck, at St. Louis, Mo., by whom it was ordered to proceed to Fort Laramie, D. T. (now Wyoming), where it arrived May 30, 1862, having marched overland from Fort Leavenworth, Kans., a distance of about 640 miles. During the summer of 1862, the Battalion was permanently detached from the Sixth Ohio Volunteer Cavalry and designated as the 'First Independent Battalion Ohio Volunteer Cavalry.' A Battalion of four companies (E, F, G, and H) was organized at Camps Dennison and Chase, Ohio, from June 26 to July 31, 1863, and the two Battalions were consolidated and designated the 'Eleventh Ohio Volunteer Cavalry.' The Second Battalion was called into service during John Morgan's raid through Ohio, and after the capture and dispersion of his force returned to Camp Dennison, O. Leaving Camp Dennison August 1, 1863, the Second Battalion reached Fort Leavenworth, Kans., on the 13th. While there awaiting supplies, the sacking and burning of the town of Lawrence, Kans., occurred, and the Battalion was sent in pursuit of Quantrill. After marching about 150 miles it was recalled, and, on September 2, proceeded across the plains for Fort Laramie, where it arrived October 10, 1863. Companies I, K, and L were organized June 30, 1864, at Fort Laramie, D. T., being composed of surplus recruits assigned to the Regiment. Companies A, B, C, and D were mustered out April 1, 1865, at Omaha, Neb., by reason of expiration of term of service. The remaining companies, being the last volunteer troops from Ohio, in service, were mustered out July 14, 1866, at Fort Leavenworth, Kans., by order of the War Department.

"The ground of the operations of this Regiment, which was never actually together during its term of service, was in the center of the Rocky Mountains and the then hostile Indian country, before the organization of the Territory of Wyoming, when nearly all that vast extent of territory was known as Dakota and Idaho. Its principal duty was to guard the Pacific Telegraph line and the overland route of communication and supply, extending from Colorado and western Nebraska and Kansas, through Wyoming and Idaho to Utah and Oregon. With the exception of Fort Laramie, the men of this Regiment erected and guarded all the military posts and stations established in 1864 and 1865, on the line of communication and supply indicated, to make the circuit of which required one thousand miles of travel. From March 1 to September 5, 1865, a single company of this Regiment erected five posts, guarded one hundred and fifty miles of Pacific Telegraph line, and its several detachments had thirteen engagements with Indians. Two companies, on an expedition to Powder and Tongue Rivers, took part in a charge upon and the burning of an Indian Village, marched twelve hundred miles and were out fifty-eight days."—*Official Roster of the Soldiers of the State of Ohio . . . 1861–1866*, XI: 547–48.

For a particularly interesting account of the regiment and its commanding officer and his son, see *Spring.*

Pages 100–01. Harry Dall was William Healey Dall, later to be a distinguished authority in the field of natural history. He succeeded Robert Kennicott as leader of the Western Union International Telegraph Expedition to Alaska. In 1870 Dall published *Alaska and Its Resources,* which was for many years the accepted authority; his greatest work, however, was done in the study of mollusks.

It was the telegraph company, rather than Secretary of State William H. Seward, that was responsible for Dall's going to Alaska.

Page 101. Samuel Findley Burtch, born in Ohio in 1828, went to Iowa in 1854, and later that year to Nebraska. He was the enrolling clerk of the lower house of the first Nebraska legislature. Later he moved to Sarpy County and held a variety of political positions. One man has commented that Burtch, although unmarried and without church affiliation, had "succeeded in living a moral, benevolent and generally useful life."

Pages 101–02. Sioux Lookout, some six miles northwest of Fort McPherson, is a high hill which affords a magnificent view of the surrounding country. On its crest there is now a statue of an Indian gazing out over the countryside.

CHAPTER XI

Pages 104–05. Bad Wound (Owashicha) was a southern Oglala Sioux chief of considerable distinction. He had been appointed by General William S. Harney to succeed Man-Afraid-of-His-Horse as head chief of the tribe. *Hyde* considers it likely that Bad Wound was killed June 14, 1865, when the Indians fought among themselves at the time of their attack upon Captain Fouts of Company D, 7th Iowa Cavalry.

Pages 105–06. General Robert Byington Mitchell was born in Ohio in 1823; after college he studied law and was admitted to the Ohio bar, practicing in Mansfield, Ohio. He served in the Mexican War as a second lieutenant, and then returned to his law practice for several years before migrating to Kansas in 1856. Elected to the legislature in 1857, he was a prominent Democrat and a delegate to the Charleston Convention.

After the outbreak of war he was named colonel of the 2nd Kansas and was badly wounded at the Battle of Wilson's Creek; he commanded, as a brigadier, the 9th Division at Perryville and soon was chief of cavalry of the Army of the Cumberland. He is credited with being responsible for much of that army's success. In 1864 he was sent west to the Department of Kansas and named commander of the District of Nebraska.

President Johnson appointed him governor of New Mexico, and he took office in July, 1866. His administration was marked by controversy, which culminated in his resignation in 1869. He died in

Washington, D.C., in 1882, best known for his energetic and excellent record as a Civil War officer. *DAB*

Page 107. Spotted Tail, a Brulé Teton Sioux Chief, was born near Fort Laramie about 1833. A warrior of proven ability, he participated in the annihilation of the Grattan command. He signed the April 29, 1868, treaty but refused to sell the mineral rights of the Black Hills. He stayed on the reservation during the 1876 campaign and was responsible for the surrender in 1877 of his cousin, Crazy Horse. Spotted Tail was killed by an Indian named Crow Dog in 1881 in South Dakota. In the years between 1876 and 1881 Spotted Tail had dominated the white agents at the Rose Bud Reservation in a futile attempt to preserve the status quo. His death made it easier for the agents to deal with the tribe, although they sorely missed his advice and influence.

His Indian name is given as Sinte-Galeshka in the *Hodge*.

Page 107. "Cooz" means coups, and is a French-Canadian term for a formal token or signal of victory in battle. There were three types of coups—killing an enemy, scalping an enemy, or being the first to strike an enemy either alive or dead. Most respected was touching a live enemy in battle, for this feat implied close combat. Stealing a horse was also a coup, as was striking a tipi in a hostile camp during a charge. Coups were counted in public, and scoring any kind of coup entitled the Indian to call himself a warrior. Red Cloud in 1891 boasted that he had counted coup eighty times.

Pages 107–08. Two Strike, a Brulé Sioux chief, was Spotted Tail's lieutenant. He was not a Miniconjou. In the later days at the agency, Two Strike stood with Spotted Tail for the status quo, and was by all accounts "a fighting man with little brain." He lived until 1914.

Pages 107–09. The great Siouan family of American Indians is broken down into the (1) Dakota tribes, (2) Assiniboin, (3) Upper Missouri tribes, (4) Lower Missouri tribes, and (5) the stragglers. The Sioux with whom Ware was in contact were from the Dakota tribes, and this group may be divided as (1) Eastern Dakota, (2) Santee-Dakota, (3) Teton-Dakota, and (4) Yankton. It is the Teton-Dakota and their subtribes that we are concerned with here, particularly the Brulé and the Oglala. (The Teton-Dakota subtribes are (1) Blackfeet, (2) Brulé, (3) Hunkpapa, (4) Miniconjou, (5) Oglala, (6) Sans Arc, and (7) Two Kettle.)

Ware's definition of Brulé is adequate. Oglala means "to scatter one's own" or, as an alternative, "village divided into many small bands." Ware is correct in saying that Lakota is the name the Teton Dakota applied to themselves; the Santee-Dakota called themselves Dakota.

See *Hodge* and *Hyde* for further information about the ethnology of these Indians.

Page 115. Woc-co-pom-any (Wakonpomny) Agency, or, more properly, the Upper Platte Agency, was located in Wyoming, about one mile west of the present town of Henry, Nebraska. It was on the south bank of the Platte, not far below Bordeaux' ranch, perhaps thirty-five miles east of Fort Laramie. *Hyde* says that Wakonpomny is from a bastard Sioux word referring to the handing out of gifts. Two of the prominent agents at this place were Thomas Twiss and John Loree; Loree was agent at this time.

Pages 115–16. The Smoky Hill trail ran from northeastern Kansas to Denver, Colorado. It ran from Atchison to the Fort Leavenworth– Fort Riley military road at Indianola (north of Topeka), thence through the Kansas River Valley to the Smoky Hill River Valley and west along that valley across Kansas to Colorado, proceeding north of Cheyenne Wells, Colorado, to Hugo and Limon and on west until it hit Cherry Creek, south of Denver. The trail could be reached by leaving the Santa Fe Trail at Council Grove, or—from Leavenworth and the Kansas City area—by going west until the road along the river valley was intersected. The present U. S. Highway 40 roughly parallels the Smoky Hill route.

The Smoky Hill route was used during the Pike's Peak gold rush in 1859, but a shortage of water and game caused many to name it "Starvation trail." It was shorter than the Platte River route to Denver, but frequently a high price was exacted for the number of miles that were saved.

The Leavenworth and Pike's Peak Express Company operated over the Smoky Hill route beginning May 17, 1859, but could not meet their expenses and sold out to Russell, Majors and Waddell. The Butterfield Overland Dispatch operated over this route first with freight and then in the fall of 1865 with passengers, but was forced to sell to Ben Holladay in 1866.

CHAPTER XII

Page 119. John K. Wright of Leavenworth and Junction City, Kansas, was mustered into the service February 2, 1864, as the second lieutenant of Company B, 16th Kansas Volunteer Cavalry. On October 1, 1864, he was promoted captain of the company. He was mustered out December 6, 1865.

After the war he entered political life and served as sheriff, probate judge, mayor; he was elected to three terms in the Kansas House and was a state senator (as Ware says), 1888–1892.

Page 119. Lieutenant Henry L. Rockwell was assistant commissary of subsistence, a staff officer of the 1st Colorado.

Pages 119–20. Captain Alfred de Watteville (or Wattewyl), a captain in the Swiss army, was on his way to visit Colonel Wilham O. Collins, commanding the 11th Ohio Volunteer Cavalry at Fort Laramie.

Colonel Collins had been collecting natural history materials for the Smithsonian Institution, and the Acting Consul General of Switzerland had asked Collins to allow Captain Watteville to join him to gain knowledge about the West and to collect natural history specimens. Colonel Collins agreed, and Captain Watteville traveled west, accompanied by Dr. Rudolph B. Hitz, who had been sent along by the Smithsonian Institution. *Spring*, p. 58.

Page 120. Lieutenant Colonel William Oliver Collins was the commanding officer of the 11th Ohio Volunteer Cavalry. Collins was born August 23, 1809, in Somers, Connecticut, and attended Amherst College, graduating in 1833. He was admitted to the Ohio bar September 9, 1835, in Hillsboro, Ohio where he was an active and successful attorney and a member of the Ohio State Senate. Appointed colonel of volunteer cavalry in 1861, his original command was the 1st Independent Battalion, Ohio Volunteer Cavalry. He was undoubtedly disappointed at being sent west to fight Indians rather than south to fight Confederates. An excellent officer, he tried to learn about and understand Indians and their problems.

The prosperous town of Fort Collins, Colorado, was named after Colonel Collins. On August 20, 1864, he ordered Camp Collins, then in the vicinity of La Porte, moved to the present location of the city. See *Spring*.

Collins returned to Ohio after his discharge in April, 1865. He resumed the practice of law and maintained a keen interest in public education and charitable work until his death October 26, 1880.

Page 120. Caspar Collins, red-headed son of Lieutenant Colonel William O. Collins, was born at Hillsboro, Ohio, September 30, 1844. Caspar accompanied the regiment west but returned to Ohio with his father in the summer of 1863 to recruit four more companies for the 11th. Caspar, then old enough, enlisted and was commissioned a second lieutenant June 30, 1863; he was assigned to Company G. On May 1, 1865, he was promoted first lieutenant and placed in temporary command of the company.

One of the important posts guarding the overland trail was located at Platte Bridge, where Casper, Wyoming, now stands. On July 26, 1865, Collins was ordered to the relief of a wagon train which was under attack some seventeen miles from Platte Bridge; he crossed the bridge and he and his twenty-five men were quickly attacked by Sioux, Cheyennes, and Arapahoes in overwhelming numbers. Lieutenant Collins after one charge ordered a retreat and took up the position of rear guard. He stopped to give aid to a wounded soldier, and his horse became unmanageable and ran away with him directly into a crowd of Indians. His mutilated body was found two days later. On November 21, 1865, Major General John Pope ordered that the post at Platte Bridge be named "Fort Casper" (*sic*), in honor of the lieutenant who "lost his life while gallantly attacking a superior force of Indians. . . ." Casper, Wyoming, named after Lieutenant

Caspar Collins, is located on the site of Platte Bridge station, and the passage of time has sanctioned the spelling mistake which changed an "a" into an "e." See *Spring*.

Page 120. The fiddler was Lieutenant Joseph Bone.

Page 121. Dr. James W. La Force (at age thirty-six) was appointed assistant surgeon on November 13, 1862. A former resident of Agency, Iowa, he resigned December 7, 1864.

James ("Jimmy") O'Brien (twenty-three years old) was another Irishman from Dubuque who was mustered into the service May 27, 1863, promoted to eighth corporal May 1, 1866, and sixteen days later was mustered out at Fort Leavenworth.

Pages 122–23. In 1864, at the time Ware writes of Mitchell, he was commanding officer of the District of Nebraska in the Department of Kansas, making his headquarters at Omaha. Although he may have spent more time out in the field than did his predecessors, the headquarters were at Omaha.

Page 122. John Pratt of Boston but living in Leavenworth, Kansas, enlisted first as sergeant major of the 2nd Regiment of Kansas Volunteers on May 14, 1861, and served until October 31. He re-enlisted November 11, 1861, as a first lieutenant and adjutant of the same regiment, and was promoted captain and assistant adjutant general of United States Volunteers on October 29, 1862. He was mustered out on December 19, 1865.

Page 126. Allen Ellsworth, for whom the town of Ellsworth, Kansas, is named, was born in Indiana. At age thirty-three he enlisted from Ashland, Iowa (November 14, 1862) as fourth sergeant of Company C. He was promoted second lieutenant of Company H, July 13, 1863, and was discharged from the army July 9, 1864. The official Iowa records do not indicate that Ellsworth was ever connected with Company G, as Ware states.

Page 126. Fort Riley, Kansas, located on the north bank of the Kansas River near the mouth of the Republican River, was built in 1853. The fort was an important frontier post, and soldiers stationed there helped to protect travelers and mail moving on the overland trail. Beginning in 1892, it was the cavalry and light artillery center for the entire U.S. Army. The fort was named after Major General Bennet Riley of Buffalo, New York. The 7th U. S. Cavalry was organized at the post in 1866 but left there 1867–1868 for campaigns to the north and west.

Page 126. Ira C. Schenck, born in New York, had been appointed second lieutenant March 6, 1863, while residing in Burlington, Iowa. He was then thirty-eight years old. Schenck was promoted first lieutenant August 20, 1864, and he resigned from the army November 22, 1865.

The author served on a court-martial with Lieutenant Schenck (see pages 208–14) without feeling it necessary to repeat or amplify his disparaging remarks.

The captain of Company C was Jonathan C. Mitchell, who entered service at the age of forty-one, from Agency, Iowa. He was appointed captain November 5, 1862, and, as Ware indicates, was dismissed August 19, 1864.

CHAPTER XIII

Pages 133–34. Jesse Howe, born in England, entered the army from Howard County, Iowa, when twenty-two years old. He enlisted March 9, 1863, as a first sergeant and was mustered out May 26, 1865, at Fort Leavenworth.

Page 134. The inspecting officer is presumed to be Major George Armstrong of Omaha. He enlisted January 14, 1864, as captain of Company A, 1st Battalion, Nebraska Veteran Volunteers, and was promoted major September 24 and transferred to the 1st Regiment, Nebraska Veteran Volunteers. He was appointed chief of cavalry of the District of the Plains, April 20, 1865, and mustered out of the service July 1, 1866.

Page 135. John Murphy, who had been born in Ireland, enlisted May 21, 1863, from his home in Hopkinton, Iowa; he was then nineteen years old. The "little young Irishman" with the "rich brogue" died of disease August 14, 1865, at Julesburg, Colorado. He is buried in the National Cemetery near old Fort Sedgwick.

CHAPTER XIV

Pages 139–40. On May 23, J. S. Maynard, the acting assistant adjutant general of Colorado, forwarded to Major E. W. Wynkoop at Fort Lyon, Colorado, this telegram from Major O'Brien at Cottonwood:

"Is there any of your command out after the Cheyennes? Reports here are that a whole company are engaged fighting 180 miles south of this post; nearly all killed."

Maynard also asked Major Wynkoop if this could be Lieutenant George Eayre's command that was hunting stock supposedly stolen by Cheyennes. Major Wynkoop replied the same day that he had not heard recently from Lieutenant Eayre, but would investigate.

On the 25th, Brigadier General Thomas J. McKean telegraphed that Eayre's detachment had been attacked by four hundred Cheyennes on the 16th, near Smoky Hill [River]. The Indians were driven from the field, with twenty-eight killed; the troops lost four killed and three wounded. According to *Grinnell,* the soldiers attacked the Indians;

according to Lieutenant Eayre, the Indians attacked the soldiers. See *Grinnell*, pp. 144–46; *O.R.*, Ser. I, Vol. 34, Pt. 4, pp. 14, 38–39, 55–56.

Page 140. The incident of the Confederate officers being killed by Osage Indians exists in several forms. *Monaghan* says that in May, 1863, Osage Indians massacred twenty-one men, mostly Confederate officers, who were supposedly in Montgomery County, Kansas, to recruit "wild" Indians to the Southern cause. *Colton*, using *Whitford* as one of his sources, says that the men killed early in 1862 were Confederates who were coming to Colorado to recruit a Southern regiment. Unnamed federal authorities sent a party of Osage Indian scouts in pursuit with orders to kill or capture the Confederates. The Indians killed them and brought back their heads as proof.

Pages 143–44. Whistler was an Oglala chief, not a Miniconjou. He was one of the leaders of the southern Oglalas who were generally friendly to the whites. Bad Wound was considered their head chief.

CHAPTER XVI

Pages 158–59. This battalion of Pawnees under North later accompanied General Mitchell and his command from Fort McPherson on the march to Fort Laramie; on their activities, see pages 165, 193–94. Ware says (page 190) that North could not control the Pawnees and that they were soon discharged but were reorganized in August at Fort Kearney with Joseph McFadden as captain and North as lieutenant. This second Pawnee scout organization served only until October before it, too, was disbanded, but according to Grinnell (*Two Great Indian Scouts*, pp. 53 ff.), North then was authorized to raise another Pawnee scouting force of one hundred men. It was this third unit that started North on his spectacular career. Grinnell's account of the earlier service is confusing and makes no mention of the fact that North had difficulty with the Indians.

Pages 158–59. On June 19, 1864, General Mitchell sent Major C. S. Charlot, the assistant adjutant general, Department of Kansas, the minutes of a council held June 8, 1864, with Brulé and Oglala Sioux.

Grinnell apparently assumes that the minutes were misdated. *Hyde* accepts the date June 8 as being correct, and in a footnote comments: "Eugene F. Ware in his book, *The Indian War of '64*, states that there were two councils and that General Mitchell was present. Ware, who was also present, asserts that Spotted Tail defied General Mitchell. These statements, and the dates given by Ware, do not agree with the official records."

Ware, of course, describes three councils (April 17, May 26, and July 19) at which the General was present, but on page 260, he refers to "*both* of General Mitchell's Indian councils" (italics added). According to the "minutes" of the June 8 council, the "Major commanding" spoke for the whites; while Ware reports that General Mitchell, not Major O'Brien, spoke at the second council for the whites. In the "minutes" are a number of errors—"Lord" for "Loree," "Henman" for "Hinman." No mention is made of any Pawnees being present.

Enclosed by Mitchell with the "minutes" is a report made June 10, 1864, to Major George M. O'Brien by two scouts who sign their names Alfred Gay and John W. Smith. They state that in accordance with instructions received from Major O'Brien on June 2, they scouted the Cheyenne country. The report is well written and may well be the work of Ware's "John Smith" and "Gray, or Hunter," reported to be on such a scout on pages 198–99.

General Mitchell could not have been at Cottonwood on April 16 and 17 since he was then ill in Omaha, but he could have been there on May 26 and July 19. Since Ware was often absent from the post in June, he may not have been a witness to the June 8 council conducted by O'Brien. See *Grinnell*, p. 151; *Hyde*, pp. 106–7; *O.R.*, Ser. I, Vol. 34, Pt. 4, pp. 458–62.

Page 165. Special Orders No. 66, Headquarters, District of Nebraska, July 14, 1864, ordered Major Wood to take two companies of the 7th Iowa to Fort Laramie.

Page 165. Captain William D. Fouts of Company D was born in Indiana, but enlisted from Albia, Iowa, at age forty-nine, being appointed captain November 18, 1862. Captain Fouts, with D Company and parts of Companies A and B, left Fort Laramie, June 11, 1865, to escort some 1,500 Sioux to Julesburg, Colorado. These Sioux had been friendly and were being moved south to get them out of the way and to place them where they could be more easily watched and controlled by the army. The Sioux, however, did not understand the reasons for this movement and regarded it as a "death march." The older chiefs—Little Thunder and Bad Wound—tried to restrain the younger men, but on June 14 firing broke out and Captain Fouts and three enlisted men were killed and four enlisted men wounded. The Indians were, at the same time, fighting among themselves, the younger men in favor of attacking the troops, the older men trying to prevent the attack. This action is called the "Battle of Horse Creek," and at least some blame must rest on Fouts's shoulders, since he was so certain that the Indians were peaceable that he refused to issue cartridges to his men; he also failed to disarm the Indians and to separate the warriors from the women and children.

CHAPTER XVIII

Pages 176–77. That Lincoln asked General Mitchell to hold a peace council with the Indians cannot be substantiated by any existing records. Nor can Ware's statements about the "preachers" urging Lincoln to allow religious denominations to control the various tribes be verified. During Grant's administration various religious denominations were given certain rights among certain tribes, but there is no reason to believe that Lincoln ever entertained such an idea.

Page 177. O'Fallon's Bluffs made a considerable impression on Charles E. Young in 1865: "O'Fallon's Bluffs (sic) was a point where the river ran to the very foot of the bluffs making it necessary for all of the trains to cross, then again strike Platte river trail at Alkali Creek. . . . The trail over the bluffs was of sand, and those heavily ladened, white-covered prairie schooners would often sink to the hubs, requiring from fifty to seventy five yoke of oxen to haul them across, often being compelled to double the leading yoke as far back as the wheelers, then doubling again, would start them on a trot, and with all in line and pulling together, would land the deeply sunken wheels on solid ground." *Dangers of the Trail,* p. 54.

Page 177. Morris passed the Bob Williams' ranch June 12, 1863, and commented on the "multitudes of sun-flowers" and on the Indian lodges near the ranch, noting that "one of the squaws was decked in a Paisley shawl!"

Clark, in 1860, mentioned that Williams' ranch was located at the foot of O'Fallon's Bluffs on the river bottom.

Pages 178–79. "Lone Star Ranche" had been kept in 1860 by two Frenchmen, Geroux (also Jereux) and Dion. It was between Bob Williams' ranch and the Lower California Crossing, according to *Clark.*

Page 179. "Ash Hollow," a familiar but precipitous section of the overland trail, was a deep canyon that led from the plateau to the bed of the North Platte. (See Ware's description, page 319.) It was named by Frémont for the ash trees which grew in the ravines. A few miles away is the site of the Battle of Blue Water Creek, or the Battle of Ash Hollow. Here on September 2, 1855, Colonel (later General) William S. Harney, leading a punitive expedition against the Sioux as a result of the Grattan fight, attacked and massacred a band of Brulé Sioux under Little Thunder. Some eighty-six Indians were killed in this affair—sometimes called "Harney's Massacre."

Page 180. Jules Beni has been described as a "sullen, bear-like French Canadian station master" who supposedly led a gang of outlaws and Indians in attacks upon the stage line that employed him. The stage company dismissed Beni and appointed Joseph A. (Jack) Slade superintendent, ordering him to put an end to the robberies. The Slade-Beni feud is a western classic—after Beni nearly killed Slade with a shotgun, Slade captured Beni near Fort Laramie, and was popularly supposed to have nailed him to a wall by his ears and, after killing him, to have carried his ears on his watch chain as a memento. It all makes a wonderful story although the bit about the ears is most likely not true.

"Jack" Slade was a man of extreme violence even in an era and country where violence was commonplace. He was finally discharged for drunkenness and was later hanged for his conduct by the vigilantes in Virginia City, Montana. Many legends of his fearless lawlessness and violence persist; in fact, Slade and Beni were more alike than unlike.

Page 181. Ben Holladay was born in 1820 and by the time he was nineteen, was clerking in a store in Weston, Missouri. There he tried his hand at the hotel, general store, drugstore, and packing businesses, and served as postmaster. During the Mexican War he entered the freighting business; his first independent venture, a train to Salt Lake City in 1849, netted him a large profit. Soon the business expanded as far as California, and Holladay became wealthy.

But Russell, Majors and Waddell (William Russell, Alexander Majors, and William B. Waddell) were the biggest freighters in the West throughout the 1850's. In 1859 they also began the overland transportation of passengers to handle immigrants bound for Colorado in the Gold Rush. They lacked capital for the new venture, however, and borrowed heavily from Holladay. They overexpanded and finally Holladay acquired the overland line on March 21, 1862.

Holladay dramatized himself, living the life of a dashing young prince. The trip that he was on when Ware saw him at Julesburg (page 423) was well publicized, and it took Holladay only twelve days and two hours to travel from San Francisco to Atchison, five days faster than the regular time.

Holladay kept the stages rolling under extremely difficult conditions: poor roads, bandits, bad weather, and the constant menace of Indian attack. Not only these hazards but the coming competition of the Union Pacific Railroad caused the "stage king" to consider selling the lines, and on November 1, 1866, he sold out to Wells, Fargo and Company. After quitting the stagecoach business he moved to Oregon and had various business ventures—a sawmill and a hotel, among others. He died July 7, 1887.

See *Frederick, Hafen,* and *Banning* for more detailed information.

Pages 181–82. There have been four "Julesburgs"—the first was Jules Beni's ranch, which became a pony express stop, then a stage station, and eventually a rough, tough small frontier community. This "old" Julesburg was destroyed in the Indian attack of January 7, 1865. Between 1864 and 1867 the second Julesburg flourished, but it was abandoned and moved to the other side of the river—the third Julesburg, one of the wildest of the Union Pacific construction camps and "the wickedest little city east of the Rockies." Gamblers, freighters, railroad men, soldiers, Indians, whores, all made Julesburg a violently picturesque settlement. The fourth and present Julesburg was founded in 1881 when the Union Pacific cutoff to Denver was envisioned.

CHAPTER XIX

Page 189. Julian R. Fitch entered the army as a private in 1861 but before the year had ended was a lieutenant in the 35th Ohio Infantry. He joined the signal corps in 1863 and in 1865 was brevetted first lieutenant and captain for distinguished service. He became a regular army officer in 1866 and rose to first lieutenant that year. His army career ended in 1873 when he was cashiered.

Page 191. "Jules' Stretch" was generally applied to the twenty-five miles of the overland trail north of Julesburg which went up Lodgepole Creek and over the high ground that separates the North and South Platte Rivers, ending on the North Platte west of Ash Hollow.

Pages 191–92. Mud Springs, about seven miles north of present Dalton, Nebraska, got its name because of a nearby buffalo wallow. The stage station there was attacked on February 5–6, 1865. Defended by hastily summoned units of the 11th Ohio Cavalry and part of Captain Fouts's Company D of the 7th Iowa Cavalry, the station was not captured, although the fighting was brisk, Colonel Collins pursued the Indians, and on the 8th fought them, with inconclusive results. According to Colonel Collins, the soldiers were outnumbered ten to one.

CHAPTER XX

Page 196. "Ficklin's" was named for Benjamin F. Ficklin, who was a director of the C. D. C. & P. P. Express Company and who handled the Salt Lake City section of the Pony Express. It was Ficklin who replaced Jules Beni with Jack Slade.

Page 197. Chimney Rock, near Chimney Rock, Nebraska, was a familiar landmark on the overland trail. Tradition has it that in 1827 Joshua Pilcher named this conical mound of reddish sandstone with a narrow shaft rising from its center. In 1842 John C. Frémont saw the rock and thought it looked like a factory chimney. Travelers inevitably commented on the unusual formation so that it became a well-known curiosity and check point. It stands about 350 feet above the river bed, and the shaft is approximately 150 feet tall—as opposed to Ware's estimates of 300 and 85 feet on pages 309–10.

Page 197. It is difficult to know who "Major Underhill" was, since the 11th Ohio Volunteer Cavalry had no such officer. The only officer named Underhill in the regiment was George C. Underhill, the regimental surgeon.

Captain Jacob S. Shuman commanded Company H, 11th Ohio Volunteer Cavalry. He had entered the army on August 2, 1863 (age thirty-seven), for three years' service, and was mustered out with the rest of his company on July 14, 1866, at Fort Leavenworth, Kansas. Company H was one of the last companies from Ohio to be discharged.

Captain Henry L. Koehne had enlisted at age thirty-two as a private October 23, 1861. He was promoted first lieutenant November 21 that year, made captain of Company A, March 13, 1863, and mustered out April 1, 1865, at Omaha, Nebraska.

Captain Levi G. Marshall had been appointed captain of Company E eight days after he enlisted on May 21, 1863. He was then thirty-two. He was promoted major on May 1, 1865, and resigned from the army March 1, 1866.

Page 197. Scott's Bluff, a butte of dominating height northwest up the river from Chimney and Court House rocks, stretches southwest from the North Platte River and reaches a height of 750 feet above the river. It was a landmark mentioned by many travelers. The city of Scottsbluff, Nebraska, is on the other side (the north side) of the river, across from the bluff.

Page 197. Fort Laramie, located at the junction of the Laramie and North Platte Rivers, was founded in 1834 by Robert Campbell and William L. Subtlette as a trading post called Fort William. It was sold in 1835 and again shortly afterward to the American Fur Company, which enlarged it and called the post Fort John. John C. Frémont recommended that the government purchase the post, and this was done in 1849. "Fort Laramie" as it was popularly called was a rendezvous for Indians, trappers, and traders, and a stopping place on the overland trail. Fort Laramie was one of the most important posts ever built in the West, and troops were stationed there until 1890.

Pages 197–99. James Bordeaux, a French trader and bourgeois for the American Fur Company, was described by many travelers—among others, John C. Frémont in 1842 (he said Bordeaux was short, stout and blustery) and Francis Parkman ("inflated with his transient authority"). Bordeaux served as a guide with Jim Bridger and was a witness to the Grattan massacre; only his friendship with the Indians and the fact of his Indian wife saved him from Grattan's fate. Bordeaux' "ranch" was some nine miles east of Fort Laramie on the south side of the Platte.

Page 199. The firm of Bullock and Ward, sutlers at Fort Laramie, was familiar to many travelers. Colonel William G. Bullock had been early on the trail and in 1868 was responsible for bringing the first permanent range herd to Wyoming. Bullock, a Virginian, had come to Fort Laramie in 1858 to join Seth E. Ward; he stayed with Ward until 1871.

Seth E. Ward was sutler at Fort Laramie from 1857 to August 2, 1867, after which he was post trader until August, 1871. Ward, too, was a Virginian and before coming to Fort Laramie had been a trader at Sand Point, at the foot of Register Cliff. An interesting description of Ward exists:

"We modestly approached the pompous Mr. Ward, who we were told was the sutler. He wore fine clothes, and a soft, easy hat. A huge diamond glittered in his shirt front. He moved quietly around as if he were master of the situation, and with that peculiar air so often affected by men who are financially prosperous and self-satisfied. He

seemed to be a good fellow and was in every respect courteous. . . ."
J. C. Birge, *The Awakening of the Desert*, pp. 178–79. Boston: R. G.
Badger, 1912, as quoted in *Ft. Laramie*, p. 349. See also *Mattes.*

Pages 200–01. The buffalo berry, which was also called the "bull-
berry," was harvested by the women and children after the first frost.
The buffalo berry came from one of two silvery-foliaged shrubs, Shep-
herdia Argentia or S. Canadensis. These berries were widely used
by the Indians in the preparation of what one authority has called
the "original K-ration," pemmican. Ware's description of pemmican
could be better: dried meat was mixed with berries or plums, wal-
nuts or pecans, or any combination of these fruits, and then thoroughly pounded and partially dried. It was stored either in a large
intestine or in a parfleche bag; these containers were sometimes sealed
with melted tallow. Under ordinary conditions, pemmican would keep
for long periods of time.

Pages 200–01. A parfleche was a container made from a single
piece of hide, usually from the buffalo. The hide was soaked and
pegged to the ground, hair side down; the outline of the parfleche
was sketched in and any desired decorations painted on. The hair
was then removed, the parfleche cut out of the hide and folded like
an envelope; holes were made for the ties. Frequently parfleches were
made in pairs, to be used like saddlebags, one on each side of the
horse.

Page 201. Julius (Jules) Ecoffey was a native of Switzerland, educated at the University of Freiburg. He was a stage station operator,
cattleman, and Indian trader. Ecoffey, whom *Hyde* considers to have
been a true friend of the famous Red Cloud, was the trader at the
Upper Platte Agency, with his own buildings and goods on the agency
grounds. He is supposed to have been killed by outlaws in 1876.

Pages 201–04. James Bridger, equally famous in fact and fiction.
Born March 17, 1804, in Richmond, Virginia, he moved with his
family to a farm near St. Louis in 1812, and Bridger left that place
with William H. Ashley and Major Andrew Henry to ascend the
Missouri River to trap furs. Bridger spent the rest of his life in the
West, trapping, exploring, trading, scouting, and spinning yarns. He
is credited with discovering the great Salt Lake and was one of the
first to enter Yellowstone and to describe it accurately. He knew
all the early mountain men and was deeply involved in the "Mormon
War" of 1857; on occasion he was employed as a scout by the army.
His biographer says that Bridger "probably better than any other
man, typified the western frontiersman, and faithfully personified the
spirit of the old West."

He was employed as a guide August 18–31, 1864, and then went
east, only to be recalled by General Dodge to scout for the Powder
River expedition of 1865. He died July 17, 1881, and is buried at
Kansas City, Missouri.

His story-telling proclivities are well known; Jim Bridger loved to tell tall tales to credulous emigrants. The "bear" story (see pages 296–97) is famous. See *Alter* and *Vestal* for biographical information.

Page 202. Leo Palladie (also Pallardy and Pallady) was a well-known frontier figure. Colonel William O. Collins of the 11th Ohio Volunteer Cavalry, in a letter of May 27, 1862, said this of Palladie:

"I have employed an excellent interpreter whom I intend to keep permanently if the Government will pay him. His name is Leo Pallardy, a Frenchman, or rather of French parentage, born in St. Louis, raised in St. Charles, Missouri, and for the last seventeen years a resident among the Indians and agent and trader. He was interpreter for General Harney and also for the Sioux chiefs at Washington City on a visit to the President a few years ago. He is about 32, a very good scholar, a capital hunter (he brought in an antelope yesterday) and thoroughly acquainted with the country and the Indians from the Rocky Mountains to the Missouri. His dress is a black buckskin hunting coat, highly ornamented, and light buckskin pantaloons with moccasins. He occupies the tent with Caspar [Collins' son] and myself and makes himself generally useful in packing, unpacking, loading, etc. etc." *Spring*, pp. 109–10.

CHAPTER XXI

Pages 210–11. Major Thomas S. Twiss came to Fort Laramie as Indian agent in August, 1855, and held this job until 1861. He was a West Point graduate and an army officer of ability. Twiss was in charge of the Brulés and Oglalas of the upper Platte. *Hyde* charges that he moved his Indians to areas where they could be attacked by troops both in 1855 and in 1857; that he attempted to obtain government funds by misrepresentation, and (quoting Sir Richard Burton) that he spent most of his time with a pet bear and his Oglala girl. After he was removed from office by Lincoln, Twiss took his Indian wife and joined the Oglalas living in the Powder River region. Hyde says further that no one knows where he died, and that in the 1930's many Oglalas named Twiss were still living.

It should be mentioned that a more sympathetic view of Twiss suggests that his Indian policy was humanitarian and that Twiss was often at cross-purposes with the military. See Alban W. Hoopes, "Thomas S. Twiss, Indian Agent on the Upper Platte, 1855–1861," *Mississippi Valley Historical Review*, XX (December, 1933): 353–64.

Page 216. Captain Jacob S. Shuman of Company H, 11th Ohio Volunteer Cavalry, established a fort originally named Camp Shuman, and later Fort Mitchell, on the south side of the North Platte just north of the bluffs.

CHAPTER XXII

Page 218. Presumably by "Horse Creek Treaty" Ware refers to what has been called the "largest assembly of Indians in American history." Some ten thousand Indians—Sioux, Crow, Shoshone, Cheyennes, Assiniboin, Arapahoes, Blackfeet, Gros Ventre, Arikari and Mandan— met near the junction of the North Platte and Horse Creek beginning September 8, 1851. The treaty which followed this council is called the First Treaty of Fort Laramie. It supposedly, among other things, put an end to intertribal warfare and provided for safe passage of wagon trains along the Platte.

Page 219. John Loree, the agent at Fort Laramie (born in Ohio but appointed from Indiana), was not a favorite of the Brulés and southern Oglalas; his main efforts were spent with the friendly Indians (*Hyde* calls them "loafers") who stayed close to Fort Laramie. According to *Hyde* the "Sioux south of the Platte and those up on Powder River hated him, openly calling him a thief and complaining that he gave trading licenses to only a few of his favorites and permitted them to charge high prices for the poorest of goods."

Page 218. On August 18, 1854, Lieutenant John L. Grattan was sent from Fort Laramie to arrest the Indian (or Indians) who had killed a lame cow which had straggled far behind a Mormon wagon train. Lieutenant Grattan entered the Sioux camp and let matters get out of hand. Apparently he opened fire with two cannons, and the Sioux retaliated by killing the lieutenant and his twenty-eight men. The fight took place near Bordeaux' ranch, about two miles from what is now Lingle, Wyoming. See *Ft. Laramie,* pp. 221–45.

Pages 219–20. William Ellsworth was first lieutenant of Company H, 11th Ohio Volunteer Cavalry. Ellsworth, at age twenty-seven, enlisted August 2, 1863, for three years of service; on September 16 of that year he was appointed first lieutenant, and on May 1, 1865, he was promoted captain of Company E.

Lieutenant Ellsworth was a principal participant in the fighting in and around the Mud Springs station, February 6–7, 1865. From all accounts, he seems to have been a very capable officer.

Pages 220–22. "Shad-blow" was George W. Marsh, a native of Pennsylvania who enlisted from Mount Pleasant, Iowa, September 23, 1861, and became a bugler in Company C, 4th Iowa Cavalry. He was then nineteen. Marsh was promoted chief bugler and transferred to the noncommissioned staff of the regiment on May 23, 1862. He was mustered out at Helena, Arkansas, October 25, 1862. Bugler Marsh, Sergeant Houghton, and the author were mustered out following the publication September 6, 1862, of General Order 126 of the War Department, Adjutant General's Office. This general order reorganized infantry, cavalry, and artillery regiments, abolishing the positions which these men held on the battalion staff; since their jobs no longer existed in the new regimental organization, they were mustered out of the service.

On June 22, 1863, Marsh enlisted for three years' service in Company H, 11th Ohio Volunteer Cavalry, as first sergeant. On October 30, 1865, he was promoted second lieutenant of Company E. He was mustered out July 14, 1866, with the rest of his company.

Page 221. Edward F. Houghton, a native of New York, enlisted in Company H, 4th Iowa Cavalry, January 1, 1862, and was immediately transferred to Company C. He was promoted 2nd Battalion sergeant major on January 15, 1862, and mustered out at Helena, Arkansas, the same day Ware was, October 25, 1862.

CHAPTER XXIII

Pages 235–36. The fortification at Samuel D. Bancroft's ranch, one mile west of Julesburg, was named Fort Sedgwick after Civil War General John Sedgwick. It was not abandoned until 1871.

Page 238. Major John S. Fillmore, born in New York, was an additional paymaster of volunteers from Colorado, August 26, 1861–July 1, 1862; on November 8, 1862, he was reappointed. Major Fillmore died on Christmas Day, 1864, a little more than two months after Ware met him.

Pages 239–40. Dr. J. F. Wisely was an acting assistant surgeon in the Army Medical Department from May 17, 1864. Assigned to the Department of the Missouri in 1865, Dr. Wisely is not identified with any specific regiment.

CHAPTER XXIV

Page 242. The Colonel G. P. Beauvais ranch (sometimes called "Star Ranch") was well known to travelers. Beauvais was an old American Fur Company man. In 1867 he was made a member of the Sanborn-Sully Commission to investigate the Indian troubles, and in 1875 he was a member of the Allison Commission which had been created for the purpose of buying the Black Hills from the Sioux.

Morris commented, June 14, 1863: ". . . we come to 'Star Ranche' or 'California crossing,' where was an excellent store belonging to Mr. Beauvais, a man who had accumulated a large fortune in the Indian trade. The ranche was kept by a half-caste young man of pleasant manners and appearance, who gave us a little music. I think I heard that Mr. Beauvais, like many of the trappers and rancheros here, had wandered down from the neighborhood of Montreal. Prices here ranged very high. Corn was 2 dolls. 80 cents per bushel, and sugar, from 12 cents at St. Joe, had mounted up to 40 cents."

On April 10, 1863, *Young* stopped at the Beauvais ranch, where ". . . there is quite a settlement about the old ranche—one big 'doby' storehouse, with three or four small 'dobys' alongside, and across the road a barrack for a small garrison now stationed here. We are given one of the small 'dobys,' which we enter by a doorway four feet high, and which has about twenty feet of depth to its ten feet of width."

Page 242. Lieutenant John K. Rankin had been a member of the 2nd Kansas, and was on Mitchell's staff at Perryville and in the Middle Tennessee and Chickamauga campaigns. He was frequently assigned as acting assistant adjutant general. He was promoted to the military staff of Kansas Governor Samuel J. Crawford, February 18, 1865, with the title of paymaster general and the rank of colonel.

Page 242. This may have been John Talbot, first lieutenant of Company A, 1st Battalion, Nebraska Veteran Volunteers. Talbot was appointed at age thirty-one from Omaha on September 24, 1864. He was transferred to Company I, 1st Regiment, Nebraska Volunteers, July 10, 1865, and mustered out July 1, 1866.

Pages 244–45. Colonel George Laird Shoup, the "rollicking gentleman," was born in Pennsylvania in 1836 and moved to Colorado in 1859. After the war he settled in Idaho and became a member of the Territorial House (1874), governor of the territory, and first governor of the state; he was United States senator from Idaho, 1890–1901. *Biog. Dir. Am. Cong.*

Page 248. The two men in the ambulance were John Lynch and William Reaucleau (or Reauleau). Lynch was twenty-one when he enlisted as a private October 31, 1861; he was mustered out April 1, 1865. Reaucleau enlisted at age twenty-six on January 1, 1863, and was mustered out at Denver, December 31, 1865.

Pages 250–51. Albert Sidney Johnston, born in Washington, Kentucky, February 3, 1803, was graduated from West Point in 1826. He became very friendly while at the Military Academy with Jefferson Davis, served in the Black Hawk and Mexican Wars (with time out to help Texas break free of Mexico), and led the ill-fated campaign against the Mormons in 1857–1858. He resigned from the army April 9, 1861, to cast his lot with the Confederacy. An extremely talented officer, he was offered the command in the West by President Davis, and accepted. General Johnston was killed at the Battle of Shiloh, April 6, 1862. Albert Sidney Johnston was the best general officer the Confederates had in the West; only Generals Joseph E. Johnston and Nathan Bedford Forrest proved to be as able.

CHAPTER XXV

Pages 257–58. Lieutenant Boyd was apparently Second Lieutenant George H. Boyd of Company H, 11th Ohio Volunteer Cavalry. He had enlisted for three years of service on June 15, 1863, at age twenty-two, and on July 31, 1863, had been appointed second lieutenant.

The Roster of Ohio Soldiers, Volume II, does not record the manner or the date Boyd left the army.

Page 260. Davis Lippincott enlisted March 15, 1863, from West Union, Iowa. He was twenty-three years old and had been born in Ohio. He was promoted seventh corporal July 29, 1863, and moved through the grades of corporal until he was made first corporal April 27, 1864. Corporal Lippincott was killed in the January 7, 1865, Indian attack on Julesburg, Colorado.

Page 261. "Sheldon" would have been George N. *Shelden,* an Illinoisan who enlisted from Davenport, Iowa, July 1, 1863. He was then nineteen years old. Shelden was mustered out May 17, 1866, at Fort Leavenworth, Kansas. The "brave little fellow Stephenson" was John Stephenson, who was eighteen when he enlisted from Muscatine, Iowa, on July 20, 1863. He was promoted sixth corporal May 1, 1866, just sixteen days prior to his muster-out at Fort Leavenworth.

CHAPTER XXVI

Pages 267–68. It is probably worth noting that McCellan was also the candidate of all the sincere War Democrats and that he repudiated the antiwar planks of the Democratic platform. The height of passion fanned into flame by the war made it possible for dedicated Republicans like Ware to believe that all Democrats were traitors. There was no understanding of what may be called "loyal opposition."

Page 268. Marcus Mills "Brick" Pomeroy was the outspoken publisher of the *La Crosse* (not Prairie du Chien) *Democrat;* whether or not his opposition to Lincoln and war constituted sedition is perhaps a matter of opinion. Pomeroy loved controversy and was an expert propagandist and pamphleteer. He later published papers in New York and Chicago and became wealthy through promotion of the Atlantic-Pacific Railway Tunnel. Pomeroy was nationally known for his belligerency and for his support of unpopular causes. In a period when political sentiment was extreme, it was easy to dislike him. *DAB*

Page 268. General Sterling Price moved toward Kansas City in 1864; he was opposed by Union forces under General Samuel R. Curtis. At Lexington, Missouri, on October 18, the Confederates forced the Union troops back to Independence. In the fighting that followed along the Big Blue and culminated in the Battle of Westport, October 23, 1864, the Union soldiers beat off the Confederates, forced them into a hasty retreat, and pursued Price to the Arkansas River. This was the last important action in the West during the Civil War.

CHAPTER XXVII

Page 280. The 1st Colorado Cavalry saved New Mexico by their actions in the Battle of Glorieta, March 28, 1862. They were the deciding factor in the victory which saw the invading Confederate column stopped and forced to retreat down the Rio Grande Valley.

Page 283. Adolphus Donley, age forty, had enlisted February 1, 1863, as a wagoner. He was born in Ohio and resided in Barclay. He was mustered out at Fort Leavenworth, May 17, 1866, spelling his name "Donely."

CHAPTER XXVIII

Page 288. Major General Patrick Edward Connor, born in County Kerry, Ireland, on Saint Patrick's Day, 1820, had been a regular army man. He served in the Mexican War in Albert Sidney Johnston's regiment and then emigrated to California. In 1861 he was appointed colonel of the 3rd California Infantry and in 1862 was sent to protect the Overland trail in Utah and Nevada Territories, with headquarters at Salt Lake City. He did a good job of policing the trail, and General Henry W. Halleck ordered him to protect the trail between Salt Lake City and Fort Kearney. In November, 1864, Connor went by stage to Denver to examine personally the trail he had been ordered to guard. When the District of the Plains was created March 28, 1865, Connor was named commander. For detailed information about Connor, see *Rogers.*

Pages 289–94. George Quayle Cannon was a distinguished member of the Mormon Church. Born in England, he came to the United States in 1842 and settled at Nauvoo, Illinois, which he left in the exodus to Salt Lake City in 1847. During his busy life he was editor of the *Deseret News,* chancellor of Deseret University, a director of the Union Pacific Railroad, and a member of Congress for four terms. Cannon died in California in 1801. *DAB*

Page 294. Alkali Lake stage station was located about ten miles east of the present town of Ogallala, Nebraska. There was a post office at Alkali as well as a telegrapher. The station was raided on October 28, 1865, the Indians destroying considerable property and killing four men. General Herman H. Heath led troops in pursuit, eventually killing twenty-nine of the raiders. *Frederick*

Pages 293–94. Frank Jenne Cannon, son of George Q. Cannon (see page 399), was born in Salt Lake in 1859 and worked as a newsman, becoming editor of the *Ogden Herald* in 1887. He was interested in local politics and, as Ware says, did attend the National Republican Convention in Minneapolis in 1892 as a delegate from Utah Territory. He was elected senator from Utah in 1896, serving until 1899; throughout the rest of his active career, he continued his interest in politics and editorial affairs. He died in Denver in 1933. *DAB*

CHAPTER XXIX

Page 298. After Sherman captured Atlanta, the Confederate Army, led by General John B. Hood, moved to attack the Union supply lines and to invade Tennessee. Sherman let them go, after detaching two corps to General George H. Thomas, the officer charged with defending Tennessee. At Franklin, Tennessee, on November 30, Hood attacked Schofield and suffered a bloody repulse; on December 15–16, Thomas attacked and decisively defeated Hood in the Battle of Nashville; it must have been the news of this Union victory that reached Ware on December 20, 1864.

Page 304. John M. Pierce, the self-acknowledged captive of the Sioux, enlisted in the 7th Iowa Cavalry, November 25, 1864. The official Iowa records state that his enlistment application had not been received at the time of his death on January 7, 1865, at Julesburg, Colorado, during the great Indian raid on that town. A diligent search of the extant records of McDonough County, Illinois (where Blandinsville is located), leaves Private Pierce as much a mystery today as he was to our author.

Pages 305–06. The captivities of both Mrs. Fanny Kelly and Mrs. Sarah Larimer are well known since both ladies wrote popular books about their experiences. They were captured near what is now Glenrock, Wyoming, July 12, 1864, and were released after some six months of captivity. No one described in either book can be identified as John M. Pierce.

Page 306. Idaho Territory—including present Montana, Wyoming, and Idaho—was created March 3, 1863; prior to that time Fort Laramie had been in Nebraska Territory, May 30, 1854–March 3, 1863. Wyoming Territory was created July 25, 1868, and Wyoming was admitted as a state July 10, 1890. Ware was correct in saying that Fort Laramie was in Idaho Territory in 1864.

CHAPTER XXX

Page 308. Fort Lyon, on the Republican River in southeastern Colorado, was built by William Bent in 1853 and leased to the government in 1859. It was named successively Fort Fauntleroy, Fort Wise, and finally Fort Lyon (after General Nathaniel Lyon, killed at the Battle of Wilson's Creek). This fort was abandoned in 1866 after the river began cutting away the bank, and another Fort Lyon was built twenty miles upstream.

Pages 309–10. Ware's description of the command hierarchy of the "Department of Kansas and the Territories" is accurate.

Page 310. Robert R. Livingston, thirty-five years old and from Plattsmouth, Nebraska, was mustered in as captain of Company A, 1st Regiment, Nebraska Volunteers, June 11, 1861. He was promoted major January 1, 1862, lieutenant colonel April 22, 1862, and colonel October 4, 1862. Colonel Livingston was mustered out per S.O. 83, A.G.O., 1865.

Page 309. Samuel R. Curtis was the first general officer appointed from Iowa. He was born February 3, 1807, in New York State, was graduated from West Point in 1831, studied law and practiced both civil engineering and law, and served as colonel of the 3rd Ohio Volunteer Infantry in Mexico. When the Mexican War was over, he went to Iowa and continued his career as an engineer-lawyer; in 1856 he was elected to Congress from the 1st Iowa district and was re-elected in 1858 and 1860. In Congress he was known chiefly for advocating a railroad to the Pacific. On June 1, 1861, he was elected colonel of the 2nd Iowa Infantry and commanded in Missouri and Arkansas, fighting bravely at the Battle of Pea Ridge. On September 19, 1862, he was placed in command of the Department of the Missouri, from which he was later removed by Lincoln primarily for political reasons. But Lincoln then assigned him to command the Department of Kansas on January 1, 1864, and Curtis is given credit for turning back Price's attempt to capture Kansas City in October of that year. He later commanded the Department of the Northwest, with headquarters in Milwaukee. He is regarded as one of the better political generals. *Stuart* has sketch, pp. 35–50.

CHAPTER XXXI

Page 318. Eugene S. Sheffield (age eighteen), a native of Indiana, had enlisted from Ottumwa, Iowa, October 1, 1861, as fifth sergeant of Company D, 15th Iowa Infantry. He was promoted second sergeant July 1, 1862, and discharged for promotion to adjutant of the 7th Iowa Cavalry on March 4, 1863. Adjutant Sheffield resigned from the army July 20, 1865.

Pages 321–22. The ten men who rode with Ware from O'Fallon's Bluffs to Cottonwood Springs were from Company B, 7th Iowa Cavalry. John Wilcox, who commanded the company, first enlisted (when thirty-six years old and living at Eddyville, Iowa) as fifth corporal of Company I, 7th Iowa Infantry, on July 24, 1861. He was promoted fifth sergeant and fourth sergeant on the same day, October 18, 1861. He was slightly wounded in the arm at the Battle of Belmont. Wilcox was promoted second lieutenant November 22, 1861, and resigned September 26, 1862. A few weeks later (October 18) he was appointed captain of Company B, 7th Iowa Cavalry; in November, 1865, he was promoted 3rd Battalion major and was finally mustered out of the service May 17, 1866, at Fort Leavenworth.

CHAPTER XXXII

Page 325. Bluford Starkey, age eighteen, enlisted from Davenport, Iowa, July 6, 1863. He was killed in action September 8, 1864, near Fort McPherson and is buried in the Fort McPherson National Cemetery.

Page 330. Charles A. Thompson, then twenty-three years old and from Omaha, was mustered in as a corporal in Company K, 1st Regiment, Nebraska Volunteers, July 21, 1861, promoted regimental commissary sergeant January 18, 1862, and first lieutenant and regimental quartermaster May 19, 1862. He was mustered out per G.O. 83, War Department, A.G.O., 1865.

Pages 332–33. The 1st Regiment, Nebraska Volunteers, was mustered in as infantry at Omaha in June and July, 1861. The regiment was mounted October 11, 1863, and their designation was changed November 6, 1863, to 1st Nebraska Cavalry. The regiment was remustered as veteran volunteers at Omaha on July 22, 1864. The 1st Nebraska Veteran Volunteer Cavalry was mustered out in Omaha on July 1, 1866.

After a number of rather minor actions, the 1st Nebraska was at Fort Donelson, Fort Henry and the Battle of Shiloh; at Corinth and in Arkansas, Mississippi, and Missouri. After the veterans returned from a furlough, June 10–August 13, 1864, the regiment left Omaha for Fort Kearney, arriving there August 23.

CHAPTER XXXIV

Page 355. Thomas J. Majors ("commanding detachments"), from Mt. Vernon, Nebraska, was mustered in as first lieutenant of Company C, 1st Regiment, Nebraska Volunteers, June 15, 1861. He was then twenty-four years old. He was promoted captain January 5, 1862, and major May 1, 1864. Major Majors was mustered out of the service July 1, 1866.

Page 355. Edward B. Murphy, a Canadian, was twenty-seven years old when he was appointed first lieutenant of Company A from Ottumwa, September 12, 1862. He was promoted captain July 8, 1863, and resigned from the army December 23, 1865. Captain Murphy was known for his aggressiveness, and the regimental commander is recorded as saying that he considered him one of the best officers in the 7th.

Page 355. Captain Isaac Wiles's Company B, of the 1st Regiment, 2nd Brigade, Nebraska Militia, was mustered into state service for four months at Plattsmouth, Nebraska, September 9, 1864. The company was mustered out February 13, 1865.

Captain Alvin G. White's Company C, of the 1st Regiment, 2nd Brigade, Nebraska Militia, was mustered into state service for four months at Pawnee City, Nebraska, September 22, 1864. The company was mustered out February 6, 1865.

Pages 355–57. Ware not only greatly overestimates the extent and damage done by the prairie fire, but incorrectly credits General Mitchell with developing the idea. The credit should go to Colonel Livingston, for the idea was his.

CHAPTER XXXV

Page 360. Andrew S. Hughes was one of the pioneers in the service of the Overland Stage Company, joining the company in July, 1861. He was the son of General Bela M. Hughes, general counsel for the company. General Hughes sent his son back East to college in 1862–1863, but from that time on Andrew Hughes was associated with western transportation. After the stage companies were superseded by the railroads, he worked for the D.S.P. & P.R.R. and the D. & R.G.R.R.

It is not possible to identify "Clift," although he might possibly have been Charles Clift, who began as a pony express rider when only seventeen years old and who was well known along the Platte.

Page 360. The singer of the Sioux war song was James G. Smith, a Virginian who was appointed second lieutenant of Company A, September 12, 1862, while living in Ioka, Iowa. He was then forty-one years old. On July 8, 1863, he was promoted first lieutenant, resigning with that rank October 9, 1865.

Pages 362–63. How Ware confirmed his suspicion about the well-armed Indian's being a Confederate emissary from Indian Territory is not explained. Like most of those involved in fighting Indians in 1864–1865, he saw a Confederate behind each bush and each Indian raid as inspired by agents direct from Richmond.

CHAPTER XXXVII

Page 380. Thomas J. Weatherwax, thirty-two years old, enlisted from Omaha on June 30, 1861, as first sergeant of Company G, 1st Regiment, Nebraska Volunteers. He was later promoted second lieutenant, retroactive to June 30, 1861; promoted first lieutenant October 30, 1861, and captain September 2, 1862. Captain Weatherwax was mustered out July 1, 1866.

Page 391. Lillian Springs was another place familiar to those who traveled west.

Morris, stopping here June 16, 1863, reported: "At this ranche I felt convinced, by a fence and saw, that an Englishman or Irishman had been at work, so I went in and found it tenanted by a North of Ireland man; he had left a good farm in Illinois on account of the war, which he disapproved of, and, as he considered talking a thirsty process, he insisted in my joining him in some whiskey, modified by a cordial much approved of, I believe, called the 'good Samaritan.' I had my fears as to the results, but they proved groundless."

CHAPTER XXXVIII

Pages 395–96. Fort McPherson National Cemetery is located some four miles south of Maxwell, Nebraska, and was originally the burial ground of the fort. It was made a national cemetery in 1873.

Page 395. North Platte, Nebraska (population 15,433 in 1950) is built upon a long, narrow delta between the forks of the Platte River. In November, 1866, William Peniston and Andrew J. Miller, learning that the Union Pacific Railroad would establish a construction camp at the forks of the Platte, moved their "ranch" there from Cold Water. The winter of 1866–1867 saw the settlement mushroom into a wild and woolly construction camp with some two thousand residents. When the railroad built westward, the town was all but abandoned, the same year the town of North Platte was made a Union Pacific division point, and its growth since then has been steady but not spectacular.

Page 398. Grenville Mellen Dodge, political leader, army officer, and civil engineer, was born in Danvers, Massachusetts, in 1831. He engaged in railway construction work and in business until he entered the army from Iowa, first serving as colonel of the 4th Iowa Infantry. Ware's comments are accurate as far as they go. Dodge was an energetic officer of considerable ability and a railroad construction engineer without peer.

The best biography of Dodge was written by J. R. Perkins, *Trails, Rails and War: The Life of General G. M. Dodge* (Indianapolis: Bobbs-Merrill Company, 1929).

Page 399. Lieutenant Edward Kimble Valentine had served in the 67th Illinois Infantry; after his discharge he enlisted as a private in the 7th Iowa Cavalry in 1863. By the time he was discharged in 1866 he had risen to the post of regimental adjutant. After practicing law in Nebraska, he was elected a judge in 1875 and then served three terms as a Representative in Congress. Valentine's last political office was sergeant-at-arms of the U.S. Senate, 1890–1893; he died in Chicago in 1916. *Biog. Dir. Am. Cong.*

Page 399. William Baumer, thirty-seven years old, was mustered in from Omaha as captain of Company B, 1st Regiment, Nebraska Volunteers, June 11, 1861. He was promoted major April 22, 1862, and lieutenant colonel October 4, 1862. He was mustered out July 1, 1866.

Pages 399–400. Colonel Preston B. Plumb, born in Ohio in 1837, had moved to Kansas in 1856, and was one of the organizers of the town of Emporia. He was United States senator from Kansas, 1877–1891. *Biog. Dir. Am. Cong.*

Page 400. Ware's trip into southeastern Nebraska carried him into northeastern Kansas (Seneca is in Kansas). Beatrice was christened

July 4, 1857, for the daughter of Judge John Kinney, one of the town's founders.

Page 403. The "medical director" was William McClelland, from Omaha. He had been mustered in (at the age of thirty-five) as assistant surgeon of the 1st Regiment, Nebraska Volunteers, July 25, 1861, and promoted surgeon on September 7, 1862. He—with the rest of his regiment—was mustered out of service July 1, 1866.

Page 404. Lieutenant Colonel George H. Hoyt, a member of the Massachusetts bar, had been assistant counsel for John Brown and, after the third day of the trial, was generally in charge of the defense. It is believed that the Yankees who had aided the old man in his foolish attack on Harpers Ferry sent Hoyt to Brown to prevent Brown's papers from being found and published. Hoyt also proposed an escape attempt which Brown rejected. It is fair to say that Hoyt's defense of Brown was not prompted by an idealistic interest in justice and fair play.

Page 404. On April 5 and 6, 1865, *Young* was snowbound at Cottonwood Springs. On the 6th shells burst over the bluffs, and a squad of soldiers fired their carbines into the air—"Richmond is taken!"

INDEX

District of North Kansas, 311
District of South Kansas, 311
District of the Upper Arkansas, 311, 312
Dobytown, Neb., 31-32, 35, 154
Dodge, Gen. Grenville M., 96, 398, 405, 414
Donley, Adolphus, 283, 287

Eagle Twice (Indian), 108
Ecoffey, Julius (Jules), 201, 252
Eight Mile Creek, 348
Elkhorn River, 12, 13
Ellsworth, Sgt. Allen, 126
Ellsworth, 1st Lt. William, 219-20, 226, 227, 257
Ellsworth, Kan., 126
Elston, Charles: and Ah-ho-appa, 412-13; at Fort Laramie, 201-2, 213-14; guides troops, 209-10, 223, 224, 226-27, 228, 230, 231, 232, 245, 342; mentioned, 201, 269, 296-97, 305, 376

Farley (a traveling tailor), 129
Ficklin's, 196, 216, 222, 227, 249
Fillmore, Maj. John S., 238
Fitch, Lt. Julian R., 189; report on the Smoky Hill Route, 419-24
Fitchie, Sam D., 71-72, 137
Forbush, Corp. Thomas, 93
Ford, Col. James H., 311
Fort Benton, 202
Fort Caspar, 216
Fort Collins, 120, 216, 312
Fort Cottonwood, *see* Fort Mc-Pherson
Fort Ellsworth, 312
Fort Garland, 312
Fort Halleck, 312
Fort Kearney: description, 31, 32-35; Ware sent to, 18, 27, 30; mentioned, 14, 39, 41, 43, 48, 53, 54, 64, 68, 70, 71, 80, 85, 88, 98, 100, 104, 122, 123, 126, 139, 149, 150, 156, 186, 193, 216, 229, 239, 243, 251, 268, 269, 279, 284, 307, 310, 311, 317, 318, 319, 352, 355, 390, 392, 396, 398, 399, 400, 401, 402
Fort Laramie: description, 199, 203; guard mount, 217; raided by Indians, 207-8; squaw camp, 200, 214, 308; Ware arrives at, 196-

97; mentioned, 100, 154, 165, 179, 181, 184, 192, 196, 197, 202, 203, 218, 219, 222, 225, 227, 228, 229, 238, 247, 248, 249, 250, 251, 252, 253, 254, 258, 269, 270, 294, 305, 309, 312, 325, 384, 397, 402, 408, 409, 410, 412, 415
Fort Larned, 312
Fort Leavenworth, Kan., 17, 31, 33, 73, 127, 305, 309, 311, 402, 404, 405
Fort Lyon, Colo., 308, 309, 312
Fort McPherson, 36, 47-49, 53; *see also* Cottonwood Canyon *and* Cottonwood Springs
Fort McPherson National Cemetery, 395-96
Fort Riley, Kan., 126, 311, 312
Fort Sedgwick, 236-38, 245-46, 272-73, 318, 320, 328; illustration, 238; *see also* Julesburg, Colo.
Fort Smith, 414
Fort Zarah, 312
Fouts, Capt. William D., 165
Freeman, Daniel, 65
Fremont, Neb., 13, 14, 27
Fremont's orchard, 312
French, Thomas, 65
French's ranch (Thomas French), 39, 41, 43, 44

Gallagher, Ben, 63, 70, 104, 167-68, 169, 178
Gallagher carbine, 6
"Galvanized Yanks," 401, 404
Gardner (supposed Cheyenne Indian agent), 75-76
Gardner's ranch, 38
Geroux, *see* Jereux
Gillett's ranch, 269, 359, 370, 377
Gilman, J. K., 51-53, 75, 76, 83, 129, 140
Gilman, Jud, 52, 65, 75
Gilman's ranch (J. K. and Jud Gilman), 44, 51, 57, 60, 61, 65, 70, 97, 126, 127, 150, 155, 170, 171, 311, 320
Gold, discovered in Colorado, 53
Gore, Sir George, 35-36, 427
Grand Island, Neb., 27
Gratton Massacre, 218-19
Gray (a scout and hunter), 136-37, 138, 143, 157